A. CUMMING
1975

Meet me off the Western Islands and...

SHIPS
AND
MEMORIES

SHIPS
AND
MEMORIES

BY

BILL ADAMS

pseud. of Bertram Martin Adams

The story of the years the author spent in the four-masted barque *Silberhorn*, running to Oregon and San Francisco, as told in his famous book, *Ships and Women*, which is reproduced in full, together with many memories and reflections from his no less famous *Letters*, the odd story and poem, with over one hundred and fifty photographic illustrations of the ships he knew and forty pen-and-ink sketches by W. M. Birchall.

WITH AN INTRODUCTION

BY

ALEX A. HURST

TEREDO BOOKS LTD.
BRIGHTON,
SUSSEX

MCMLXXV

ISBN 0 903662 02 7

Filmset in 12pt Times Roman by
Photocomp Limited, Birmingham
Printed by Clarke, Doble & Brendon Limited
Oakfield Press, Plymouth

CONTENTS

SHIPS AND WOMEN

MEMORIES

LIST OF ILLUSTRATIONS

VII

INTRODUCTION

Different ships: different long splices' is a well-known nautical saw, but it holds equally good of other spheres of activity and is certainly true of writing.

When it was suggested that I edit this book, it was pointed out that Bertram Martin Adams, who was always known as 'Bill', does not maintain many of the accepted rules of syntax, and I suppose it was thought that I might virtually re-write his book and articles. In fact, I have done nothing of the sort and have altered very little. Where I have made amendments, they have been very minor, and often to correct the spelling of ships' names, which may have been the results of printers' errors. Otherwise, I have occasionally inserted into *Ships and Women* a few lines here and there *in his own words* from his *Letters* to the Blue Peter in those instances where the two over-lapped: when the letter expanded the theme, and when the inclusion of both accounts *in toto* would have been repetitious.

Adams never set out to write in the high stylism of—say—Conrad in *The Mirror of the Sea*, but to set forth his experiences rather in the form of a yarn, as he might have spoken it. Both books are classics of their respective types, and I doubt if either has ever been surpassed in its own sphere. *The Mirror* is a marvellous book to read, but its matter would seem stilted and pedantic if spoken by its author, impromptu, as he smoked his pipe or leant against a bar. *Ships and Women* is precisely the opposite, being written in that informal way in which a sailor speaks, and for this reason I deemed it to be sheer desecration to alter and amend it. Only in the highlands of Scotland do people customarily speak aloud with a full regard to grammar and syntax without sounding oddly formal, and it was by writing his book in the way that he did that Bill Adams created such a wonderful atmosphere that he can transport his reader away from his chair and back through time to the very decks of the *Silberhorn*.

Adams not only loved his sea, but sensed the very soul of his ship. Some people may deny that ships have souls. Whether they have 'souls' or 'personalities' I will not argue, but the fact is that sailing ships *did* possess this characteristic, though it was something that not everyone who sailed in them appreciated. Only those who achieved that understanding and who came to grips with the souls of their ships arrived at a real *rapport* with the sea.

I am fortified in my belief that the idea of editing *Ships and Women* is fundamentally wrong by an incident which occurred soon after I had left school and was working, temporarily, in a City office in which I was in charge of the 'Captains' Room'. The captains, in this context, were the masters of colliers running into London River, and my job was to provide them with money for their ships' wages; deal with their tonnage and light dues, and with other aspects of their ships' business.

They were a strange mixture of men. Some might have risen to command ocean liners, but had taken to the coastal trade in the mistaken belief that seafaring and marriage could be reconciled thereby, whereas others had obviously reached the peak of their careers. My own ambitions had extended far beyond the sea horizons since the age of seven, and I had soon separated the sheep from the goats—the latter, in my book, being those who had served in sail! Generally I would draw these men out as far as possible, though most of them suffered from that inhibition which suppresses the expression of any deep feeling, found so commonly among Northern peoples. Moreover, it was obvious enough that many of the steam-trained men tended to resent that line of conversation, for it was a time when service in sail was no longer held to be necessary, but it still held a grudging respect, and a lack of it in older men created some secret feeling of inferiority whenever the subject arose.

One of these latter was a big Geordie, who had joined a certain collier as a deck-boy, long years before. He had worked his way up through the foc's'le to the bridge and, having served in no other vessel, he was now her master. It was a great achievement, but he knew nothing of the soul of the sea or of any ship, and he found himself in good company!

One morning, there was a whole crowd of them, spilling over the bench space provided. Business was finished, and they were sitting and standing around, smoking and chatting. Most of them I knew well. There was an old master who had been in the *Knight of the Thistle*: another who had been in de Wolf's *Glenalvon*, of the same company as the *Silberhorn*, which forms the burden of this book; there was an old fellow with long, white walrus moustaches who had served in Fenwick's barque *Ethel*, and he had been in their ships ever since. (Later, I saw the *Ethel's* bones, half-buried, on the other side of the world.) Another had been in Dunlop's smart *Clan MacFarlane*, and there were others, most of whom were contemporary with Bill Adams and had served their time at the turn of the century. A few were younger but, apart from one who had been in the *William Mitchell*, not many of these had been in sail.

On the whole, these fellows were no more articulate than the average man, in the sense that they had the ability to hold an audience spell-bound, yet I could still sense a certain resentment from the steam-trained men in the room. There was one stranger there: the master of a chartered vessel, who sat listening, silent and attentive. He was a smallish man, with a clipped, grizzled moustache.

Then, in a break, he began to speak: first, briefly, of a departed square-rigger in which he had served his time, and then, at greater length, of his time as second mate in an old clipper ship—the *Sam Mendel*. It was no polished, after-dinner speech of well-turned phrase, but a man speaking colloquially from his very heart, yet stirring his memory not only to speak of the events of his voyages, but of all the minor and splendid sights and impressions—the way the spray looked as it flew up to soak the leeches of the courses: the way the ship herself sensed the weather, sometimes in the thundering might of the Westerlies or sometimes in the splendour of a steady Trade: in a dripping fog in soundings or as she gloried in a fine wind while sail was piled on her when leaving port. He spoke of the sight of the sails against the rising dawns: the relationship of the men aboard and of so much more that most men who have felt deeply about such things normally keep locked away, lest they expose their own souls to view. He must have spoken for well over half an hour, quietly, unostentatiously, and almost as though under some spiritual influence, yet always with that inherent pride in ship of the real sailor. In all that time, no-one spoke or shuffled and one might have heard a pin drop. The Office Manager had entered but he, too, stayed silent, mesmerised by the force of the man's description. That collier master knew *all* about it: *he* knew that ships had souls (though he never said so in so many words), and he even moved the steam-trained men to sense the sheer wonder of it all. For me, it was a golden morning whose gleam has never faded yet. Had he been asked to write it all down, I am convinced that he could never have achieved the same effect. In retrospect, I wish it had all been taped, for every man listening to him was transported away from the dingy city office, and we were all aboard the *Sam Mendel*, so long vanished from the face of the sea, sensing her every scend and pitch.

(Oddly, within twelve months, I was in a four-masted barque threshing her way up towards Copenhagen under lower topgallant-sails, gradually overhauling that man's ship all one long afternoon. I would lay any money that the sight of us kept him on his bridge, and I wished that I could let him know that I was aboard!)

To edit Bill Adams would have been as wrong as to have asked that collier skipper to express himself on paper. He could have done it, but all the spontaneity would have been lost. I had read Adams before I went to sea, and I discovered all the magic then. I read him when I was actually in sail, and the impressions were no less. Even now, years afterwards, I still find his descriptions so powerful that I find myself *there*.

Perhaps I feel a certain affinity with Bill Adams. We both went to sea rather later than most, at nineteen, and we had both been to public schools, which was unusual in square-riggers. Like him, I stood six feet three and, whereas he was some 187 pounds, I scaled well over 200 but, like him, I revelled in pulling fore-hand and equally enjoyed a certain prowess in feats of strength and in the sheer physical contest demanded by the deep-water sailing ship. Like him, I delighted in these ships, and in feeling them under my control, whereas so many regarded their tricks at the wheel as so many 'chores'. Granted that his decade of sail was a richer one than mine, but I also found that same understanding with the sea and with the souls of ships though, fortunately for me, I never knew the pangs of vertigo. My ships were under-manned, and I was aloft and taking my wheel within twenty-four hours of joining. Like him, I had to leave the sea, if for less dire reasons—(I could no longer pass the statutory sight tests)—and, once again like him, I have lived long on memories of days in those splendid square-riggers. Thus, where ships are concerned, I touch his mind. As for women, some readers may find less than they expect (or hope) from the title! Here again, if for different reasons, I find that his re-actions to the fair sex were much the same as my own. To me, ships and women were simply not compatible, though I would be the first to admit that this opinion is supported neither by the majority nor by history!

Some may think it odd that a young man who battled so long with vertigo should develop such strong feeling for his ship. This does not seem odd to me. Long before I went to sea, I was going out with tugs as they towed tall ships in and out of port, sometimes being so horribly sea-sick that I was still green about the gills when I arrived home! Invariably, my parents advised against repeating the performance, but the magic of great masting had made itself manifest to me, and I was drawn back as if by an unbreakable cord. Oddly, I was sea-sick on my first day at sea, but never again thereafter, save occasionally when sailing in some yacht with an outside ballast keel, but I know very well that, to those who come under the spell of tall ships and high canvas, there can be no physical barrier to destroy their relationship.

Bill Adams wrote nothing until years after he had had to leave the sea and, when he did start to put pen to paper, he first wrote stories. Admittedly they were sea stories, some being based on events which subsequently became set down in sequence in *Ships and Women*, whilst others were so fanciful that they might almost be deemed to be Fairy Tales.

Thus his writing is that of an ageing man, describing events seen in retrospect and, if any reader quibbles with his veracity, I would remind him of the words Shakespeare gave to King Henry V before the battle of Agincourt on St. Crispin's Day:

> *He that shall live this day, and see old age,*
> *Will yearly on the vigil feast his neighbours,*
> *And say: "Tomorrow is St. Crispian":*
> *Then will he strip his sleeve and show his scars,*
> *And say: "These wounds I had on Crispin's Day".*
> *Old men forget; yet all shall be forgot,*
> *But he'll remember with advantages*
> *What feats he did that day . . .*

Not long ago, a retired captain commissioned an artist to paint his old ship—a great, box-like, brutish full-rigger. When the picture was half done, he protested that the masts were not tall enough, and persuaded the artist to alter them. Yet the artist had been right in the first place! Old men forget . . . or become confused! Thus, in checking some of the facts written by the author, I have let all stand. This is a book of reminiscence, which gives an unparalleled description of the men, the ship and the whole life and sailing of his ship. He himself was writing in a remote village in the Californian Sierras far from the sea. Even had he wished to check his memory, there was no Maritime Museum at the Foot of Polk Street in San Francisco in those days and, if lapses exist, they are not of the sort that should make any reader wish to unhorse him.

His description of the sinking of the *Chanaral* is accurate enough, but at that time the *Silberhorn* was climbing the North Pacific and but three weeks off San Francisco. She was certainly not in the Channel that night, but I have no doubt that the author did see the ship. Such things are of little consequence when *'all shall be forgot'*.

The *Silberhorn*'s logs have vanished in the limbo of time, but I have had access to some of the relevant Crew Lists, Consular documents and so forth, relating to Adams' time in the ship. Certainly names and events aboard check very well with his account. Occasionally there is a measure of doubt, and in such instances I have inserted a foot-note. However, he does seem to have become chronologically confused sometimes where he lists ships in port or in company with his own

XVIII

vessel. This is not a matter of 'remembering with advantage', but merely of memory. On one occasion, many of the ships he mentioned as being in 'Frisco were scattered about the seas and ports of the world, but further checking elicited that he probably was with these vessels in the course of his time in the *Silberhorn*. Thus I have not amended the text. Reminiscences seldom constitute history and few voyage books provide dates and passage times. It is Adams' book—not mine. The actual passages of his ship, while he was in her, as culled from Lloyds, are included as an appendix.

In one account, his school-master took him to see a stranded ship in the Avon: in another account it was his father. It is of no consequence. Perhaps I should mention the incident of the brig which fell down on the *Silberhorn* in Barry Roads and sank, since I can find no confirmation of the affair, though a schooner called the *Grimaldi* did fall down on her as described at that time, but she did *not* sink and, after the ships had been locked together for some three hours, the tug *Glenrosa* towed her away, *sans* mainmast, towards Watchet.

I cannot possibly check his tale of the Greek brig, in *Corinth Helen*. Again, it makes no odds, but there is no doubt that brigs did hold an allurement for many a big square-rigger man. He would seldom account a fore-and-after as being the 'real thing', but a brig, with her small size and easy working, provided some sort of temptation to which few of the men of the big ships actually yielded. They represented a rather different life, in that final fling of sail. Those who did break into print so often conjured up a brig, as if to appease some unsatisfied craving, and it is perhaps significant, if not purely coincidental, that the one incident in Conrad's *Mirror of the Sea* which has eluded all research and which appears to have been a purely fictional or hearsay story, is the sinking of the Danish brig!

So far as his letters to the *Blue Peter* are concerned, I have sometimes deleted or withheld large sections, simply because they are also contained in *Ships and Women*, but there is no doubt that an event has the greater force if told by a witness, or if the *raconteur* has some personal recollection upon which to stand his assertion. Thus Adams sometimes gives himself a little licence, and transports himself about the world to places he never visited! When he says that he read of the

1. The GOLDENHORN, sending down t'gallant-masts prior to passing under a bridge.

death of his first mate in Santa Cruz, it does not alter the fact that the point of the story is true enough. If men like Bill Adams had known that sleuths would check their every word, they would never have written anything at all! They did not know: we can give thanks that they did write, and we must accept the spirit in which they wrote.

It is, perhaps, unfortunate that the small camera was not in general use in Adams' day, since I can find no trace of pictures taken aboard the *Silberhorn*, save one of a group which is reproduced, nor yet of any of her under sail. The book has been illustrated as relevantly as possible.

The *Silberhorn* was one of three sisters, of which the other two were the *Matterhorn* (which is mentioned several times) and the *Goldenhorn*. They were built in 1884, 1883 and 1882 respectively, for Charles E. de Wolf of Liverpool. The *Goldenhorn* was wrecked on Santa Rosa Island, near San Pedro, after nine years of life and some six years before Adams went to sea. All three were built by Russell's, of Port Glasgow, and really represent the second transition stage from the clipper to the big carrier. The four-masted barque of iron or steel was a relatively new innovation, and the first of them, the *Tweedsdale*, had been built in 1877, though, of course, the Americans had produced wooden vessels of this rig prior to this date.

Many people today think of the four-masted barque in terms of the later ones, which were huge, by sailing ship standards. The whole building of the modern square-rigger, from the clippers to the last big nitrate vessels, to all intents and purposes occupied little more than half a century, and in that time she suffered several metamorphoses.

The *Silberhorn* and her sisters were really a great deal smaller than the ships which followed in the nineties, when freights had fallen and large hold capacity was the order of the day. They were nice looking vessels, if not so attractive as those with masts of unequal height, and they were rigged with royals over single topgallantsails, as distinct from the later vessels—even in their own company, such as the *Lyderhorn* and *Englehorn*—which had double topgallant yards. Certainly it was an age when there was still plenty of pride in the ships of this type, and it was equally an age when there was a lot more character both in the foc's'les and on the waterfronts than in that last decade of sail which so many young men have recorded so often.

Captain Robert Gibson joined the ship in St. Nazaire in 1893. On her previous voyage, when running before a fierce gale around Cape Horn, the upper topsails had just been lowered prior to making them fast, when the ship was badly pooped, washing the two men from the wheel. One, an apprentice named Whaley, went clean through the poop rails (with a ventilator) into the sea and was lost, since the weather was too bad to launch a boat, and the other landed up by the mainmast. No doubt she had lost speed with the reduction in sail.

Outward bound, she had been laid on her beam ends off the Falklands and, after leaving Hong Kong in September 1894, she encountered a typhoon and was brought down to goose-winged main and mizzen lower topsails. Later, passing through the strait between Formosa and Samasana, she was caught in a seven-knot current in a big swell with no wind whatever and with no anchorage. There was nothing to be done, so the boats were cleared away and, as a last resort, the longest line was bent to the anchor. So she drifted towards the land in a clear, moonless night in a silence which created an awful tension, broken only by the sound of Mrs. Gibson sobbing as she paced the poop. Then, at 4.30 a.m., when they could hear the breakers ashore, a catspaw came and the yards were squared, after which she just got clear, to encounter a good deal of heavy weather on her seventy-day passage to the Golden Gate.

Previous to Adams' first voyage, the *Silberhorn* had run out from Sharpness to Melbourne, leaving in August 1895; then she had loaded coal in Newcastle, New South Wales, for Antofagasta, after which she had loaded saltpetre in Iquique for Hamburg, then moving back to Liverpool in January 1897. There Adams joined her.

The ship was finally lost in 1907. She had left Newcastle, New South Wales, for Iquique with a cargo of coal on June 12th, and was never seen again. On August 27th, the German barque *Anny* passed a burning sailing ship towards dusk in hard weather near Juan Fernandez, and the only clue that could be made out as to her identity were the letters '-ool' on her counter—presumably Liverpool, the *Silberhorn*'s port of registry. Newcastle coal was very prone to spontaneous combustion, and many the tall ship which was lost through this cause. Three years later, when the big four-masted barque *Lord Shaftesbury* called at Pitcairn, she learnt that one of the *Silberhorn*'s lifebuoys had been washed up on the beach there. That is all that can be said of the loss of the ship.

The *Matterhorn* foundered two years later, in April 1909, with the loss of her mate and five men off the Umatilla Reef, when bound towards Ipswich from Portland, Oregon.

Captain Robert Gibson, who had left the *Silberhorn* the voyage before her loss (when she was commanded by Capt. Warren, who had come from the *Matterhorn*) died at an advanced age around 1926-7. He was then about 75 or 76. Adams wrote: "He often took me out in his big car and would calmly open it up till it was making seventy miles an hour. He was arrested for speeding on one occasion, and fined fifty dollars, but I always felt perfectly safe when he was at the wheel. When, on the other hand, I took him in my car, he was amusingly nervous and absolutely refused to let me go more than fifteen or twenty miles an hour. Good old Stormy!'' Seventy miles an hour was no mean speed in those days!

Sometimes I have stepped aboard a sailing ship's deck in dock and sensed her spirit instantly—and let it not be thought that it was always a beneficent spirit! I have known men who could do this infallibly, and who always proved to be right. This is *not* a romantic idea: these men were ship-masters of great experience. I have also known men who have had no experience of sail and who have barely been afloat, yet who also understand these things and who would, I am sure, discover all that Adams discovered had they but the opportunity. They will appreciate all that he writes the more.

Those who deny that ships have souls or that men can reach a *rapport* with their vessels may content themselves with criticising the grammar or, better still, they may lay this book aside and turn to one closer to their own understanding. Bill Adams' Crispin's Day lasted the full four years that he served in the *Silberhorn* and, for the rest of us, I believe that he has feasted his neighbours with all the honour and glory of it, whilst catching the whole spirit and soul of the sea. It lived with him all his life inland in California, and he speaks from his own heart in the poem reproduced in this book:

> *There's an ache in my heart . . .*
>
> *Dear God! But I'd give my soul to go*
> *To the open sea and the wind and snow . . .*

If he has written his accounts just as he would have told them to us, man to man, that is our immeasurable gain!

Alex. A. Hurst.

WM BIRCHALL 1935

W·M·Birchall.
'1924

ACKNOWLEDGEMENTS

THE PUBLISHERS wish to thank all those whose help and co-operation has made this book possible. We have much appreciated the kindness of the Peninsular and Oriental Steam Navigation Company Ltd who have allowed us to reproduce the various articles, poems and letters by Bill Adams which appeared in their magazine, The Blue Peter, together with *The Grain Ships* by Capt. A. E. Dingle and the attractive sketches by that splendid marine artist, William Minshall Birchall. At the same time, we are equally indebted to Peter Davies Ltd for their permission to use the material previously published by them as *Ships and Women*.

We also wish to thank everyone who has assisted in helping to trace photographs which are relevant to Adams' theme and, in particular, to those who have allowed us to use pictures from their collections, viz: Herr Gustaf Alexandersson, of Saltsjöboo, Sweden (Plate I): Mr. R. M. Cookson (5-11-19-32-53-62-65-73-77): the late W. Dewar Brown (14): The Dept. of Maritime History, Merseyside County Museums (110): the late Cdr. H. O. Hill (121): The San Francisco Maritime Museum [80 (Harry Dring Coll.) 50-89-105 (Hester Coll.) 40 (Historical Section, Union Title Insurance Co, San Diego) 58-59 (Mrs. A. Y. Hughes Coll) 56 (Gilberg Coll) 132 (Livingstone Coll) 27-141-144 (Morrison Coll) 134 (Wm. Muir Coll) 2-61-131-135-146 (Plummer Coll) 132 (J. W. Procter Coll) 22 (W. A. Scott Coll) 88 (Dick Schiach Coll) 48-105 (Wilton Coll) and also Plate 71]. We should like to express our especial gratitude and appreciation to Mrs. Mathilda Dring, of the San Francisco Museum, for all her tremendous efforts and trouble throughout, and particularly during a time of crisis when a packet 'went missing' in the labyrinths of the International postal system, when publication was imminent!

Many pictures were contributed from more than one source, and we thank all those people who went to such trouble on this score, together with the many persons, in various fields on both sides of the Atlantic, who gave us much assistance in our quest to discover Miss D. I. Adams, Bill Adams' daughter.

The cover picture is a detail of a water-colour by the Liverpool artist Sam J. M. Browne in the possession of Mr. Alex. A. Hurst, and the endpapers have been specially drawn for the book by Mr. Andrew Cumming, of Lenzie, who has taken for his theme the valedictory words of one of Adams' letters: "Meet me off the Western Islands, and we'll roll up the Channel together." Most readers will echo the ensuing final comment: "Would that we might!"

2. *"Out beyond the Golden Gate, shaping course off Farralones."*
The skysail-yarder LYNTON, sister to the QUEEN MARGARET.

THE GRAIN SHIPS

Tall ships, long ships, full-built ships and clippers,
  Loading up at Crockett Docks with barley, wheat or corn;
Manned by 'long-shore hoboes and wild apprentice 'nippers',
  Officered by men of iron, racing round the Horn.

Out beyond the Golden Gate, shaping course off Farralones,
  Hobo crews a-sweating blood—wish they'd ne'er been born:
Harassed mates a-cursing them, damning them to Davy Jones,
  Grand old 'Frisco Grain Fleet! Racing round the Horn.

Bracadale and *Marlboro' Hill*, *Combermere* and *Talus*,
  Tamar and *Queen Margaret*, and lofty *Silberhorn*,
Nimble *Banklands* leading them, and dainty *Euryalus*:
  White-winged, swift-heeled beauties! Racing round the Horn.

Southward through the summer seas, clouds of canvas gleaming;
  Royals straining at the trucks, jibs like wings of morn;
Lifelines! Close-reefed tops'ls! Decks with grey spite streaming!
  Growl, but take it as it comes, racing round the Horn!

These be dreams of long ago, grim motor ships or steamers
  Bear the freights of three tall ships, barley, wheat or corn;
Gone from sea the old romance, lost to all but dreamers—
  Only ghosts of clipper ships race around the Horn!

A. E. DINGLE

XXVII

W.M.BIRCHALL.
1928

SHIPS AND WOMEN

To

DOLLY'S DAUGHTER

DOROTHY INEZ ADAMS

W.M.Birchall. 1925

CHAPTER I

YONDER'S THE SEA AND A SHIP

I suppose I ought to start my biography at the very beginning. All that I know about it is that the doctor who was present when I arrived said that he did not think it would be possible to rear me. I was very diminutive. I have heard that the nurse set me aside in a two-quart jar on a shelf; and that I was forgotten till a week later, when I was found sucking one of my toes, apparently lost in deep thought. I think that perhaps that was so, for I have ever liked to think my own thoughts, and if you're not a bit contrary in this world may Heaven pity you! And then, too, there's nothing like getting a good start. The nurse, who was not really a nurse but only the village midwife, said, "Well, s'elp me if 'ere ain't that there babby! W'y, the little cuss, 'e'd ought to have been dead an' all dried up by this time!"

I might begin my biography with the three pigs that lived in a sty at the back of our little house in Berkswell. One was black and big, and its name was Father. A smaller one, spotted red and white, was named after my brother Geoffrey, who was two years older than I. I was about four. The littlest pig was named after me. It was Geoffrey who named them, and Father thought his idea very good. Sometimes the pigs escaped from their sty, and Geoffrey and I had a lot of fun driving them back. Father was seventy-one, and, while very active, could not run fast enough to be much help. One day three men came and caught Father and laid him on his back on a bench and one of them stuck a knife in his throat. He squealed very deliciously for a long time; his squeals growing gradually feebler and feebler, till at last they ended in a sort of hopeless gurgle. Then he was taken from the bench

1

and Geoffrey was laid on it. When he had stopped squealing, it was my turn. After the knife was stuck in my throat, I managed to wriggle off the bench and ran away. But they soon caught me, and put me back on it. Then we ate chitlins, pig's pudding, and fresh pork pies for many days. Pig-killing time was in November and, after our pigs were killed, Geoffrey and I went from one nearby farm to another to watch the pig-killing. When a pig was dead, it was hung by its hind-legs to a branch of an apple tree, over a great tub of scalding water. Its bristles were scraped off, and it was cut open and its insides were taken out. They were all bubbly-looking and whitish and very exciting. The world was a delightful place at pig-killing time.

The three pigs did not belong to us, but to my step-brother Frank who lived some miles away. He had a large house and kept seven female servants and a footman and a butler, and a tiger to polish the shoes and silver and door knobs, and so on. A tiger was a little boy. Our house was small, and we had only one servant, and a nurse to take care of Geoffrey and me. Sometimes our nurse took us for a walk, and very often a man from the village would meet us in the lane and put his arm round her. They would go through a gap in the hawthorn hedge, the man telling us to stay where we were. Then Geoffrey and I would pick primroses on the lane banks and bluebells and dog violets. We would hear our nurse giggle and say, "No". When they came back to the lane, she had a red face and looked excited and happy. The man would kiss her and go away, and we would continue our walk.

My mother was always in bed upstairs. I remember her only once at Berkswell. She was sitting propped up on her pillows. Her jet black hair was hanging in a cloud about her shoulders. Her blue eyes, large and very big, were looking right at me and she was smiling. It made me feel very happy. Except for one other time, I do not remember her at all. She had been engaged to a Congregational minister when she ran away and married my father when he was sixty-four years old.

Maybe I could begin my biography with the other time I remember my mother; because it is the plainest of all the memories of my childhood. It was a grey day, with low clouds and now and then a sprinkle of rain. I don't know where Geoffrey was. Maybe he was away at Albert Villas, which was a private school for the sons of gentlemen, at

Clifton. Our two aunties owned it. They were not really our aunties. They were our step-sisters, and Frank's sisters; the daughters of my father by his first marriage. Their names were Auntie Kitty and Auntie Polly.

I was alone, digging for worms in the wet cold earth of the back yard. There was a high brick wall round the yard. Everything had a sombre feeling; a feeling of loneliness. But I dug a good many worms and put them in a can before, drawn by I can't say what, I set the can down and went into the house. There was no one about. The window blinds were down, the house was dark. I went upstairs and into a bedroom. In it were two chairs, and on them was a long wooden box. I had to tiptoe to see into the box. I looked into it for just a very few moments. And then as I went from the room, I met two servants in the hall. One looked at the other and said, "He's seen his mother." I don't know where it happened. And though, since I grew up, I have several times tried to find it, I have no idea where her grave is. She was thirty-five when she died.

My memories of Warwickshire, which we left after my mother died, are few but very distinct. I remember Guy Fawkes' Day, when Geoffrey and I followed the village lads, who carried an effigy of Guy Fawkes and finally set fire to it, standing in a ring round it and singing:

Oh, don't you remember the fifth of November,
With gunpowder, treason, and plot.

I remember the Maypole dances; and Good Friday morning, when, before daylight, village lads and girls came from house to house singing:

Hot Cross buns! Hot Cross buns!
One a penny, two a penny, hot Cross buns!

I remember Kenilworth Castle, very very plainly, and Coventry streets, too. Lady Godiva and Queen Elizabeth were real to me when I was only a little lad.

It was while we lived at Berkswell that I first saw Dolly. She was the fourth of Frank's five daughters. He came to Berkswell one day with her and Ede, the fifth daughter. Geoffrey and I had each a glass jar in a sunny window, and in the jars were flies and other winged insects

3

we had caught. Dolly took the lids off and set all our insects free. I was very angry and hated her, and told her that I did. But I know that even then, deep down inside me, was a sort of respect for her. I was a barbaric, cruel little boy, and she made me conscious of it, and that she was gentle and merciful. She was eight years older than I.

My father had long silky white hair that hung down over his shoulders. He wore a pointed white beard, in which was a tinge of ruddiness here and there. His big moustache was also ruddy-tinged. His eyes were deep blue, bright as those of an eagle. The veins on his wrists stood out, high and cordy. One day, while I sat on his knee, I lifted his beard. Under it was a wide livid scar running from close to his ear down across his throat. An Arab spear had made it long ago. As a lad he had quarrelled with his father, run away from home, and enlisted in the French Foreign Legion. When the Legion lost its colours in battle, he recaptured them. Then he was colour-sergeant of the Legion. But after a while he grew tired of being a Legionnaire and deserted. Captured, he was sentenced to be shot. On the night before the execution was to be, he escaped and swam almost a mile out to sea, where an English ship lay at anchor. So he returned to England. There he obtained a position as French tutor in a private school for young ladies, owned by a lady whose two daughters helped with the teaching. One morning a few weeks after he obtained the position, one of the daughters did not appear. Nor did he. They had eloped to America. The daughter with whom he ran away had been engaged to a man named Ben Sarsons, and was to have been married in a few days. She was the mother of Frank and my two step-sisters. My father took out his naturalization papers at Elmira, New York State, on April the ninth, 1845. He did many things in America before he went back to England. He was a backwoods school teacher, and for a time he practised law. When he returned to England, the Crimean War was starting. His elder brother was a general and commanded the Guards Brigade at the battle of Inkermann, dying of wounds after the battle. Father rode with the Heavy Brigade and was with it on Balaclava Day, when it charged through thirty thousand Russians, wheeled, galloped back, and repeated the charge twice more. I used to have his sword, but lost it long ago in my wanderings. After the Crimean War he

4

returned to America, where he later rode with General Sherman from Atlanta to the sea.

After my mother's death Auntie Polly took charge of Geoffrey and me. My father had no money and was cared for by Frank. I hated Frank, because he always teased me. I hated him more after Auntie Polly took me to Albert Villas, because she made me wear my hair in long curls; and that made him tease me still worse whenever he came on a visit. But I loved his wife, Auntie Clarissa. I was afraid of Auntie Polly. There was a sort of wall between us. It was many years ere I knew why that wall was. I don't know where my father was during my first years at Albert Villas. Auntie Polly kissed me a great deal and taught me to say prayers at bed-time. All the twenty-two gentlemen's sons at Albert Villas hated her, and took out their hate by teasing me. And Auntie Polly, to show how just she was, and that she showed no favours, was stricter with me than with any of them. Geoffrey was afraid of her, too. On the morning of the day he died he was sick; and because he was afraid of being punished if he made a mess, he kept the sick in his mouth. He died when he was nine. Auntie Polly never meant to be unkind. She was just a Victorian old maid who, loving children, knew nothing of what went on in their hearts.

At Albert Villas I was put in charge of a servant named Ada. When Auntie Polly was busy, Ada heard me say my prayers and put me to bed. One night, before she blew out the candle, she said, "If ever I find your hands below your middle, your fingers will be cut off and you'll be fed on bread and water." I was terrified, and kept my hands as close under my chin as I could. And when, on waking next morning, I found that my bed was wet, my terror was ghastly. I carefully pulled up the bed clothes. Maybe no one ever found out about it, for nothing happened.

Auntie Polly spanked me very often. I seldom knew why. One night when she was spanking me, I struggled so that she struck me on the back of my head to make me be still. A ring on one of her fingers left a scar I still have. That night when she was gone, two of the servants came in and comforted me where I lay whimpering in the dark. It was soon after that Auntie Polly took Geoffrey and me to church to be baptized. I can still see the clergyman, in his long white surplice,

5

and feel him putting the mark of the Cross on my forehead. The church was dim and smelt musty. It was sombre and cold. On the way back to Albert Villas it rained, and Auntie Polly talked about 'the sweet Jesus'. I can still hear the clop-clop of the horse's hoofs, and I remember wishing the sweet Jesus would make the sun come out.

One evening Auntie Polly took me for a walk along the top of the high cliffs above the gorge of the river Avon, a little way from Albert Villas. Above the muddy water far below I saw what I took to be pieces of paper floating on the still air. "Look at the pieces of paper," I said.

"They are not pieces of paper. They are sea-gulls," said Auntie Polly, and, pointing far away, toward a level grey expanse in the west, added, "And yonder's the sea, and a ship." And then, as I looked to that level grey expanse in the west, out to beyond where lay that ship at anchor, a something stirred in me. An unrest came upon me, a desire. Not yet had I heard the names of Drake and Frobisher and their companions. Yet in me, a little lad of five or so, stirred that same unrest that once had stirred them also. And I remember that that night, putting me to bed, Auntie Polly taught me:

> *Gentle Jesus, meek and mild,*
> *Look upon a little child.*

I wondered what 'meek and mild' was.

And I mind a later day when all the school walked along the road that ran beside the river, at the foot of the cliffs. It was my first time to walk there. My second time to see the river. And there were ships. And again that something stirred within me. And then, a while later again, while we walked by the river, a ship named the *Beatrice* ran aground on the other bank and stuck so fast that the tug boats could not move her. And when we came back to Albert Villas that day, my father was there. I told him of that ship, and next day he took me, alone, down to the river. The *Beatrice* was still there. They had cut away her three masts short off at her deck. She was lying far over to one side, and beside her were lighters into which men were unloading her cargo of rum, sugar, and coconuts. And my father said, "She's from the West Indies, my son." Ah—the West Indies!—When he spoke those words I had a sort of vision. Stronger yet, that something stirred within me. And then my father said, "Some day, my son,

6

3. *Barque EMIGRANT, built in Bremen in 1847, ashore in the Avon.*

perhaps you'll see something more than a river with muddy banks!"
And what with the *Beatrice*, and the rum and coconuts, and the ships
that came up and went down that muddy river, and those words 'The
West Indies'—well, it was as though a something were pulling at me
somehow.

When next the holidays came, Geoffrey and I went to stay with
father at Bowers Farm, in Herefordshire. It was owned by the aunt of
the assistant teachers at Albert Villas. A white house on a hill, with a
tree-bordered drive leading down to a deep lane. Across the lane were
the farm buildings. Stables, cowsheds, pigsties, barns, cider mill,
granary, and the cottage where lived John Thomas, who worked on the
farm, with his wife and fourteen children. Horses, cows, calves, colts,
pigs, chickens, ducks, geese, sheep, lambs. Delicious smell of fresh

manure, and hay, and horse's sweat, and the breath of cows. Daffodils, dog violets, primroses, cowslips, meadowsweet, ragged robin. And no one to interfere with a small boy! No prayers to learn. No spankings.

Father used often to visit John Thomas' cottage, and I'd go with him, while Geoffrey played with Thomas' oldest son. One day I heard father say to Thomas, "Thomas, my man, you ought to go a bit easy on the missis. It's hard on the women, man!"

And John Thomas replied, "It be a' right for foine gintlemen to talk, maister, but it be different w'en I be abed wi' the missis." I wondered much what that mysterious conversation meant.

The harvest-time came, and Geoffrey and I followed the wagons up and down the sunny fields. After the wagons came the gleaners, girls and women, to gather up what was left for their own. Often the labourers worked far into the night, lest wet weather come. Then the women and girls did the milking. When the men came from the moony fields, maybe a girl would hang her milk pail to the cowshed wall, and go to meet one of them. Then they would go up the ladder, to the hay-loft. Presently they'd come down again, and kiss, and go their separate ways, whilst I'd wonder in a sort of vague child way. Not wonder exactly. But there'd be a consciousness of some mystery.

When term started again Geoffrey and I were back at Albert Villas, learning about the sweet Jesus, and being taught a hymn at bedtime. Soon we both had the mumps. One evening when we were getting better, he was in the little tin bath-tub in the middle of the bedroom. The doctor came into the room while he was there. A woman doctor, unmarried, elderly. She had a pet pug-dog with her. Auntie Polly, who was bathing Geoffrey, had a pet pug-dog, too. They forgot about Geoffrey and talked about how nice dear little pug-dogs were, while he sat shivering in the chilling water. Next day Geoffrey was worse. He was still ill in bed when I went to Bowers farm for the holidays, and then he died. Father left to take the train to go to his funeral ere I was awake. I woke to find myself alone in the great four-post bed in which we slept together. Frightened by death, I cried. Then a woman came in, the sister of the assistant teachers at Albert Villas, and crossly told me to be quiet. When she was gone, I

4. *Norwegian barque MONARCH, built in 1856 as the British LANSDOWNE, in Bristol.*

lay wondering if Geoffrey was with the sweet Jesus, and if there would be pigs to chase, and rats to hunt with terriers, and lambs, and colts, and puppies. If there were none of those things where the sweet Jesus lived, I thought that Geoffrey would not be very happy there.

When my father came back and asked me how I'd been, I told him of that woman. He said to her, "My God, woman, if ever you have a child it'd serve you right if it had a hare lip and bandy legs!" She cried. And some time later she did have a child, and it did have a hare lip and bandy legs. I heard Father say to John Thomas, "If the woman hadn't slept with her cousin and then had to marry him it wouldn't have happened." I was puzzled about that, too. We moved the day after father came back, because of his anger with that woman. We went to live at Low Cop farm. There were no children there, but there was a brook in which grew yellow flags and golden king-cups. There was golden gorse, too, on the hill slope below Low Cop. And there was my father. So I soon forgot Geoffrey.

9

It was when we were at Low Cop that the first American mowers and reapers came to the English countryside. One day an angry crowd of farm labourers came, demanding to see 'the damned old Yankee'. Father asked them all into the stone-floored kitchen and told the farmer's wife to bring ale and bread and cheese, and soon they were all talking and laughing. When they went away, one of them took off his hat and held it high and cried, "Three cheers for t'owld gintleman!" And I can still hear their cheers ringing amongst the gnarled old apple trees that stood all about the farmhouse.

One evening at sunset father took me down to the river Wye that flowed maybe a mile away. The sky was all shining gold. The air was motionless, and no bird sang. No sound came from the farm animals. The golden light glowed on the yellow gorse on the hill slope. All the world was silent and golden. It is the first sunset I remember. As we walked to the river, the lights faded. The air grew cooler. On the river bank father stripped naked. He walked in, and swam to the far bank and back, his long white hair floating out on the water behind him. And then he made me strip, and led me into the cold clear water. I learned to swim that evening. The Roman cavalry had splashed across that river, hunting the fleeing Britons. Norman knights had forded it, harrying the Saxons. King Arthur and his knights had ridden there. Father talked of them while we rubbed our white skins dry, our feet deep in meadowsweet and ragged robin.

While we were at Low Cop, father became acquainted with Mr. Pellew. George Israel Pellew, rector of Peterstowe parish. He was tall as my father, who stood six feet three. His head was bald, his hair snow white. His eyes were pale blue. His hands were rheumatism-twisted; his shoes slit along the sides to let his bunions out. His voice was as a clear bronze bell pealing gentle yet very strong from a belfry of white marble. We went often to the rectory to visit him. While he and father talked, I sat in a great rocking-chair, which, as I rocked, moved slowly about the room. On the wall was a large picture of the bombardment of Alexandria, with Admiral Pellew, Mr. Pellew's uncle, on his ship's quarter-deck; a drawn sword in his hand. I pretended that my chair was a line-of-battle ship. Sometimes Mr. Pellew would say, "Captain, cease fire! Can't you see the enemy's forts are in ruins?"

10

Oh—Captain!—I liked that! *Ships and the sea!*

When I was a bit past nine, Ben Sarsons, to whom my father's first wife had been engaged, died. He had never married and, dying, he left all his fortune to Auntie Kitty and Auntie Polly; left each of them seventy thousand pounds in direct legacy; as well as the residue of the estate when all was settled. The residue almost doubled their legacy. He had been going to leave all his fortune to Frank, but he was a very strict member of one of the nonconformist churches and, when Auntie Polly told him that Frank drank too much, he changed his will. And telling him that, Auntie Polly set for all time a curse on his money. For it was only in her prudish mind that Frank drank too much. My aunts gave away their school to the assistant teachers. I was to go to Albert Villas and be taught free. Almost at once Auntie Kitty married a man named Robert Latham Frere. A man with a dark face and dark heavy-lidded eyes. It was said that he came from Louisiana, but no one ever knew for certain, nor where Auntie Kitty met him. She bought a fine house six miles from Peterstowe. Spacious lawns and shrubberies, flower beds in wide terraces, fruit and vegetable gardens, greenhouses, and a gardener's and a coachman's cottage. Auntie Polly bought a place called High House, at the edge of Peterstowe common land. Two big apple orchards, shrubberies of laurel, laurustinus, and lilac. Rowan-berry trees, and holly. A great garden with box-bordered paths. Madonna lilies, crown imperial, peonies, wallflowers, narcissi, and a hundred more.

So now Auntie Polly had father and me to live with her. On Sunday I must go twice to church, and on Wednesday evening to prayer meeting. And no more could I play with the village children. I was a 'gentleman's son'.

I mind a summer morning when I woke early, and, because my way downstairs led through Auntie Polly's bedroom, climbed down the branches of an ancient spreading pear-tree that was nailed against the back wall of the house. I took a market basket, and went mushrooming in the dew-drenched fields. By and by, when I was far wandered from High House, a farmer came running and waving a stick and shouting. He asked who I was.

"I'm from High House," I said.

11

"W'oo be 'ee?" he asked.

"Mr. Adams' son," I said.

"Not t'owld gintleman's?" he asked, a puzzled look on his face.

"Yes," I said.

"It be'ant legal, be it?" he asked. I did not know what that meant.

"I don't know," I said.

And he told me to fill up my basket and welcome, and take the mushrooms to t'owld gintleman, wi' his respecks, by Goad! When I got back to High House, I hid my basket and climbed to my room by way of the pear-tree. Later, I fetched my basket, pretending I'd gathered the mushrooms in the morning. If ever I have been a liar, Auntie Polly made me one. And that day at lunch I told father and Auntie Polly of what the farmer had asked me. And father beat his fist on the table and guffawed for a long time. But Auntie Polly went red as a beet. I wondered what it was all about.

Sometimes father and I stayed a few days at Auntie Kitty's. Once while I was playing in the hay-loft, I looked from the window and saw Uncle Robert kissing the gardener's daughter. She tried to push him away, but he held her fast, and set a hand on her breast and, in a minute, he drew her into the coach house. After a little he came out alone, a smile on his face, and went off through the thick shrubbery toward the house. Then the gardener's daughter came, her face very red, and tears on it. She stooped to wash her face at the trough where the horses drank; then tossed her head and walked off, looking very angry. I was puzzled.

It was soon after that that father ceased to visit Mr. Pellew, and Mr. Pellew ceased coming to High House. Trouble was come between them, because, while Mr. Pellew had been told that Auntie Kitty was going to marry Uncle Robert, it had been kept secret from my father. I heard father mutter "bloody old rip". And then soon Auntie Kitty and Uncle Robert went away, to live in Paris. I'd sometimes see Auntie Polly on her knees, crying, and praying to the sweet Jesus. She took me into the garden one day and made me promise never never to be alone with Uncle Robert. In the way that small boys learn things, I came to know that Uncle Robert was squandering Auntie Kitty's money. I heard 'Monte Carlo' and once I heard my father mutter, "the damned Frenchwomen". I wondered what 'Frenchwomen' might mean.

One day a telegram came, saying that Frank had died. And he died very poor, having lately lost all his money. I wore a band of black round my sleeve when I went back to Albert Villas. Then, one day, I got a good idea. A man named Cook used to come to teach us Latin; a simple sort of man whom the boys teased. I began to cry hard one day during class. He came and bent over me and asked very kindly what was the matter. I pointed to the black band on my arm and cried louder. He, sorry for a small boy who had lost someone he loved, excused me from class. I worked that trick a number of times, and squared my account with Frank for having teased me.

It was almost worse at Albert Villas after my aunts left. The teachers made my life miserable by making sneering remarks about my aunts before the other boys; who would look at me and snigger. Then I knew why my father had always disliked the women and had referred to them as 'common stock'.

Mr. Cook left Albert Villas after a while and was replaced by Mr. O'Leary, who supported an aged mother by teaching. A black-haired man he was, with a lean face and flashing impatient black eyes. A restless-seeming man, as though some curb held him in check. On one of his first days at Albert Villas he caught me drawing the picture of a ship on my slate. It was a grey windy day, and in the gas-lit class room we could hear the distant whistles of the tug-boats on the river. He lifted my slate and brought it down on my head with such force that it broke and my head went through it; the frame resting on my shoulders.

"Don't draw ships! Draw anything you like, but not ships!" said Mr. O'Leary. And much I wondered.

When Mr. O'Leary took us walking, he never asked, as did the mistresses, where we would like to go. Always he took us by the road along the river. And always he stared at the ships, a sort of hunger in his dark eyes. He never spoke to us, and did we ask a question often he would make no reply. So we discussed the ships amongst ourselves. Not only English ships came up the river. Sometimes there would be a French or a German, a Swedish or an Italian ship. And now and again there would be a ship with swarthy men on her decks, and a red and yellow flag flying. Then one of the older lads would call, "Look! It's Spaniards!"—*Spaniards, eh?*—And there at once was Francis Drake, with Frobisher and his companions, and the sails of the Armada coming up from under the rim of England's sea. Aye, there was then a sound as of a drum beating!

There were steamers, too, but they interested me less. Lacking in grace, they were, and had about them a sort of smoky cocksureness. Yet there was one that brought with her always the sound of a bugle. The *Argo* her name was, and long ago she had carried troops to the Crimea. Seeing her come round a bend, a lad thought of such words as Sebastopol, Inkermann, and Balaclava. There was a quick vision of six hundred horses at the gallop, manes tossed, sabres shining. Then soon she would be gone by, and the bugle's note was stilled.

One evening a steamer called the *Dumbrody* ran her bows in the mud on the nigh side of the river, and, borne by the tide, swung across the stream till her stern took the other bank; blocking all traffic. All up and down the river then whistles hooted, warning that traffic was blocked. Stevedores came from Bristol and drove the red Kerry cattle from her far-heeled decks into the water. It was dusk, and great bonfires were lit on both river banks. The cattle's eyes bulged in terror as they swam ashore and floundered up the muddy banks. Dogs barked, dashing hither and thither. Winches on the grounded steamer groaned. The bonfires flared, sparks flying high toward the waking stars. The cattle bawled. Mr. O'Leary stood watching, like a man in a daze. And after the *Dumbrody* was floated and gone on her way, with her back broken, he still stood staring at the ships that came hurrying to make up lost time. It was long past the right time when he took us back to Albert Villas. I walked at his side, and until we were at the school door he said no word. Then, with all the other boys gone in, he suddenly laid a hand on my shoulder; gripping me tight. "Salt water, my boy! Salt water—*and ships!*" he murmured. And then somehow I seemed to understand him, and I liked him well. For bringing us in so late he lost his position, and I saw him no more.

In place of Mr. O'Leary a young soft-spoken man named Hook came to teach us our Latin. I liked him from the first, and I think that

14

5.   *Bristol Docks in the 1880's.*

6. *COUNTY OF LINLITHGOW in the Avon.*

he liked me. One Saturday afternoon he invited me to his home, and asked the headmistress if I might go. Because he said that I was doing very well with my Latin, she let me go. I had tea and cake with him and his white-haired mother. Then he bought a bag of bananas and took me down to the docks. He hired a rowing boat and, while I sat in the stern eating bananas, rowed all up and down the docks. Then there came to me a feeling of release, of great freedom. Under the figureheads of ships we passed; figureheads representing women, and warriors, and goddesses. One ship had a red and yellow dragon for a figurehead, I mind. There was scroll work about the ships' bows, in gold and bright colours, and some ships' names were in gold lettering. There was a scent of tar, of cordage, of brine. Sails hung to dry flapped gently in a little breeze. Men high on masts called one to another, in words un-intelligible to me. As we passed beneath the bow of one great ship

16

7. *German ship HENRIETTE, ex British STRATHEARN, in the Avon.*

a sailor seated beneath her boom called down to me, "Hey, Shipmate! How about one of them bananas?" I tossed him one. He caught it, peeled it with a quick jerk, and crammed it whole into his mouth. *'Shipmate!'* A sailor had called *me* Shipmate! Ah, I cannot tell you how it was that then I felt! I was overjoyed, and I was filled with longing inexpressible to go with that sailor whithersoever he and that great ship of his might be going. But then soon I was back at Albert Villas, and the headmistress was saying something sneering about my aunties; and the other boys were sniggering. Oh, a lot I cared then! *'Hey, Shipmate!'* No one knew that I had been so hailed by a sailor! And there were names in my mind, too. Ah, names! Rio, Calcutta, Cape Horn! Names of places far beyond that level grey horizon in the west.

It was soon after that that the holidays came, and now Dolly

17

came into my life again. She was about seventeen or so. Auntie Polly and I drove to Ross to meet her train. On the way back, I sat beside her. I had never seen anyone so beautiful. I wanted to be near her all the time she was at High House, but Auntie Polly told me to go away and not to be a nuisance. I hated Auntie Polly, with a jealous hate. I wanted Dolly to myself, alone, and one night I had her to myself, for I had a frightening dream, and woke up in terror, and cried out. Auntie Polly called to ask what was the matter from her bedroom on the landing below, told me not to be silly and to go back to sleep. Then, in a minute, there was a soft foot on the stairs, and a glow of candle-light. Dolly was come. There was kindness in her eyes, and pity for a small boy afraid. She asked if would I like her to read to me and, when I said "yes", read to me from *Pilgrim's Progress*. But I did not hear a word. I lay looking at her, worshipping her; adoring the sweet tones of her voice. She kissed me at last, and left me, whereupon I went to sleep as children in heaven go to sleep. It was last night, so real it is still. But many, many nights are gone since then, yet I see and hear her still. Oh, many, many nights! A river winding to the sea. Cowslips in green meadows. Daffodils, primroses, wood anemones, dog violets. Blackbirds singing, and thrushes at the dusk. Lambs gambolling. Scent of sweet hay. Old Mr. Pellew's voice, a clear bronze bell. Labourers raising a cheer for my father: a small boy lost in wonder at the meaning of beauty, at the meaning of loneliness, at the meaning of hunger for a thing hid; and always a consciousness of names—of ships, and salt water. Rio, Foochow, Cape Horn. Always that level grey horizon in the west. Ah, ships!

CHAPTER II

YOU'LL FIND IT A HARD LIFE, MY SON

If Auntie Polly could forbid me playing with the villagers' children she could not prevent father associating with the villagers, for he spent hours seated on the bench in the cobble-stoned yard of the Yew Tree Inn, chatting and drinking ale with the farmers and yokels, often answering questions about America. "A wild lot, Sherman's bummers. But we had a great ride." If old Pellew, as my father now called him when he did not speak of him as "that bloody old rip", passed, he ignored him utterly.

Time passed, and things were better at Albert Villas. I was getting well up in the school and one of the older boys now. If I tried to, I could always be at the top of my class. I did not always try. My dislike for the women forbade it. Boy pride. But now I was allowed at times to go out alone, and ever I went by the river or docks. My lesson books were covered with drawings of ships.

Sometimes by the docks I dared to speak to a sailor, but sailors seemed never to have much to say to a young lad. Yet there was a day when one did speak to me. I was wandering one late afternoon along a dock, when I heard loud words harshly spoken across the street; and I saw a big man quarrelling with a little woman. Cursing her he was, and beating her with a stick. So over the street I strode, large as round thirteen or so might be, and began to take the woman's part. At once she turned on me, and the two of them, shouting, threatened to cut out my lights and my liver; and called me by many names the like of which

19

I had not heard before. Then it was that three sailors came across the street. While one knocked the man down, another walked off with the woman who now was all smiles.

The third turned to me, looked at me solemnly, and, speaking in a slow drawled voice, said, "That's life fer ye, sonny boy! W'en a big man's fightin' a little man, take the little feller's part, sure enough. W'en two big or two little fellers is fightin', let 'em fight an' settle it. But w'en ye see any kind uv a man at all, big or little, raisin' hell wid any woman at all—lay low an' vast heavin'; or ye'll have the two of 'em down yer neck, an' the woman furdest o' the two. 'Tis jest a way they have, sonny. Ye kin pin yer trust in a ship, but don't be pinnin' it in no woman. Have ye a pocket knife, sonny?"

I handed him my pocket knife, and he cut a chew of tobacco from a black plug, put the rest of the plug in his pocket, and my knife with it, and walked off.

"Please, sir, you have my knife," I called.

To which, looking over his shoulder he replied, "No, sonny. 'Tis mine now fer th' advice I give ye." Then I saw the first sailor come from the house into which he had gone with the woman, and the second go into it. To the man with my knife the first called, "Eh, Jock, lad! Ye'd best be comin' over!" To which the man with my knife called back, "Naw, shipmate! I've the wife to home."

Then to me he called, "There's a bit more advice fer ye, sonny! W'en you find the right gal—stay wid her!" And, wondering much what it was all about, I went back to Albert Villas.

It was soon after that that the son of the woman who owned Bowers arrived at the school. I'd not seen him before. Round maybe twenty-five or so he was, and a sailor, and his ship had come to Bristol. Next day one of the women, having some parcels to take him and needing me to help carry them, took me to the docks. His ship was named the *Tythonus*,* and was in from South America. He showed us over her, and I can still see every foot of her decks. Asking no questions, I listened like a weasel. "Madeira" he said, and "Santos", and "Bahia". I seemed no longer a schoolboy: I was far off, where islands were in a wide sea. And I knew that I belonged on that sea: though I could not have voiced it. Had anyone asked me of what I was thinking I'd have

---

* Built in 1862 by Pile, Spence of Sunderland and of 1152.N.R.T., the *Tythonus* was owned by Gillison and Chadwick, of Liverpool. [Ed.]

8. *American ship JOSEPH B. THOMAS at Bristol.*

replied, shyly, "I don't know," or, more likely, "Nothing."

Before long the *Tythonus* was gone down the river, gone 'neath that level grey horizon in the west, and I was nigh fourteen, and in a world filled with mystery. Adolescence approaching. The older boys talked of new things. I mind a night when one asked, "How do women get babies?" And another replied, "They go into a dark room and pray." However it may be today with youth, in that day we knew naught save what we might imagine. About that time there came to the school to teach us our Latin a woman. The other women were round maybe forty or so, but this was not much more than a woman grown. Flaxen hair, she had, and keen blue eyes in which was a sort of smoulder: a

21

long mouth, and a queer way of smiling when she took us walking. There was about her a something that disturbed us. There was rivalry as to who should walk with her. Our rivalry made her laugh, and her laughter increased our rivalry. Did her shoe-string become loose and a boy kneel to tie it, there was excitement in tying it: a vague, disturbing thing. Yet definite, too. She would lay a hand on a boy's head when he knelt, or would tweak an ear gently, saying "Thank you". And there would be in her eyes that smoulder. It made one restless. Yet not restless exactly. Just a something. At the school, in the class rooms, with the other women about her, her face was frigid, unsmiling. Her eyes were cold. We could not understand.

When I was fourteen, I left Albert Villas and took an examination at one of the great public schools. Passing it gained me a scholarship that took fifty pounds a year off my tuition fees for three years. Uncle Robert had run through all Auntie Kitty's fortune and she was now drawing on Auntie Polly. Thus I must win a scholarship, to save Auntie Polly expense. Sometimes Auntie Kitty came to High House and they talked far into the night. One night I heard Auntie Kitty say, "Mary dear, I've never been a wife to him." It puzzled me. How could she be married to him, and not be his wife? I wondered. I heard her say once, too, "I believe in God. I believe in the devil." She had always been kind to me, and now she believed that God and the devil were one. Much perplexed, I was. I never asked my father anything. He never told me anything, save once to say, "My son, be a good boy. Be a good man." He spoke in a matter-of-fact fashion, as though meaning, "Take life as it comes. Don't get all fussed up."

Auntie Polly was delighted that I had won the scholarship. To have pleased her didn't give me any particular satisfaction, but my father's commendation made me feel proud. Also I had pride of my own. But when I went to the school, my pride left me. I found myself looked down on by the other boys for the reason that my sitting for a scholarship implied that my people could not afford to pay my way. I was humililiated, and rebellion woke in me. Silent rebellion. At Albert Villas I had enjoyed the school games, cricket and football. Now I found that to play them three times a week was compulsory. They ceased therefore to be games. I shirked them, and was looked down on the more by the mob for so doing. I was in the Headmaster's house, with some sixty other boys of from fourteen to nineteen and twenty. The Head was a short man with a huge belly, and hanging jowls. A pimple on the ridge of his nose became fiery red when he was angry. As was the case with all the other masters who had houses, he was an ordained clergyman. Each morning before classes all the school gathered in the assembly hall, and there were prayers. Psalms were sung. One of the elder boys read a chapter of the Old, another a chapter of the New Testament. Last thing at night the boys of the Head's house gathered in the big dining room for prayers. The servants were there, the matron who looked after our clothing, and the house-maids. The Head's wife was there, with their four daughters. Duckfoot, Little Widow, Snoots and Tootsie. Some of the elder boys had secret assignations with them; the matron carrying notes. In each dormitory was a prefect, whose duty it was to keep order. Smoking was an expulsory offence. If a boy was heard to swear he was called before a meeting of the prefects, in the head prefect's study. He was given his choice of being reported to the Head, or of writing a thousand lines of Virgil on the next half holiday, or he could take a prefect's 'johnning' — so many blows on the side of his head with the prefect's flat hand. It was the johnning that was always chosen. Such boys as lacked the guts to take a johnning were never in trouble.

A worse humiliation to my pride was the matter of pocket-money. At noon on Saturday the Head assembled the boys of his house and gave to each whatever sum of pocket-money his parents had arranged for him to have. Auntie Polly allowed me none at all. I alone of the sixty boys had no money wherewith to buy tuck at the school tuck shop. The curse on Ben Sarsons' money again.

The school was close to the sea. It was visible from the upper windows, and from the playing fields. Ships passed along the horizon, out beyond the wide bay. While the other boys swarmed in the tuck shop or played the compulsory games, I'd go off alone and gaze at the horizon.

On Sundays all the boys of the Head's house walked to church at the town's other side; walking along the sea-front. They went in twos and threes, chums together. I walked alone, or with a boy named

Redman, who, like myself, had no chum. He was the son of a small farmer who worked in his own fields and hence was not a gentleman. We always walked in silence, having no liking for each other, yet it was better than walking alone, and being conspicuous. Yet, at times I chose to walk alone. Redman scowled at me then. Sometimes on a dark Sunday evening, on our way back from church, two girls would be waiting at a street corner. Two of the prefects would disappear up a side street with them and, going by a short cut, be back at the school with the rest of the boys.

The school terms came and went. The seasons passed. When I came home for my holidays, my father would be sitting in his great high-backed chair by the open fire. As I entered the room he'd look up.

"Is that you, my son?"

And then, "Tonight I shall sleep like a top."

I was his all. He mine. And if I had troubles, I told him naught of them. They mattered not at all when I was nigh him.

Villagers died and were buried. Always when one died the sexton tolled the church bell, once for each year of the life that was over. If a child of one died—one slow clang of the bell. If a gaffer of eighty, the sexton stood long at the bell rope. *Clang—clang—clang—clang.* Eighty times. In winter the foxhounds often swept through the High House apple orchards, in full cry; men in scarlet coats and top hats, ladies riding astride, wearing bowler hats and black habits, leaping the hedges. In Autumn each parish held its Harvest Thanksgiving, according to when the crops were in. Peterstowe might hold it this week, Bridestowe next week, Hentland the week following. The farmers bought the best of their produce to the church. Sheaves of heavy-headed wheat, oats, barley, rye. Great shining apples, red, russet, yellow, green, and pears. Turnips, carrots, beets, mangold wurzels, swedes, cabbages—whatever grew in the rich acres of Peterstowe parish. The women brought their choicest flowers. Children gathered long trailing tendrils of clematis from the hedges. In the deep stone windows all along each side of the old church were set the sheaves of golden grain, the fruits, the vegetables. The stone font in which, through hundreds of years, Peterstowe children had been baptized

24

was twined about with clematis, with crimson-leaved Virginia creeper, and hops. The high oaken pulpit whence Mr. Pellew leaned down on Sundays was creeper-twined, flower-garlanded. The farmers and labourers came with their wives and children, filling the old oaken benches. Mrs. Thomas, Mrs. Evans the charwoman, and others such, sat with their dresses open; feeding the labourers of a future day. Voices rang, far-echoing over field, meadow and pasture, over the woods and bubbling brooks where golden king-cups grew.

> *The sower went forth sowing,*
> *The seed in secret slept*
> *Through weeks of faith and patience*
> *Till out the green blade crept;*
> *Till warmed by summer sunshine*
> *And fed by winter rain,*
> *At last the fields were ripened*
> *To harvest once again.*

And old Mr. Pellew's voice would ring, high above all other voices, his twisted hand upraised, the sunshine streaming in through the leaded window upon his bald head,

> *Then thank the Lord,*
> *Oh, thank the Lord*
> *For all his love.*

With the harvest done, there'd be a concert in the great barn behind the rectory. Lanterns hung along the white stone wall, and above the platform at the barn's far end. Farmers and labourers from all the parish crowded the backless wooden benches.

> *D'ye ken John Peel with his coat so gay?*
> *D'ye ken John Peel at the break of the day?*
> *D'ye ken John Peel when he's far far away*
> *By the cry of his pack in the morning?*
> *'Twas the sound of his horn called me from my bed,*
> *And the cry of the pack that he oft times led,*
> *Peel's View-halloo would have wakened the dead,*
> *Or a fox from his lair in the morning.*

Later, Mr. Pellew would stand in the wide door, and hold out his

25

twisted hand to his people, pat little children on their heads, saying "God bless you all!" while off into the dimmy starlight would wander village lads and lasses. Then there'd be laughing in the lanes, and a sound of quick kisses. The tearing of a dress maybe. Long sighs. And maybe "No, you don't."

There came a day when, with Auntie Polly gone to visit Auntie Kitty in London, my father sent me with a letter to Bridestowe rectory. "Give it to the rector with your own hand, my son," he said. And next day the rector of Bridestowe came, and I stood outside the door to listen. Then I heard my father make the Bridestowe rector promise him that when he died he should be buried in Bridestowe churchyard. I hurried away, leaving the Bridestowe rector to find his own way out. On me fell a great cold dread.

Time passed. I was a sixth form boy, and allowed to carry a walking stick, as was the sixth form's privilege. But yet I had no chum. I could read Cicero, Sallust, Virgil, Horace, Ovid. Long since I'd marched with Caesar's legions over Gaul and Britain; seen British spearmen fall before the broadswords: seen captives walk in Roman triumphs. Over the sea was a new land where my father had ridden 'neath a new flag. 'The bloody owld Yankee.' Tea chests, in Boston harbour. Indians yelling, tomahawks in red hands. The Matabele war was just over. Lobengula, the Matabele chief, had been to London. Not long since, Gordon had died at Khartoum. Not long since a man named Stevenson had written a book, *Treasure Island*. I watched the ships pass.

A school-house boy had been found with a girl in Two Mile copse, and expelled. The Headmaster had chanced to enter the lavatory on the playing field, where smutty rhymes were scribbled over the white-washed walls. The head prefect had come round the dormitories that night, warning. The walls were newly white-washed.

And then there came a holiday when I went to London to stay a while at Auntie Clarissa's. Dolly was there: twenty-five now: soft-voiced and grey-eyed. I felt abashed in her presence. She was different to all other girls. Her sisters went to music halls with men, danced, and told risqué stories. I overheard Ede say one evening, when she thought I was not within hearing, "Isn't he oddly unsophisticated?"

9. French barque MARÉCHAL DE GONTAUT in the Avon Gorge.

I wondered what it meant, and when I went back to school and other boys that night talked smut in the dormitory, I stuffed my fingers in my ears. Fresh-come from altar steps.

Golden gorse along the sea cliffs. Skylarks singing. Blackbirds whistling. In Two Mile copse I found a bullfinch nest one day, and as I came back schoolward, two girls leaned from a window, their bosoms bare, their eyes mocking. I was seventeen and wondered how a girl's bosom would feel beneath my hand. I reddened, and went on; hearing their mocking laughter. That night the dormitory prefect walked out in the dark, to where Duckfoot waited by the playing-field hedge. When he came up to the dormitory no boy spoke. A sort of thrill ran through the dormitory when he put the gas out.

A letter came from Auntie Polly. Which did I want to do; enter Guy's Hospital to train to be a doctor, or go into the paymaster department of the navy? She sent me literature. From being a clerk in the paymaster department I could work my way into the combatant

27

branch of the navy. Drake and Frobisher—Jarvis, Howe and Hood—Collingwood and Nelson. I knew the names of all.

I gave away my silkworms, my pet grass-snake, and my box with lizards in it. No time for aught but study now. In due course, I went to London, took the exam. and failed. Eight vacancies, a hundred and twenty candidates. The Head frowned at my failure; not at *my* failure, but because I'd failed the school. But in London one night, while I was walking in the Strand, a girl had touched my arm, laughed up at me, and asked, "Want a sweetheart, dearie?" I told my dormitory of it, and was in some degree a hero now.

My scholarship three years being done, Auntie Polly could not afford to keep me at school to prepare for the second exam. in November. My failure was a sore point with her. My father said, "You did well to pass as high as you did, my son."

Auntie Polly engaged a young clergyman who lived at Ross, three miles away, to cram me for the November exam. Day by day I walked the three miles and back. Home by one o'clock, to study all afternoon. Going and coming, I leaned on the parapet of the old stone bridge that spanned the river; said to the flowing stream, "Tell the sea that I am coming soon."

Blinx followed me daily, flying along the hedges, or perched on my shoulder. He was a jackdaw a village boy had taken from its nest in an elm behind the church. At night he slept on my window sill. At dawn his cawing woke me, to go to my books before breakfast. While I studied in the afternoon he perched on my shoulder, and gently pecked my ears.

Came a Sunday when I walked with Auntie Polly down the hawthorn-bordered lane. I carried her prayer book. In a way I had ever loved her. Aye, loved her much I had. For was she not my kin? And now she said to me, as though she voiced what long had been in her mind, "You must be a good man, dear. You mustn't be like your father."

Every light went out. A wall of frozen stone stood between her and me. I could not speak. Naught to speak of. "Do you hear, darling?" she asked.

I said, "I heard you." And in silence we entered the church, that she might pray, and sing hymns, to the sweet Jesus.

10. *British full-rigger WISCOMBE PARK in the Bristol Avon.*

August came, and my father saddled the pony and rode off to visit
friends in Hereford. Eighty-seven years old, an eleven-mile ride.

There came a day of wind and driving rain. Just back from Ross,
I sat at lunch with Auntie Polly. The dining-room door opened. My
father stepped in, mud from shoulder to foot. I helped him to his
chair, filled and lit his pipe. He had been riding slowly, a mile from
home, his feet not in the stirrups, the reins not in his hands, when a dog
ran from the hedge and leapt at the pony's nose. Leaving him lying
on the hard road, the pony trotted home. He walked the last mile,
alone. Undressing him that night, I asked, "Do I hurt you, father?"
He answered me, "You never hurt me, my son."

For a time he walked as far as into the garden. Then, staying
always indoors, he sat smoking in his great chair. Days passed. His
bed was brought to a downstairs room. He went forth and back

29

between sitting-room and bedroom unaided for a while. A day came when he stayed in his bedroom. Now I hurried home daily, never pausing to send a message to the sea. Came a day when he sat on the edge of his bed, his great chair empty. Next day he stayed in bed. And that day I stayed home.

Auntie Polly said, "You must go to your tutor, dear."

"No. I stay with my father," said I. And, noting my tone, she was silent.

"Why are you not at your studies, my son?" he asked one day, waking from stupor.

"I'm not going in the navy. I'm going to sea in the merchant service, father," I said.

"You'll find it a hard life, my son," said he, and in his voice was a ring of pride that his son had chosen a hard life. They were the last words ever he spoke to me.

That afternoon, wandering, he cried a woman's name. Not that of Auntie Polly's mother. Not that of mine.

"My rose of roses!—Oh, my dear rose of roses!" he cried.

"Some old flame," said Auntie Polly, scornful-voiced. But I— what was it to me? Naught. It was my father's business. Who shall come between a lad and his sire?

Later that afternoon the door of his bedroom opened. Mr. Pellew entered, stepped to, stood beside my father's bed. Aware of someone, my father murmured, "Who is it?"

"Me—Your old friend Pellew."

My father reached out a frail hand, felt for Mr. Pellew's twisted hand. Their fingers met. "I'm glad to see you, old friend." He never spoke again.

Clang—clang—clang—clang, eighty-seven times. The church bell pealing over the meadows, the fallow fields, the woodlands, the brooks, the sere winter hedges, of Peterstowe parish.

It was November, with snow falling. I stood by his coffin. In the stone-floored kitchen sat his bearers; eating, in the Old Country fashion, cold roast beef and bread and cheese, washing them down with ale. Presently the bedroom door opened, and Jones of Low Cop, Thomas of Bowers, Bill Weevin, shepherd at Flann farm, Jack Evans,

30

wagoner at Flann farm, Badham the blacksmith, Jimmie Link the poacher, and Jack Hall of the Yew Tree Inn came in. In silence they lifted, in silence bore him away, down the stone front steps, past laurel and lilac, out to the lane. Walking alone, I followed. Behind me my aunts, his daughters. Behind them Polly Dobbins, the servant girl. No others. In deep snow we walked slowly, the bearers with their black hats in their hands. A little way from the churchyard gate Mr. Pellew met us, snow falling on his bald head, on his long white surplice. *"I am the resurrection and the life."* He turned, and I followed him into the churchyard through a great crowd of villagers, who, staying without, came none of them into the churchyard.

"Come, darling," said Auntie Polly, laying a hand on my arm.

"Go. I stay," I said. And for a little I stood alone. And then I went from the churchyard gate without which yet stood that great crowd of silent villagers. A farmer looked at me coldly.

"'Twarn't roight!—T'owld gintleman 'ee wanted to be putt i' Bridestowe," said the farmer. And then I knew why they had stayed without the gate.

I said, "No. Father and Mr. Pellew made it all up. It's all right."

And they pressed toward me, hands outstretched. "Goad bless 'ee, young maister," they said, gripping my hand. "Ah didn't knoaw. We didn't none o' us knoaw."

Next day I went to Hereford to stay a while with my father's friends. Three days later a letter came. Blinx was dead. He'd refused to take food from anyone; had sought me everywhere, cawing. A little black bird dead for the love of a lad.

I came home to High House. My father's things would be there. His pipes, his walking sticks, his slippers, his old muzzle-loading gun. They would be mine now; my own dear treasures. All of them. I, his son.

And I found nothing. High House had been swept and garnished. He might never have been. There was no thing of his, no sign that ever he had been there, and I knew that Auntie Polly had done away with all that had been his, hoping to wean me from his memory. Thereupon a great blackness came to my heart. But I said nothing. Not a word. I hid the thing I felt.

CHAPTER III

RISE AND SHINE

I had thought that there was nothing more that Aunt Polly could do to take my breath away, but she had another shot in her locker. She said that it would be beautiful for me to be a curate, and that we would go to Ross together to consult my curate tutor about my preparing for the ministry.

"I'm going to sea," said I.

She thought that I was referring to the navy clerkship and that I had not realized that, through having missed the November examination, my chances there were done. "You can't go to sea, dear," she replied.

"I'm going to sea in the merchant service," I retorted.

Whether she was then aware that I was my father's son, or whether she realized that after all for me to go to sea would cost her a lot less than preparation for the ministry, I don't know. She toddled off to visit an old fellow who lived not far away and was interested in a Liverpool shipping firm. He'd been friendly with my father, and he told her he would write to the son of the head of the firm on my behalf. After a week or so there came a letter from that young man, saying that he had found me a berth as an apprentice in the ship *Helenslea*, bound for West Australia. Then again I had names in my head. Ah!— I liked the name Helenslea. There was music in it, and also there was music in West Australia. I dug out the atlas and pored over it, while I remembered Mr. O'Leary, and was very sorry for him. But in a few days there came another letter telling me that after all I could not go in the *Helenslea*. A lad whose parents had influence with her owners

33

had been given the berth that was to have been mine. My disappointment was bitter.

Disconsolately I wandered the winter roads, wondering should ever I get to sea, and very gloomy I was when I saw the *Helenslea*'s sailing reported in the shipping column of the newspaper. You cannot always tell, eh? From that day to this no eye has seen the *Helenslea*.*

A letter came from Auntie Clarissa, inviting me to go and stay with her for a time, and very glad I was to go. I was gladder yet when I found that Dolly was there. She was more than ever lovely. Loveliness born of bitter grief. She had been in love, and the man whom she loved had died. In her bitter sorrow she had tried to end her life, that she might go to him. Now she had gone to the Bible for solace, prayer the fountain whereat she drank deep. Knowing that I also was alone, she looked at me from soft tender eyes. I was shy in her presence, yet liked to be near her. Yet also I liked very well to be with Ede, her younger sister. Ede and I went to cheap music halls together, where girls in tights danced and sang suggestive songs, and we sat up late, by the drawing-room fire: till Auntie Clarissa would call down the stairs, "You children *must* go to bed." I'd sit in her bedroom, while she took down her hair; smiling at me from sly eyes. I'd sit till she'd say, "Now trot along, sweetheart! You're a nice boy, but I'm going to take off my petticoat." And I'd go, puzzled; led on, then told to trot along. Photographs of three or four men in her bedroom made me jealous.

After a while there came another letter from that young man. I was to join a ship in Liverpool in a few days. And the ship's name was nicer than even Helenslea. The men who called on Ede looked at me condescendingly—a sailor! City men, content with the gas-lit offices of foggy days. Men to whom such words as Rio, Callao, Cape Horn were naught but mere names.

The night ere I returned to Peterstowe to get ready to go, Dolly called me to her bedroom. I see it yet. The snow of her pillow. The Bible on the chair beside. She had been away that day, visiting Auntie Kitty in London, and while she was there, a package had come to Auntie Kitty from Auntie Polly. A golden ring, set with pearls. Something more for Auntie Kitty to pawn, to raise money to satisfy

* In fact, she was wrecked on Inaccessible Island but, as it was some time before her fate was known, she was believed to have gone missing. The *Helenslea* was a steel barque, owned by Chadwick Wainwright, of Liverpool. [Ed.]

Uncle Robert's lust. Auntie Kitty had pawned the ring, and Dolly had taken from her the pawn ticket; and later redeemed the ring. "It was your mother's, dear," she said, and gave it to me. Never had I had aught that had been my mother's. Bidding me goodbye next day, Dolly kissed my cheek.

When I came to Peterstowe, Aunt Polly saw the ring on my finger, and said sharply, as though I were a small boy who had done something wrong, "Give me that ring at once. Where did you get it?"

"I don't give you my mother's ring to pawn," I retorted. And she said no more, for the tone of my voice was a tone new to her.

The night ere I left to join my ship there was a concert in the rectory barn. I was late getting there. It was crammed with the people of Peterstowe parish. But when I appeared, a farmer took my arm and led me to a seat that had been reserved for me. I heard a voice say, "Young maister, 'ee be gwine away come marnin'."

The rafters shook, to the voices of Peterstowe parish.

> *D'ye ken John Peel with his coat so gay?*
> *D'ye ken John Peel at the break of day?*
> *D'ye ken John Peel when he's far far away*
> *By the cry of his pack in the morning?*

And,

> *I'll never never part by a sale or a swap*
> *From the filly that stands in the stall at the top.*

And then a farmer rose and walked to the platform, and, with kindly eyes turning to me as he sang, sang a song such as never before I had heard in the rectory barn:

> *When his ship is trimmed and ready*
> *And the last goodbyes are done,*
> *When the tug boat's lying waiting,*
> *And Jack aboard is gone,*
> *Then the lasses fall a'weeping*
> *As they watch his vessel's track,*
> *For all their landsmen lovers*
> *Are nothing after Jack.*

And then, again,

35

With a long long pull, and a strong strong pull,
Cheerily, lads, yo-ho!
And we'll drink tonight to the midshipmite,
Cheerily, lads, yo-ho! Cheerily, lads, yo-ho!

I knew then that the concert was being given for 'young maister', who was to be gone in the morning, and there was a lump in my throat.

"God bless you, my boy. I hope you'll succeed. I know you will if you try," said old Mr. Pellew, taking my hand in the doorway. And I walked from the barn, and turned from the rectory drive, through the gate into the churchyard. And I paused by a grave.

"You'll find it a hard life, my son," I heard. Pride in the voice.

Aunt Polly was gone to bed when I came in. She called to me to come to her bedroom. Reading her prayer book, she was. She bade me kneel, and we said the Lord's Prayer together. Then she made me promise that I would not smoke, nor drink any liquor, nor play cards till I was twenty-one; and that I would not marry till I was thirty. She kissed my cheek, and I hers. How I wished that that wall were not between us! For she was my kin, and I was dire lonely. Only I knew of that wall. She was unaware of it.

Next day I came to Liverpool, and found that young man. Gilson, his name was. He had been a sailor but was retired from the sea to be in his company's office. They owned a fleet of tramp steamers. He took me to the Sailor's Home and helped me to purchase my sea gear; paying for it with the money that Aunt Polly had sent him. "You don't need to buy a sea chest. I've got one I'll let you have cheap. And I've a pair of good sea boots you can have cheap too," he told me. After my outfit was bought, he told me to meet him next morning when he would take me to the office of the owner of my ship.

I sat at the end of a long wooden bench, before an open fire, in the Sailor's Home that evening. Outside, the night was dark, and rain drove by. At the other end of the bench sat another lad, rigged out as was I in the uniform of a sea apprentice. Eight bright brass buttons on a double-breasted blue serge suit. A blue cloth cap with a shiny leather peak; and the company's house flag above the peak, circled by gold braid.

Full of sailors the great room was. Tall men and short, broad and narrow, old and young, bearded and shaven. Tanned faces, and far-seeing seeming eyes. Stoop-shouldered a little, most of them. Some played billiards. Some stood in groups, talking. Some sang, gathered about a piano that a young man strummed merrily. A strange song, with wind in the words and a slap of water. A rolling care-free chorus.

The door opened, and a lad with a laughing face entered. You might have said, "He owns the earth," so twinkle-eyed he was. He also wore an apprentice's uniform; but the buttons were tarnished, and the braid of his cap faded. He came straight to me, and sat down.

"Going to sea?" he asked.

"Yes," I answered.

"Don't go. The sea's hell," he returned.

I said nothing. He asked the name of my ship. He said, "That's my ship too. She's a hard, hungry old bitch. Go back home."

Again I said nothing. He remarked, casually, "You call the carpenter Chips, and the sailmaker Sails." Then he rose, winked at me, and added, "Got a date with my girl." And away he went.

The lad at the other end of the bench moved over to me. "Do you suppose it's as bad as he says?" he asked.

"I don't know," I replied. I didn't feel attracted by him and soon I rose and went up to my cubicle on the topmost of four galleries that encircled the large building, but all night I scarce slept. For all night there was the click of billiard balls, the strumming of the piano, the singing, and always a murmur of voices. Names, endless names. Taltal, Anjer, Frisco, Rio—the Horn.

Next morning the owner of my ship looked at me from satirical eyes. I didn't like him. A pallid clerk set on the counter before me my apprentice indentures, whereby I was to bind myself to serve the owner for four years with no pay at all.

The said apprentice to furnish all sea bedding and wearing apparel, and faithfully to serve his said Master, his executors, administrators, and assigns; to obey his and their lawful commands, and keep his and their secrets; and not absent himself from their service without leave; nor frequent taverns nor ale houses unless upon their business; nor play unlawful games. In consideration whereof the said Master covenants to teach the said apprentice, or cause him to be taught, the business of a

37

seaman and provide him with sufficient meat, drink, and lodging and medical and surgical assistance and to pay said apprentice the sum of thirty pounds.

I took the pen, to sign my name. The owner said, "Better read your death warrant before you sign it." His satirical voice riled me. I signed it, unread.

"I'm going down to the ship. He can come with me," said the owner. Mr. Gilson wished me good luck. I followed my owner to the windy street. There were low dark clouds scurrying overhead, and in a moment, turning a corner, I saw a forest of spars and masts above the warehouse roofs. The wind buffetted us.

"Going to be lively outside, if this keeps up," said my owner, speaking to himself. Outside!—Ah!—Salt water!—*Sailor, sailor, sailor!*

We passed through a gate. Forty years are gone since that morning. But I see her still, just as then I saw her. Her stern toward me, on it her name in golden lettering. *Silberhorn.*

Her beauty smote me. Sky-pointing masts, low hull, wide tapering spars. Perfection of symmetry. And *mine*. Ah—salt water and ships at last! "You'll find it a hard life, my son." I did not think of those words then.

My owner led me along a rope-littered deck on which sails lay outspread. Riggers were aloft, getting her sails up; shouting to one another. Should ever I be able to learn *that* language? My owner led me to a small man amidships, and to him said, "Think you can make a sailor out of this fellow, mister mate?"

The mate* glanced at me uninterestedly, looked aloft and shouted to a rigger. My owner turned and went. A rope falling from aloft dropped heavily on my head and shoulders, knocking my cap off and almost knocking me down. Another, running through a block, tangled my feet. I fell, and rose red-faced. The mate said, "You can come aboard tonight." I was relieved to go ashore.

It was dark when I went aboard again, a porter carrying my sea chest. I with my canvas sea bag on my shoulder. In it my oilskins, sea boots, blankets, tin plate, tin pannikin, tin knife and spoon. I entered a tiny alleyway whence on each side a door opened into a tiny room—

* John H. Lowry of St. Mawes, aged 30.

11. *Salthouse Dock, Liverpool, in the 1890's. On the left, the Shaw, Savill full-rigger WELLINGTON lies ahead of the HELENSLEA. In the centre the 4-m. ship HIGHFIELDS lies outside the MELANOPE, with the white Russian schooner ZERIBA inside her. The vessel in the immediate foreground is the LADAS.*

the apprentices' half-deck, just behind the mainmast. Four lads each side. In each side just room for four narrow bunks, and four sea chests set about a tiny table hinged to the outer bulkhead. I saw the black-haired lad who had asked, "Do you suppose it's as bad as he says?" I saw that other also, and he saw me.

"You damned fool! I told you to go back home," he said, but spoke with a laugh in his eyes. Glynn Williams, his name was. He had been at sea a year. So had two others, Hickley and Barford. Thompson had served a year in a different ship. Taylor and Douglas had been for two years in a training ship anchored in the Mersey. Only Wood, the black-haired lad, and I were quite green.[*]

Having had no sleep the previous night, I was very tired. But they sat talking till midnight. Then I was asleep the moment my head touched my pillow. The straw mattress, the 'donkey's-breakfast' on which I lay, was more comfortable than my feather bed at Peterstowe ever had been, but in a minute I was awake again. Ten to five of a dark February morning, and my birthday. The watchman was lighting our lamp. He had set a large tin pot on the table. I dressed as did the others, in dungaree jumper and trousers, and drew my sea boots on. No one drank any coffee. I tried to and could not. The pot looked as though it had never been washed. The coffee was bitter well nigh as aloes.

"Turn to! Wash the decks down!" bawled a surly voice outside. I followed the others to the dim deck, my eyes heavy with sleep.

"Jesus Christ! Wot in hell d'ye think ye are? Get out o' they glad rags!" The second mate, speaking to Wood who had dressed in his nice new uniform. He crimsoned, and hurried back to change. Apprentice uniforms are for shore use only.

Three hours of passing heavy wooden buckets from hand to hand, the second mate taking them from the last passer and slapping the water on the deck. Four lads with long-handled brooms scrubbing. In less than half an hour my arms and shoulders ached. My palms were a mass of blisters from the wet rope handles of the buckets.

"Jesus Christ! Step along wi' them buckets!" from the second mate. I stepped along. Wood's face was corpse-like.

At eight, breakfast. The same bitter coffee in the same dirty pot

[*] Hickley was born in Somerset, Williams and Adams in Kent; Barford in Berkshire, Wood in Derby, Thompson in Essex, Douglas in York and Taylor in London, according to the articles. [Ed.]

12. *SILBERHORN.*

and to eat, only hard-tack too flinty for strong young teeth to break. One dipped it in the coffee. From eight forty-five till noon, hauling on grimy ropes, with hands on which the blisters were long ago broken. At noon, tough beef, ill-cooked, and soggy ill-cooked potatoes in their skins. From one till six, hauling on grimy ropes again for a purpose quite unknown, at least to Wood and me. At six, supper. The same dirty tin pot, with a thin brown drink. They said it was tea. Skilly, they called it. It had no flavour save of the dirty pot. Dry hash, made of the dinner leavings, was edible. Glynn Williams said, "There'll be no hash when the old bitch is at sea."

I was about to roll into my bunk after supper when the mate looked in. "Shift ship!" he said, calm as though farmer Jones of Low Cop might say, "Let's us go pick some o' they musherooms."

We moved the ship to the dock nearest the river, to be ready to go out at dawn. No machinery of any sort to help us; we eight lads, with the carpenter, and the two mates, dragged on great ropes till nigh midnight. The ship three hundred feet long, by some fifty wide, by twenty-three feet deep in the water. Three thousand tons of cargo in her holds. We were almost done when the crew came aboard. Singing, shouting, cursing, they rolled drunkenly into their quarters in the forecastle; a deck-house just behind the foremast.

At midnight, my bunk at last, and, blowing the lamp out, Glynn Williams, asking merrily, "Who wouldn't sell a farm and go to sea?"

Then, before dawn, "Turn to! Rise and shine! Shake a leg there! No time for coffee this morning."

Wind cried by. Chill rain drove. I mind a muddy river, and lights winking along its shadowy shores. Then a grey tossed sea. Ahead of the tall clipper a tug boat with smoke pouring from her funnels. I don't know how that day passed. Once I saw, on the poop, a man of medium stature, dour-faced, thin-lipped; with eyes that seemed to say coldly one brief word: *'Obey!'*

"That's the damned Old Man," Glynn Williams told me. I'd seen my captain, the skipper.*

It was nigh dark when MacDonald,† the second mate, dragged from the sail locker two stowaways. Far off a lighthouse winked through the cold evening's scud. As MacDonald came from the locker, each big hand clamped on the neck of a scared young landsman, the Old Man shouted, "Let go the tow boat's line!"

Scowling at me as I passed, following the crew up to the forecastle head, to let go the line, MacDonald growled, "Ye'd moike a bloody foine possenger." I had known that a long time since.

The tug came as close as she dared in the tossed sea, maybe fifty or sixty feet from the ship's side. MacDonald tied a rope round a stowaway, hove its other end aboard the tug, shouted, "Haul in!" and lifted and dropped the screaming stowaway to the cold winter sea. The other struggled, too scared for any screaming but, in a minute, the

* Robert Gibson was 52 at this time. [Ed.]

† Alexander John MacDonald was 23, and came from Deptford. [Ed.]

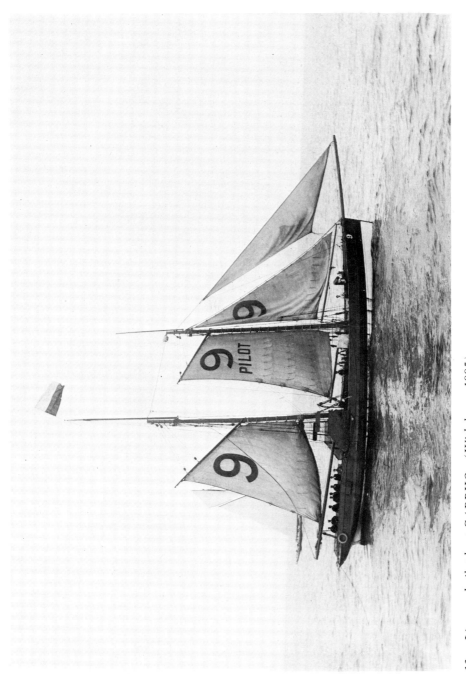

13.   *Liverpool pilot boat SAPPHO. (Withdrawn 1885).*

tug boat men were hauling him in too. The tug turned on her heel, tooted her whistle thrice in farewell, and was gone. We were free, before us fourteen thousand miles of unfenced salt meadows. I'd forgotten Mr. O'Leary and Peterstowe, long ago. All I knew was a great ache, and hunger also. And yet, too, I was aware of something: aware of a strong majesty in my ship, throwing the sprays high, seeming to challenge the long inrolling ocean swells. No ragged robin now, no meadowsweet, no wood anemone, nor bluebell, but bronze bells clanging, sonorous across a sullen sea and, as a sail went threshing and flapping to its mast-head, a deep voice singing; and a roar of windy voices coming in on the chorus of my first sea chantey,

> *And I give you fair warning before we belay,*
> *Waye, aye, blow the man down!*
> *And I give you fair warning before we belay,*
> *Oh, give us some time to blow the man down!*
> *Don't ever take heed of what pretty girls say,*
> *Waye, aye, blow the man down!*
> *Don't ever take heed of what pretty girls say,*
> *Oh, give us some time to blow the man down!*

Girls!—the word seemed incongruous. I wanted vaseline for my broken blisters, hot food for my hungry young belly, sleep. Finally, being allowed to go below for supper of skilly and the last dry hash, since I had no vaseline, I rubbed salt pork grease on my sore palms.

What next I recall is that I was standing at the foot of the poop ladder, on the quarterdeck, with one of the older lads when he cried, "God! Look out!" It was pitch dark by then. There was a roar of blasting wind, and a great sea crashed over the bulwarks, while from high aloft came a report like the crack of a cannon. A sail ripping, though I did not know it then. The older lad leapt up the ladder; but that sea caught me and swept me from my feet and to and fro; me clinging to a stanchion with both hands, water down my neck, my clothing all soaked, my sea boots full of water. Utter darkness and, just audible in the wind's savage roar, shouts. I made my way up the ladder at last, and someone bumped into me, and a voice shouted, "Who is it?" I shouted my name, and the voice shouted back, "Stay where you are! Hold on!" The Old Man. And I clung there, in the pitch dark, with

44

14. *A hard initiation. (View aboard the Finnish barque WINTERHUDE).*

the ship rolling till I knew that she would roll right over and never come up. Now and then a half-heard cry in the darkness. Now and then another report like that of a cannon. I was not afraid. I was past that. I was numb. Mind and body numb, in that utter darkness and that continual savage roar. I didn't think. I just clung, waiting for the ship to roll over. But at some time in the night one of the older lads was with me on the main deck, and we were making our way through water that tore at our thighs toward the half-deck, he with a hand clutching my arm. We entered the half-deck, and I saw that it was Glynn Williams, "You damned fool, what did I tell you?" he shouted, merry-eyed. In the half-deck two feet of water swirled to and fro with each mad roll of the ship and, lapping up to my straw mattress, soaked it. But that didn't matter at all. I fell onto my mattress. Ah, *sleep!*

And next thing I remember is that it was day, and I was on the poop. The ship was rolling her rails under in quick succession, one after the other; her decks a rage of rushing white water. On each mast was one tiny sail only, and yet she was running like a stag with the hounds at its heels. Near her was another ship, and *her* masts hung in wreck, and she was flying a distress signal. All we could do was to run on, leaving her to her doom. At some time in the morning the mist cleared, and right ahead of the ship was a fanged black coast; rocks reaching out to bid her welcome. Just time to turn away, only just time. Mates shouting, Old Man shouting. Weary sea-soaked sailors yelling at the ropes, and then she was running again with the wind-hounds at her heels. That night lights winked ahead, and soon after midnight her anchors were down. They still speak of that gale along those coasts. Eleven ships were lost that night. We saw one, as we ran past Lundy Island, hard on the rocks, her masts gone, her decks beneath the sea, no one on her.

It was only when I opened my sea chest that I, had I then known how to curse, would have cursed Mr. Gilson. Its contents were sodden, all of them. Not till then did I find that there was a long crack all along the bottom of my sea chest. One of the other lads, noticing my sea boots, said, "Good God! What in hell did you get felt-lined sea boots for?" Felt-lined sea boots, once wet, never dry till fine weather. Mr. Gilson had no doubt used them in a steamer, where they would be right enough. It was just one more example of the curse on old Ben Sarson's money, Auntie Polly having asked Mr. Gilson to spend no more than needs be on my sea outfit because of Uncle Robert's needs! Since the things in my sea chest were not quite so wet as those on my body, I changed into some of them.

We were anchored in Barry Roads, off the Welsh coast. Fifty

46

miles or so away was Peterstowe, where soon now spring would come marching with its daffodils, and bluebells, its dog violets and primroses; its song of thrush, blackbird and yellowhammer. I did not think of Peterstowe. It might have been a thousand miles away. I rolled into my soaked bunk and slept, and knew nothing, till at ten to five came MacDonald, bellowing at the half-deck door, "Wash the decks down! Jesus Christ! Step along!" He talked of Jesus almost as much as did Auntie Polly. So out we went and found we had to wash the decks down with no help from the crew. The crew had mutinied. They'd told MacDonald to go to hell and take the bloody ship with him. I mind one of them well; the rest indistinctly, a mob of weary faces, sullen-eyed. A sea had crashed into their forecastle; had smashed the door from its hinges. There wasn't a donkey's-breakfast left in any bunk, not a blanket, nor anywhere a tin plate left, nor a pannikin, nor a fork nor a spoon. Their clothes were gone. Everything was gone over the side to the sea. The forecastle was gutted. They'd slept on the bare hard planks of the forecastle deck that night, all soaked to the bone, and now "T' 'ell wi' t' bloody bitch!"

So soon the Old Man came forward to see about talking some sense into his sailors. "Come, men, what's all the fuss about? Get along now, and turn to!"

Then that one man I mind stepped out from the others; a giant of a man he was, with a bushy red beard, and a mop of wild red hair, and big glittering hard blue eyes. He faced the Old Man, looked him straight in his eyes, and he said, "Ye think *we'd* take yer bloody unlucky owld bitch round the Horn, do ye? Ye think that, eh? By God, go on an' think wot ye bloody please, Captain, an' no damned offence meant, by God! Yer bitch is unlucky, an' she'll never get round the Horn, an' to hell with her! We'll touch no rope of her more, an' be damn to her! Aye, we've had all we want o' *this* bitch!" And a murmur of approbation rose from the sullen-eyed men at the big man's back, and then the Old Man said, "You've signed articles. It's duty or jail. Take your choice!"

And at that the big man cried loud, so that his deep voice rang the ship's length, "I'd sooner be six bloody years in any bloody jail than head south for the Horn in *your* bitch, Captain! An' that goes for me

47

15. One of de Wolf's older ships, the ERIN'S ISLE, built in St. Johns in 1887.

mates too—" and he turned and looked at his scowling fellows, and from them again came another loud murmur of approbation. At this, the Old Man turned and walked aft, and the men went back into their forecastle and sat on its hard bare planks, leaning their wet backs against its cold iron bulkhead. Not so much as one pipe amongst the mob of them. Not a crumb of tobacco. Nothing. And in mid-morning a tug boat came off to the ship and they went aboard her, and she took them and the Old Man ashore. We saw no more of them. Six months in jail they got, for refusing duty; and we heard that that big red-bearded man, on hearing that sentence passed, cried to the judge, "Yer a damned fine man, Judge: Good luck to ye!" *

MacDonald let us have a full hour for breakfast that day instead of the usual three-quarters. And then out we went, and down to the sail locker to drag great rolls of sails about, making them handy for the riggers to get aloft in place of those that had been blown away. It took all morning, and how the afternoon went I know not at all. Too tired to know anything, I was. But night came at last, and then it was the long night in; save that two apprentices must stay on deck, for two hours, to keep anchor watch. The older lads drew lots to see which two should take which hours, and it fell to me to take the watch from midnight till two of the morning. But for my partner, I had, by good luck, Glynn Williams. I liked him best of them all. But when we turned out at midnight in the cold rain, he curled up in his oilskins in the lee of the deckhouse, and left me to stand watch alone. "The old hooker's all right," he said, when he wakened at a bit before two. "The rain's quit and the night's clear. Sit down and make yourself at home." So I sat down by him, and he asked me about my people, and did I like girls, and what in God's name I came to sea for. I'd little to say of my people, and less of girls, for I knew not a thing of them, and his last question I left unanswered. He laughed, and said, "It's in a damned fool's blood I guess, and he can't help it."

Next morning letters came off, and parcels for some of us. I'd a parcel from Mrs. Hall of the Yew Tree Inn. A big round fruit cake, and butter, and two loaves of Yew Tree bread, and a ham from a Peterstowe pig. Not a one of them had so fine a parcel as had I. Also I'd a letter from Auntie Polly, who wrote that she thanked the sweet

* All 14 of them were jailed in Penarth. [Ed.]

Jesus for having taken care of me and for bringing me safe in from the terrible storm.

Ten days we lay in Barry Roads, while stevedores took out damaged cargo and carpenters repaired the forecastle. One of the hatches had been smashed by a sea, and water had got down into the hold. Riggers came off too, and sent down what few ragged remnants were left of her split sails, and sent up new in their places. New sails came off too, for the law said that a ship must have three full suits, and we'd lost almost one whole suit. We lads dragged the sails from the locker for the riggers, and we stowed the new sails in it, and when we were not at that we were kept busy polishing brass work, and cleaning rust spots from the bulwarks—a tedious job that Polly Dobbins or any little housemaid could have done! Every night Glynn Williams and I kept anchor watch together. We'd sit on the rail and gaze shoreward. Lights winking. Warmth, over there. Wide fireplaces and good things to eat. All we ate during the ten days was just what we should have eaten had we been at sea. Salt pork, salt junk, pea soup, bean soup, and, except for potatoes, no vegetables at all. The potatoes were always ill-cooked and soggy. The grub in our parcels we kept to eat during anchor watch. Glynn had but a small parcel. Sharing mine, he said, "You're a damned good shipmate, Bill!"

And I liked that. *Shipmate*, eh? I minded that sailor who long ago in Bristol dock had called me by that name. One night Glynn found an extra pipe and gave it to me. "You'd best be learning to smoke," he said. "A pipe'll damn near save a chap's life sometimes." And I said, "I've got no tobacco."

Glynn said, "You've the picture of a damn pretty girl in your bunk. I'll give you a pound of 'baccy for it." And I gave him Ede's photograph. I had no picture of Dolly, and had I had, I'd not have traded it for anything at all.

In the evenings we'd sit in our half-deck. Some would write letters home, some talk. Sometimes there'd be singing. Wood never talked, never joined in any song. Utterly miserable, he looked always. He was twenty-two,* older than any of us by several years. Glynn told me one night, "If you're going to be a sailor, you want to start young. Wood's too old."

* Richard Vincent Wood was born in 1877. [Ed.]

Wood came from a wealthy home, an only son. He'd tried his hand at several things and had not liked them. And then he'd tried his hand at several more things and had not liked them either, so then he'd taken a notion he'd like to be a sailor. Then, to find out if he really liked the sea, his father sent him across to Canada and back, first cabin passenger in a fine liner. When he told that, the older apprentices hooted with laughter. He had not brought even a razor with him, thinking there'd be a barber in a sailing ship. There was another thing he had not brought, but that we did not find out about till later. MacDonald never looked at Wood without scowling.

My hands healed while we lay off Barry. Maybe it was not going to be so bad! I was content enough. With her brasswork gleaming in the wintry sun the ship was beautiful. A great deal of it she had, more than most ships. I could not help but see her beauty, and she looked so strong, so like a confident bird; at rest on the quiet water.

There came a morning when a little breeze blew from the easterly. It was the first quite clear day since we anchored, and out there came from all the ports along the Bristol Channel the many vessels that had run for shelter from the great storm. They came in a long line, ships, barques, brigs, brigantines, barquentines, topsail schooners, ketches. Vessels of almost every European nation. Coasting vessels mostly, but here and there a tall deepwaterman. Whenever a deepwaterman passed us by, her crew would gather in her rigging and cheer us. *"Three cheers for the Silberhorn!"* And we lads would give her back her three cheers. Then she'd give us one cheer more, and be gone. There are no mornings such as that today, for sailing ships are gone, and steamers have our sea. By and by that lovely fleet was gone save for a few last loiterers, and then the breeze fell quite away, and the sea lay flat. Right ahead of us was a lofty brig. The sun gleamed on her. She was a lovely thing, a seaward-sailing bird. We gathered in the bow, to watch her come; her people working hard to get her anchor over. Something was wrong. Before they could get her anchor over, she was upon us, broadside on. Our boom end struck her mainmast fair, and down it came with a long splintering crash; snapped like a match, the sails upon it all tearing, and then our sharp bow struck her side, and cut deep into her. She might have been a cheese, so deep it cut, crushing

51

her to below her water line. And down she went, her people scrambling to our head rigging. Her skipper looked from our high forecastle head, to where she'd been, then turned to our Old Man. "She was all I had," he said. Our Old Man took his arm and led him away to the cabin. A grey-headed very wrinkled captain, with tears in his eyes. *

Next day our new crew came off. I mind a few of them. There was a lanky Scot named Alexander,† who looked as though he'd read Shakespeare. He didn't, but he sang. He was a chanteyman. There was a little stubby stubbly fellow with one eye; a hideous socket where the other should have been. Smith his name was. Bald, with a big bushy grey moustache. He and the Scot were chums. He looked up and down the deck and grinned, and rubbed his horny hands together. "I 'opes she makes a long voyage. More days, more dollars," he said. There was a young lad named Erickson, from Helsingfors, who knew no English. A youth glad to find other youths aboard, he smiled at us apprentices, a shy soft smile. There was a German lad named Furst, and there were Billings‡ and Thornton, old chums. Billings was pock-marked, with red bleary eyes and a continual sneer. Short and square, he was. Thornton was taller, sallow-faced, but with the same sneer. Seeing us lads, he looked at Billings, winked, and said, "Look at the maiden's choices!" And there was a huge hulking loose-knit yellow-headed man who might have voyaged with Leif Ericson. A giant Norwegian. Johansen.‡ Others I have forgotten. They came aboard toward evening, and lugged their sea bags to the forecastle. Soon afterwards the mate came forward.

"Man the windlass! Heave the anchor in!" shouted the mate.

Tramp, tramp, tramp. Twenty-three pairs of sea-booted feet tramping round and round the windlass on the forecastle head. Men, apprentices and second mate. Ahead the tug boat lay, ready to take us out.

* See Preface, p. XIX. [Ed.]

† Alexander, from Edinburgh, was 29, and had come from the *Wileapauke* with Thornton, from Goole, aged 33. John Smith was from Goole, having left the *Falklandbank* and gave his age on the articles—for what it was worth!—as 48. There is no-one named Erickson on the articles. The name should probably read Bargison, aged 22, from the *City of Truro*. Furst spelt his name Först, and was also 22, his last ship being the *William Anning* of Cardiff. [Ed.]

‡ George Billings, 38 of Salisbury gave his last ship as the *County of Cardigan*. The Norwegian's name was John Hanson, 45. For the rest, there was a Dutchman, a Swiss, a Dane and the rest were British—14 in all. The carpenter was a Finn, the sail-maker a Norwegian and the Cook a Chinaman from Hong-kong. The carpenter had been with the second mate the previous voyage in the *Camp Hill*, the sail-maker had come from the *Fort Douglas* and the cook from the *Acanthus*. [Ed.]

"Sing! Someone sing! Let's hear a sailor sing!" cried the mate. And Alexander sang,

> *Oh, where are you going to my pretty maid?*
> *And away, Rio!*
> *Oh, where are you going to my pretty maid?*
> *And we're bound for the Rio Grande!*
> *And away, Rio! Away Rio!*
> *Oh, fare you well, my pretty young girl,*
> *For we're bound for the Rio Grande!*

Verse after verse, and all hands coming in on the chorus. Tramp, tramp, tramp, and the windlass pawls clinking and the great chain cable clanking slowly in. A hum of wind in the rigging. The tide slapping by. The tug boat's smoke blowing seaward, and you could feel the eagerness of the ship! A bird, waiting to fly!

"Bully boys! Walk her up!" from the mate.

> *In Amsterdam there dwelt a maid,*
> *Mark well what I do say,*
> *In Amsterdam there dwelt a maid,*
> *And she was mistress of her trade,*
> *And we'll go no more a ro–o–vin' with your, fair maid!*
> *A rovin', a rovin', oh, rovin's been my ru–i–in,*
> *We'll go no more a ro–o–vin' with you, fair maid!*

Once again, verse followed verse:

> *I touched that maid upon her toe,*
> *Mark well what I do say,*
> *She said: "Young man you're rather low!"*
> *And she was mistress of her trade,*
> *And we'll go no more a ro–o–vin' with you, fair maid!*
> *A rovin', a rovin', oh, rovin's been my ru–i–in,*
> *We'll go no more a ro–o–vin' with you, fair maid!*

Stamp and go! Stamp and go! Round and round with each verse touching some higher part of that maid's anatomy, the words a far cry from the old concerts in the Peterstowe barn:

> *Mark well what I do say,*
> *She said: "Young man, that's my main hatch!"*
> *And she was mistress of her trade,*
> *And we'll go no more a ro–o–vin' with you, fair maid!*

A rovin', a rovin', oh, rovin's been my ru–i–in,
We'll go no more a ro–o–vin' with you, fair maid!

The lights of Barry winking in the dusk. And fifty miles away was Peterstowe. Through Peterstowe's green trees the wind that blew the tug-boat's smoke was wailing. Goodbye! Goodbye to daffodil, to wood anemone, and bluebell, to thrush and blackbird singing! *Oh, sailor, sailor, sailor!*

Next came the Old Man's voice, in tones impatient, sharp as a hammer's blows on metal, *"Loose the topsails!"* And shadowy forms swarmed up the shadowy rigging to shake her first wings free, and we were on our way.

The next two weeks are but a hazy memory. There never was a sky, nor any sun, nor star. The storm winds blew. Sweeping the long decks over, the wild seas roared. My feet were never dry, and always I was weary. Four hours on duty, four hours off; and never quite four hours sleep at once. It takes a lot of getting used to. I mind a pitch-black night when we hauled on ropes by the foremast; clewing up the fore topgallant sail, a hundred and fifty feet or so high on the reeling night-hid mast. I mind the mate bumping into me, asking who I was, and saying, "Hop up and lend a hand with that sail!"

It was my first time off the deck, and as I climbed into the rigging a spray lashed me, soaking me through. The wind howled, and presently I came to that wide platform round the lower mast-head that's called the 'top'. You have to sway outward there, your head much farther from the mast than are your feet. Somehow in the darkness I made my way over the top, and started up the topmast's slenderer rigging. It swayed beneath my weight. The wind tore at me, and soon I came to the topgallant crosstrees where again you swing outward, your head much farther from the mast than are your feet. I reached my hands up, clutched the rigging above the crosstrees, started to drag myself over them—and lost my feet. And there I clung, and kicked, and kicked again; seeking a foothold. Eternally I clung, gasping, breathless, in the inky night. Finally then I found my feet, and started up again, but then a sailor's boot struck my mouth, so that I tasted blood. The men who'd gone aloft, old seasoned sailors, had furled the sail and were coming down. "Get t'ell out th' way, damn ye!" from one. And from

16.   *A tall ship going the other way.*

another, "It's one o' they blasted green apprentices. Get t'ell out th' way, will ye, damn ye!" And somehow I swung my shuddering self out of their way, and down they went past me. And then, going down myself, I found descent worse than the climb had been.

I mind an afternoon of haze, but with a lot less wind now and all sail set. Suddenly, the mist thinned on a patch of sea near by. The sun broke out upon those few acres of rolling water. And there, shining in that little patch of sudden sunlight, rode a tall ship going the other way. Someone cried, "A homeward-bounder! Look!" And then, all in a tick, the haze rolled over that sun patch, and she was hidden again. A homeward-bounder, eh? And when should *I* come home?

I remember well a day of no cloud, when all the sea was blue. The wind was light. Some work was to be done upon a topsail yard, a hundred feet or so above the deck. Sailors were up there. And the mate said to me, "Hop up and lend a hand there, you, boy!" So up I went, my second time aloft, and now I knew night had been merciful. My head began to swim when I was scarce half way up the lower rigging and, as I higher climbed, all things became a blur. I shook. I shivered. *Vertigo!* I somehow made my awkward way above the top. Once there, with terror on me, I stopped, and did not dare look down. I felt that I must jump. There was an awful sense of down-drawing, and then I knew—*I was not fit to be a sailor!* And then there came a mocking voice, and, looking up, I saw the sneering eyes of Thornton. "Get down," he said, "Afore ye fall an' make a bloody mess on deck!" *So I went up.* And when I came to the topsail yard no one noticed me. And I thanked God for that. I thought myself a coward. A coward, because I could not go high up without that vertigo.

I hated Thornton for a thing he'd said one night. We'd hauled the braces tight, and he and I and Billings were coiling up the ropes. Their forms were dim, but voices sounded plain. And I heard Thornton say, "All wimmen's just alike. There ain't none different."—All women evil in their secret hearts? All women slaves to lust? Just find the way, and any woman's yours? Well, all my lights went out. For, being young, I thought that that old sailor who'd travelled all his life about the world must know whereof he spoke, till then there came to me a memory of Dolly's face, and all the lights were bright. I knew he lied.

56

17. *LYDERHORN—one of
de Wolf's later ships.*

I don't remember much how passed the days of those first few weeks. I mind the meal times best. Hard-tack for breakfast always, and bitter coffee, and on alternate days, at dinner time, salt pork and split pea soup; or boiled salt horse and bean soup. Never a change till Sunday came. For supper hard-tack and skilly. On Monday eve each man and boy was served a half pannikin of canned marmalade, and the same amount of sugar, to last till Monday next. For each four apprentices there was a bottle of vinegar. At noon each day a half gill of lime juice for everyone, to ward the scurvy away. We called it monkey's water, and sometimes drank it and sometimes threw it to the sea. On Sunday was our treat. That day we had the meat called Harriet Lane. It came in tall blue corrugated cans; stringy lean meat coiled down into the cans in stringy coils. It tasted something as a wet rope smells. In some ships it was known as Fanny Adams. Long ago there'd been two street women murdered in Sydney sailor-town, and it was never known what became of their dead bodies.* So rumour

* Harriet Lane was the other! [Ed.]

ran that they'd been canned for sailors. Tough girls they were, yet tasty to a sailor once a week.

Sometimes we'd pound the hard-tack into fragments, mix them with scraps of pork, have the cook heat it for us, and call it 'cracker hash'. Or we would dip a hard-tack into water, hold it there a few seconds, and take it to the cook to go into his oven. When it came out it was a soggy mass, four or five times its dry diameter. And that was a 'midshipman's muffin'. They bloated you, filled you tight with wind, so that you had to let your belt out. We'd make them Monday eve, and on them lay our full week's whack of sugar, and on the sugar all our marmalade. One good square supper a week. One muffin was all that any lad could eat. We called the hard-tack 'pantiles'. Sometimes a sailor'd varnish a pantile, then paint the picture of a ship on it. Or else he'd maybe paint two hearts, an arrow through them and blood dripping. Girls liked such curios when a sailor came to port.

Later, when we'd been long at sea, the pantiles grew soft and crumbly. We'd crumble them, and shake the fat white maggots out; eat what was left. And sometimes we would gamble. Two lads would pick a maggot that looked like a fast crawler. We'd stick two pins at each end of the little table, for goal posts. And then we'd race our maggots, pricking them on with pins. We'd bet our tobacco, matches, and even underclothes. One night Glynn Williams bet Ede's picture, and lost it to Chinaman.[*]

There came an evening when all the wide bright sea was blue, with gentle white caps flashing in the sun's last light. Under full sail the ship pitched easily, to scend and pitch again at each long scend's soft ending. Gently she rolled, her lofty mast-heads swaying. It was as though she danced, greeting the coming night. Her brasswork flashed and all her teak wood shone. All the west was golden, and, the golden lights slowly fading, there came vermilion in the sunset sky, and lights of opaline, of topaz, of amethyst, and ruby. Set clear against that majesty of light, set in the midst of that slow-darkening sea that slowly passed from azure to dim indigo, there stood a gem-like island;[†] its outlines soft against the many-tinted sky. Sailors and young apprentices, mates, carpenter, cook, sailmaker, steward, and our Old Man, and his Old Woman with him, stood gazing in the soft sea-murmurings

[*] Taylors nickname.
[†] Probably one of the Cape Verde group. [Ed.]

while sea and sky grew dim. The island vanished, merging in the night. The stars came out.

Clang—clang—clang—clang the ship's bronze bells crashed out, while from the forecastle head a sailor on look-out cried, music-voiced, "All's well, sir."

The mate replied, "All right."

All gathered on the hatch, beneath the stars, we sang;

Merry are we, merry are we,
There's no one on earth like a sailor at sea.

M BIRCHALL
'928

CHAPTER IV

MERRY ARE WE

Wood had a stubbly beard. Three weeks from Barry, and never yet a shave. So Hickley said one evening, "I'll shave you, Wood. What say?"

Wood sat on an upended bucket, very pleased. He'd felt himself a scarecrow. One side of his face Hickley shaved, the other side of his moustache; then said, "Well, that will do for now." Wood pleaded. Hickley said, "Another time, old son. Good Lord, my wrist is tired! You grow some beard!"

And then MacDonald's whistle blew, for an apprentice to go to the poop. "Your turn, Wood," said Hickley. And up he went, crimson-faced because the Old Woman was there walking with the Old Man. She looked at him and laughed.

Wood was not one of us. And now it was discovered what he'd left behind as well as a razor. The weather was hot, the ship in the tropics, and in the half-deck was a rank sour smell.

"My God, Wood, do you ever wash or change your clothes?" asked Hickley. Supposing there'd be a laundryman aboard a sailing ship, he'd brought no soap to sea. The older lads dragged him out to the deck, stripped him and scrubbed him with a stiff-bristled deck broom. He came nigh weeping. And, washed, he knelt on the deck and scoured his sweaty clothes with soap they gave him. "My God, Wood, we can't have the half-deck stinking. It isn't a sailor's way."

The vertigo was always with me when I had to go aloft. Height was my utter horror. I dreaded taking sail in, dreaded setting it. On deck I loved my ship, but up aloft I feared her with a ghastly fear, and

God knows how I hid it. Sailors don't notice things perhaps. At any rate none ever knew of it. I lived with horror ever at my elbow. So did Wood. He suffered just as I, but he let others know. Day time was worst; but night was bad enough. I mind the first time I went to a royal, the highest sail of all, above the big topgallant. I went up on the mainmast. The ship was racing through a windy sea, sprays flying high. Hickley went first, ahead of me. Two lads to a royal. I somehow made my way to the high spar, a hundred and seventy feet from the hard deck and farther from the sea that waited me. I set my foot upon the swaying footrope, no thicker than my thumb; and I walked out along it. I could not see a thing with any clearness. All was a dim and sickening blur. The tall mast swayed through a terrific arc. I don't know how I did it, but I gathered up the flapping sail, lashed it, and came down. And, God, how good it was to feel the solid planks beneath my feet again! *I was not fit to be a sailor!* I did not wonder could I ever live it down. I lived just day by day, and night by night. When at work on deck I put it out of my mind, or did so mostly. I could have told the mate, of course, and he would have been easy on me. But I kept my fear a secret hidden thing, because of pride; deeming myself a coward. Wood told MacDonald of his dread. MacDonald said, "Why, Jesus Christ, forget it! Hop up aloft and overhaul that mizzen royal buntline!" And up went Wood, shaking like any leaf, a hundred and seventy feet or so, and all alone. Death at his elbow.

Pleasant it was upon the tropic sea. We sat upon the hatch at evening, singing. Sometimes we danced, for Alexander had a queer old fiddle made of coal oil cans. We boxed, we wrestled, had tugs of war, played leap frog. Billings and Thornton often sat apart, talking of 'hoors'.

"Remember Katie Jacobs on the Boca, Buenos Ayres?"

"Aye, an' Liverpool Liz? Is she in Portland yet, d'ye s'pose?"

They spoke of 'Number nine' in Yokohama. They said, "Them coolie gals is swell out in Calcutta."

I liked the names of ports, not women. The half-deck was a decent sort of crowd, all innocent still. "Thornton's a dirty bastard," Hickley said. It was our common judgment.

And then one sunny afternoon I sat out on the boom's far end with Douglas, fishing for bonito. They sported in their thousands under our bare feet, leaping, playing. And now and then a school of flying-fish flashed from the sea to dart away down wind. Seated out there, we could watch the tall ship coming, her cutwater lifting, up, up, and up; then pitching deep, deep down. Dancing she came, and swaying lightly with a gentle roll. Oh, lovely thing! And I forgot my vertigo in her great loveliness. Oh, yes, I loved her well.

Then Douglas spoke, "A few more weeks and we'll be off the Horn."

The Horn! There was a sort of something in that name. A dread. Or, call it challenge. And could I meet that challenge? I said no word. I wondered. Cape Horn. Vertigo.

"You'll find it a hard life, my son." Funny! I'd never thought of that, not even when I'd trembled up aloft with vertigo.

Well, I forgot Cape Horn. For when I went on duty the mate said, "Get down the fore peak, you boys. Get up a barrel of pork, and one of junk, and fill the harness casks."

The harness casks were two fine teak-wood casks that stood on top of our half-deck. Bound with wide bands of brightly shining brass they were. The varnished teak-wood glistened in the sun. And when we opened up the barrel of pork, a reek spread all along the lovely ship. A stink of rotten pork. We took it from its barrel piece by piece, and piece by piece we put it in the harness cask, and then, for many days, we ate it. Putrid pork, while back in Liverpool the owner ate roast beef, and maybe Yorkshire pudding. We didn't think of *him*. We damned our grim Old Man, blaming it on him; as we blamed all things hard, never realizing in our hot youth that he as much as any of us was the sea's slave, serving a shipowner.

We ran from the tropics, and came soon to the roaring forties. Rain beat down. Wind blew cold. Sailors and boys knelt in a long row on the rain-wet planks, each with a bucket of salt water and a large flat sandstone. To and fro, to and fro, we pushed the holystones, scouring her long decks white. Monotony, day after day. A housemaid could have done it. "Who wouldn't sell a farm and go to sea?" One does not love his ship on days like those days were. But the mate says, "Come on, now! Keep those holystones moving!"

63

And soon we were preparing for Cape Horn. Lashing the weather boards to the taffrail, to make a solid bulwark lest the seas burst on the high poop. Long ago the most skilled of the sailors had got all her rigging ready for the hurricanes.

Darker the dark sea grew while each day passed. Colder the air. June. Midwinter off the Horn. The Old Man's eyes were solemn. The mate was mute. MacDonald cursed more mightily than ever. Flocks of little black and white sea pigeons circled all about the ship, and now and then came larger birds. Cape hens and mollymawks. At dusk one day a pod of sperm whales passed within a hundred yards. They rose to spout, and dived, and rose again. Playing as trout play in a mountain pool, they sported. One monster bull leapt from the sea, his whole bulk leaving it; and falling back to his cold element brought down his flukes with a great crash, flat on the sullen water. A bull sperm whale, ninety feet long or more, with bulk of four or five big elephants. They passed, sporting towards Cape Horn.

That night MacDonald looked in at an open port. "Aye, sing, by God! Sing now ye've the chance!" he said. For Glynn Williams was singing:

Merry are we, merry are we,
There's no one on earth like a sailor at sea.

Wood's eyes were as the eyes of a poor rabbit that the snake approaches. And as for me, I wondered.

Another evening came. The wind was fallen quite. The sea was level. The clouds hung high and dark, without a break; a canopy of omen. The horizon a sharp line around a solemn sea. The ship lay motionless, her sails all hanging flat. Sea pigeons in hundreds sat on the dark water. A few Cape hens and mollymawks and one lone snowy albatross. All utter still, to fly an effort on the windless air. And from the distant west there rose a slow-upcreeping glow; a fan-shaped lurid light that slowly spread from the sharp-cut horizon toward the higher sky. The centre of that glow, where the cold winter sun was setting, was a ruby light. The outer glow was as slain bullocks' blood. The ruby faded, and all the western sky was one great bloody light. Old blood, and dull; not from a fresh-made wound. It was as though the gods had slaughtered bullock herds for sacrifice, and their hot

64

blood had dripped and soaked into the canopy of cloud, empurpling it. Old Man, mates, apprentices, sailors, gazed at that bloody west. Sheer silence. No voice. No footfall. No rope creaking. And then the lights went out, as though a curtain had been dropped. The sun was gone. The cook came from his door and flung a hunk of pork rind to the sullen water. An instant flurry rose, of hungry birds all winging toward the rind. They screamed and fought above it. The albatross winged thither, and lesser birds made way for his white majesty. The silence fell again. The Old Man turned and murmured to the mate. The mate came down to the main deck.

"Clew up the royals!"

The royal yards slid down, to rest upon the heads of the top-gallant masts. We waited word to go aloft and furl them. Instead came, "Clew up the topgallant sails!" Their heavier halliards groaning, they slid down. Again we waited word. Instead came, "Clew up the cross-jack!" We hauled that great sail up, a hundred feet across its head, by forty-five or fifty deep. And after it we hauled up the yet larger mainsail. The foresail next. And then we lowered the upper topsails, and slid the staysails down. Then the sole sail left set was one small narrow strip upon each towering mast. Three narrow strips of board-hard canvas. The lower topsails. It was pitch dark by now. Nigh to five o'clock. And then the order came to go aloft and furl the lot of them, and up we went and gathered in her wings, the canvas rustling in the sheer sea silence. Blocks creaked, and sailors cried, *"Ho, roll and bunt her!"* And *'Yo—ho—ho—roll her, bullies!"* And Alexander sang, *"That's the way we'll pay Paddy Doyle for his—"* — rolling the mainsail up he sang that, and all hands, giving the sail a last roll, roared together, *"Boots."* Of a sudden I remembered my felt-lined sea boots and wondered how I'd fare off the Horn. We stripped the ship of almost all her dress, left a scant-clothed lady on the hidden sea, and all night long there was not any sound nor any motion. Only her clanging bells, to tell the hours away. Only at each hour's passing the look-out man's clear high cry, "All's well, sir." Then the mate's quiet answer, "All right." Her sidelights gleamed, throwing a red and a green glimmer on the forward water. We saw some sea birds floating, red and green. There was an eeriness about the night, but just ere I went below to roll into my bunk at four of the freezing morning, there came a sort of moaning from the far dark west. The sound of a great gale yet far away, and when they wakened me for breakfast, there was a thundering outside our half-deck. A rage. A roar. The ship was labouring. I heard water crashing to and fro upon the deck. It was my day to fetch the breakfast coffee from the cook's galley. I stepped from the half-deck door into barbarous fury. The sky was inky, close on the reeling mastheads. The lower topsails strained, tighter than war drums. I could not see a hundred yards away on either side, for mountain seas black as the lowering sky. I ran for the cook's door, and passed the carpenter's. He stood in his door. He looked at me, and shouted. Winds swept his words away. But I just caught them. *"This is the Horn!"*

All day it blew, and all the next, and all the next, and all the next; and then blew on, and on, and on, and ever on. Oft times the snow whirled by. Darkness till nine, and dark again soon after four. Salt pork, salt junk, pea soup, bean soup, and Harriet Lane on Sunday. And margarine in place of marmalade now when Monday came. And vinegar, of course, and daily lime juice. And no man had a dry rag on the second day. Though all wore rope yarns tied about wrists and ankles, about the oilskin trousers and the jacket sleeves, to keep the water out, water got in. We call those rope yarns 'Soul and body lashings', because they keep our souls and bodies in one piece. We stuffed towels within our oilskin collars, to keep the water out. They didn't, for you can't have great seas sweep over you and water not get in. Everybody's sea boots, as they stepped, went 'squelch'. Felt linings didn't matter very much.

Day upon bitter day, we hauled the braces tight to hold her rolling spars from having too much play. Sails worked loose from lashings. We went aloft to lash them. One yelling day the galley stove was swamped because the cook, for just a moment's space, left his door a half-inch too wide open. We ate hard-tack at every meal that day. The thick skin on our palms split open at every finger-joint, in the barbaric cold. Beneath the splits we saw the raw red flesh. The sails, with ice upon them, knocked our knuckles raw; bare to the cold white bone. Our oilskins, chafing at wrists and neck, caused salt water boils. Poor

18. *Cape Horn sea.*

sons of Job were we, and kin to Lazarus. But they had sun, ashore!
Yet still we laughed at one another, too, mocking a comrade's miseries.
Seeing a comrade knocked down by a boarding sea, and soaked afresh,
we'd yell, "Why didn't you stay on the farm, you clumsy lubber?" I
had that yelled at me many times. But Wood yet many more. His face
was a ghost's face. When in the evenings we were all together in the
half-deck, the ports closed, our pipes puffing comforting smoke, he'd
sit and stare straight before him and never speak a word. If spoken to
he'd often never change that stare nor say a word.

One evening, looking at Ede's photograph hung in Chink's bunk,
Hickley said, "My God, I wish I had her in my bunk with me. I'd be
warmer then."

And Glynn replied, low-voiced, "Dry up! She's one of Bill's
relations."

Then Hickley said, his face gone lobster-red, "Sorry, Bill!"

So then I asked him, "Got a fill of 'baccy?" And, making amends,
he gave me a fill quickly: though always a bit close with anything he had.

At last there came a morning when the wind was low, out of the
frozen south. We put some sail on the ship. I went aloft to loose an
upper topsail, and had that vertigo. On the rigging there was ice, and
on the sails. I almost slipped and fell from the ice-sheathed rigging,
and then I all but fell from the frozen footrope of the frozen sail. It
would have been quite bad enough without the vertigo. God knows
how I got up, or how came down again. I did, and that is all I know.
We hoisted that topsail in a lightly falling snow, and Alexander sang,

> Boney was a warrior,
> To me waye, aye, yoh!
> A warrior and tarrier,
> A long time ago.

Then, as the mate called, "Good! Make fast there!" the snow
ceased. And, about to walk off, old One Eye turned and gazed across
the northern water, and all hands stopped, and gazed where he gazed.
There I saw a hard black triangle of land, a dark hill snow-capped.

"Cape Stiff!" said One Eye, and, looking round at us, he grinned
and rubbed his horny hands together, saying, "I 'opes she makes a long
voyage. I'm goin' to save me pay-day. More days, more dollars, b'ys!"

68

Then snow came back, and hid Cape Stiff. Before the day was gone, the wind was savage as ever. On, on, and ever on we fought the hurricane, and I lost count of days, of weeks. So, too, did everyone, save One Eye maybe. Sometimes, in lulls, we set a little sail and all hands sang. You cannot hoist a sail without a song for sailormen to pull by:

> *Oh, blow today, and blow tomorrow,*
> *Blow, boys, blow!*
> *Oh, blow for all poor tars in sorrow,*
> *Blow, my bully boys, blow!*

There came a murderous day when we were taking in an upper topsail. All hands were at the gear. Great flakes whirled by. The bitter sprays beat on us. "Aloft and make it fast!" MacDonald shouted, when it was ready for furling. The crowd climbed into the reeling ice-sheathed rigging till only Glynn and Wood and I were left on deck.

"Get up there, you!" MacDonald bawled to Wood.

But Wood was beaten. He could not face the Horn's mad music any more. He ran, and vanished through the half-deck door. I felt like following, God knows. But Glynn, catching my eye, laughed merrily and cried, "Who wouldn't sell a farm and go to sea?" Then he leapt for the rigging, and I leapt after him. And that time I had no least touch of vertigo. The first time yet.

One night a flat calm fell upon the hidden sea. The ship lay still. Pitch black, and somewhere below zero. At two that morning the mate cried, "Wash the decks down!"

We fetched the deck buckets, the brooms, and we fetched sand. We hung a lantern in the icy rigging. We flung the sand upon her planks, and scrubbed the green sea slime away, making them safer to walk upon. With that green slime, they were grown treacherous. You could not move along them, unless you gripped a lifeline. Next day the hurricane was back.

Six bitter weeks we fought the blasting Horn. Forty-two days. And no man ever had a dry rag. And no man had palms that were not red and raw. Always hungry, and never rest enough. And never, never for a moment warm. Yet there was amongst us one contented one. Old One Eye'd wink his solitary orb, and grin, and say, "More days, more dollars, b'ys!" He'd save his money now, for his old age ashore.

At last there came an evening when the sky was high. There seemed a sort of benison of peace upon the sea. We piled full sail on her at last again; the first time in six full weeks. She seemed to say, stealing all eager over that quiet untossed sea, "Give me a wind behind! Oh, do let me go!" And not far away, upon the starboard quarter, lay a small group of tiny islets.

"Diego Ramirez," the word went round. Those tiny islets lie fifty-eight miles sou'westward from the Horn. Then Stiff was left astern! We were gazing at them when then there came a sudden ringing cry from our high forecastle head where the look-out man stood: "Sail right ahead, sir!"

We had not seen a ship in many a day, and ran to see her come. The light was fading. But soon we saw her name, *Aladdin*. She hoisted flags, and we the same. Word went round that she was out from Callao, and then we saw a sailor stand upon her rail, and on her deck behind stood all her company. His voice broke out, clear-ringing over that still peaceful sea:

> *Goodbye, and farewell to you, fair Spanish ladies!*
> *Goodbye, and farewell to you, ladies of Spain!*
> *For we've received orders to sail for old England,*
> *But we hope in a short time to see you again.*

And in a moment then the crews of both tall ships were singing:

> *We'll rant and rave and we'll roam across the wide ocean,*
> *We'll rant and we'll roam o'er the waters so blue.*

Soon the *Aladdin* was gone. We saw her bright lamp winking for a little space, and, as we turned away, with darkness falling, Johansen, that huge Scandinavian sailor, said, "Vee beats der Horn, py Gott!" and all hands laughed, because he spoke so funnily. Then I was glad that I had come to sea. The first time I had ever known that I was fully glad. We'd won our victory, and I'd been there. *Oh, sailor, sailor, sailor!*

But Wood stood like a corpse. He had not stood out to see the tall *Aladdin* pass. Now Glynn said to him, "We've beat the Horn, old

70

19. *ALADDIN, with t'gallant-masts housed.*

son!" He stared at Glynn, as though he did not know whereof Glynn
spoke at all. He'd never been aloft since shirking that upper topsail.
MacDonald had not ordered him to go.

Now the good winds came, and day by day she flew northward
and ever north. And still the flocks of white sea pigeons followed her,
and grey Cape hens, and mollymawks, and many albatross. The wind
came ever warmer as she flew. Presently there came a ramping night
with a wild wind that whooped from dead astern. That night she staggered, running like a stag with hounds too close at heel. Going below
at dark, the Old Man said, "Take nothing off her, mister. She can stand
it." The sprays whipped over her. The seas came roaring in across her
rolling rails, her long decks deep in water. We laughed. We shouted,
"Go!—Go!—Go!" And when the day came back there was no bird
at all on all the warm blue sea. They were gone back, to watch while

71

other ships came battling out around the Horn where their homes were.

I polished brasswork now and scoured the rust away from rails and deck-houses. The elder apprentices worked aloft, helping the men repair the damage of the Horn's barbarity. I envied them, and yet, fearing that vertigo, was glad to be on deck. I envied Glynn the most. He was a monkey in the swaying rigging. He'd hold with one hand to some slim rope a hundred and sixty feet up in the webby rigging, and laugh and jest if anyone should say, "You're too damned careless, man!" A *sailor*, Glynn was.

The Horn had bound us all in comradeship. We knew each other now. Men chummed in pairs. Thornton and Billings ever had been chums, and so had One Eye and the lanky Scot. And now young Erickson and Furst were close as brothers. They never were apart when evening came. Glynn and I were chums too, I a bit shy because he was my senior. We were a happy crew. At evening time we gathered on the hatch and sang, and danced bare-foot. "Hurrah! We'll soon be in!" said Glynn. Then we would often sing that song of merry sailors. Young Erickson had picked up English well. We'd make him sing it. He'd blush and shake his head; then urged by Furst, would sing:

Merry are vee, merry are vee,
Dere is not on eart' like zee sailor at sea.

We'd laugh, and clap him on the back; and he and Furst would hug each other, laughing. Even Wood was less corpse-like now at last. A little light of hope was come into his eyes.

We'd crossed the line, and left it far astern. The wind blew pleasantly, driving her on at maybe ten knots. That night all hands were more than ever merry and Erickson stood up, and sang unasked. MacDonald, passing, stayed to hear him sing. "Bully for you," he said. Erickson, smiling happily, replied, "I verree merrie, sir. Yow bat I am."

The mate's watch went below at eight that night. I wakened suddenly. A cry. A shout. A shout not heard. The words, swift-breaking in upon my sleep, indistinguishable. But yet, I somehow knew and in an instant we of the watch below had all dashed to the

20. *LORD RIPON—a very lofty ship.*

deck. Black dark the night was. They'd stopped the ship, and all were running now toward the quarter boat. The Old Man shouting, "Lively! For God's sake lively!"

We swung the boat away. The mate leapt into her. Billings and Thornton leapt, and Johansen, and Alec. The stoutest of the crew, most brawny-armed. We saw her for a moment. Then she was gone.

"Who is it?" someone asked.

And someone said, "It's Glynn."

MacDonald's watch had been furling the royals, and Glynn had gone up to the fore royal yard. He'd fallen from it. The look-out man had heard him cry out as, falling, he struck the bellied canvas of the foresail; and bounced off to the sea. The foresail had broken his fall. The helmsman heard him yell as the ship drove past him. Someone had flung a lifebuoy to the sea. And that was all that anybody knew.

"Coil up them ropes, lads!" ordered MacDonald. Whilst coiling a rope, I heard Glynn's voice beside me in the dark.

"He isn't gone! He's here!" I shouted. They gathered round.

Glynn said, "It's Furst. He went aloft with me. I heard him curse the flapping sail, and then I heard him scream."

We stood beneath the lantern, hung in the mizzen rigging to direct the boat back. And no one spoke. Silence. Above us on the bridge our Old Man stood. I saw young Erickson, his face as white as chalk.

Erect she lay, and still upon the soughing sea. The wind thrummed drearily in her webbed rigging. We waited on, and on. We peered into the night. Silence. An hour dragged by. Another. The Old Man, leaning toward us, asked, "Could he swim?"

And someone answered, "Yes, sir. He was a very fine swimmer." We hoped.

By and by, we saw a speck of white upon the night-hid sea. It dipped to a sea hollow and was lost. It rose again. We heard the solemn-seeming *clunka-clunka* of the oars. The boat came in. We gazed down into her, counting—one—two—three—four—five. No more. They climbed aboard, and still no one spoke. In silence we hoisted and swung her to her chocks, the water dripping from her mournfully to the mournful deck.

We gathered underneath the bridge-head. All hands there. Our

74

Old Man spoke.

"Anything more you want me to do, lads?"

Johansen replied, "Nuddings more to do, sir."

The Old Man said, "Square the main yard!"

The ship sailed on.*

There was a hush upon the ship next day. Alone upon the fore-castle head, young Erickson sat weeping. He was excused from any work that day.

When the evening came and seven of us lads were in the half-deck we were silent. Wood's face was ghastlier than ever it had been. At that moment Glynn came in, after two hours at the wheel.

"Well," said Glynn, "I guess it is the sailor's way." And no one spoke. Then Glynn smiled, and spoke again. And at his words Hick-ley said, "Glynn, you damned fool, you've got a crazy rhyme for every-thing."

Glynn had said, "Man that is born of woman has but a short time to live. He goes up like a main topmast staysail, and comes down like a flying jib."

At this the funereal air was broken, and we played cards, and talked, and put the memory of death away. It has to be the sailor's way, or we should mourn too often.

Next morning when I went on duty, the order came to loose the royals. I was nearest to the fore rigging. He who is nearest the rigging when such an order comes is the one who goes aloft. And a cold horror came on me. But then Johansen strode up, and to me he said, "I goes to dere fore royal, mine poy. Dot yard is cursed. Ven from a yard falls a sailor, den der yard is cursed. But not can dot yard scare *me*. Yow see? I goes. Yow stays der deck on." And up he went, and oh, how glad I was I did not have to go to that cursed yard whence Furst had fallen to his death.

---

*The official log is no longer extant, but there is a consular note of this accident. [Ed.]

WM Birchall 1925

CHAPTER V

THE FLYING JIB COMES DOWN

There came a morning I was at the wheel when night gave way to day. I'd never steered till we were past the Horn. Since then I had, taking my regular two-hour trick with all the crew. Only Wood didn't steer. I loved it. That morning all the sky was hung with stars, save far ahead. With all sail set she seemed to dance along the murmurous sea. There seemed a something different about her somehow; an eagerness; yet, too, about her seemed a sort of peace. I did not sense a sternness in my ship that morning, as at times I seemed to do. I was most happy standing at her helm. At my least touch she'd shift her long lean shape, swift-answering me. I loved my ship. Maybe I could not then have said it. Today I know I did. Youth's unvoiced love for what is beautiful. The dream the soldier knows, thinking he has a holy cause. The dream that brings the quiet to priests' faces; be they right priests, and not the belly kind. The dream that makes the tailor cut with eyes contented, shearing his finest woollen goods to shape. To each man his own calling. There is no calling like the sailor's was. Today the steamers have our sea.

I stood there, humming that old merry song that Erickson had sung the night that he lost Furst. And soon I saw ahead of her, far off, a great mass of tumbled cloud that rose in a dark wall from the horizon. The mate had seen it too, and he went down to the main deck and forward; and stood upon the forecastle head a while. I just could see his shape in dawn's first opalescent light. A sudden fragrance came, filling the air, and then I heard a little fluttering sound. A tiny land-bird settled on the deck before me! And then there came from the look-out

77

man a high ringing cry, *"Land-ho!"*

The crew came running, eager, to the deck. The mate spoke down the tube that led to our Old Man's pillow. "The land's ahead, sir."

More than five months since we'd left Barry Roads! There is not anything in all the earth as wonderful as that first scent of shore to sailormen come in from deep sea voyaging: except it be a woman's kiss, if she's the right woman.

Dawn opened swift, bursting its banners out. The sea, no longer deep sea blue, gleamed emerald. To any coming from the shore it would have seemed blue water. But we knew blue where real blue seas roll by, mid-ocean's blue.

She shone in beauty. Her brasswork flashed and glittered in the sun. Her teakwork gleamed, with two fresh coats of varnish. There was a lot of that most lovely eastern wood—chart room, and skylight, taffrail, poop ladders, fife rails, and the big after-hatch; and a round beading running the full length of her bulwarks on each side. All pumice-stoned it was, before the varnishing: now smooth as glass, and throwing back the sun. Her boats and bulwarks were a dazzling white. Her deckhouses and bulkheads a pale cream. Her masts and yards were lovely with new paint. Her long lean decks, all holy-stoned and oiled: you might have eaten from them without a table-cloth. Long labour it had been to make her as she was, and many a day we'd cursed the toil of it. Now we were proud of her. "Py Gott," Johansen said, his blue eyes shining, "Vee gots der dandy sheep!"

There was a new stay spliced at the high jigger masthead, above the poop and quarterdeck. And when you tuck a splice in wire you serve it, wrapping it round and round with spunyarn, tight as tight; then rubbing tar with varnish mixed in it into the spunyarn, to keep the moisture out and save the splice from rusting.

"Johansen," said the mate, "go get a tar pot. Hop up aloft and tar that splice. That's the last touch to finish her." So up Johansen went, a tar pot in his hand. There is no rigging on a jigger mast high up. You have to swarm, your legs about the mast. That day she was rolling quite a bit, and pitching to a long slow ocean swell, and, somehow, as she took an extra sharp deep pitch, Johansen clinging there, holding with toenails and eyelashes as we sailors say, let that tar pot fall.

21.   Another of de Wolf's—the PENTHESLEA in the Fowey River.

Down it came, now upside down, now right side up, and landed on the white poop deck. And everywhere, on teak and paint and boats and bulwarks, were a myriad little spots of utter black.

"Well, Jesus Christ!" MacDonald roared.

The mate said quietly, "I don't think Jesus had a damned thing to do with that."

The Old Man, his eyes the eyes of some old savage shark, a man-eater, said, *"My God!"*

At once everyone was called on deck, men and apprentices, carpenter, sailmaker, and even the steward. There was no four-hour watch below for anyone that day. All day we scrubbed and scoured. Had Johansen killed his father and his mother, wife and babies, in a drunken fit, he'd not have looked more desolate. By night we had her

79

as she'd been at dawn, and all was well again. "Tomorrow we'll be in," we said, and our eyes shone. Only Johansen's didn't. His comrades in the forecastle could not cheer him. He sat alone and brooded.

At dawn next day a tug-boat picked us up off Flattery, to take us up the straits of Juan de Fuca. The order came to take all sail off her and send it down, so I went up aloft with the rest. On either side the forest grew down to the water's edge. That strait was as a road to Paradise, for beauty. Yet I scarce saw it. For now I had, and worse than ever yet, that vertigo. I shook and trembled. All up the long Pacific I had fought it. And here was I, and all my fighting it no use at all. *I'd never make a sailor!* It ruined coming in to my first port. And Wood, of course, was just as miserable, and everybody saw him. No one guessed my misery. I hid it somehow. God knows how. I don't.

A Saturday it was we moored the ship. We had her moored by dusk. Then the Old Man sent for us apprentices, and gave us each a dollar from our premium money, so off we went ashore, all dressed in our shore uniforms. The shore folk stared at us, so brown we were, so bright of eye, so happy-seeming. Into a restaurant we went, and gathered at a table. A snow white table-cloth, and finger-napkins! Glasses, in place of dented rusty tin pannikins! A waitress came to take our order. And Hickley spoke for every one of us.

"Ham and eggs for three on one plate," said Hickley.

"Sir?" said the waitress.

"Ham and eggs for three on one plate," he said again.

And she said, "Sir?" again, "I don't understand, sir."

"Well, then," said Hickley, "bring me three servings of ham and eggs all at once on one plate, and bring the same for every one of us."

And how those shore folk stared!

She went to give the order; but ere she went she set two long brown loaves of crisp French bread upon the table, all nicely sliced. Having given the order, happening to glance our way, she saw no bread. So she brought more, supposing she'd forgotten, but when she looked again there was no bread. Six loaves we ate before our order came, and didn't leave a crumb. Then we went out and wandered round the town. We didn't need a cent for any entertainment. We'd stand and stare to see a street car pass. We'd call to one another, "Look!—A horse!" We'd gaze at children who'd gaze back at us. More than five months at sea, and now ashore again! Our legs felt odd. We couldn't walk aright. The sidewalk should have rolled. Then we'd have been at home. It was a merry night, during which we entered a saloon to have a glass of beer together. When we came out, Wood stayed. The bartender was from his own home town in Derbyshire. We left them there, their elbows on the bar; their faces close together.

I forgot to say that when we moored the ship, letters came. I'd one from Aunt Polly. Mr. Pellew was dead. He'd died soon after I sailed. There was a new rector, 'a dear young man'. Since my ship had been so long without bcing reported, Auntie Polly had had him pray at Sunday service, publicly, and ask sweet Jesus to take care of me. We all read snatches of our letters out. All but Wood, who sat apart in silence; never one of us. When I read about sweet Jesus taking care of me Glynn said, "Well, maybe he did, by God! Who knows?" And then he laughed and said that silly rhyme of his, "Man that is born of woman has but a short time to live. He goes up like a main topmast staysail, and comes down like a flying jib." And Hickley said, "You damned fool, Glynn. You haven't any sense."

When we came back aboard that first night we had no money left. There'd be no more till Saturday came round again.

When Sunday morning came Billings and Thornton were gone, and some of the other men. There were whores for Billings and Thornton, and for any who wanted it plenty of work ashore. They could afford to desert and leave behind the little pittance owing them for, having drawn two months' advance pay ere we sailed, they had but three months' pay left. Two pounds ten shillings a month. Not worth bothering about. Alec stayed, and old One Eye who, being our oldest man, was picked for nightwatchman while she was in port. Erickson stayed. Johansen didn't. I heard the mate say to MacDonald, "My God, I tried to talk the big fool out of it! He wouldn't listen. He said he 'voss too shame'. We've lost a damned good man. If he'd not spilt that tar pot he'd have stayed."

And Wood was not aboard when Sunday came. He had not slept aboard. We washed the decks without him. And after breakfast the mate called me to the quarter-deck. Our Old Man was there in the cabin doorway.

"D'ye know where Wood is?" the mate asked me.

"I saw him last, sir, at the Poodle Dog," I answered.

"Go fetch him down aboard," the Old Man growled, his voice a mastiff's.

So off ashore I went, and to the Poodle Dog. The bartender said, "Sure. He's up in bed. We slept together. A damned fine lad, he is."

And up I went, shook Wood awake, and said, "The skipper wants you." As we walked down to the ship together, neither speaking, there came to me a memory of that boy with whom I'd always walked to church on Sundays at my school, but now, as once my schoolfellows had looked down on me as different, I looked down on Wood. The world's all tooth and claw. The strong wolf eats the weaker.

From that day on Wood was never allowed ashore again. The Old Man was a martinet in that. No apprentice must ever sleep save aboard the ship. So when we went ashore on Saturday evenings, each with a dollar in his pocket, Wood must stay. No one to talk to but old One Eye. One of us asked one day, "One Eye, do you yarn with him?"

"Hell, no. He ain't no good fer yarnin'. He jest sits an' stares at nothin' till he rolls into his bunk," One Eye replied.

The ship's food was vile. Hunks of the toughest beef, and only little hunks. Tough as old sea-boot leather. Sweet potatoes, because they were cheaper than the Irish sort. We'd never seen nor tasted, and scarce could stomach them. Breakfast and supper, pantiles only; unless we could contrive to save a little of the dinner beef, for the cook to make dry hash of. We very seldom could. So we were ravenous.

There was a night when Glynn and I were ashore alone together. We wandered here and there, peered into restaurants and sniffed delights within. We saw the bakery windows and the candy shops. Our belts were tight, drawn in to their last holes for hunger, and presently we came to a shop over the door of which hung the three balls of a pawnbroker, so I said, "Come on in, Glynn."

I'd kept my mother's golden pearl-set ring safe in my sea chest while at sea. But in port, going ashore at evening, I always put it on. I took it off now.

22.   *A vessel very similar to the SILBERHORN—possibly GOLDENHORN.*

Glynn said, "Christ, no, Bill!"

And I said, "By God, we're starving."

I set it on the counter, before a little bald-headed man with ferret eyes and a skull cap.

"What will you give me for it?" I asked.

He said, "I giff you vun dollar."

And Glynn and I went to a restaurant and filled our bellies tight. Glynn said, "You're a good shipmate, Bill!" And that was what I liked. *Shipmate!* He was the first chum ever I had had. *Oh, sailor, sailor, sailor!*

At last a day came when the ship's wide holds were empty. They yawned cavernous. Soon now we'd go round to the Fraser river to load for Liverpool. A tug-boat took us from the wharf. We dropped the anchor, and rested out in the quiet harbour, waiting.

Glynn and I were by the main hatch one morning. I mind that we were jesting about some little thing, his face all merry fun. Mac-Donald passed.

"Get down below, you boys! Take brooms and sweep the hold out. No damned loafing now!"

Then he went on.

Glynn said, "Slip in the half-deck, Bill, and get some smokes. No one'll catch us in the hold."

So I went into the half-deck, and he down below, but as I stepped back to the deck I heard the order to get the gig away. The Old Man was going ashore. I ran to help, not eager for the hold. A ship's hold is a dim-lit, shadowy musty place. From it you cannot see the shore or anything.

Then, with the gig gone, I started forward to go down the hatch where Glynn was gone, and I met Douglas running, and his face was white.

"What's up?" I asked.

And Douglas said, "Glynn's killed."

I raced to the hatch, dropped down the ladder to the hold. There, lying outstretched on the floor of the lower hold, was Glynn, a red trickle at the corners of his mouth and at his nostrils. He'd stumbled in the dimness and had fallen from the between decks to the lower hold.

Sixteen feet!

The mate came down, and others. We lifted him. I bore his drooping head. His blood reddened my hands, red blood of my first chum.*

Next day we were his pall-bearers. We buried him in a shore cemetery, with pines about it. A little wind went soughing through the pines. Our Old Man was there, and his Old Woman. Just those two, and we his apprentice comrades. And the preacher began:

Man that is born of woman has but a short time to live.

And we caught one another's eyes, and hung our heads; because somehow we could not help but let the smiles come to our faces. And that was sacrilege.

Only Wood was not there. He wouldn't come. He sat alone, and shivered in the empty half-deck; his face was ghost white.

* There is a Customs House note, in Vancouver, of this incident. [Ed.]

H·M Birchall. 1925

W.M.Birchall.
1925.

CHAPTER VI

THE ROVING EYE

The fishing village where we went to load was a dismal place. A collection of unpainted wooden huts, and shacks built of old coal oil cans all rust-covered. We moored the ship beside a salmon cannery. The air reeked of decaying fish-guts. At low tide enormous heaps of them were exposed beneath the cannery floor. We ate and slept in the reek. The river was cheerless and muddy. Muddy dykes traversed the village. On most days fog hid the flat island behind it. There was neither scenery nor clean air; and sailors live on both. But there was one compensation, we found on our first night ashore. In the centre of the village was a huge rambling wooden store kept by an ancient Jew. Above his door a sign said, 'Everything from a needle to an anchor'. So we strolled in, and asked for an anchor.

"I haff not vun. Maybe I gets," said he.

"Why, you old goat, the blasted thing'd weigh three tons," said Hickley.

He shook his head, and said, "Dot breaks mine floor." And then we found his barrel of dried apples. He tried to push us from it; for between us all there wasn't one red cent. Then Polly Thompson found two dozen alarm clocks and, unseen by the old man, set them all jangling. The old man ran to stop them. Barford, taking a banjo from the wall, began to play and we began to dance. Shouting, "Viley!— Viley!" the old man ran to the street.

Wiley, the village policeman, came in, and with him, arm in arm, MacDonald, the two of them a little merry from a few drinks. Wiley stood six feet four and was broad in proportion. Barford stopped

87

playing, but he cried, "Make that damned banjo play!" We'll show you how to dance!" So he and MacDonald did a tap dance on the wooden floor, and Polly started all the clocks again and everyone but the old Jew was merry. Beyond devouring a good many of his dried apples, we never harmed him; but we kept him nervous.

Long wooden chutes were run from the wharf down into the ship's holds, and down them all day long slid salmon cases in a ceaseless stream. Always there were two apprentices in the hold to nail up any cases that jumped the chutes and broke, but always when a case was broken, we, ere we nailed it up, took out a can or two and hid them beneath our jumpers; and when no mate was about, slipped up and hid them in the half-deck. Those not in the hold did pottering jobs about the deck, polishing brass, wiping paint, keeping the ship clean. A ship's just like a woman; forever being touched up.

On Sundays we wandered about the island. Nothing to see but a flat plain, and dykes, and musk-rats; and here and there a farm. One Sunday, Polly and I came to a farm where apple trees stood in a row before the house. A grey-haired woman opened at my rap.

"Lady, we're sailors. We wondered might we have an apple or two?" said I.

She sat us in her parlour, brought tea, bread and butter, and jam. Watching us eating, she seemed doleful, very. When we rose to go and I thanked her, she ran at me, and flung her arms round me, and kissed my cheek. She said, tears on her withered face, "I had a son who was a sailor. We never knew what happened to his ship."

Beyond the village was a little church. Old Donaldson, the minister, came to the ship sometimes with a big basket filled with vegetables. A shy old chap, he gave them to the cook, then hurried off with no word to any of us. When Sunday came we went to church at evening, really to show we liked his vegetables; just by way of thanks. We crowded in the back pew, now shy ourselves; and found it a bit hard to sit still for so long. But at the end of the service, when he had preached a sermon we didn't listen to, he gave out a hymn. And his congregation, a few women and children, turned to stare at us, none of them singing that hymn. For that was our hymn. We made the rafters ring.

23. *The full-rigger IMBERHORNE in Cape Town.*

Eternal Father, strong to save,
Whose arm hath bound the restless wave,
Who bidst the mighty ocean deep
Its own appointed limits keep,
Oh hear us when we cry to Thee
For those in peril on the sea.

Then we slipped quietly out.

There was a ruddy, jovial man they called the Judge. I think he was their Justice of the Peace. He lived alone in a small two-room cottage. He hailed us as we passed one day, and asked us in. Then he introduced us to the Major, another jolly man. We never knew what he was Major of, unless it was the Judge's beer bottles. They opened beer for us and asked us of the sea. The Major said, "Judge, let's have Simp-

89

son here!" And the Judge called to a passing fisherman, "Hey, Jake! Send Simpson here, will you?"

Simpson came in. We knew him at once. We knew his English eye, and English Adam's apple. He had been reared as we had, far away. He was our breed. The Major whispered to me, "He was captain of his school cricket team. Went to Eton and Oxford." Now that remittance man lived with a young Siwash squaw, in a shack built of old coal oil cans.

Wiley dropped in. "Why, hello, sailors!"

"Let's have some singing, boys," the Judge said. We sang for them, 'Rolling home across the sea', and 'Sally Brown was a gay mulatto'. And then the Major said, "Come, Simpson!" And Simpson rose and sang,

> *D'ye ken John Peel at the break of day?*
> *D'ye ken John Peel with his coat so gay?*
> *D'ye ken John Peel when he's far, far away?*
> *By the cry of his pack in the morning?*

And there was hunger in his voice, and in his eyes, for meadowsweet, and hawthorn hedges, and the fallow fields. As for me, I was back in Peterstowe, seeing the hounds cry by.

"Say, Judge," said Hickley, "that old wood barn out at the edge of town? It's got a sign above the door says 'Opera House'. Could we have it to give a minstrel show?"

"Of course. That would be great, by God!" the Judge said, and gave us the key. And then we held rehearsals nightly. The Judge, the Major, Wiley, spread the word for us. A landsman came aboard one day and told us he'd a son 'could speak a piece', and would assist us gladly. We thanked him, and told him that it was a sailor's show. He seemed offended.

Another ship came in, a lovely one, *The City of Benares*. She'd four apprentices, and they joined in with us. But on the afternoon of the day the show was to be, one of them came hurrying aboard. They couldn't come. A young first voyage apprentice had fallen from their mast and was dead.

"Damn it, there's always someone getting killed," said Hickley, and I'd a sudden horror of that vertigo. When would my turn come?

90

24. *CITY OF BENARES off Gravesend.*

We blacked our faces for the show. Every seat was taken. Our Old Man sat in the front row with his Old Woman. We'd given them free tickets. Beside them sat the Judge and Major, and Wiley, but Simpson sat on the far back seat. A broken gentleman; yet still, because he knew his shame, a gentleman. We sang 'Swanee River' and 'Poor old Jeff' and 'Dinah Dinah Do'. We tap danced. They clapped, and someone called, "Hey! Give us a sailor song!" So we sang 'Jack's the Lad', and 'When the Ship is Trimmed and Ready'.

Then a woman rose, and called in a soft voice, "Please show us how you hoist your sails when you're at sea." Ah—*then* we gave them 'Roll the Cotton Down' and 'A Black Ball Ship Came Down the River' and 'Blow for all Poor Tars in Sorrow'. They clapped and cheered, and many cried 'Encore'. So then we made the old barn shake, singing 'The Maid of Amsterdam', and in the chorus many of the fishermen joined, and Wiley roared the words:

91

When they were all gone we counted out our gains. Just fifty dollars. A fine fat fortune for six hungry sea apprentices. Going down to the ship, we talked of what we'd spend it on. Someone said, "Let's give it old Donaldson. He's a good sort!" and, after some arguing, we agreed to keep just fifty cents apiece and give him all the rest. We'd put it in the plate next Sunday. "We'll give the old boy a surprise," we said.

Wood had no part in our show. He'd never come to church. Though now allowed ashore, he seldom went. That night he took old One Eye's place as nightwatchman, that One Eye might be there. All through the voyage we'd laughed at One Eye; rubbing his horny hands together when the winds were light, saying, "More days more dollars. I'm goin' to save me pay day." Even down off the Horn he never had complained. He knew full well that soon he'd be too old for sea-faring, and wanted a long voyage, to save towards his old age. Since we were come to port he'd never had a drink. "The bloody booze is wot puts sailors on the bloody rocks," he said.

We didn't see old One Eye when we came aboard that night, but soon after we were in our bunks, Wood came in and turned into his. One Eye was come, he said. Next morning we slept late. No one wakened us till MacDonald came bellowing at our door: "By Jesus Christ! What's come o' Smith? Turn out, Gawd dommit! It's nearly eight o'clock."

One Eye was not aboard. We sought him everywhere. But while we washed the decks down, the cook came from his galley to throw some refuse to the river. He called the mate. A cap was floating, down beneath the gangway. Later Wiley came, the Judge and Major, with some fishermen who brought grappling hooks. They fished old One Eye up. His face was bloated. In each pocket was a beer bottle.

It was a Saturday night the stevedores completed her loading. They worked till long past dark, by lantern light. Polly and I were in the hold, and each swiped one whole case that night. By now we had, hid everywhere about the half-deck, salmon enough to make sixteen

25. *Off the Straits of Juan de Fuca, the barque ALFHILD makes sail.*

full cases. Cans under our straw mattresses, in our sea chests. We would not have to eat much ship's food on the road home.

That Saturday new sailors came to take the places of those who had deserted her and, save for Polly and myself, all hands were busy getting sail aloft. On Sunday they were busy too, and I had to help. Oh God, that vertigo! I had not been aloft in many weeks. It all came back, as bad as ever. I hid it somehow. Wood was kept on deck, to slack the ropes away as needed. Lord, how I envied him! I thought of Furst and Glynn, and that *Benares* boy. But evening came at last, and I was still alive. We went to church, and sang *'Eternal Father, strong to save'* and put the forty-seven dollars in the plate from our minstrel show, and old Donaldson asked God to bless us, and keep us safe upon

93

our rolling sea. He met us at the door, and shook our hands, and thanked us. His eyes were a bit dim. And I'd a sudden memory of Mr. Pellew.

"God bless you, my boy. I hope you'll succeed. I know you will if you try." And I wondered would I ever be able to conquer that awful dizziness that came on me aloft.

A tug-boat came to take us out next day. The *City of Benares* gave us three cheers, and we gave her three back.* And both ships beat their bells. The Judge, Major, Wiley and Simpson were on the wharf; and a crowd of cannery hands and fishermen to wave us farewell.

Salmon's what I remember best of that voyage home. Salmon and vertigo. We ate salmon three times a day, and never touched the ship's hard fare; unless to nibble hard-tack now and then. So I had no complaint about the grub. But I had that great dizziness aloft as bad as ever I had had it at the very first. How would I ever be a sailor? When Glynn was living, though he never spoke of it, I thought some-times he was aware of my trouble. Having him for my dear chum had helped a lot. Now there was no one. All of us were chums, but he had been my one dear closest one. I managed well enough upon the lower yards, the foresail, mainsail, crossjack. They were but fifty feet or so above the deck. The topsails were troublesome. But when I had to go above the cross-trees, that was hell. The royals were my horror.

We'd crossed the line when Douglas got a boil upon his knee. It laid him up. He had to go to the cabin twice a day for the Old Man to dress it. He was no sooner well than one of the others got a boil. Too much salmon. And by the time that we were toward the tropic's lower edge, only Hickley, Wood and I were eating it. Three times a day we ate it.

There came a sunny day when I was at the wheel. A bowhead whale appeared beside the ship. A monster. He swam so close that I could have dropped my hat on him. He'd dive, come up the other side, and dive again to come up where he'd been. The bright sea was all sun. There was no cloud at all except that fleecy rim of tender little clouds that ever hangs all round the wide horizon where the trade winds blow. The sun dipped low. The gentle white caps tossed their snowy heads. I was alone, no one upon the poop. I could see no one

_____
* The *City of Benares* sailed 11 days later. [Ed.]

26.   *Two more of de Wolf's fleet: the GLENALVON and . . .*

27.   *. . . the GLENESSLIN, wrecked on the Oregon coast in 1913.*

on the ship anywhere. I steered a fairy ship along a fairy sea; watched by a mythical monster. Happy? Yes, save that, upgazing to the royal high above, I would remember Furst and Glynn; and wonder would my turn soon come.

The sunset flame gave way to sapphire tints. The darkness fell. Stars winked. And soon a voice cried "Light ahead, sir!" And as we veered a little from our course, and brought the light abeam, a sailor asked, "By God, d'ye smell them pineapples?" Another said, "Aye. And I smells oranges too, and bananas."

High up above the sea, upon the island's ridge, the light flared toward the stars; a signal bonfire to let us know that we were seen. We stopped the ship and let her ride erect on that warm scenty sea. And then we soon heard voices, and the *clunka-clunka* of long oars,

> *Rock of Ages, cleft for me,*
> *Let me hide myself in thee!*
> *Let the water and the blood*
> *From thy riven side that flowed*
> *Be of sin the double cure,*
> *Save me from its guilt and power.*

And then two whaleboats swung in alongside the ship and we were gazing down into the upturned faces of the sons of mutiny. The Pitcairn Islanders, who were come off with boats loaded to the gunwale with fruits to trade. Soft-spoken, very gentle men, they swarmed up to the deck. They asked for linen sheets, and pillow cases, for their womenfolk. They asked for scented soap. We had not those, but what we had they traded liberally for. And if they'd hear us curse, they'd say, "Oh, sir!" or "Please, sir!"

Out on the deck I heard MacDonald say, "They're Jesus-lovin' bastards, ain't they?" Bastards they were, of course, originally; born of the union of mutinous sailors with native girls. But who's not a bastard if his lineage were traced back far enough? Now they were Jesus-lovers surely. No more religious people on the earth. When, in an hour, the order came that they must go, my bunk was piled with pineapples, green coconuts, oranges, mummie apples, and bunches of bananas. I'd scarce a rag of clothing left save what I stood in. My sea chest was nigh empty. I had more fruit that anyone else in the half-deck. A lot I cared that Cape Stiff lay ahead!

96

We swung west next day, and took the west wind on our quarter. Turning the wheel over to me, the helmsman said, "Sou'east—for the Horn, son." And then in a few days the mad Horn gales were yelling after her. But this was summer time. December now. Daylight till ten o'clock, and light again soon after one in the morning. We shortened sail to six topsails and the foresail and let her run like that. And how she ran! In those vast troughs she looked no larger than a walnut shell . . . and, roaring up astern, their crests long miles of wind-flung flying foam, the mighty rollers cut all wind from out her topsails. Eighty feet from the deck her topsails were, and lying in the troughs her topsails hung flat on her masts for just a moment. Then as she rose, the whooping wind would smite her and we could feel her lift, jerked forward bodily; all her own weight and the three thousand tons of cargo in her hold—jerked forward in a rush by just the topsails. "Go, old bitch!" we yelled. And go she did, like a stag with the hounds at heel. MacDonald shouted, "The Liverpool girls have got hold of the tow line!", but I, with no clothes, shivered and shook. All one long day we sailed through ice, and all that day all hands were kept on deck. Berg after berg rolled by: the big ones ponderous and motionless, lying on the sea with no roll or movement at all, and the sprays flying in white sheets hundreds of feet high on their pinnacles; but the smaller ones rolling and lumbering about in the sea troughs, smashing the emerald water to dazzling white foam in a lather all round them.

"Jesus Christ and General Jackson," said MacDonald, "it's a gawd dom good thing it ain't night." And so it was. And cold though I was, I still had plenty of fruit and plenty of salmon.

Wood was forever mute. He had to go aloft again now, on the homeward passage. MacDonald didn't spare him. One sailor shirks, another must do the thing he leaves undone. I mind a day when we were past the Horn and piling sail on her. There was another home-bound ship in sight and we were racing her. MacDonald shouted, "Hop up there, Wood! Loose that mizzen royal!" The ship was surging through a noisy sea, and rolling hard. The Old Man, on the poop, watched the rival ship. Wood started up toward the swaying spar a hundred and seventy feet from the deck. He went halfway and stopped.

"Get up, Gawd dommit!" bawled MacDonald.

97

He went a little way, and stopped again. And then, despite Mac-Donald's curses, he started down. He came down slowly. MacDonald waited for him, beside the rail. He lowered himself gingerly from the rigging to the deck. "Well, wot t'ell—Gawd, wat d'ye mean, eh?—" began MacDonald savagely. Wood looked him full in the face, and, with a crazy grin upon his lips, clapped his hands together and started jumping up and down on both feet.

"By Gawd! The lubber's loonie!" said MacDonald.

And so he was. His mind had broken. Wood was mad. Made mad by horror of the rolling spars. It wasn't nice to see. Yet he was harmless, and so did not have to have the irons put on. There was some talk of that at first. From that day he never worked at all, just wandered here and there about the ship, and sometimes stopped to clap his hands and do that crazy jumping up and down. He still ate salmon. So did Hickley and I.

It was a few days after Wood lost his reason that the mate called to me, "Hop up and loose that fore royal!" And up I started to the spar whence Furst had fallen. I reached it somehow. I mind how far, far, far away the narrow deck looked from the rolling spar. I mind that sea and sky shone dazzlingly. And that is all I mind, save that my limbs all shook; and that I seemed to hear Furst's falling scream. I don't know how I loosed the sail. I did, though. And I came down again. Sailor? How would I ever be a *sailor?* And yet the sea held me in thrall.

We came in at last, and let the anchor drop down to the Mersey mud. Wood's father came. Wood looked at him and grinned and clapped his hands, and jumped up and down, and did not know him. That day at breakfast Wood and I had finished the last can of salmon. Hickley had had to quit a while ago because of boils. I've never eaten salmon since. Wood's father took him off ashore. 'Twas better in the half-deck with the madman gone.

Next day we docked, and I took train for Ross. It was eleven at night when I came back to High House. I went in the back way, and found the kitchen lit; and Polly Dobbins there. She started when I entered without rapping. Her mouth fell open. She stared at me from her big eyes of pigeon blue.

98

28. *German barque HEDWIG, ex ANTILLES, at sea.*

"W'y maister, 'ow you've changed!"

"Polly got anything to eat?" I asked.

She fetched me bread and cheese, beef, pickles, and a big jug of milk. Seated on the table edge, I gorged while she stood staring, incredulous to see so much food go down.

"You'm belly must 'a grow'd a sight, maister."

And then she took the plates and things away, and I began to ask about the villagers. And then a voice called down the stairs:

"Polly, who are you talking to?"

"It's me, Auntie," I called, and down she ran, and threw her arms round me, and kissed me. And I kissed her.

"Oh, darling, I'm so glad you're home again. Tomorrow's Sunday. You'll be able to come to church with me," she said.

And—oh, well—sailors being trained to do their thinking quick, I said at once, "Auntie, you know—at sea we live on salt pork and salt junk. We get an awful lot of salt. And when a sailor comes ashore, the first thing that he does, he takes a dose of epsom salts to get the salt food out of his system. So I can't come to church, you see, Auntie."

Her face fell. And when I started up to bed she gave me a glass of epsom salts.

"Thanks, Auntie. I'll take it when I tumble into bed," I said.

Of course, I opened my bedroom window and poured it out over the ivy that clung to the house wall.

I stayed late abed next morning, you can bet. Linen sheets in place of mouldering blankets. Ah, luxury! And Auntie Polly was gone to church when I came down. The size of a sailor's belly amazed Polly again. All day I wandered about the village.

"You'm seed a' many queer things, I warrants me, young maister," said the villagers.

And I told them of whales, sharks, and flying fish. And by the end of day I felt quite bored. I wanted something, and did not know what.

And when another morning came, I set out for Hereford, eleven miles away, on my old bicycle. The village was too still. I had to move. There was a restlessness upon me.

And as I rode through High Town, round four o'clock or so, thinking I'd best start home, I passed two girls. I'd never thought of girls. They'd been just girls. I'd never kissed a girl. You think that funny, eh, and me nineteen? Think what you please. It's fact. And now I saw a girl who smiled to me. A smile half shy. I see her yet. A lot of soft brown hair, and soft grey eyes. She had a bow of pale blue ribbon on her hat, and I was six foot three, and wore a sea apprentice uniform, and had, maybe, a slightly roving eye. Most sailors have it. And sailors never were in Hereford.

"Darling, where *have* you been so long?" asked Auntie Polly when I strolled in at after two in the morning.

I'd left Annie at a bit past ten. But it had rained hard on the way home, and the night was dark. Slow going; walking much of it. And, too, I'd stopped at the Red Lion Inn a while, and talked to yokels there of whale and shark and flying fish.

100

"Night and day are all one to a sailor, Auntie," I said.

"But, darling, you are wringing wet. Why, you're wet through!"

"Oh, am I? Why, I hadn't noticed that!" said I.

Nor had I. What's a little wet to a sailor? So then I had to spin her a long yarn of how I'd met a chap I liked. "Nice sort of chap. His name is James. He's very interested in the sea and ships." And Annie really was, though her chief interest was a young sailor, and her name *was* James. Auntie swallowed it!

Almost three weeks I was in Peterstowe, and every blessed day I rode to Hereford. If high wind blew and rain lashed down, I put my oilskins on. I'd often walk as much as I would ride, and I was never home till, at the earliest, midnight. Every blessed night Auntie sat up to wait till I came in. Auntie Kitty came on a brief visit. I heard them talking. "He's got a friend, a man named James. It makes me nervous, Kate. He says his friend's a Catholic. The Catholics proselytize."

"I wouldn't worry, Mary," Auntie Kitty said. "The boy's got sense, I'm sure. And after all, a boy does need a friend." She was a good old scout.

And then there came a letter from my owner saying, "Join ship on such and such a day." It was the day after the morrow. Annie cried that night. We lay on the green grass, under a hawthorn hedge, and did a lot of kissing. Nothing more. There might have been—but I was innocent and didn't even dream of anything more. You think that funny, eh? A sailor, and nineteen. Think what you please. Next morning luckily, I was at the kitchen door when the letters came. One for Aunt Polly, postmarked Hereford. She had a friend there, a sharp-faced woman whom I did not like. I thought, "By cripey, I bet that's who it's from." And whether ethical or not, I opened it, to find it was all about me and Annie. She'd seen us lying by that hawthorn hedge. She said that Annie was a 'bad girl'. She said, too, that Annie was the daughter of a poor man; not a gentleman. It made me see red. I put it in the fire. That night I stayed with Annie till nigh midnight. Kisses, nothing more. The morning of the day I was to leave to join the ship there came a telegram. I opened that too. "Did you get my letter?" I put it in the fire, and then I went to Ross and took the train and left the train at Hereford, of course, and fooled about with Annie all the afternoon, and took a later train. I see her yet, upon the station platform, tears on her pretty cheeks. She'd given me a photograph, and on my wrist I wore a silver bangle she had put there.

"You'll wear it for me, won't you, darling?"

I watched her waving till my train went round a bend.

And then—I was a sailor. Who would be in the half-deck now in place of Glynn, I wondered, and of Wood? The previous night, ere I came in from Hereford, I'd been down to the churchyard. I'd stood there a little while. "You'll find it a hard life, my son." And hard it surely was. Those awful swaying spars! But, standing by that grave, I did not think of them. I should have been ashamed to own my fear to him.

CHAPTER VII

THE SILVER BANGLE

It was pitch dark when I came aboard. My sea chest contained an entire new outfit. "Whatever did become of all your clothes?" Auntie Polly had asked. And I had told the old apprentice yarn we ever told, of how a sea had flooded the half-deck and washed my clothes all overboard.

A light shone in the half-deck, and on the mainmast a few feet from the door. I saw that great steel mast uptowering to the night. And fear came over me. I put it away, went in and asked the question a sailor always asks: "Where are we bound this voyage?" We all had hoped to go out to the Colonies, or maybe to Calcutta, or perhaps to China. Sailors call Australia the Colonies.

"Portland, Oregon," they told me. And I said, "Damn!" Cape Horn again, and in the winter.

Polly Thompson was there, and Chinaman, and Douglas. Hickley* was to be third mate, share the second's cabin and eat at the saloon table. Barford had transferred to our sister ship† just in from China. Tattersall, one of her apprentices, had traded with him. There was a tousle-headed young first voyager with questioning blue eyes. An Irish lad, O'Brien.‡ There was a fat lad who reminded me of cows and pigs. He was a farmer's son. Then, too, there was a lad with thick curly black hair and very deep blue eyes that looked right into mine. Seeing him, I knew at once I'd found a chum. Later he told me that he had felt the same, the moment he saw me.

We tumbled out next morning at the usual time, five o'clock. Both mates were new.§ The second was a fellow with a face just like

---

* Hickley was then 21. [Ed.]   †The *Matterhorn*. [Ed.]

‡According to the articles, born in Guernsey. He was 17. [Ed.]

§The mate was Robert Burns, 31, of Rochester, from the *Arconcania*; the second, Frank Howell, from Sussex, 27, from the *Dunderdale*. The crew were mainly Scandinavian. [Ed.]

a rat's. We didn't like him. We didn't judge him smart enough for our ship. He irritated us. He had no pride in ships. We had, and he could see it, and so we irritated him. We old hands grinned at the new lads' struggles with the heavy deck buckets. By night they were utterly weary, and we yet quite fresh. I wrote to Auntie Polly when quitting time came; told her of the girl, and of the letter and telegram I'd burned. I said, "She's a liar. My girl's all right. Your friend's got a nasty dirty mind. That's what's the matter."

I wrote, "I'm sorry I had to keep it all from you; but I knew you'd make a fuss. There is no need to fuss. My girl's a fine square girl."

We sailed next morning. The same old song and dance. And I had a most happy feeling, for I felt at home. I put away my fear of the tall swaying spars, and loved the ship and loved the sea. And, loosing sail, I managed well enough. The dizziness was there, but yet I managed. Maybe I'd conquer it upon the long wet road to Oregon. And what if not? Of that I didn't think. One day, a day.

Bond was my new chum's name,* Irish he was, from Dublin. He seemed a quiet sort. We passed a word or two on that first day, and every word we spoke seemed to draw us together.

And when the evening came we sat in the half-deck and talked of home.

"How was it, Bill? Did you have a good time?" asked one.

I brought out Annie's picture. The old hands gathered round.

"By God, a dandy little clipper, Bill! Say, what'll you take for that picture, man?"

I said, "Give me your marmalade for the first three weeks at sea, and your Harriet Lane the first two Sundays, and it's yours."

We made the trade. Chink hung up Annie's picture in his bunk.

One day soon after sailing, the Old Man, while I was hauling on a rope beside the jigger mast, saw Annie's bangle on my wrist.

"You, boy? What's that rubbish you're wearing?"

I said, "It's a lucky sign, sir. It will bring us fair winds to Portland."

The Old Man scowled at me, but said nothing. Maybe he thought, "Fair winds, eh? Well, we'll see." In any case it wasn't his affair.

Maybe it was my bangle, maybe not. We ran, and ran, and ran,

*Born 1880, from Longford. [Ed.]

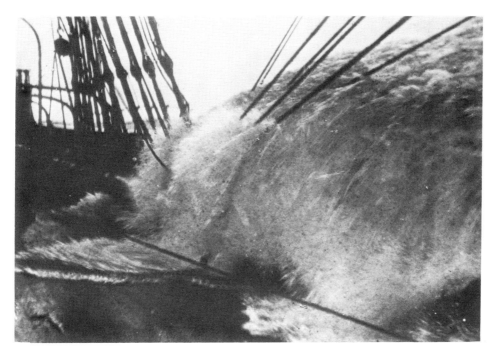

29. *Cape Horn sea boarding the ELGINSHIRE.*

with bully breezes driving the old ship along. We crossed the line in less than twenty days. Being an old hand now, I did less common deck work; less brass polishing and scrubbing rust away. The new lads did all that. I worked aloft with one or other of the sailors, repairing rigging; learning to splice and knot, and all the thousand little tricks that go to make a sailor. The height horror was there. At times most terrible; at others not so bad.

In fifty-three days we came to the pitch of the Horn. The same old song and dance. Ice on the shrouds. Seas crashing over the decks and deck houses. Toil, toil, toil. Clothing all sea-soaked. Hungry all the time. Sheer misery. But we had fair luck and spent but eleven days battling the hurricanes. And then one day when past the Horn we lay all day in a flat calm. Dark sky, dark sea. No break at all in all the sea or sky's monotony until, toward dusk, we saw, all of a sudden,

105

in the far south, a white edge in the sky; and under it a white line on the ocean.

"All hands shorten sail!" We had not got the royals furled when the buster smote her. A 'southerly buster' straight from the South Pole. The sails ballooned, the ship began to roll, the skipper shouted orders and we got sail off her without losing one, and then we let her ramble; with only her big foresail and six topsails set. She rolled her railings under in quick succession; flooded her whole deck's length. Two men stood at her wheel. No one man could hold her. When the morning came I was the weather helmsman, the old ship in my keeping. The wheel tore my arms well nigh from out their sockets. I sang, I laughed, and said, "Go! Go, old Bitch!" You don't look up when you are steering ships in that weather. You keep your eyes glued on your rolling compass. Snow squalls yelled by, hiding the world away, and then they'd clear and all the barbarous sea would shine and sparkle; with here and there a glint of sun from some cloud rift. The compass-card swung through a horrifying arc. To hold her on her course took every ounce of strength and all the skill of the man at her wheel. It was bitterly cold—fifty-six south latitude. July; wind off the polar ice-cap. If I dared to glance up for an instant it was to see a world of green and white water, with, above it, a hard, white yelling sky— either that or else nothing but a whirl of roaring whiteness, for snow-squalls constantly obliterated everything.

My arms began to tire, but I didn't mind that. I was in the prime of my youth and I wouldn't have traded my hold on those wheel-spokes for the softest job ashore. But all of a sudden the enjoyment passed from me as a man lifts off a portion of his rainment; my heart went cold as the snow on my shoulder.

At my shout, the skipper leapt from the chart-house and ran to my side. I shouted half-a-dozen words to him, "Ship hove-to dead ahead, sir!"

Glancing up from my compass, I'd glimpsed her for an instant only, lying full upon our track maybe a mile away, under main lower topsail and fore and main topmast staysails, her bow brought to the gale to ride it out. Some ships dare not run before that sort of wind. Even as I glimpsed her, snow hid her: hid the sea before me: hid our boom and fo'c'sle head; hid our fore and main masts and the straining sails upon them. Above my head the mizzen topsails were become a dim, grey blur.

Well, we could do nothing. You cannot alter a ship's course when she is running before such a gale as that one was. Try to, and she will get away from you, and that's her finish. So it was hit or miss. The Old Man stood before me, silent, grim.

When, for an instant, I dared glance up again, the snow had thinned a little. I saw the mainmast and the sails upon it. To starboard I saw a monstrous, great, green sea lift up its thundering crest of snarling, broken, white, lathered water. High on the lathered crest, there rose the sharp bow of the hove-to ship. For one grim instant her boom-end hung almost above our very rail—and all but fouled our trailing cro'jack braces. We were at that moment rolling—rolling away from her. I was aware of the stiff, grey belly of her fore topmast staysail, but I'd scarcely caught the rusty letters of her name when she was gone—the ship *Yarana*. We'd missed her by a mere matter of inches. I've never seen nor heard of her again. Her boom missed our rigging by a few feet only. There was a man on look-out on her fo'c'sle head, but I never saw her whole length for the whirling snow-flakes.

By now, she was gone astern, and all was well. Had she, instead of scending, been pitching, diving her sharp bow down, and had we rolled toward, instead of away from, her—well, I'd not be sitting here to tell of it.*

For two full days and nights the buster raged, and then we picked up a brave wind from the westerly, and off we went, with all sail set. We never had to take a sail off her till we were come far north of the line, beyond the region of the north-east trade wind. We were going to make a record run, and everyone was gay. The Old Man's eyes shone. He came to me one day where I stood splicing a rope on the poop. He looked at the silver bangle on my wrist, and grinned.

And then one evening came the Booby birds; those simple, silly birds that, alone of all the sea birds, will settle on a ship. They settled on her spars in scores. Big birds with plumage white and brown. Sailors don't like them much, because when morning comes the decks are dropping-spattered. But no man harms a sea bird. Or I, at least,

---

*The *Yarana* was a steel full-rigged ship built in 1892 and owned by S. Clink of Greenock. Generally slow ships, their fleet was named after famous racing yachts. The *Yarana* went missing in 1900. [Ed.]

have never seen one harmed.* But while we all sat yarning on the hatch that farmer's son went up aloft, unseen by anyone. The wind was blowing fair and the old ship was running through a singing sea, and we were happy, very. A record run! We'd show our sister clippers something this voyage! And then we saw the farmer's son come down, and in his hand he had a Booby.

"You damned young fool, what did you kill it for?" we asked.

He said he'd skin it for his sister.

Polly said, "Damn your sister!"

And right then, before he had begun to skin the bird, the mate cried, "Lee fore brace!" The wind was shifting.

We trimmed the sails, and sat to yarn again. And then again the mate cried, "Lee fore brace!" And ere the dark came the ship was off her course; the wind from dead ahead. That damned young farmer's son had brought us evil luck. We cursed him. We would have kicked him, too, but chose a bitterer punishment. We put him to Coventry. No one spoke to him. And did he speak, no one would answer. That's hard when you are in a ship at sea. It cuts a man. It makes him a pariah. We'd see the lubber crying. "Blubber, you little bastard!"

We came to Oregon in a hundred and ten days. It would have been in something more than ninety, but for that damned young lubber. We'd made the fastest passage of the year; but not a record.

In from our sea we came, and came to Paradise. All one long lovely day we towed up the Columbia, often the pines so close that their green foliage brushed our yard arms. Above, a crystal sky; below, a wide calm river. And, of course, the old ship dazzling. No speck of rust or dirt. We sent her sails down, stowed them in their locker. Working aloft I plucked a sprig of foliage from a tree. The height horror was not there at all that day. And working by me, Paddy sang that song he always sang at dog-watch time. A song called 'Paradise Alley'. I'd found a chum; a very merry chum, and I was very happy.

"I wonder what the Portland motts are like," he'd say. He called girls 'motts'. He knew a lot about girls, and I knew naught, save Annie: and didn't know her really. He'd been *with* girls, and somehow when he talked of that I did not take it in. It was beyond my ken. I'd

---

* French ships, in particular, often killed albatross. [Ed.]

30. *EURYDICE.*

have been shocked to hear some other talk of girls as Paddy talked. But somehow he didn't shock me.

Letters had come aboard at Astoria, and on the way up river the Old Man sent them to the half-deck. I'd one from Auntie Polly. She had left Peterstowe. She'd let High House and had moved as far away as she could get without going out of England. To some place I had never heard of. Some place in Cornwall. She'd moved to keep me from Annie when I came home again! Why, I'd not thought of Annie since I don't know when. Probably not since I'd finished the marmalade and Harriet Lane I'd swapped her pretty picture for.

In our last port there'd been no other ship save the *Benares*. But coming to Portland we saw a spar forest. Ship after ship. I mind their names, and they are music to me, as to any sailor. To a landsman a ship's name means not a thing. Listen then: *Euphrosyne, Lady Isobel,*

Eurydice, Cambrian Chieftain, Melanope. You've never heard the beating of ships' bells; nor seen their signal flags a-flutter on a high sea wind. The loveliest things that by the grace of God's good hand the hand of man has ever fashioned. And now they are all gone, and steamers have our sea.

We moored the ship. A little fat fellow, with bleary eyes and pudgy hands, and jowls that hung, came to our half-deck. And he passed cards around. 'The Golden Eagle'.

"Nice girls at my place. All young and pretty. Crazy for sailors. You come and see, eh?"

And when he went another man came in with other cards. 'The Elegant'. He said, "I've got 'em fat or not fat. Some lads like 'em skinny—and I've got 'em that way too."

And when he went another man came in with other cards. 'The Senate'. He said, "You come an' see my gals. I give 'em Spanish fly. You'll like 'em. Come see, boys, eh?"

We went ashore and to a restaurant and ordered ham and eggs for three on one plate again. We stuffed the crisp bread down and filled our bellies tight. The shore folk stared. And then, when we went out, Paddy said, "Let's go see the motts, Bill." I went with him, down to the 'Golden Eagle'; leaving the stony streets for sailortown. The other apprentices went on, to stare in shop windows and revel in the simple things that gave to simple lads come in from sea their simple pleasures.

One girl sat playing a piano in a big room's corner. One girl danced alone, out in the centre of the room. They wore long flowing gowns of gayest colours. Their hair was short, showing their slim white necks. Their white throats showed. Their slender arms were bare. There were no other men there yet. They gathered round us.

"Why, hello, sailor!"

And one girl said to Paddy, "Got a dollar, sailor?"

Well, somehow I felt shy when Paddy left the room. The girls winked at each other, seeing my red face, so I went out, and walked up and down outside till Paddy came.

"What did you go out for, Bill?" he asked.

I couldn't say.

And when we came down to the ship that night, the others did the

110

31.   *CAMBRIAN CHIEFTAIN* at a voyage end, and . . .

32.   *. . . anchored off Wallaroo.*

good and Godly act, and sneered at us; saying we'd been with whores. Paddy only grinned and didn't care, and because Paddy was my chum, I let them think I'd done as he had.

All the six weeks that we lay there, beside the Portland wharves, unloading and loading, I went with Paddy up to sailortown each night.

I'd say sometimes, "Paddy, let's go and see the park. They say it's pretty there. The squirrels come and eat out of your hand."

But Paddy said, "Ah, let's go see the motts, Bill."

But there was a night I did persuade him to cross the river bridge, and go to the fine residence section over there. The rose gardens were wonderful. You never saw such blooms. I made him hang around till dusk was come; and then we filled our arms with stolen blooms.

"Ah, hell, Bill, what good's roses? Let's go and see the motts," he said. So when we'd filled our arms with stolen roses, we went to sailortown.

"Oh, God! Look at the roses!" cried a girl, and ran and buried her face in the roses that I held.

And I said, "Would you like them?"

"Me?—My God!—will you give them to me, sailor?" she asked.

And I said, "Yes, of course."

And she said, "Sailor—?" and nodded toward the door that led upstairs.

But I said, "No. You can have them as they are. Just your roses." And she began to cry.

But Paddy gave his roses to a laughing black-haired girl, who led him, laughing, from the room. She said, "Four bits, sailor, and an armful of roses."

The dollar given us by the Old Man on Saturday night did not go far in sailortown and, since the places where we went were always full of sailors from other ships, who stood us drinks, we needed money. You can't take drinks and not give drinks back. So one night Paddy said, "Bill, I've got a brand new pilot jacket. I paid forty shillings for it in Liverpool." And down we went to Uncle Block's one night, and Paddy took a dollar for his pilot jacket. I pawned my silver watch and chain for fifty cents. Then we began to sort our clothing out, to see what we could spare. We even pawned some blankets from our bunks.

34.   *EUPHROSYNE, at Crockett, San Francisco.*

33.   *MATTERHORN, sister to SILBERHORN.*

Huge all wool blankets for a dollar and soon there came the time we had naught left that we could spare. Then we prevailed on Chink and Polly to let us pawn some things for them, on ten per cent. commission. They didn't go to sailortown. They used the money to buy grub with. We made but very little money that way. Our comrades looked down on us, doing the good and Godly act, and sneering, because we spent each night in sailortown. Paddy didn't care. I wasn't keen on sailortown myself, but went because I liked to stay with my chum. Often enough, after midnight, I'd get him on my shoulder and pack him down to the ship; half seas over, too drunk to walk. But I was never drunk. I saw to that. One night there were some soldiers in the 'Golden Eagle'. I counted how many times the drinks went round. Just twenty-two. I sat close by an open window and, when no one was looking, poured out my beer. By closing time the place was like a madhouse. Soldiers singing, sailors dancing; some girls singing with the soldiers, others dancing with the sailors, and two girls having a fierce fight in the centre of the big room. Ginger and Cork Fender, their names were. Always there was one girl called Cork Fender in a whore-house. A cork fender is a great soft mass of cork, within a strong rope netting, and it is lowered between a dock and a ship's side to take the jar from the ship's side as she grinds against the dock edge. The girl called Cork Fender is always a fat girl. This one's name was Rose. The singing and dancing stopped while everyone gathered round to watch them fighting. Then the door opened and in came the second mate of the *Primrose Hill*. He was Cork Fender's fancy man. He grabbed the ginger girl, and laid her on his knee, and spanked her hard; her stern exposed, while everybody laughed. She kicked and screamed. Then he stood drinks to all, and then he winked at Rose.

"Good luck, Cork Fender! You've got a dandy sailor! See you treat him well!" someone called after them. And Rose called back, "You mind your damned business. I'll mind mine." And then the crowd laughed louder yet and someone cried, "I bet she will."

I wished to God that we were out of Portland, on the good clean sea yet, somehow, I could not tear myself away from Paddy.

There was a place called the 'Seaman's Bethel' close to sailortown. An old chap with grey hair and a sad face was manager. The

35. *PRIMROSE HILL.*

Reverend Fletcher. Paddy and I and other laughing apprentices would pass at night, and he'd be at the door.

"Oh, my dear lads, please go no further," he would call.

He took my arm one night and begged me not to go beyond the Bethel's door, murmuring words about the 'dreadful women lost in sin'.

A few days later I was ill and had to lay up in my bunk. It was most cold and miserable in the half-deck. My head and all my limbs ached. The Old Man came.

"Come now, young fellow! You're needed on the deck! Can't have a sailor loafing!"

And that afternoon there came a great basket of grapes for me. Cool, purple grapes that soothed my throat. There was a little note came with them, tied to the basket handle, "Love from Vernie." One of the 'Golden Eagle' girls. As I ate them, in old Fletcher came. He sat down and started a long pow-wow about the evils of the port, and how he prayed that I would keep away from sailortown when I was well. He didn't see the grapes at first, the half-deck being dim. But when he did, he eyed them hungrily.

I said, "Have some. Just help yourself, sir."

And the old chap sailed right in. I guess he never had much luxury at the Bethel. He swallowed pips and skins and smacked his lips, his eyes ashine with pleasure. And when he rose to go he asked, "Where did you get the lovely grapes, my dear young boy?"

Said I, "A girl up at the 'Golden Eagle' sent them to me, sir." He paled, and left me.

And later Chink came in. "By gad," said he, "what in all hell was the matter with that old devil-dodger? He made a beastly mess out on the deck. Sick as a dog."

How is it that the preaching people are at times that way? Aren't whore's grapes just as good as any grapes? And can't whore's have hearts as kind as other women have, and, maybe, even kinder?

Well, we towed out at last, the ship's big belly full, and anchored in the river. That night our new crew came off. The outward crew had all deserted her the day that she came in. No sailor stayed with any ship in Portland those days.* 'Twas Larry Sullivan who saw to that. He kept the only sailor's boarding house there was. Each time a ship came in he'd go aboard, with bottles in his pockets, and give her men a drink; and tell then what fine jobs there were in Oregon; that only fools would stay in a damned ship. A sailor coming in from five months on the sea is easy keeled. One beer will make him feel a trifle jolly. Two make him start to sing. At three he owns the earth. So off he'd take them to his boarding house; and there would keep them keeled until a ship was laden, ready to go out. Then Larry'd go and see her skipper. No skipper could get sailors any other way. The skipper paid for every man what was called 'blood money'. If sailors happened to be plentiful it might not be more than twenty-five dollars. It went as high as fifty. Usually Larry'd take a ship's crew to her roaring drunk. Each man would draw a full month's wages in advance, and he would pocket it; guiding their hands if they were too drunk to guide their own

* Oddly, Adams does not mention that Hickley was paid off at Astoria. His indentures were dated July 9th, 1895, so he would have finished his time. [Ed.]

36. *French ASIE capsized in Portland two years later.*

while signing over to him their advance notes. In three years Larry
cleaned up eighty thousand dollars shanghaiing sailors. When last I
heard of him, he was in a penitentiary. I hope the louse died there.

It was a dandy crew that Larry brought us. Liverpool Irish,
every one. They came from his boat roaring drunk, singing, shouting,
cursing. A few had to be dragged aboard, with ropes about them.
They rolled into their forecastle and sang and cursed for half the night.
At dawn the mate went to rouse them to heave the anchor in. They
damned him. But he was wise and said, "You're a poor looking lot.
I bet there's not a man can sing a chantey." And out they came, all
bellowing, "By God, we'll show ye."

So we went tramp, tramp, tramp around the windlass, while a
small pock-marked fellow roared out 'Rolling Home'.

> *Far aloft amongst the rigging*
> *Stretches out each snowy sail,*

117

Like a bird with outspread feathers
Flies our ship before the gale,
And the billows sweeping past us
Seem to whisper as they flee,
There's a welcome sweet awaits you
In the land where you would be.

And then the chorus came, and all those Irishmen, and we apprentices, and the old carpenter, and the sailmaker, joined in:

Rolling home, rolling home,
Rolling home across the sea,
There's a welcome sweet awaits you
In the land where you would be.

"By gad, I didn't think you had it in you," said the mate, drily, "Let's hear another now!" And then it was:

Goodbye, fare you well!
Goodbye, fare you well!
Hurrah, my lads, we're homeward bound!

I wish that I could give you the lilt, the eager quaver, the rolling roaring music of that last line. I can't. The only place to catch it is on a good ship's forecastle head. Soon the ship was gliding down the river, and other ships were cheering her, and we were cheering back. We anchored off Astoria that night, and I forgot the girls, the booze, the singing and the dancing in the 'Golden Eagle'. Oh, I was glad to be away off to my heaving sea! But Paddy muttered, of five damned months at sea and never a mott; still hankering for the lips of his girl Dot, a little frizzy-headed whore who'd had a case on him toward the end, and called him 'honey boy' and meant it.

It's hard to be a man when you stand six feet three, and have clear eyes, and muscles like steel wire. Yes, I was very glad to be away again, out to my good clean sea. I was a different lad, yet I was not. And Paddy was, of course, in no way changed. What I had found was old, old finding to him.

The crew refused to heave the anchor in when morning came. The Old Man went to talk to them. They damned him to his face. He went ashore and brought the consul off. They damned the consul. He fetched the sheriff then. They damned the sheriff louder. And so the Old Man frowned, in a deep quandary. There were no other sailors to be had just then. If he sent these to jail, he'd have to wait no telling how long, and Larry'd charge him no telling how much blood money for new men. Larry had a branch house in Astoria, and it was empty now.

Consul and sheriff went ashore, and the Old Man went with them. Soon he was back, bringing a gang of longshoremen to help us boys to heave the anchor in. Not one of them could sing a chantey, but Polly sang. Then, when the chorus came, those Irishmen came swarming to the forecastle head and made the chorus ring from side to side of the Columbia's wide mouth. Soon the longshore crowd all went ashore, and we went out; the tug ahead of her. The Old Man thought when we were once at sea the men would turn to. They didn't. They loafed in the forecastle, and laughed at us apprentices; pulling our arms out, hoisting the heavy topsails. They never touched a rope, while, one by one, we gave her all her wings. "Look at the damn bridge ornymints!" they jeered; making great fun of us, who each some day would be an officer.

We piled on all her sail. The tug-boat left us, and there she was, a tall four-master, to be handled by eight apprentice lads! And, by the Gods, we handled her! For ten whole days and nights we tore our arms out of their sockets; hauling the braces tight, dragging the jerking sheets hard home. The Old Man looked at us complacently, taking it all for granted; and never smiled nor said a single word. We were, it seemed, no more than part of the ship's gear. We cursed our hard Old Man, and yet were proud of him. We didn't want his praise. To hell with it!

Then one night a hard squall came shrieking from the night-hid sea. Over the ship went, till her long lee rail was scooping water, and all her long length groaning. In a trice, out came those Irishmen and took their places: as though they'd never done a thing but take them. An order was obeyed almost ere it was given. Wild weather sailors, all. Such was the way with Liverpool Irish sailors. Fine weather and they'd growl and swear at officers. But let wild weather come, and they were like a lot of boys let out of school. And after that they gave no trouble much, save that the little pock-marked man would curse the second mate to his face. We hoped there'd be a fight. There never was. The

119

second was a rat. He could have whipped the little pock-marked man and, had he done it, he'd have made a friend.

Tom Swift,* the little fellow's name was. He took a liking for me. When he was with his fellows in the forecastle he'd damn and curse, talk soot, and jest of women he had known the world across; his every other word a swear word. When first he spoke to me I was upon the forecastle head, and it was dawn. The dawn came grey, all pearly clear above a pearly sea. And then it changed to opal. The sky was filled with tender streaming banners of soft cloud. 'Twas then Tom Swift came up and joined me. His eyes grew soft. He looked at me and shook his towsled head. And there was reverence in his bleary eyes. He never said a word, nor did I. But after that, he'd seek me in the evening when the day's work was done. He'd never curse, nor say a word about the women then. He'd say, "Me lad, Tom's goin' to make ye somethin' like a sailor," and he would teach me all the tricks of seamanship he knew; telling me just how certain sails could best be set; and how a splintered mast could be sent down, in a mad sea, repaired, and sent back up. He'd been a sailor in some famous tea clippers. All the long road from Oregon he taught me seamanship. It was against the rules for apprentices to fraternize with common sailors. My older comrades sneered at me, saying, "Tom Swift's no better than a pimp. Good Lord, why do you chum with him?" I never told them why. I minded that still dawn when he'd looked at the sky. And I was glad he was my friend, my *shipmate*, sharing all he had to share with me.

We met a good many ships that voyage on our road home. We'd see at dawn a tiny speck upon the sea ahead; the royal of a ship whose hull was hid 'neath the horizon. Bit by bit we'd lift her from the sea. We'd see her topgallants, and then her topsails, and then we'd see her hull. By and by she'd be beside us, both ships running neck and neck. God help the helmsman who didn't steer her true when those times were! I mind a dandy barque that lay abeam one dawn. She'd sailed from Oregon a day ahead of us. A strong wind blew, piping a high tune in our rolling rigging. Both ships were carrying full sail. Great sprays drove over them. They rolled and pitched, and fought to shake the rival ship away. The wind came harder as the day drew on. The sky grew dark. Big inky clouds came scudding from the sea's far rim. Our

* Aged 31 (by the articles), of Liverpool. Most of this crew are noted as having served last in 'American Ship'. [Ed.]

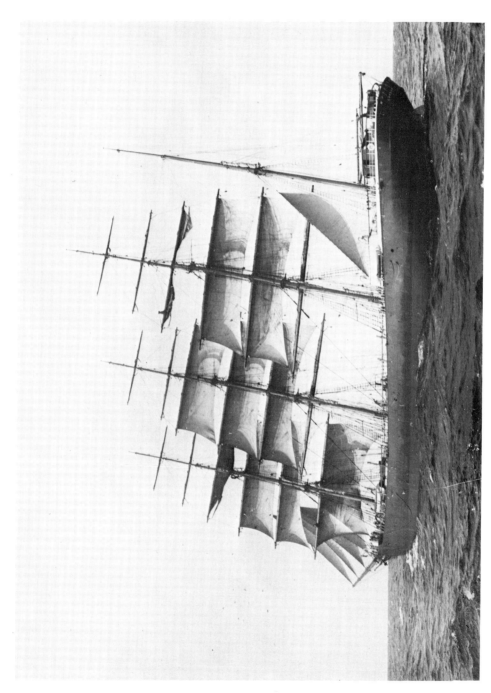

37. *MUSKOKA.*

38. *CISSIE, ex DRUMBLAIR.*

ship lay down, with half her deck submerged. Then a mad squall smote her; and hailstones battered down, leaping from mast and spar and deck-house. So dark it was you scarce could see her length. We thought a mast must surely splinter and go overboard. At each mast, at each sail's gear, a sailor stood ready to lower away quick as the order came. I heard the Old Man say, "Take nothing off her, mister. She can carry it." All through that day we drove, her whole length trembling to the mad squalls' beating. The night came down. All night we saw the winking red port sidelight of that other ship, still running neck and neck. And day came back, and still the two ships drove.

We raced that ship three days, three nights; and then the wind changed and we ran away from her at last. You don't see sights like that today. For steamers have our sea. That was but one race of many that we had upon that homeward voyage.

No ship ever got away from our tall clipper. She was a queen, to fly.

39.   *PROCYON—a big barque.*

"Go! Go, old bitch!" we'd yell. "Oh, go, go, go!"

We damned her for the hardness of her food. We damned her high ballooning sails that tore at us; toiling with all our strength high up above the raging sea. We damned the good old ship for everything. We damned her, and we loved her. That vertigo was bad at times, but I was conquering it. A long slow bitter battle. It was Tom Swift who helped me more than anything. I could not let him see it. I had to live up to his confidence. He'd call to me when sail came in, "Hey, come on you! I'll show ye somethin' now!" And then, of course, I had to answer to his challenge. Often it was dire. I did it, though. *Oh, sailor, sailor, sailor!*

It was mid-morning when we sighted Pitcairn Island. There was a piping wind and we were running fast. A little way astern another clipper followed. She'd been there yesterday, and all the starry night. She was so close that we could see the long lift and the pitch of her sharp cutwater, and almost hear the breaking music of her bow-wash. Pure white, her hull was. All her masts and spars and blocks and deck-houses were white. There was not anywhere a patch of colour on her. She was a tall white bird, fast hovering at our heel. Our Old Man scowled at her, and we scowled, too, fearing what he would do. Just thirty days we'd been at sea. The hard-tack was all weevils. The pork was rancid. Oh, pineapples, oh, oranges! And then of course, the Old Man did just what we feared he'd do. We damned him mightily, and yet, we did not damn him in our hearts. A sailor may be hungry, but he's a sailor still.

The islanders had seen us and were coming off to meet us. Their boats were stacked with fruit. We saw their piles of golden oranges, and yellow bunches of bananas, and heaps of sweet green coconuts all full of luscious milk, and the green leaves of mellow pineapples. And our Old Man *sailed on!* We passed the boats so close that we could hear the natives calling, above the sea's high sough, the wind's high pipe. There was a girl in one boat. Paddy threw her a kiss and shouted, "Hey! Meet me off the Horn, and warm me up a bit!" On we flew, and on came that white clipper after us. You don't catch clipper captains halting in a race to let their crews munch fruit! And then we heard the mate say, "Well, I'm damned! They're chucking all the fruit into

124

40.   *One of the smart white "Sierras"—the SIERRA ESTRELLA.*

41. A passing full-rigger.

the water!" And how we damned that tall white clipper then! We raced her two more days, then lost her in a wet wind from the westerly. She'd never gained a foot.

There came a pitchy night when we were running east, under topgallant sails. The ship was driving bravely. Just ere the dark fell, I was at her wheel. The old girl wrenched my arms.

The second mate came, asking, "D'ye need a man at the lee wheel?"

"No, sir," said I.

And then he went, and I was all alone. And then there came six snowy albatross.* They sailed upon the wind in a straight row, each with his six foot spread of wing outstretched, no pinion moving. They

---

* It used to be thought that the 'snowy albatross' was a separate type. Actually, albatross become whiter as they grow older. [Ed.]

42. A ship in company—probably French.

hung, they floated, just above my head and just beyond the rail. It seemed that each of those great snowy birds turned down a beady eye, to watch me steering her. They say that when a sailor dies his spirit goes into a sea bird. I don't know. Six long-drowned skippers, maybe? And I cried, "Go, old girl! Show them a sea bird's flight!" So dark came down, and in the last dim light I still could see those hovering watching shapes.

Just as I left the wheel, the order came to furl topgallant sails. The wind was freshening. All shouting at the ropes, we clewed them up. "Aloft and make them fast!" the mate cried. I jumped into the mizzen rigging, and as I started up a fist beat on my ankles.

"Get up, ye bloody farmer! Can't ye bloody move!"

It was Tom Swift. How I ran, to keep ahead of him! I quite forgot that vertigo, I came to the topgallant yard, and he came too; but then no other. It takes four hands (a man's a hand) to furl a big ship's 'gallant. And so we had the work of four to do. We fisted the wild sail, and fought, and fought it. We had it gathered close beneath our breasts, ready for lashing down, when came a puff that tore it free again. And then I heard the voice of the Old Man, from the bridge far down beneath us. A few pale stars were gleaming, so he could see our shapes against the murky sky. "What's the matter up there? Why don't you get that sail furled?"

And then I lost my wool with my Old Man. I let the sail go loose, and I leaned back and downward. Clinging with one hand, I set the other to my lip, and bawled at him, "If you're in such a damned big hurry why don't you come and show us how to furl it?" Tom Swift let out a jolly yell. Then we fought the sail again and picked it up and lashed it.

We were about to start down to the deck when, dazzling our eyes, a flare lit all the sea and sky. It scarce was gone when came another flare. The thunder rumbled, a long continual growl. On, and on, and on, the lightning flared, and lit the rolling ocean and the scuddy sky, and every rope and every inch of all the straining ship. There, maybe, half a mile away, was that white clipper; running neck and neck, taking in her topgallants, too. We saw her hands up on her rolling spars; just saw their little shapes; black dots with waving arms and bobbling heads, like spiders in the night. Maybe a mile beyond that clipper was a darkling shape, on which great breakers flung themselves as high as any tall ship's masts.

"The bloody Horn!" said Tom.

So we, instead of going down, stayed there a while to watch the fiery skies and roaring seas, and our old enemy Cape Stiff, and I had quite forgot that vertigo! I never thought of it. And was I gay? *Oh, sailor, sailor, sailor!*

Suddenly we saw that tall white clipper let her topsails go, and up her crossjack went, and then her mainsail. She was stopping.

Tom Swift cried, "She's lost some poor beggar overboard!"

Later, when we were come to port, we heard about it. She'd seen

43. SIERRA NEVADA.

in the bright lightning flares an open boat upon the roaring Cape Horn sea, so she had stopped and taken up the men from it. Five men. Three dead, and two so nearly dead it hardly mattered. One of them lived though. Their ship had struck on the Diego Ramirez, five days ago. They'd been adrift without a bite of food or drop of water; all that got off the wreck. And that's the sailor's way!

When I came down, I had to go up to the poop to coil the ropes there. The lightning had quite ceased. The night was pitchy. In the chart-room doorway, clear in the lamplight, stood the Old Man. I had a chill, you bet! I'd sworn at him. Now I should catch it if he saw me. He saw and called to me.

"Yes, sir," said I.

But all he said was, "Boy, go get me a cigar from the saloon."

I fetched him a cigar, and as I handed it to him he looked at my bare wrist. "You, boy—where's that fool bangle that you used to wear?"

I said, "I sold it, sir, for money to buy food in port." And that gave him a stab. It wasn't his fault that the grub was as it was. He was the owner's slave as much as we. A look of gloom came to his eyes.

And I had lied, of course. For Vernie now was wearing the silver bangle Annie had given me—and not for food.

CHAPTER VIII

EVERYONE KISSES A SAILOR

From Cape Stiff till we were well up in the trade winds once again nothing much happened. We shook the maggots from the hard-tack, and in the evenings puffed baccy smoke into the crevices to drive the cockroaches out. We'd kill enough to fill a gallon can. We gambled, betting matches, baccy, marmalade and Harriet Lane. The same old song and dance that sailors know.

But when we began to get the pretty clipper ready for port again, the Irishmen began to kick up a rumpus. They said, "The hell, we ain't no bloody painters nor no paint scrubbers."

They didn't want to do the common deck work. 'Twas sailor work for them, or no work and, since the rigging was all in good shape, there was no other work to put them to. The day the mates ordered them to scour the rust from the rails, they refused point blank. The Old Man went to talk with them. They laughed at him. But presently a big man named Reuben got a notion, and when the Old Man had been gone a while, they all came out and went to work. But every man had his pipe in his lips. Smoking's not allowed when you're on duty. The mate said nothing. The Old Man scowled. Big Reuben, laughing, said, "All right, me b'ys! We'll clean the hooker up and paint her, but we'll do it our own way." Then day by day the whole crew smoked their pipes while working. Not only that, They'd talk to one another in loud voices, tell sailor yarns, and gossip on the girls of sailortown. A man aloft would shout down to a man on deck. The ship was like a madhouse, with their noise. We apprentices, of course, worked in our usual way. No smoking or talking.

131

We made a long, slow passage through the trade-wind seas. They stretch from tropic edge to tropic edge. Three thousand miles or so. We'd little balmy breezes all the way. The sun was warm. The sea was warm. You never wear a shoe, nor anything but just a pair of trousers rolled up to the knee, a little undershirt, and some old shady hat. You watch the dawn blaze out, and see the great round golden sun lift from the sea's clear rim. You see the evening's quiet many-tinted glow. Day after day for weeks. Maybe there'll be a moon. And in the quiet night each rope, each block, and every part of all the towering ship will be as plain almost as in the day. Our Old Man never let us sleep out in the moon's full light. We thought him foolish, but the sailors said that he was right. A man who sleeps out in the full moonlight goes moonblind. He cannot see by night. By day he can.

In those still, moonlight nights a voice would sound from end to end of her. A footfall too. One night the mates were talking. I heard the second say, "That long-legged Adams, by God, I think he's got a flock of bats in his belfry. He'll stand and stare for hours together at the stars." And so I would. Sometimes I'd climb aloft and lie on that wide platform round the lower mast-head upon my back, and gaze up at the sky all through my four-hour watch on duty. There would not be a sound, save for the little ripple of the bubbles at her side. I would think that I was sailing *through the stars*, and quite forget the sea. The ship seemed disembodied from her element. Her sails would arch above me, gently swaying. There was not anyone in all the universe but me, and I was sailing in a ship star-voyaging. Then maybe I'd hear Tom Swift call my name and down I'd go.

"Where was ye, son?" he'd ask; and when I told him he would stare at me, and nod his tousled head, and seem to understand.

"By God, ye'll make a dandy sailor, son, some day," he'd say. "It's in yer blood."

I saw a shooting star one night when I was at the wheel. The second mate leaned drowsing on the taffrail. The crew all lay asleep about the deck. The only man awake save me was Tom, keeping look-out upon the forecastle head. That shooting star illuminated all the sky. It put out all the stars. It lit the whole horizon's circle bright as noon almost. Later Tom said to me, "By cripes, I thought as Jesus

132

Christ was comin', son. By God, I did."

"What do you know of Jesus Christ?" I asked.

"Damn little, son," said he. "I 'eard some yarns of 'im w'en I was just a nipper. I 'ad a mother once. Now ain't that queer? By God, ol' Tom come out a woman's belly! An' look 'ow 'ard e's got! She says to me one day as Jesus Christ'd come w'en none was lookin' for 'im."

"See, son," he said. "Just you an' me was all as was awake. You're but a kid, an' I ain't no one no'ow. An' she says too as a bright star'd be we'en 'ee was comin'—or some such tale as that. That's w'y I thought as Jesus Christ was comin'."

So I said, "Tom, you've got it mixed a bit. That star she spoke about was one that shone when He was born on earth. The Bible tells of it."

"Well, anyway, that bloomin' star it comed, and now it's gone," said Tom. "An' Jesus Christ ain't come. Let's see you tie a mast-head knot, me son. That's more important. The Bible ain't a-goin' to 'elp ye get your second mate's ticket. Tom Swift is. 'Ee's better'n the Bible w'en it comes to seamanship. Let's see you tie that knot."

Each evening in the dogwatch men and boys would gather at the hatch and sing and dance. There was an evening when two men had quarrelled in the day, shouting across the deck to one another. They'd talked about a girl called Tess in New Orleans. One said her hair was black, the other yellow. They called each other liars and damned each other. When evening came they stripped their shirts off, to fight it out. The crew all gathered round. The deck grew blood-spotted, and neither could beat the other. They fought till they gave out. You think them savages? Maybe they were. But I at school had read how Catholics and Protestants had burned each other at the stake, owing to differences. High dignitaries of the church abetted it. What's the difference? Two common sailors fight about a whore's hair colour. Others make prostitute religion, and fight about it. When you sail the high seas and watch the sun and stars come up and sink, and see the moonbows arching in the mist, it makes you wonder about things. Anyway, since Quayle could not beat Harris,* and Harris not beat him, none of us ever knew for sure what colour Tess's hair was. Who knows which church is right?

* Henry Quayle, 31, was a Manx man; Harris was 22, and from Liverpool. [Ed.]

At dogwatch time we tried our strength, man against man. I was just turned twenty, and there was but one man in all the crew could handle me. Reuben, his name was; a giant of a man. But when it came to mast-head races I left him behind. He was too heavy. At "Go" we'd jump into the rigging to see who first could come to the royal-mast head and down again. Polly and I could never beat each other at that. We both stood six feet three. We beat the rest, our reach was in our favour.

They say the sea's monotonous. Maybe it is. I never found it so. I never did grow tired of watching sea and sky. Paddy was bored, though. He'd sit when the red sun was sinking in a bank of ruby cloud, and talk about the motts. One evening Reuben said, hearing his talk of motts: "After a voyage as long as this, by God, anything that wears a skirt does me." As he spoke, the Old Woman appeared upon the poop to take her evening stroll. Then Reuben sang:

> *Johnnie, get yer gun!*
> *There's a hoor in the garret!*
> *Johnnie, get yer gun!*
> *There's a row downstairs!*

While the Old Man scowled, the Old Woman went hurrying below. A mad wild lot those Irish were. Yet one morning, soon after dawn had burst across the scarcely rippled sea, there came a little bird that fluttered at her sides. It was exhausted and could not fly high enough to reach the rigging. It fell into the sea. All hands ran to it, and Quayle, who'd fought about the colour of Tess's hair, slid down a rope and saved it. He held it safe in his cupped hands and hurried to the cabin door with it, and rapped. The steward came.

"I want the skipper's wife," said Quayle.

When the Old Woman came, he held the bird out to her. She looked at him and smiled and took it. And soon she brought it out and set it on the after hatch, where all the crew could see it, in a cage. The man who came from steering passed it by. When he joined his fellows they would ask, "'Ow's that there little bird?" and from that day when the Old Woman came to take her evening stroll, no sailor ever sang that song; or ever sang a chantey with a sotty line to it.

We came up channel by and by, and had our orders from the

Lizard signal station to go on to Antwerp. A fresh wind blew, and, as we passed steamer after steamer, we yelled taunts at them. Dirty tin kettles, fouling our clean sea! We saw the little white-washed cottages, set in the April fields. And all the air was sweet with earthy scents. At night we saw the winking lights of towns. There's no one happy as a sailor coming home. At dawn next day we saw that tall white clipper once again. We sailed beside each other, so close that we could shout. 'Twas then we heard about the boat that she'd picked up.* The one survivor from the lost ship's boat was steering the white clipper home. She turned away, for London, Two nights later we docked our ship in Antwerp, late at night. Tom Swift sang 'Sally Brown', for us to heave her cables taut.

> *Sally Brown, would ye marry a sailor?*
> *Way, aye, Sally Brown!*
> *Sally Brown, would ye marry a sailor?*
> *I spent my money on Sally Brown!*
> *For seven long years I courted Sally,*
> *Way, aye, Sally Brown!*
> *And when I asked her would she marry*
> *I spent my money on Sally Brown!*
> *For answer she showed me a nigger's baby,*
> *Way, aye, Sally Brown!*

And then Tom Swift was gone, as all his fellows were. Gone in a tick, the instant that the mate cried, "That will do!" I tried to find him, but I was too late. He'd gone to find the Sally Browns of Schipper Street.†

> *Tom's gone, what shall I do?*
> *Hilo! Hilo!*
> *Tom's gone, what shall I do?*
> *Tom's gone to Hilo!*
> *Where Tommy's gone I must go to,*
> *Hilo! Hilo!*
> *Where Tommy's gone I must go to.*
> *Tom's gone to Hilo!*

But I have never seen Tom Swift again, by any sea or shore. Maybe he wings it off Old Stiff today, his sailor spirit in some great white albatross; looking for a clipper to drive by; watching for me. But steamers have our sea.

---

* The facts of this incident seem to be a little elusive. [Ed.]
† But he turned up at the Shipping Office and received his pay and fare to England! [Ed.]

Next morning, in a smoky London station, the shore folk, crowding to their dingy offices, all stared at us. City men. Top hats, and bowlers. Kid gloves and shiny shoes. And troubled eyes, and pasty faces. Minds upon pennies set. We were sea-brown, and springy on our feet. "Poor bastards," Polly said.

I went to Aunt Clarissa's for a day or two. Dolly wasn't there. Ede was. She looked at me, and smiled. She said, "Who was the girl? I think you've lost your—" and at that moment Aunt Clarissa came into the room. Ede finished with "your boyish look."

Later she asked again, "Tell me about the girl."

I said, "There wasn't any girl."

She laughed at me, and I was glad that Dolly wasn't there.

The place Aunt Polly had moved to gave me a chill feeling the minute I arrived. The little railway station was a terminus. Beyond it was the Atlantic whence I was just come. There was a tiny town that made one think of widows, so sere it was. Aunt Polly had rooms in a farmhouse some two miles up the coast. It stood in a dell, hills all round it. No horizon. Just hills. On the way thither I recognized golf links, on which was a pavilion. The cabby told me that in summer many Oxford men came to spend the summer in the town. Then the widows took boarders, and the place was gay. But this was late winter. What the devil could a sailor find to do in such a place?

Auntie was overjoyed to see me, and said no word of Annie. She had that much sense. I filled my belly with tough cakes and Cornish cream, and sat talking to her of the sea. Next morning I pottered about, watching the shepherd with his lambing ewes; looking at cows and horses. By noon I was sick of the farm. I rode to the town and found that there was a little haven in which were a few coasting vessels. Their crews did not know my style of ship. But we were all one breed. I spent the afternoon yarning with coasting sailors. Yet it was dull. There was a restlessness in me. I'd been over a year away, and only sailors to speak to. It was dusk when I started home. When we left the ship in Antwerp we were told we'd have a month ashore. What could a sailor do in such a place for a month?

Then, turning a corner, I saw a girl. She smiled to me. I jumped from my bicycle took off my hat, and said, "Hello!"

136

She said, "Hello yourself and see how you like it. There's no one can learn *me* anything."

Well, Ede had been wrong. I hadn't lost my innocence; for I didn't catch on to the girl's meaning. I said, "Let's take a stroll."

She gave me a cold stare and said, "What sort of big fool are you?"

I said, "If that's how you feel, I'll bid you good evening."

She called after me, "Hey—wait! Haven't you got a shilling you want to spend?"

Pretty as a skysail in the sun, she was; but her words gave me a nasty feeling. She was Paddy's sort, not mine.

In a few minutes I passed two more girls walking arm-in-arm. They smiled to me. I got off my wheel, took off my hat, and said, "Hello!" One of them looked at me from bold eyes. The other blushed, and said to her companion, "Come on."

The name of the girl that blushed was Judy. She was smallish and had a lot of soft brown hair, and big bulgy blue eyes. Her mouth was very little. It was ten that night when I left her. I asked her for a kiss. She said, "No."

"Why not?" I asked.

She said, "Of course not. What do you think I am, kissing a man I've known only a few hours?"

I said, "Everyone kisses a sailor. Come on. Don't be silly."

She said, "I'm not everyone."

I said, "I know. That's why I want a kiss. I'd not kiss everyone."

She said, "No" again.

So then I said, "See here. Be a good sport. Let's toss to see if you kiss me or not. Heads you do, tails you don't.

She said, "I like your cheek."

I said, "I like your cheeks too. They're the prettiest ever I saw. That's why I want a kiss."

I had to argue a long time ere she let me toss a coin. I told her I might be drowned on my next voyage, and then how would she feel when she heard about that? I said, "Sailors have a hard life and there's never any telling when a chap will get killed or drowned. My best chum got killed." That made her look a bit tearful. I brought out a coin and said, "Heads I win, tails you lose."

137

And she was so simple she didn't see the catch in that.

When the coin came down heads I said, to prove I was square, "We'll toss three times and go by the best of three if you like."

Then I said, "You lose again. Now we'll have that kiss." She tried to back out, but I said, "You can't do a thing like that. It's not square." And at last she let me kiss her, and gave me a shy little kiss.

When I reached home, Auntie wanted to know where I'd been so late. I told her I'd been to the haven, talking with sailors. "I'll take you there tomorrow," I said. Next morning she walked to the haven with me. The chaps on the coasters treated her as though she were a queen. Sailors are that way. They made her tea, brought out a can of sardines and a loaf of fresh bread. She was delighted. They asked her to come again and she said she wished it were not so far to walk. So now I had a tip-top alibi, and spent every evening with Judy. She soon learned how to kiss a sailor. It's not the same way you kiss a lubber. Not on your life.

Judy was a housemaid, and I a gentleman's son. In England a gentleman's son doesn't run round with a housemaid. But a lot I cared. Besides, she wasn't the usual sort of housemaid. She was of gentle blood that was come on hard times. She hadn't any education, but she liked the right sort of things; like wading at low tide in the rock pools and poking about amongst the sea anemones. "Aren't they pretty?" she'd ask. Sometimes when she had to lift her skirt high she'd say, "Please look the other way." I'd do so. But a sailor can see from the back of his head. She didn't know that. Sometimes we'd take long walks into the country. Often we'd sit under a tall hedge. I'd tell her about the Horn, and she'd look at me from her big round eyes; and there'd be a look of dread in them.

One day she said, "I wish you weren't a sailor."

"You wish I wasn't a sailor, do you?" I asked. Then she snuggled her little brown head on my breast.

I'd been at Bude ten days when a wire came, ordering me to join the ship. Ten days! I wrote telling my owner I'd understood I was to have a month ashore, and that therefore I'd not had my teeth attended to, and that they needed a lot of attention. Could I have a few days extra? He wired back that I must join the ship at once. So I had

138

44. *HUTTON HALL—another of de Wolf's ships.*

Auntie write him. She swallowed it about my teeth of course and wrote a long pow-wow about how her dear young brother's teeth were much in need of attention before he went back to sea. It worked. The owner wired, allowing me one more week. I went to the dentist, who looked my teeth over and said they needed nothing at all. Fine. Judy and I had a grand time.

On the afternoon of the day before I was to leave for Antwerp, an old maid she knew called and told Auntie that it was all over Bude that I was going to marry Judy Terdrey. Auntie was in the deuce of a stew, never having heard of Judy. I got her smoothed down after a bit. "Don't worry, Auntie. My girl's all right. And anyway I'm going to sea right away. No harm done." I had a date to meet Judy at nine that night. So at eight-thirty I said, "It'll be a long day tomorrow, Auntie. I'm going to bed now." I went to my room, and she to hers. After a bit I opened my door to go down. At once hers opened. "Where are you going?" she asked. I told her I was going down to the bathroom. I did so, and made a lot of slushy noises and came back. Looking from my window after a bit I saw that Auntie's light was out. I opened my door again to go down. At once hers opened. I said I couldn't sleep and was going down to walk on the lawn. She said she'd come too. It was close to nine. After a bit I said, "I think I'll sleep now," and we went to our rooms. And then I remembered my sailor's sea chest. A sailor lashes his sea chest with a gasket; a long rope about about as thick as your thumb. I took the gasket from my chest; dropped it from my window; slid down and ran. I met Judy in the lane, crying her eyes out. It was long past nine. We sat in the pavilion, my arm round her.

"Know how to kiss a sailor, Jude?" I asked.

You bet she knew! I felt her little body tremble. I heard her little quick breaths. Good for her I wasn't Paddy! Ede had been wrong about me.

It was after one in the morning when I walked with her toward her house, over the soft green grass mattress.

"You'll write to me to 'Frisco, won't you, Jude?" I asked. She threw her arms round my neck and began to cry. I felt her little breasts pressed close to my strong chest; felt her little body quiver. "Cheer up,

Jude! Show me how you kiss a sailor," I said. She said, "I won't! It isn't *a* sailor. It's only you. It'll never be anyone but you!" I took out my handkerchief, dried her pretty eyes and kissed her goodbye at her gate.

I got back to the house, climbed up the rope to my room, and found Auntie Polly sitting in it waiting for me. She said, "I wish I'd never let you go to sea."

I said, "You didn't let me. I'd have gone whether or no. Cheer up, Auntie. What's all the fuss about? Maybe I'll be lost overboard this voyage, and then you won't have to worry."

She didn't say anything; just look stumped. A hen with a duckling. She went sadly to her room and I followed. She reached for her prayer book and read awhile. Then we said the Lord's Prayer together. She kissed me sadly, and I kissed her.

Next evening I was in Liverpool Street Station, London, with a two-hour wait for the train for Harwich, and nothing to do. Soon I saw a girl with yellow hair and blue eyes that had a sad look. She came to me and shyly asked "Can you tell me where I'll find Geoffrey Clarke, please?"

I said, "Who's Geoffrey Clarke? I never heard of him."

She said, "I thought perhaps you were from the same ship. He's an apprentice in the *Largiemore*."

I said, "The *Largiemore's* an old tub. My ship can sail rings round her; mine's the smartest clipper out of Liverpool. A girl like you oughtn't to be bothering about a chap from a tub like the *Largiemore*."

We got along in great style. When my train pulled out I had in my pocket the photograph she'd brought to give Geoffrey Clarke. He watched me kiss his girl goodbye. I'd taken her to supper while he'd been hunting round for her. At the first stop he came to my compartment and said, "Damn you *Silberhorn* chaps." We talked and laughed all the way to Harwich.

On the boat going over from Harwich were a couple of girls on their way to Brussels. Clarke and I walked the deck with them *all* night. Mine was a dandy little clipper. Petite. I always liked them that way. She had grey eyes and butter-coloured hair. When we parted

141

next morning at Antwerp I had her photo in my pocket, with Judy's and Clarke's girl's.

The Old Woman was at the cabin door when I went aboard. She called to me.

"I'm sorry you've been so ill, Adams."

"Thank you, Mrs. Gibson," I said, "It was only me teeth."

When I strolled into the half-deck where my comrades were at breakfast they asked me where in hell I'd been. They'd been pulling their arms out for a week, getting the old ship's sails aloft ready for sea. They had all her sail aloft but the big crossjack. I told them of the trick I'd worked on the owner and they damned me. All but Paddy. He grinned.

We hoisted the crossjack after breakfast; a sail a hundred feet wide by some forty-five or fifty deep; a great sail with heavy iron rings at each corner and heavy steel wire stitched all along its edges. Alongside our ship lay a ship called the *Cumbrian*. Her Old Man called across from his poop to our Old Man, "I wish I had your apprentices, Gibson." Our Old Man replied, "You ain't the only one." Oh, yes, we were a proud lot of young sailors!

At quitting time Paddy said, "The Antwerp motts are swell, Bill. You don't have to have any money."

After supper we all went ashore together. Our way led through sailor-town, of course. We stopped at the *Sausage Pan* estaminet to have a glass of bock. There was a girl called Irish Mary, and another called Cork Fender. There was a pretty little whore called Pauline, and a big blond deep-bosomed one called Cookie. Cookie looked at me hard. But when Chink and Polly left the place, I went with them. Paddy tried to get me to stay.

"It's nix batal, Bill," he said.

But I was too fresh from Judy's lips. Chink, Polly and I wandered round town till late. It was midnight when we passed the *Sausage Pan* on our way to the ship. The estaminets closed at midnight. Paddy came out and went off with Irish Mary. All the girls came out, each with a man but Cookie. Cookie ran to me, took my arm, and said, "I been vaiting for you, nice Eengleesh apprenteece."

"I've got no money," I said.

142

45. *CUMBRIAN.*

Cookie said, "Nix batal." Nothing to pay. But I shook her hand from my arm and went on with Chink and Polly. Chink said, "By God, Bill, you've got a lot of strength of mind." It wasn't strength of mind. It was just me.

We pulled out next evening and dropped anchor in the river; ready to go to sea at dawn. The crew came aboard as we passed out to the river. I remember a few of them. There was a long-limbed man with a narrow chest and a white face. As he came over the rail the mate said, "By God, we've got a corpse aboard." After him came a short squat man with the most enormous shoulders I had ever seen. He was bow-legged. His dark eyes had a queer set hard stare. Kylon, his name was. A Finn. The tall man was a Swede, Shelberg by name. They went straight into the forecastle. The rest of the men stood on

143

the fore deck calling goodbye to a crowd of whores on the pier-head; laughing and joking.

We'd one new apprentice, to take the place of Douglas who was to be third mate. His father was a wine merchant of Brussels. We were allowed no liquor in the half-deck, of course. But the kid brought a whole case of champagne aboard. That night all the apprentices but I got tight. I was always careful of booze because when I do a thing I'm thorough. I didn't want to wreck my career by starting to drink. We dubbed the Belgian kid Alphonse. It wasn't his real name. But he looked as though it was. At dawn we hove the anchor up, Chink singing the good old 'Maid of Amsterdam'.

> *In Amsterdam there dwelt a maid,*
> *Mark well what I do say,*
> *In Amsterdam there dwelt a maid*
> *And she was mistress of her trade,*
> > *And we'll go no more a ro–oving with you—fair—maid,*
> > *A roving, a roving,*
> > *Oh roving's been my ru–i–in,*
> > *And we'll go no more a ro–oving with you—fair—maid.*

And I wish I could tell you how the lilt and swing and lift of that old chorus goes. But I can't.

That night a hand fell on my arm. A friendly voice asked, "How's Judy?" It was the new second mate. A slight chap, with hard bright, brown eyes. He'd seen the last letters go ashore, and amongst them mine to Judy. The minute he spoke I knew I'd found a chum. Willie Clegg, his name was.

It was evening when we slipped under full sail in a light breeze through the Downs, through Dover Straits. To starboard shone the high white chalk cliffs at which Napoleon had gazed so hungrily. To port was the low beach whence he had gazed. Roman galleys had furrowed the still water on which we sailed so softly. Hengist the bloody, and Horsa, had urged their oarsmen hereabout. The sun had flashed on Norman shield and sword and spear. The fleeing Spaniard had lumbered by here, hastening to his doom in Calais roads, and now a tall Cape Horner was on her seaward way, while all was peace. There was no sound. England lay still beneath her canopy of evening cloud,

46.   A homing clipper—the German ANENOME, ex MACCULLUM MORE.

and soon the dark came down, the bells broke out. "All's well, sir!" cried the sailor on lookout.

The mate replied, "All right!"

When the morning came we saw the white-washed cottages again, the bright green April fields. Steamers sped by. A fleet of warships passed. The sea was dotted thick with brown-sailed fishing boats. A homeward clipper passed, and cheered the outward bound. We cheered her back. The long lean sailor walked the deck that evening, the Finn beside him. They scarce ever spoke. There seemed a silent camaraderie between them. While we gazed shoreward to the land that would be gone when morning came, they paid no heed. This was no shore of home for them. They did not turn as did all others when the second mate, as dusk began to hide the shore of home away, broke into song:

145

What would I not give to wander
Where my old companions dwell?
Absence makes the heart grow fonder,
Isle of beauty, fare thee well.

A fine voice Willie Clegg had, with a haunt to the tone of it. And as his song died, we lads turned and went into our half-deck; upon us that sadness that comes over the outward-bound sailor.

I brought out my photographs. Judy, and Geoffrey Clarke's girl, and the girl from the Harwich boat. I laid them on the little table. My comrades gathered round.

"God, you've got your nerve, Bill! Three at a time, and all of them clippers! What are their names?"

I said, "I call 'em Fore, Main, and Mizzen." Then, holding up the picture of the girl on the Harwich boat, I asked, "What'll you give me for Mizzen?"

I got three whacks of marmalade for Mizzen. And then I held up Geoffrey Clarke's girl.

I got two whacks of marmalade, and one of Harriet Lane, and a half plug of Black Admiral tobacco for Clarke's girl. Then Chink reached for Judy's photo. But I said, "Hold on! You leave Main alone." And holding her photo high I asked, "What do I get for Main?" And in stepped Willie Clegg and asked, "Am I allowed to bid?"

"Yes, sir," said I. "The highest bidder gets Main. She's all to the merry, what?"

And Willie Clegg gave me a half-pound of Navy Cut tobacco, three new sail needles, and an old palm for Jude's picture. The other apprentices said it wasn't fair for the second mate to butt in. I said, "All's fair in love."

Then, when Clegg was gone, Alphonse opened his sea chest and brought out a large photograph of a girl with very scanty clothing on her pretty limbs. We stared.

"Well, I'll be damned," said Chink. "The little lubber! And only a first voyager too! How old are you, Alphonse?"

I had to translate for Chink. Alphonse was just seventeen, and the girl was his mistress! Well, that was a new one on us; for English

146

47. *A high 4-master—the MARLBOROUGH HILL.*

boys of seventeen don't keep mistresses. Chink said, "You damned little Turk!" It somehow made Alphonse seem senior to us all save Paddy. Paddy laughed and said, "Good kid! You're all right, Frog!", but I got an idea. I said, "See here, Alphonse, you give me that picture and I'll teach you English." He grinned delightedly and gave me the picture. I didn't want it for myself. I took it to the room that the sailmaker occupied alone. He was a foul old devil. I said, "See here, Sails! How's this for a clipper, eh?" He grabbed for it. I said "Hold on. You keep your shirt tucked in in windy weather! Make me a hammock and the picture's yours."

Sails said, "By God, I will."

I could have made a hammock for myself, of course, but had been too lazy to bother about it. He brought me a dandy hammock in two days, brass eyelet holes for all the lanyards, and varnished teak-wood stretchers. And off he went with the photograph of the

147

Frog's mistress. He kept his porthole open always. But that night it was shut, the curtain drawn. I think he was performing some strange rites maybe. Paddy was sorry to see the picture leave the half-deck. But I said, "Paddy, when we're in the trades we'll sling the hammock beneath the forecastle head and have a dandy place to sleep. It's yours as much as mine."

Paddy and I were like that tall sailor and the Finn. We never seemed to need to talk. There was a silent friendship between us. It was more than friendship. It was love. I don't know why it was so, but so it was. When we came down to the warm trade wind weather we shared the hammock; just as we shared everything else. When he was on duty, I was off; and vice versa. The hammock was never cold. There's no nicer place to sleep than under a ship's forecastle head, in a hammock. You hear the breaking music of the bow wash all about you. You are right up in the bow of the ship, and you feel her pitch and scend. No one else slept there. We had that lovely place all to ourselves.

The other apprentices disliked Clegg from the first. I don't know just why. Perhaps it was that he took too keen an interest in the ship, and was so keen to see her fly; and that they looked on him as an outsider, deeming her his. A sort of jealousy. I liked him from the minute he first spoke to me, and he liked me. I'd spend all the four hours of my night watch on the poop with him. He was a dandy sailor, twenty-seven years old.

He said, "I'm going, by God, to make a sailor of you, Bill."

And I replied, "Go ahead! That's what I came to sea for."

Sometimes I regretted having spoken so, for he'd no mercy on me. My vertigo was little trouble now, ordinarily, but he brought it back. He'd send me aloft on tricky jobs with the ship dancing wildly in a lumpy sea. He sent me up to blacklead all the brace-blocks. To do that you must sit astride the yard arm, far out above the sea. You have a little pot of black lead tied to your belt. You have a hammer, a cold chisel, and a punch. And when a man on deck lets go the brace that holds the yard steady, you have to haul it up to you till you can reach the block. Then you must knock the pin out of the block, give it a good coat of black lead, and put it back. It takes all your strength to haul the block up. It takes all your agility to hang on, gripping the

48. BALCLUTHA.

yard arm with your thighs while the ship rolls and pitches. And if you
drop a tool to the sea, God help you! With the brace loose, the yard
swings jerkily to and fro. You're like a cowboy riding a wild colt.
There were five braces to each side of each mast and I did all the black
leading. God knows how I hung on. I don't. But Clegg never knew
at all what hell he put me through. I never let him know. In later days
I found out things about him. He'd been second mate of the *Balclutha*
his last voyage, and one wild squally night a man had fallen overboard
from her. Clegg jumped after him, found and upheld him till the lifeboat came. It was a crazy thing for him to do. Had he not done it
the skipper would not have put a boat out, so wild the night was. But
with two men gone, he took a chance. And Clegg too had been second
mate of a tramp steamer, on a voyage across the Western Ocean in
the winter time. She'd sighted a schooner in distress. A German liner
had sighted the schooner a few hours previously and had left her to
her fate. Clegg's skipper would have left her too, had it not been for

him. Clegg had asked what any officer has a right to ask—for volunteers, and a chance to save the doomed vessel's crew. A skipper can't well say "No". Two boats were smashed, but Clegg got away with the third, made his way through a mad sea to the sinking schooner, and brought her people safe aboard the tramp. Then, like the merry fool he was, he made a second trip—to save the schooner's cat and her skipper's sextant. He had a big gold medal on which were the words, 'From William McKinley, President of the United States, to William Clegg, for gallantry at sea'. The schooner was American. I'll tell you later how I came to know of that. It was a man from the *Balclutha* who told me of the other thing in later days, after I'd lost all track of Willie Clegg.

Paddy hated Clegg. I don't know why. Maybe jealousy. Nor could Clegg ever see why I loved Paddy. "He's not a sailor, Bill," he'd tell me. It was true enough, that, in a way, Paddy was not a sailor. He lacked all eagerness. There seemed no pride in him, hardly. He had to make a living, so he came to sea. The motts were all he thought of. Clegg was as wild about the girls as Paddy was, but in a different way. He had a girl in Liverpool. "You ought to see her eyes," he'd say to me. "They're like two big round moons when I am kissing her!" He was going to marry her as soon as he had his Master's ticket. Meanwhile he'd quit playing about with the girls in sailor-town. He'd known a lot of them. He said, "There was a coolie girl in Calcutta, Bill—my God, those coolie girls are beautiful!", and then he'd maybe start to sing 'Absence makes the heart grow fonder'. After that he'd say, looking into my face, and smiling happily:

"Say, won't it be a day when I get my Master's ticket, eh, Bill? I'll come from the exam. room with it in my hand, and Mabel will be waiting for me outside. And then I'll say, 'Ahoy, Mabel!—Salue, Mabel!—I've a ring for your finger'."

Next, he'd clap a hand on my shoulder, and say, "There's lots of girls, Bill, shipmate. But there's only one *right girl!* And when you find her—*put the ring on her finger and stay right with her!*"

Clegg was a daredevil from sole to crown. He liked to drive the ship. There was a night when a cold moon was sinking in the west, behind a bank of angry cloud; and there was a low moaning all across

150

the sea. The old girl had topgallants set; the royals furled. At a quarter to midnight he said to me, "Let's put the royals on her, Bill!" I said, "Suits me, sir!" And as we hoisted the last royal to its masthead down came the wind from where the moon had sunk, and over went the ship. She flew. She staggered, each block and sheet complaining to the strain; and her lee rail so deep that half her deck was under water. The Old Man's whistle blew. Clegg laughed and stepped to the speaking-tube that led from the Old Man's pillow. "My God, what are you trying to do with the ship?" bawled the Old Man. Then the mate's watch came on deck as midnight struck, and the mate shouted, "Clew the royals up!" And men and boys of the mate's watch, all sleepy-eyed, cursed Clegg because they had to go up to the royals the minute they were from their cosy bunks. That was the sort of thing that made him disliked by my apprentice comrades. "You'd think he owned the ship, by God!" they sneered.

We were down in the hot tropics when that tall, lean man laid up. He had become far leaner. His face was chalky white, with on each cheek a spot of livid red. He coughed and coughed. Soon after he laid up, because his coughing so disturbed the other sailors, a place was fitted for him in a locker room under the forecastle head. Sometimes the Old Man would go to have a look at him.

"You must get well, my man. You're needed on deck."

And that tall lean man would look up at the skipper and would say, "Aye, aye, sir. Soon I be all right now, sir."

The steward took him fancy food from the cabin. A little dish maybe of canned liver and bacon, or a plate of beans. He had marmalade all the time, and often the dish called 'strike-me-blind'. Boiled rice, with black-strap molasses on it. Fine cabin fare. He often never touched a bite of it. Some sailor, seeing him asleep, would wolf it down. The Finn was always with him when off duty. He'd sit beside, and stroke his skinny hand.

That voyage the food was even worse than usual. Some of us lads had brought a small store of food from home. I'd talked Auntie Polly into letting me have a case of canned milk and some jars of pickles. Chink, who was in my watch, had some shore food too. So we lived well enough at first. Later we said, "Let's keep the rest till

151

49. *Burial at sea (aboard the LOCH TAY).*

we are off the Horn. We'll need it worse down there." So we stored what was left in a locker at the end of the half-deck, and starved on rotten pork and maggoty hard-tack, until one night I said to Chink, "Chink, the after hatch is open. The steward's taking the cabin food to the galley that way, from the store room. We could raid the store room some dark night." Chink said, "No good. If we get caught we'd be in a hell of a mess." So we let the plan go. But, as days passed, we kept thinking it over.

At last came a night when we tossed to see which two of us should raid the store room. I went, with the farmer's son; each taking a gunny-sack. While Chink and Pat O'Brien kept watch lest an order come, we stole into the dark hold and on into the pitch dark store room; striking matches for light. We filled our sacks with canned liver and bacon and beef essence and pickles and canned milk and some big cans of ship's marmalade. We made a bully haul and, back in the half-deck, we filled our bellies tight. Next night Chink and O'Brien went. That was Saturday night.

On Sunday morning we'd washed the decks down, and were sitting in the half-deck waiting the time to call the second mate's apprentices, when a shadow darkened the door.

"Which of you young blackguards has been stealing my stores?" asked the Old Man.

Well, a sailor learns to do his thinking quick. I pointed to our private stores and said, "Sir, we've got stores of our own. We don't have to steal. We're no thieves, sir."

"I'll treat you all alike till I find out who it is," growled the Old Man, and was gone. We looked at one another gloomily. And then there was a stir in the other side of the half-deck, and in came Polly, Paddy, Tattersall and Alphonse.

"Which of you damned young thieves has been swiping the Old Man's stores?" I asked.

Shiver my topsails, if they hadn't overheard my suggestion to Chink and acted on it, keeping their raid secret from us just as we'd kept ours secret from them. We didn't tell them we'd been raiding at first. We heard their story. During that Saturday night, while two of them had been in the store room, the mate had blown his whistle and, hurrying to the deck, Tattersall had dropped a can of tripe in the hold. The steward had found it. So Chink, whose father was a lawyer, said, "By God, you're guilty. We'd have been found out, of course, but technically it's you four who're guilty." So they decided they'd better load up the stolen stores and take them to the cabin. The Old Man met them at the door. He growled, "You've stolen it. You can keep it and take the consequences." So back they came and we all feasted, and made the best of it. But soon the steward came. The Old Man had discovered what a lot was missing and had climbed down from his high horse. The stores were to be taken back. Oh, well, that made me sore. I took two cans of marmalade and hid them in the sail room, and so hateful it was to think of taking them back, I threw over the side a

153

dozen cans of beef essence. Later, when I went for the marmalade, some low thief in the crew had found and had stolen it.

After the stolen stores were taken back, nothing at all happened. We were treated as usual. But there was a cold dread on us. Would the Old Man give the thieves bad references at the end of their apprenticeships? If he did, their careers were ruined. One thing we, of the second mate's watch, agreed upon, and we agreed without being asked by our comrades of the mate's watch, who had taken the blame. If the Old Man gave them bad references we'd own up and all be done for together.

We did the usual things. Holy-stoned the decks, prepared the rigging for the Horn, cursed the food, damned the ship and the Old Man, while ever the tall lean man grew leaner. A day came when the Finn was told to stay with him all the time. Day by day as we stood south the weather grew colder. Paddy and I unslung our hammock and stored it away till we should be in the tropics again.

Alphonse was picking up English fairly well. Sometimes he grew angry, saying, "I veesh zee Eengleesh learn. All you say ees Goddam an' Jese-krise. 'Ow een zee 'ell you teenk I learn spik zee Eengleesh?"

"Alphonse, that's all the English you'll need to know when we come to the pitch of the Horn," we told him.

One morning the Finn came running from the sick man's room. He stared about him, stared at the ship, at us, at the sea, at the unheeding sky; and rushed back. We went to see what was amiss. The sick man's pillow was crimson with blood.

That night I was at the wheel. Clegg came to me and said, "The poor devil's gone, Bill." The sailmaker sat long stitching; sewing by lantern light the dead man in canvas, and that night a great gale blew up. All hands were called on deck. We took off all sail but the lower topsails. It was bitter cold. We were come past the corner of Staten Island. Ninety-eight miles away in the south-west was Cape Horn. The air was snow-laden. There was a slither of ice on the reeling rigging. Sky and sea were inky when morning came.

At eight bells in the morning four sailors came from under the forecastle head, bearing a stretcher. Clinging to the life lines, they came slowly to the quarter-deck; two others holding the ensign over the

154

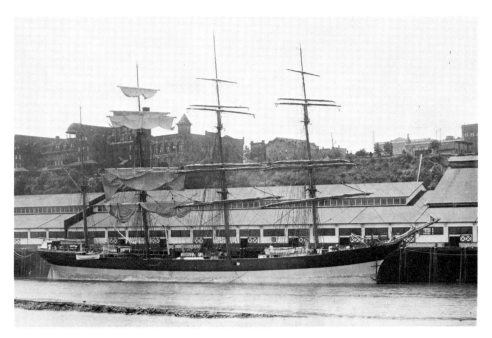

50. *HOWTH—a well-known 4-m. barque.*

dead man. Behind, came the rest of the crew; men and apprentices.

The Old Man came from the cabin door to the quarter-deck, a prayer book in his hand. Of all, he alone was bare-headed. The stretcher-bearers laid the dead man's feet upon the quarter railing.

The Old Man lifted the prayer book and, at that moment, a great sea thundered in over the quarter rail and foamed about the thighs of the crew. A stretcher-bearer lost his footing. The corpse fell from the stretcher. Another sea roared aboard. The corpse vanished to re-appear on the deck's other side. Men dashed toward it. It was swept from side to side of the ship as she rolled. It rolled over and over. The Old Man, who had stepped a little way up the poop ladder, stood watching, the prayer book in his hand. A sailor grasped the corpse, lost his feet and fell on it. Living and dead were swept across the deck, now one, now the other, uppermost. At last they brought the corpse back to the quarter railing. They set it on the stretcher. A sailor who

155

had saved the ensign laid it and held it down on the corpse.

The Old Man came down the ladder. The ship took a terrific roll. The mate shouted, "Watch yourselves!" The Old Man cried in a loud voice, "Our Father which—" A great sea swung its white crest toward the quarter railing. The Old Man made a hopeless gesture, with an uplifted hand. The man with the ensign drew it quickly from above the corpse. The stretcher-bearers hastily tipped the stretcher. The corpse fell to the sea. The wind lulled at that instant. The great sea that had threatened to break aboard swung harmlessly under the ship. The Old Man went up the ladder and disappeared into the chart-room. The crew dispersed, making their way forward on a comparatively dry deck. All but the giant Finn. The Finn climbed to the quarter railing, kneeled on it, stared down at the dark sea. Suddenly he raised his hands, and with clenched fists began to curse the sea. He shook his huge fists at the sea. He waved his great arms, yelled, screeched, screamed curses. The ship took a quick roll, a sea swept aboard, hiding the Finn utterly in its broken raging foam. It passed over him. He reappeared. He stepped down from the rail, set his hands to his face, and broke into sobs. With water washing to his thighs, he made his slow way forward, his hand on the lifeline, the tears streaming from his eyes, mingling with the salt water that dripped from the brim of his sou'wester.

CHAPTER IX

GOLDEN GOWN AND BARRACOUT

Maybe an hour or so after we'd dropped that lean man to the sea, there came a little lull in the wind's roar. The clouds above our mast-heads opened. The Old Man made haste into the chart room. Having looked at the barometer, he strode out to the deck and bawled stentorian-voiced, "Loose upper topsails!" We loosed them, in a sea less violent. The water swirled about our thighs, yet lacked the savagery it had had before. All hands were called, both watches, and carpenter, sailmaker, steward and cook. And all hands roared the chorus of the chantey-man:

> *As I went a'walking down Paradise street,*
>   *To me waye, aye, blow the man down!*
> *A trim little packet I chanced for to meet,*
>   *Oh, give us some time to blow the man down!*

And then Clegg cried, "Oh, grab and walk her up, sons! *Walk away!*"

Hauling no longer to that chantey's tune, all hands tramped merrily along the rolling deck, singing gaily:

> *John Brown's wife drinks whiskey in her tea,*
> *John Brown's wife drinks whiskey in her tea,*
> *John Brown's wife drinks whiskey in her tea,*
> *As we go rolling home!*
>   *And it's glory, glory, hallelujah!*
>   *Glory, glory, hallelujah!*
>   *Glory, glory, hallelujah!*
>   *As we go rolling home!*

157

A sudden little burst of sun broke through the scurrying clouds. A sailor yelled, "Fair wind! Fair wind for old Cape Stiff!" And every sailor took the cry up, yelling it.

"Give her t'gallants! Crowd the sail on her!" the Old Man shouted. And how we ran! We had full sail on her in just a little while, and off she went. You could feel the actual joy in her, could sense the gladness in her leaping bow, and if you think a mass of planking, metal, rope, and wire, and cordage cannot feel—well, you ask any sailor! Aye, sure a ship can feel! Away she flew, and the wild tumbled snowy clouds came driving after us from out the crystal north. Great seas rolled emerald in the wintry sun's pale light, their mile-long crests and mad cataracts of lathered surging foam, their swirling valleys flecked with twisty greens, sapphire, and blue. The air was full of velvety Cape pigeons, mollymawks, Cape hens, sooty and snowy albatross. We saw a sea-lion lift his whiskered head, and heard his bark. A flock of penguins swam beside her, and presently three whales came sporting by, and stayed their speed a while to pace with her. We cheered, and waved our hats, and our Old Man stood grinning. *A fair wind round the Horn!*

In all this the Finn came out from that lone locker room, where yet a pillow lay with blood upon it. He looked about; gazed at the sea, the sky, the reeling masts, the circling birds, the whales. He said no word.

"I wonder what it was that turned poor Kylon's mind," Chink said to me; for we had ever known that he was mad a bit. Hearing Chink speak, a sailor said, "A woman, maybe. They'll do it to a man. God knows they will."

When the mate went forward to gather up the dead man's scant belongings he found a bundle of old letters in his sea chest. They were in a foreign lingo. The mate took them to the Old Man, up in the chart house. The Old Man said, "There's other Swedes amongst the crew. Send a Swede here." So then a fellow named Olafsen went to the chart room. Later we heard about it. Clegg told me. Kylon had been engaged to marry Shelberg's sister, and gone away upon a long deep-water voyage. When he came back he found she'd wedded with another man, and died in childbed. 'Twas that that sent the Finn out of his mind.

51.   *HOUGOMONT.*

We romped past old Cape Stiff that afternoon. And as we drew almost abeam of it, the land perhaps five miles away or so, the order came to furl the royals. I went up to the main. The wind whooped after her. The whales were long since gone, but myriad birds were circling all about. I gathered up the sail, and sat awhile to watch the scenery. I thought about Tom Swift and wondered where he was. I thought of Glynn. My chums were gone, but I had other chums. I could see from that high perch the world's round curve. You always can, when high aloft, see the world's curve. You know the world is round. It's just a sort of star, wheeling midst other stars. When I came down, I went to coil the ropes up on the poop. The Old Man stood nearby, and his Old Woman with him. The Horn was snow-capped, and behind it rose peak upon dizzy peak, minarets, domes, in range on snowy range; all shining now in sun and now all shadow-darkened. The Tierra del Fuegan mountains seemed as though they were not of this world. The sea we sailed alone was as a mythic sea, and all our crew stood gazing, silent, awed. I heard the Old Man speak in a low voice his woman's name. "Sophie!" he murmured, then lifted up a hand and pointed to the shore. They stood there, grey of head, his arm about her. "Sophie—my God!—the New Jerusalem!" he said. I'd never heard a soft word from his lips till then.

By way of celebrating a fair wind round the Horn, the Old Man ordered us a special treat for supper. We filled our bellies tight on 'strike-me-blind'. It's good when you are hungry.

The morning after we were past old Stiff, we set the royals again. Hoisting the fore royal, I pulled forehand; pulling straight down upon the halliard fall. The fall passed through a block upon the deck, the others pulling lengthwise on it. Just when the sail was almost up the fall gave way. The heavy wooden block dropped on my head, from many feet above. I fell. I've often heard men say they wonder what one thinks of when he's dying. I mind, as I lost consciousness, I thought, "What'll Dolly say when she hears?" They lifted and bore me to the saloon. When I came to, I was in a chair and the Old Woman was washing my split head. It was a nasty wound. My blood flowed freely. When she was done and I was swathed in bandages she asked, "Do you think you could eat a little bacon and some doughnuts,

160

Adams?" I said modestly I thought I could. The cabin breakfast was not cleared away. She sat me there. Oh, glory! Bacon and doughnuts! And when I rose to go she said, "Come back this evening and I'll dress your head again." You may be sure I went directly after cabin supper time. It worked. I ate again. My head ached horribly. What's a headache to a sea apprentice when there's food in sight? Yet I felt deathly sick; and staggered as I walked, a little bit. But there's scant mercy in a ship at sea. If I had been a lad ashore I should have been in bed; maybe in hospital. I kept the deck and, early in the night, Clegg shouted, "Hop up and loose the crossjack, two of you!" I was the nearest to the rigging. So up I went. And God knows how I did! I couldn't see a thing. Clegg shouted, "Can't you move up there? Wake up! Are you asleep?" I loosed my half the sail, and crawled down somehow. No one said a thing, nor asked me if my head hurt. You take what comes at sea. It's part of being a sailor.

Each day for a full week I went to have my head dressed. Each day I feasted twice on cabin leavings, and then, fearing my wound was healing, I gave it a good scratch to open it up again.

It was that day that the Old Woman said, while dressing it, "Adams, you don't know how glad the Captain and I were that you were not amongst the boys who stole our stores."

And I the instigator of the raid!

I said, "Yes, Mrs. Gibson. Thank you."

When I came into the half-deck, I said, "You damned young thieves! I'd be ashamed, by God, if I were you." They cursed me, when I had told them what she'd said to me. Living on mouldy hardtack, old stale salt pork—and I on cabin leavings! But no good thing can last forever, and when I scratched my head a second time it didn't work. We never had a bit of trouble from our theft. There was no punishment of any sort at all.

While we climbed the long hill to the equator, Kylon grew ever more strange. He'd sit alone at night, and talk.

"Who are you talking to?" Clegg asked one night.

"I speaks mitt mein goot vren', sir."

"He doesn't answer you?" asked Clegg.

And Kylon said, "Yow bat. He talk me mitt, sir."

Sometimes he'd lie upon the sea-wet deck, and writhe, and call aloud a woman's name. Often he'd weep. He took to eating ever less, and less. His huge frame wasted. Yet still he was the strongest of the crew. If in the dog-watch we held trials of strength and he would take part, no man could handle him. I was a child in his great grip. Strain as I might, I was no more than just a ten-year lad. There came a day when he refused to work. Well, no. He didn't refuse exactly. But when Clegg gave him a job to do, he looked Clegg in the face and muttered, "Dot should haff been mein baby." There was a set fixed stare upon his face. His eyes were glittery. Some of the men grew scared, and went to ask the Old Man that he be ironed. Clegg and the mate walked forward. The mate said, "Hold out your wrists, Kylon. We'll not harm you." And, docile as a lamb, he held them out. They led him off and locked him in a room beneath the poop's break. His wrists in irons, he sat and never stirred all day. That night, each time a mate called up a light to look at him, he yet was sitting so. Next day the Old Man said, "Take off those irons. My God, the fellow's harmless." They took them off, and he walked slowly forward and went into that room where Shelberg died. He never worked again. He wandered here and there, and never spoke to anyone aboard. Only to Shelberg when the dark was come. And all the time, because he scarcely ate, he grew yet thinner. His cheek-bones stood out sharp, his shoulder blades. His wrists were naught but bone. He was the shell of what was once a man. His eyes were lighthouses of harmless madness. All day, all night, he did just as he pleased; and no one bothered him. The mates were kindly. The Old Man said, "You'll see that no one troubles that poor mad fellow." There was no need for him to say it.

My vertigo was little but a memory now. *Oh, sailor, sailor.* I owned the world. Sometimes I'd think of Vernie, and wonder about girls. Paddy never wondered. Paddy knew. Chink, Polly, Tattersall, would ask him of them. Laughing, he'd say, "Why, sure! They're all the same. Just girls, and we're just men. Have a good time, *I* say." Alphonse would say, "Mine meestress she voss verree sweet. I gets anuzzer ven ve gets back home." I'd taught him lots of English. I'd maybe think of Judy, and wonder what she'd be like now had she been Paddy's girl. And on the poop at night Will Clegg would say to me, "By God, Bill, you ought to see her eyes when I am kissing her! They're just like two big moons!"

And often Clegg would say, "Ah, shipmate—wait till the day I say, 'Ahoy, Mabel!—Salue Mabel!—I've a ring for your finger!'"

One day I came to well-nigh hating Clegg. He'd often tried me sorely by picking for me all the hardest jobs aloft. Of course he never knew a thing about my vertigo. I'd never spoken of it, and now he gave me a small pot of gilt paint, and a paint brush. "Hop up and gild the trucks!" he ordered me: as though to gild a truck were just as simple as to go picking roses.

There was no wind. The ship was pitching like a hurdling horse to a long, high, steep-sided swell. One minute her stem would lift almost clear of the water, her bow go soaring up. Next instant down her bow would go until the water gurgled to her forecastle head. You scarce could walk along the deck for her wild pitching. And when a man's aloft it's pitching that he feels far worse than rolling.

The highest part of a ship's mast is called the pole. The pole goes up from where the rigging ends, up to the topmost summit. Some ships had but a foot or two of pole, and some but a few inches. A short pole gives a ship a sort of stumpy look. A tall one finishes her with perfect symmetry. Our poles were ten feet long. And since there is no rigging on the pole you have to go up monkey-fashion. The pole ends at the truck, a rounded wooden ball. Our trucks were kept gilded. These gilded trucks were her last fancy touch.

So up I started and, knowing that I had a dizzy job to do, began to tremble. The vertigo was back. I thought of Furst and Glynn. Was my time come at last? I took the foremast first, and far below me I saw Willie Clegg; and came nigh hating him. I had a touch of that same feeling that my comrades had for him. I thought him too damned smart.

I passed the place whence long ago Furst fell from. And I went on. The pole looked like a mile. I clenched my teeth, and started up it monkey-fashion. Once when she took a wild pitch I thought my time was come, and almost yelled. A hundred and ninety feet below, the deck was waiting me. "Get down afore ye fall an' make a bloody mess!" I seemed to hear. Well, somehow I gilded that fore truck. I

163

don't know how. And down I went. And when I reached the solid deck there wasn't any peace; because I knew that I'd gild three more ere I was done. So up I went again, the same thing over on the main-mast. And down I came again. I was half done. As I started up the mizzen mast I saw the Old Man on the poop near by. And he saw me. He didn't see my fear, because I didn't let him. To brace myself I sang.

Tom's gone, what shall I do?
Hilo!—Hilo!
Where Tom's gone I must go too,
Tom's gone to Hilo!

And, hearing me, the Old Man called, "You—Quit that singing and get on with your work!" So then I ran, despite my blurry eyes, my horrid fear. I went up like a frightened monkey, determined that he should not guess my fear. I saw the hard old devil eyeing me. I saw him turn and speak to his Old Woman. "That lad can climb, eh, Sophie?" I bet that's what he said. When I came down and went up to the poop, to start to climb the jigger mast, he saw my trembling. "What's the matter, boy?"

I said, "I'm trying to see how fast, sir, I can gild the trucks. I'm out of breath a bit."

He said, "You see you gild 'em properly, and don't miss any place!"

Though shorter than the other masts, the jigger is the worst. It has a longer pole. I thought of Johansen, and of how he'd dropped his tar pot from the jigger. Suppose I dropped my gilt? Some other would be sent to do the job instead of me! But—*sailor, sailor, sailor!* You have a thing called pride, and pride is stronger than your fear of death. So up I went, and down I came at last. The Old Man was gone. I leaned against the mast, all shaky-limbed. Then, seeing Clegg coming and taking the gilt pot from my wrist, I bowed my head; hiding my face from him. He said, "By gad, Bill, but you're fast! You're a damned handy sailor, aren't you, eh?"

So then I had to look at him, and laugh. I said, "If I'm a sailor it's your doing maybe, sir."

He said, "Oh, no! You've got the breed in you, old man."

164

52. *KENILWORTH.*

That night Clegg told me that he got a wigging from the skipper for sending anyone aloft to gild the trucks when she was pitching so. And I said, "To hell with the skipper! I got 'em gilded, didn't I? What's all the growl about?" And that was not all brag. I loved Clegg then more than ever yet I'd loved him, somehow. Why?—Just think it out. It's easy. *Oh, sailor, sailor, sailor.*

One night soon after that, while I was talking with him on the poop, Clegg said, "By God, Bill, I feel ill." He said he had a sort of weak all-over feeling. Next day he laid up and Chink took his watch. We were a week or two from 'Frisco, and everyone was busy getting the old girl into fancy dress for port once more. I'd see him now and

53. KENILWORTH making sail.

then at night for just a bit. His face was pale. His strength was gone. He'd lost all eagerness.

We sailed in through the Golden Gate one sunny afternoon and dropped the hook. The port was full of ships. A row of ships at anchor. Along the waterfront a forest of tall masts and spreading spars. *Euphrosyne* was there, and *Illawarra, Melanope, Corunna, Eurydice.* Oh, I could name the names of sixty ships. But they'd mean naught to you.

A little distance from us lay the great barque *Kenilworth*, of Maine. We'd heard of her. All sailors knew her well. A brutal Yankee hell-wagon, where men were treated worse than any dogs ashore. Her mates wore knuckle-dusters, carried belaying pins. Her skipper was a devil out of hell. God help the sailor who didn't do his work! No mercy for him. And did he do it, mercy scant enough. We saw that she was laden, ready to go out.

166

54. EUPHROSYNE.

The minute we'd our anchor down a boarding master came aboard. He went toward the forecastle where our crew were gone. And on the way he met with the big Finn. "Hello, my hearty! And did you have a good time off the Horn? God, you're a husky sailor! Here, have a drink on me."

And Kylon sent the rot-gut bottle to his lips and took a long, long swallow.

"Go on! Drink hearty, sailor! That's the real stuff! It warms a sailor's blood when he's come round the Horn."

So Kylon tipped the bottle up again. And then the boarding master had him by the arm.

"Come on, my lad! I've got a dandy berth for you, my bully boy!"

Thus Brown, the boarding master, took off that wasted, rot-gut-fuddled Finn to the hard *Kenilworth*. He sold him to her skipper, who'd been waiting for one man to fill his crew. Then she hove her

167

55. 'Frisco grain fleet waiting to load in 1902. Foreground RELIANCE (with awnings), DUMFERMLINE to left, DOWAN HILL beyond. Looking towards Benicia.

anchor up and stood away to sea. We never heard of Kylon any more.

Letters came off. I'd one from Auntie Polly. She'd moved again, to get as far from Judy as she could. The half-deck rang with laughter. I'd one from Judy. She wrote, "Your picture's always on my dressing table. I kiss it when I wake, and when I go to bed at night. And close above my heart I wear the lock I cut from your dear head that day." I felt a little bad. I wrote to her, "Lord knows when we'll get home. They say maybe the ship will go to China. I'll bring you back a silk scarf if she does." I knew quite well of course that we'd not go to China.

We docked next morning, and Clegg was taken to hospital. He said to me, "So-long! You'll come and see me, eh?"

"Yes, sir," I answered him.

168

Lifting a feeble hand, he said, smiling to me, "Cut out the 'sir', old man. We're *shipmates*, you and I. They call it 'chums' ashore, but *shipmate* means far more than any lubber's word could mean, eh, Bill, old man?"

'Twas Sunday when we docked. We had her moored by noon, then went ashore. There was a Seaman's Institute in 'Frisco. The chaplain was the finest sort of chap. My comrades started thither. But Paddy said, "Let's go have a beer, Bill." We went to the 'Last Chance' saloon down at the foot of Market Street. The Institute was just around the corner. We had two beers apiece. Then Paddy said, "Let's go and see the motts." But I said, "No. Let's first go to the Institute." And so we went.

When we reached the door we saw a little chapel at its left. An altar with a snow-white altar cloth and two silver candles on it. Before us was a flight of stairs, so up we went and, when we reached the top, we met a lady there. She held her hand out and she smiled at us. Paddy took her hand, and then I took it. But meet her eyes I couldn't. Two beers will make a sea apprentice just come in from a long voyage a little squiffy. I felt too much ashamed to meet her eyes.

I don't recall how that afternoon passed. But well I recollect that night. Paddy and I, and several other lads from other ships, went off to sailor-town. The others wandered on ahead of me and Paddy, and we were all alone. Then a window opened, and a soft voice spoke. Soft scent was on the air.

"Come on, Bill," Paddy said.

So we went in. One girl was there alone. She kissed me first, then Paddy. Her gown was of pale gold. Her hair was golden. Her eyes were ocean blue. Her slender arms were bare. Her hands were soft. Oh, very. And that neat little room, with carpet and with cushions, with pale pink wall paper, dim-lit by a warm roseate little lamp, was, ah, so different to our cramped half-deck with its rusty stains, and cockroaches, and our old oilskins hanging everywhere. She took our fingers in her soft scenty hands and looked at our cracked palms; our scars from cold Cape Horn.

She said, "You poor dear boys."

And then she kissed my palms.

169

"Minnie will kiss your hurts away, and you'll forget," she said.

By and by, I went out to the street. Dim street, with far-spaced, rosy little lights. Paddy came later.

"She was all right, Bill, wasn't she?" he said.

I mind next morning, while we washed the decks, I leaned on my long broom. Lost in wonder, puzzled. The mate called, "Wake up there! Come, move that broom along!" Yes, I do mind that morning, just as though it had but been today's. Paddy joked and laughed. He didn't know what things were in my mind. He only knew that he and I were chums. And so we were. I loved him. Why? God knows. Ask God. I only know I did.

But when, that night, he said, "Come on. We'll go and see the motts," I said that I was going to the Institute. So he came too. The Chaplain asked us of our homes, and of the voyage we'd had. And that same lady came and sat by me.

She said, "It's hard to be a sailor, isn't it? It's very hard at sea?"

And I said, "Yes"—I thought "It's hard ashore too."

Each night at closing time the Chaplain held a little service in the chapel. That night, when we trooped down, two score or more of sea apprentices, Paddy and I, and that same merry crowd we'd been with yesternight, were last. I was the leading one. Come to the chapel door, I paused. "Come on," said Paddy, "We'll go see the motts and have a time."

But I turned in, and sat on the rear bench. Those others all went on, out to the street. The chaplain came, bent over me, and said, "*That* takes strength of mind." But he was wrong. It wasn't strength of mind. It was only just me, puzzled, and wondering. And from that night I said to Paddy, "No. You go your way. I'll go mine." I never went to sailor-town again. It made no difference to our chumminess. Not one bit. And that's what friendship means. Oh, call it love.

When Sunday came I went to see Will Clegg. I found him fast asleep, upon his back, one arm outstretched. I sat by him, and waited. And presently he moved that outstretched arm, and turned the clenched fist over, knuckles down. And then that fist went open. And—there I saw a large gold medal in his open palm. I bent above it. It was that medal that I told you of. *"For gallantry at sea."* So then I rose, and

170

stole away; and came back presently, and coughed. He woke, and closed that hand and drew it in the bed.

"Why, hello, shipmate! What's doing down aboard? How's everyone?" he asked.

And then he said, "The doctors tell me that my heart is crocky. They say—that I—can—never—go—to—sea—again."

I can't tell you of the tone in which he said those words! I felt ashamed of my great strength. Before another Sunday he was gone to New York, upon his homeward, broken way to Liverpool.

Often at night Paddy and I would go ashore and wander here and there. He never tried to get me to go to sailor-town. I never tried to get him to the Institute. We'd stroll about, look in the shops, and watch the queer shore people. Sometimes he'd say, or I would, "You take this side of the street and I'll take that. We'll meet at Third Street. Maybe we'll find some money in the gutter." One good night I found a dime and he found fifty cents. There was a restaurant in those days on Third Street, where you could get for fifteen cents soup, fish, meat, and dessert. So we'd have thirty cents left when we'd eaten. But Paddy, who was always very spick and span, said he must have a shave before we ate. I said, "You silly ass! Why didn't you shave aboard?"

"My damned old razor's dull," said he, and walked off toward a barber shop some distance down the street. "A shave's only a dime," he said, "We'll have two beers apiece before we go aboard."

While waiting for him, I thought of those fine flower-stalls up on Kearney Street, so I went and bought a bunch of violets. A lovely bunch. I parted it in two, one for my chum and one for me. We'd still have money for a beer apiece.

"And where in hell did you get the violets?" asked Paddy when he came.

"I bought them for a dime," I answered him.

He said, "You fool, we're broke!" And so we were. For in the guileless fashion of a sailor he'd inadvertently gone into the toniest barber shop on Market Street, under the Palace Hotel. His shave had cost four bits.

The 'Frisco waterfront was lovely in those days. Why, you could walk for blocks beneath the long jib-booms of clippers stretched across

171

56.   *Figurehead of RAJORE and . . .*

57.   *. . . of CAMBRIAN CHIEFTAIN.*

the street. You'd see their figureheads. A dragon, one ship had, its red maw open and its white fangs showing. And some had knights and warriors, with spears and swords, and shields. And many ships had women for their figureheads. Ours was the fairest figurehead of all. A white-robed woman with her white breast bare. One arm out-stretched, a finger pointing to the far away. And in her other hand she held a long silver horn to her lips, about to blow on it. "That is the prettiest ship of all," you'd hear the shore folk say, taking their Sunday stroll along the waterfront. Although we damned her for a 'hungry bitch', we loved and were proud of her. We were a husky lot, and in our pride we challenged all the apprentices of all the ships in port. We won the tug-of-war. I was our anchor man, being the heaviest. Chink won the boxing match, Polly the mast-head race. And then one day a dozen ships lowered their gigs, and in each gig's stern that ship's stern skipper sat. Ours was a teak-wood gig, four-oared. I pulled stroke oar. The Old Man looked into my eyes. "Show 'em!" he said. We showed them. There is no pride such as a sailor's in his ship; except it be the pride that comes at last, when the right woman's found, and right lips meet. *Oh, sailor, sailor, sailor!*

In due course the good day came again when we were homeward bound. Two other lofty clippers put to sea with us. The fine four-mast barque *Seafarer*, and the full rigger *Wayfarer*. We were all Falmouth bound. And when we hove our anchor up we made the wide bay ring,

> *California's lovely daughters,*
> *We must now bid you adieu,*
> *But it's long that we'll remember*
> *Happy hours we've spent with you.*
>> *Rolling home, rolling home,*
>> *Rolling home across the sea,*
>> *Rolling home to merrie England,*
>> *To the land where we would be.*

And Amsterdam, of course, Always the good old 'Maid of Amsterdam', the bravest chorus of them all:

> *A'roving, a'roving,*
> *Oh, roving's been my ru–i–in,*
> *And we'll go no more a'ro–oving*
> *With you—fair—maid.*

173

58. WAYFARER.

We had for second mate in place of Clegg a little squatty man named Pengelly; a fellow no one liked but me. I don't know why I liked him. I think that I liked almost everyone. I think that liking, or trying to like, was habit with me. Natural. He was a sotty-minded little man. He said to me, "Two days. Just two days is enough. W'en I have known a gal two days, if I can't have her then I'm done wi' her, by gad." But he was a good sailor, though not so keen as Clegg. And Lord, how he could swear. I'd never heard a man could curse as he could, did anything go wrong.

It was the same old song and dance as usual. We'd see a ship, and race, and leave her far astern. We'd shake the maggots from the hard-tack, and curse the smelly pork. But now the older apprentices were grown more serious. Chink, Polly, Tattersall, and Douglas, who

174

59.   SEAFARER.

was third mate, would be out of their time when we came home, and
so they studied navigation in the dogwatches. Next voyage there'd
be a lot of green kids in the half-deck. I didn't like the thought, for
you can't sail three years with comrades in a half-deck and they not
be a part and parcel of your life. Oh, well, I'd still have Paddy. So
nothing mattered much. Love as you may your comrades, there must
be one best loved. Often those studious ones would say, "Paddy, for
God's sake dry up! You make too damned much noise! To hell with
your Paradise Alley." Then he'd laugh, and he and I would go out and
walk the deck. When the fine weather came, we slung our hammock
under the forecastle head again, and on that homeward voyage I gave
him my marmalade each Monday. For it he gave me his Harriet Lane
when Sunday came. If I lacked anything and he had what I lacked,

175

there was no lack for me. The same did he lack anything. He'd lost his tooth brush, and so we shared my own when Sunday came. That's when you scrub your teeth, if you're a sea apprentice. Fresh water's scarce. You shave, and wash, and scrub your teeth on Sunday morning, unless there comes a rain. Forever skylarking, my chum was. There never was a merrier lad upon the sea. Sometimes he'd even prevail on the three serious ones to quit their studying, and then we'd have a sing-song in the half-deck. Chink's song was always 'The Lost Chord', but that song somehow made me sad. I liked the song that Tattersall always sang:

> *My gal's a high-born lady,*
> *She's dark but not too shady;*
> *Feathered like a peacock, just as gay,*
> *She's not coloured, she was born that way!*

Polly would sing that song of 'Poor Old Jeff'. And then the farmer's son would sing, and we'd all laugh and say, "You bloody farmer!"

> *Tam Pearce, Tam Pearce, lend me t'owld grey mare,*
> *All along, down along, by a long lane,*
> *For I want to go to Widdecombe fair,*
> *All along, down along, by a long lane.*

We'd cheer when Alphonse sang:

> *Malbruck s'en va t'en guerra.*
> *Mironton, Mironton, Mirontaine . . .*
> *Malbruck s'en va t'en guerra,*
> *Ne sais quand reviendra.*

The meaning of the words was not clear to most of the half-deck, but they all joined in the 'Mironton . . .' chorus so that it almost raised our deck-house roof—

> *Pour chanter la victoire*
> *Mironton, mironton, mirontaine . . .*
> *Pour chanter la victoire*
> *Que Malbruck remporte bis.*

The baccy smoke would swirl and wreathe. I'd see my comrades' shining eyes. And maybe the old mate would pause in going by, and we would call him in. He was a quiet old chap with a much wrinkled

176

60. *Apprentices and mates aboard the SILBERHORN, 1899. Back row, L. to R.: Hickman, O'Brian, Mansen (Alphonse), Bond (who fell from the Royal yard) and Taylor. Front row, L. to R.: Bill Adams (with dog), Tattersall, Pengelly (who took Clegg's berth), Mr. Sutherland (the mate), Douglas and Thompson.*

face. "Please, sir, give us a song," but he would shake his head, and say his singing days were done. Then we would say, "Come on, sir. We know you can!" And then he'd take his pipe from out his lips and smile, and say, "All right, lads. How goes this?"

Merry are we, merry are we,
There's no one on earth like a sailor at sea.

A merry crowd we were, and happy as the day. We had forgotten Furst, and Glynn, and Willie Clegg; the tall man, One Eye, and poor Wood. Oh, I might think maybe of Glynn at times, and might miss Clegg a bit. But when you're young you don't cling to your grieving. It looks too bright ahead. Seeing the studious ones, I'd think, "It won't be long now. My turn's coming soon. When I'm a second mate I'm going to stay with her. I'll ask the Old Man to keep me on as second mate." Oh, yes. I planned to stay with the old girl till Paddy's time was up. We often talked of it. We'd stick together, he and I, through all our days at sea.

I mind a night far down in the Pacific. I was asleep, but Paddy woke me up. Behind him were Chink and Polly, both their faces merry.

"What's up?" I asked, for you don't wake a sailor in his watch below.

"Paddy's up to some of his cracked Irish tricks," laughed Chink. But Paddy's face was white.

"My God, I've heard the Banshee!" Paddy said.

"You silly fool, get out of here. Get out and go to hell and let me sleep," I laughed.

But Paddy said, "You come on deck and listen!" So I rolled out and followed them.

You know what's meant by Banshee? It is a ghost the Irish talk about. You hear the silly thing and—well, look out! The Irish say it means you're going to die. The one who hears it first, he dies.

The night was very dark, with a low wind; the old girl sailing slowly on a gentle sea, with all sail set. "Oh, hell. My bunk for me, you crazy Irish ass," said I. And then I heard it. We all heard, far away, a sort of moaning sound. As we stood there wondering what it was, the carpenter, awakened by our voices, looked from his door.

178

61. *American 4-masted barque DIRIGO making her departure.*

"You blasted fools! It's just a block aloft as needs a grease dollop. Didn't ye ever hear a dry block groaning?" he said.

Chink said, "It's whales, of course." And we all laughed at Paddy, and I went back to my bunk. We never gave it any thought again. Not even Paddy did. He said, "I guess I was a fool, Bill! Say—do you remember how that girl looked in that golden gown? And weren't her legs pretty? Say, wasn't she all right, eh?"

We stopped at Pitcairn and filled our bellies with its fruits again. We drove her towards the Horn. The mountain seas came rolling after her. The snowy albatross hovered above her rail. We met an outbound ship one howling day. Hove-to she was, our brave fair wind her head wind. We saw the seas go crashing over her, and pitied her poor devils. At dogwatch time that night we sang:

We've crossed the line, and the Gulf Stream,
Been down by Table Bay,
We've rounded the Horn and we're homeward-bound,
And that is the sailor's way.

When we were come to the sunny seas and bright blue skies again, we did the usual thing. Always when we had passed the Horn and left it well astern we sent down, one by one, her strong storm sails; replacing each with an old sail fit for the trade wind weather. It was a pleasant sort of job. It told of many weeks ahead in balmy breezes.

I came down from the mast one day at noon, to go off duty. The mate's watch came on deck. The ship was still, upon a windless sea. No white cap anywhere. No cloud in all the South Atlantic sky. Her sails hung drooping. High, high above her mast-heads I could see a solitary marline-spike bird; a white bird with a long white tail feather. I just could hear its screaming, and far away a pod of whales was spouting. Entering the half-deck for my dinner I met Paddy in the doorway. It was Sunday. He said, "My Harriet Lane is in your plate, Bill." And I said, "All right, Paddy. Thanks."

Chink and the farmer's son, O'Brien and I sat down to dinner. We had been working hard all morning, and were tired. We didn't speak.

Suddenly there came a shrilling scream. All terror in it. Up we leapt and out we rushed before 'Man overboard' had ceased its ringing.

180

The crew were racing for the boat. It wasn't necessary to stop the ship, for she was utter still on that blue limpid sea.

I sprang into the jigger rigging and raced up, clear to the truck. That's what one man must always do if anyone goes overboard by day. You go up there and thence direct the lifeboat toward the man who's in the sea. I looked all round the still blue limpid sea. The rowers in the boat looked up at me. The sea was empty. I heard that bird's faint scream. The whales were gone, and soon I said, cool as though it didn't matter in the least, "Another poor devil gone," as down I came. The boat was in beside the ship, and they were hoisting her. Since I wasn't needed I went to the half-deck to finish my Harriet Lane and, by the door I met with Chink. I asked, "Who was it?"

Chink said, "Paddy."

It didn't bother me at all at first. I ate his Harriet Lane and put my plate away. Then I walked forward to the hammock that he'd risen from a little time ago, but on the forward deck I met the mate. He asked, "Did Bond have any people?" And then it got me, and the horror came.

Oh, well, a sailor sleeps through anything at all. I went on to our hammock. The dent of Paddy's head was in the pillow still. I laid my head there and I went to sleep. And then—I wakened suddenly and I was running from beneath the forecastle head; and in my ears there rang *Man overboard!* The mate was on the deck, and saw me coming.

"What's up?" the mate asked. I turned and went back to our hammock, and that was how it was many times. I'd wake to find my-self running, that cry in my ears. It was some days ere I got over that.

That evening in the dogwatch I sat all alone, out on the rail, think-ing of my chum, when Polly came to me. "Come on, old chap. We're going to have a sing-song in the half-deck!" How I hated him, and all my comrades! A sing-song, with Paddy being nibbled by the barra-cout. I turned away, and Polly left me there, without another word. Then, presently I noted that there was no singing in the half-deck, so I rose and went there. Chink, Polly, Tattersall, were poring over navigation books. The younger lads sat silent, smoking. Chink looked up, and "Want a fill, old man?" he asked, and pushed his baccy pouch toward me. Polly fumbled in his pocket for a match. Tattersall said, "Curses! I can't get my giddy figures right tonight!" And then I knew—that they only thought to have a sing-song thinking to cheer me up. So I sat down and filled my pipe and smoked while no one spoke. The ship lay silent on the listless sea. The darkness hid her. Over her tall masts the stars shone bright. At the hour her bells clanged, and then I heard the voice of the look-out man ring.

"All's well, sir, and the lights are bright."

The mate replied, "All right."

And then I heard my father say to me, "You'll find it a hard life, my son."

Soon I went to the wheel, and stood there my two hours; and thought of Paddy, and the 'Golden Eagle' girls, and Minnie, and the violets I'd bought. I seemed to see his smile, to hear him singing that 'Paradise Alley' song and somewhere, far below me, were the barracout.

CHAPTER X

CORINTH HELEN

A wind blew up that night and the mate's watch took the royals off her. But when I came on duty soon after dawn the wind was gone again. Only a little breeze was blowing. And presently the second mate sang out, "Loose the royals!" When that order came I was beside the foremast, alone, no other near me. When an order comes the man who's nearest to the rigging goes aloft to carry out that order. So, from force of habit and of duty, I climbed into the fore rigging. And then it came to me that I was going to the place whence Paddy'd fallen. My limbs began to shake. I could not see, and I remembered what Johansen'd said, "Dot yard ees curst." I might have come back down, and told the second mate; and he'd have understood and sent some other up, but there is a thing called pride, and it is stronger than your fear of death. I mind my coming to the royal mast-head. I stood upon the place that Paddy'd fallen from, and somehow I climbed out along the thumb-thick footrope, out, and on out, till I was out above the waiting sea. I don't know how I loosed that royal, but I did it somehow, and somehow I came down. I'd never had the vertigo like that before.

The ship sailed on, and we began to make her ready for her home-coming. The winds were fair and carried her along till, sixty miles north of the line, they left her one hot dawning. There was a long, slow swell. All day she tumbled to it, her sails all slatting heavily against the spars and rigging. All night she tumbled to the long, slow swell, and when another morning came we clewed up all her sail, to save the canvas chafing. Canvas costs money. And all her white wings

183

62. *HAWAIIAN ISLES, later STAR OF GREENLAND, later ABRAHAM RYDBERG.*

hung, festooned along her spars. But later in the day the swell died down. The sea fell mirror-flat. She rode erect, the hot sun blazing on her. Some blackfish came, and sported round her bow. Small whales, they are; the bulls perhaps twenty feet long. And there were cows and calves. They nuzzled one another, playing. We saw one calf suck milk from its old cow. Then a little shark appeared; and all the whales were gone, speeding away. A sailor fetched the shark hook, begged a hunk of pork from the cook, and hooked the shark. The sailors feasted on shark meat that day. Foreign sailors mostly. But we lads in the half-deck wouldn't touch it. The day passed, oven-hot; the decks too hot to walk on barefooted. The pitch came bubbling up from every deck seam. And all night long the ship lay motionless upon the mirror sea; a great round moon slow-passing o'er the sky. All night long the tropic lightning played round the horizon, and when day came again it was as yesterday. Next night was yesternight again, and on,

184

and on, and on, the days and nights passed by. There came a day, when water was served out at four o'clock the carpenter told the old mate the water tank that he'd been drawing from was well nigh empty. So next day we drew out water from the other tank. She had two tanks below, and they were full. We'd never drawn from it, and when he drew from it the carpenter took a swallow of the water.

"God, but I'm dry," he said. And then he swore and spat.

"My God, the bloody rats have got into the tank," said he.

So, it seemed, they had. We could not drink the stinking water and had to go back to the nigh empty tank. Our water allowance was cut down to a bare minimum. We must go thirsty till a rain should come. There was no water now for morning coffee or for evening skilly. To save the precious water, the salt pork must be boiled in the pea soup, the salt horse in the bean soup. That made the soups too salt. We cut off buttons from our shirts and dungarees, and kept them in our mouths to keep saliva flowing. Morn after morn we scrubbed the long white decks. Eve upon eve, when the cruel sun was sunk beneath the mirror sea, we slapped sea water on her long white decks to cool and keep the seams tight. All day we worked out in the cruel sun. No shadow anywhere, because her sails hung all festooned along the lifeless spars. There was no dancing when the dogwatch came. There was no song. The hard-tack swarmed with fat white maggots. Night upon night we threw sea water over one another, seeking some cool. But there was never any cooling from that hot tropic sea. On Sunday we dared not wash, nor shave, nor brush our teeth, and men grow quarrelsome in times like that. One day two sailors fought, with hateful eyes. They were Norwegians. They fought barefoot and naked to the waist. We gathered round and hoarsely laughed at them; for those chaps from the northern countries don't know how to fight with fists. Their blood spattered the deck; their lips and noses dripping. They fought till they gave out. We slapped sea water over them, and hoarsely urged them on, but they had had enough.

Twenty-one days, twenty-one nights, the old girl lay becalmed. No flick of any breeze. Bodies were gaunt. Our lips began to swell. Our eyes were sullen, and our faces stubbly. Our hands were thick with paint, with tar, and varnish. Always the old mate when on duty,

185

always the second mate, gazed o'er the sea and whistled for a breeze. The Old Man's eyes were like a dog's eyes; a savage dog, almost too old for fighting.

At dawn of the twenty-second day a long black cloud appeared along the western horizon. We fetched the rain sail up, and stretched it in the mizzen rigging, from side to side of her, and pushed its canvas hose down in the all but empty tank. We stripped off all our clothes, and gathered by her rail. Fourteen stark naked sailors, seven stark naked apprentices. Dry-mouthed, voiceless. Lips swollen.

We watched the cloud advance, a wall of solid black. We saw the rain fall in a solid sheet. Flying fish leapt in myriads at its foot. Dolphin, skipjack, bonito, albacore, and barracout leapt up to take them on the wing. Sea birds dropped on them from above, wheeling, screaming.

The Old Man spoke two words, "Sheet home!"

We grasped the long idle sheets, and sheeted sail after sail home. No shouting on the ropes. We could not shout. The dry blocks groaned. The dry sails rustled. Now and again some sailor tried to shout, and cackled hoarsely.

We lay upon the deck, outstretched, our mouths wide open. The rain beat down, poured on our naked bodies, streamed from the deck out to the hissing sea, and soon we laughed and jested. Naked, we slapped each other's naked buttocks, flat-handed, mirthfully. A light wind puff came. The sails jerked full. The old girl heeled far over, bubbles racing by. The old mate said, "The Liverpool girls have got hold of the tow line."

From that day we held a bully breeze and she ran finely. She ran beyond the northern tropic's edge, and came to the Sargasso sea, and never once with a wind that was not a fine hard wind, and so, because he hated to lose any time at all by taking even one small sail off her, the Old Man told the mate to leave the light fine-weather canvas on her still. Under her old worn sails, we drove her on toward the stormier seas. All day we sped through the Sargasso sea, with clumps of amber weed in long, long lines stretching for mile on mile. We'd drop a hook and fetch a clump of weed up and lay it on the deck. Every clump was full of tiny crabs of wondrous colouring. Red crabs and green, and

63.   *L. to R.: SLIEVE ROE, CITY OF BENARES and GULF STREAM.*

yellow. No larger than your thumb nail, and there were little twisty shell fish too. One sailor said, "By God, them weed bunches is like a sort o' mermaid mistletoe." And so they were. Day after day, night after night, we swept across that fairy sea.

And then one evening, just ere dusk, the wind fell suddenly, all in a tick. All the air was utter still, and so the seas, hitherto driven on by that warm wind from southwest, having now no force to push them, toppled, and flopped up and down confused and aimless. That is a curious thing to watch. One of the most curious things you find upon the sea. Then a great dark bank of cloud came sudden sweeping from the northwest and, before we could get a sail off, smote her. Down she went, but her old worn sails began to split. So she came up again, and in a little while that wild wind from the north had stripped the old girl naked. Not a sail left. Just shreds and ribbons streaming from her spars. So, all night long, working by full moonlight, we dragged her stout storm canvas from the locker and hoisted it. It was a merry night, for we were homeward bound. We worked barefoot, and many

187

64. Smart Norwegian full-rigger SIAM.

of us naked to the waist, the weather being yet warm enough for Cape Horn sailors. We laughed, and sang, and shouted. But when the dawning came we had the old girl dressed, and under lower topsails in a hard full gale. The combers raged. The sprays flew over her. The North Atlantic tried to emulate the Horn. It never can do that, but gives a fairish imitation. Then, when dawn was wide, a sailor shouted from the foremast. We ran. We stood beside the rail, and saw a ship pass by—and she was bottom up. Her bottom was not weedy. Then she was late from port. "Lost with all hands." Capsized the previous night, when caught with too much stout sail upon her. It makes a sailor feel a little queer to see a thing like that.

When that gale died we were well up, past the Azores, but then a clear wind came from the north-east, and that was not so good. For we must go north-east. Day after day, night after night, we tacked and tacked again; trying to claw up toward soundings, cursing the north-east winds, that mocked us day by day, holding us far beyond the Channel's mouth. Day after day we tacked, and tacked again. Alone

65.   FRANCE, of the Bordes company.

—no other ship in sight by day or night. From round Cape Horn—
sea-weary, weary for home. We'd never seen the *Seafarer* nor *Way-*
farer, and wondered where they were. The skippers had a bet. Two
hundred dollars to the ship that came to Falmouth first. Our Old
Man's face was glum. Ten days we tacked her to and fro while that
north-easter blew, and then a mist set in, and from the south-west
came a pleasant breeze. So off we went again. Next day we ran under
full sail in thick, grey weather. Once, in the afternoon, the mist
thinned suddenly a little. We glimpsed, but lost at once, another
homeward-bounder. Once, in the night, the look-out man reported a
green light. No one else saw it. But when the morning came, with
thinner mist, we glimpsed, and later lost, four homeward-bounders.

We heard a fog horn blaring from close by. Then we heard
another, and soon from all about us came a constant blaring. We
answered with our own. That night the mist cleared off, and we all
saw sidelights winking on a clearing sea. Another morning found a
dozen ships about us. I mind their names, or some of them, today—

189

66. YOLA.

Gulf Stream, La France, Rajore, Wayfarer. All day we picked up ships. All night we saw red lights and green and white. Next dawn was almost calm. A smart Norwegian full-rigger, with painted ports, sailed close on our port beam; to starboard, a hulking great German saltpetre-man. Astern came *Lady Isobel,* with her dull yellow masts and spars and deep green painted hull. *Melanope, Yola, Sardomene* were there. When next day broke, we saw the Lizard. The sun was not yet up when I went aloft to furl the fore royal. Morning was clear and bright. When the sail was furled, I sat upon the yard to count the long, far-stretching line of homeward-bound square-riggers—fifty-two sail. Ships from the West Coast and the Colonies; from 'Frisco, Oregon and Puget Sound—the grain and salmon fleets. Ships from around the Horn and round the Cape; some bound into Falmouth 'for orders', others bound on up-Channel.

190

68. *CHANARAL.*

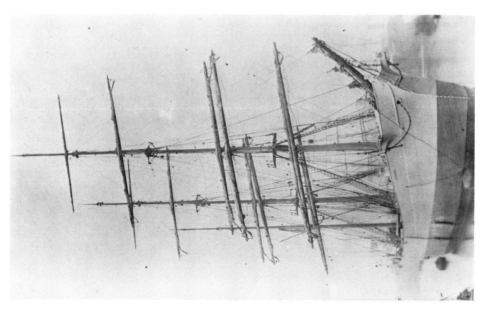

67. *INVERURIE.*

Fifty-two square-riggers coming up-Channel all together on a bright March morning! Where are they now?—Everywhere, ahead, astern, on either side, were homeward-hurrying clippers. We saw *Euphrosyne* and *Illawarra*. We saw *Melanope* and *Inverurie*. Oh, I could name a score of ships we saw that day. But they'd mean naught to you. Only I mind we passed a lovely French full-rigger, the *Chanaral*. She cheered us as we passed close by and we cheered back. All through the day we sailed amongst a homing fleet, and ship by ship we passed our rivals by.

"By gad, where's *Seafarer?*" the Old Man growled, "I ain't afraid of *Wayfarer*, but *Seafarer's* a fast one."

At times the bells clanged out, striking the hours away. The whole sea echoed with the ships' bells striking, and each ship flew her ensign. We flew our best, and it was made of silk. We shouted, "Go, old girl!" We waved to lads we knew. And they waved back to us. When night came down again, all the sea was dotted with the winking sidelights, green and red, and white stern lanterns, and all the night was musical with bells.

"All's well, sir, and the lights are bright!" we heard the look-out's cry.

There's no one happy as a sailor coming home; except it be a sailor when he meets his girl, be she the right girl. Yet Paddy Bond was gone, and I was sad.

Then I went up to that same fore royal yard again, to that accursed yard whence Furst and Paddy'd fallen. But I did not have any vertigo that morning. I furled the sail, and sat to watch the scenery, and counted half a hundred square-riggers on the sea. Ships from the west coast of America, with wheat or barley; and from Australia with wheat or wool. Calcutta ships with jute, and ships from Chile with saltpetre. German and French, Italian, Danish, Swede and Norwegian: but mostly British ships. There'll never be a sight like that again! The steamers have our sea.

So we sailed into Falmouth and let the anchor go, but not a word there was of *Seafarer* or *Wayfarer*. It was that night when *Seafarer* came in. *Wayfarer* came in next morning. All three ships had crossed the line in the Pacific the same day, and all passed the Horn on the same

69.   *Lizard Head, showing the wreck of the CROMDALE (1913).*

70.   *MOUNT STEWART, sister of CROMDALE and last of the wool clippers.*

day, and also the line in the Atlantic. And all that fourteen thousand miles not one of the three ships had seen another of the three.

Chink, Polly, Tattersall and Douglas went to ask the Old Man for a reference. Their time was out. He gave them each the same. "This is to certify that the bearer has served his apprenticeship in the ship *Silberhorn* under my command. I have always found him attentive to his duties and strictly honest. I think he will make a good officer and it is with pleasure that I give him this recommendation."

Then, remembering the stores we'd swiped, we said, "By God, the Old Man's square!"

Gay my old comrades were, but I, thinking of my next voyage with them all gone, was sad. There'd be green kids in place of them, and the old girl would be a very different ship. I thought of Glynn, and how he'd said to me so long ago, "Don't go to sea. The sea's hell!"

Oh, well! Just one more year! I'd stick it out somehow! And then *my* turn would come and I also would take my exam. for second mate, and be an officer! But I'd not stay with the old girl. Not much! No, not with Paddy gone!

We sailed for Hull on the North Sea coast one fair bright morning. Just ere we sailed, the *Chanaral* went out. We heard the frogs all roaring out a queer French happy homeward chantey chorus, heaving their anchor in. We cheered her as she passed, and she cheered back. And then we roared the good old 'Maid of Amsterdam', and followed her. And off we went, and saw the white-washed cottages again, set in the fair green fields, while all the air was full of earthy scents. We saw the towns slip by, and lighthouses. Early in the night a wind came, yelling from southwest. The old girl leapt to it, the Old Man keeping her with full sail set. He said, "She knows she's going home, and she can stand it." All her rigging thrummed. I mind I went down from the poop with Pengelly, that foul-mouthed cursing little second mate we had in place of Clegg. We went to pull together on a rope, and as we pulled a cold sea raised its head, came lopping in, and soaked us to our hides. I said "God damn!" I shouted Jesus' name, and cursed with every cursing word I knew, and I knew plenty. Then Pengelly said to me, "My God, Bill, but I'm sorry to hear that from *you*. I been respectin' you the most of anyone aboard since we left 'Frisco." And, Lord, how bad I felt! I'd never cursed at all since leaving 'Frisco. That little chapel, with that little altar, and the snow-white altar cloth had somehow broken me of cursing. I said, "I'm sorry, sir." It was too late, I guess.

When we came into Hull, after a savage gale in the North Sea that kept us all on deck through four long days and nights with scarce a wink of sleep, we heard about the pretty *Chanaral*. That squall that drove us flying up the Channel had struck her on her way across to Nantes. Had struck her not astern as it struck us, but full upon her beam. And she capsized and sank. From six in the evening till after ten next morning her mate clung to one of her upturned boats. No other man was saved. Well, that's the sailor's way. You never know.

I went to Aunt Clarissa's first. Fagged out I was, and limp, from that long North Sea gale. Ede was there, and Dolly. And they all saw how utterly tired I was, and how dispirited. I didn't want to talk. I ate in silence while they waited on me. And then I said, "Please, may I go to bed?" The light was not yet gone. In clean white linen sheets I slept the clock round. I knew naught, nor dreamed any dream. A sailor, exhausted from the old fight with the sea. A lad, tired by life's puzzling struggle, yet life but scarcely begun. When I wakened, Dolly stood by my bed with a cup of tea.

"Thank you," I said.

And Dolly said, "You're unhappy, dear."

"My chum was drowned," I answered.

"I lost a chum too, dear," she murmured, soft-voiced; and stooped and kissed my cheek. There was peace in her kiss, kiss of a comrade. She went, and Ede came in.

"Well, how are the girls?" asked Ede.

"There aren't any girls," I muttered. I wanted to forget some things.

"Silly boy," she laughed, and put an arm round my shoulder. Her hair was soft. About her was fragrance.

"Haven't you a kiss for me?" she asked. I kissed her.

"Why don't you leave the sea?" she asked.

"I can't leave the sea," I answered.

195

"Don't be so silly," she said.

There I sat, with her arm round my shoulder; thinking of Glynn, of Clegg, and Paddy. One after another, the sea had taken my shipmates. I had no chum for next voyage. But again I said, "I can't leave the sea."

"You're a fool," said Ede.

Then I pushed her arm from my shoulder, and I said, "Maybe. And I'd rather be a fool than a pasty-faced clerk like Art Norrington. Is he still trotting round after you?"

That afternoon Dolly and I went for a walk. It was spring. There were primroses and dog violets. I didn't see them. I told her of how Paddy was lost, and of my vertigo that had been so hard to conquer. She spoke a few words of her chum; her lover who had died. Very soft words. She said, "You love the sea, dear, don't you?" She understood. The next day I went on my way.

Auntie Polly had taken a house fourteen miles from Plymouth: a lonely place away out on the moors. My tiredness was gone. I was myself, and spring was on her tiptoes, with her robe rain-wet, and spring was in my blood. What the devil excuse could I dig up for going to Plymouth? Twenty-eight miles there and back over a hilly road. Well, it was simple. It's always simple when you're young.

I said, "Auntie, I'll soon be out of my apprenticeship. There's a navigation school in Plymouth, and I ought to start to study for my second mate's exam."

It was tommy-rot. No apprentice bothered about going to navigation school till his time was up. But she didn't know that. She said, "Oh, I ought to have gone nearer Plymouth. It's so far for you to ride."

School was over at three in the afternoon. That left plenty of time. There were a dozen or so chaps attending school. Some getting ready for mate's, some for second mate's tickets. One or two for master's. A sailor knows all other sailors. I was gay-hearted. After school the first day I went up and sat on Plymouth Hoe. I looked away to the horizon and saw galleons coming up from under the sea rim, a great fleet in the shape of a half moon. Behind me was a statue of Francis Drake, with a bowl in his hand. "We'll finish our game," said Francis Drake.

196

71. *PENDRAGON CASTLE, here seen in Puget Sound as the German LISBETH, was famous on the 'Frisco run.*

Maggie Cuddeford was a short, stumpy girl with grey eyes like big round moons. They call the Devon girls 'Devon dumplings'. The name fitted her. We went out to a little coppice near where she lived, in the country beyond Plymouth. We sat amongst the primroses on a bank above the river Tamar. A breeze ruffled the Tamar. Long ago the Phoenicians had come up the Tamar, seeking Britain's tin. I could see the sun on their sails, could hear the *clunka-clunka* of their galley sweeps, and I was one-and-twenty, and the sun shone bright upon the buttons of my uniform and the braid of my cap.

Maggie Cuddeford lay back amongst the primroses. I picked one and tickled her chin with it. She pushed it away and looked at me from her round grey moons. I leaned on an elbow above her while she pursed her lips toward me. I kissed them and said, "The sun's getting low, and I've fourteen miles of hilly road to ride," I rose, took her hands, and pulled her to her feet. Frowning, she asked, "Are all you sailors alike?"

197

"Not by a long chalk," I answered. "My ship's the smartest clipper out of Liverpool and I'm her eldest apprentice."

"I don't think you're so smart," she said.

"Tomorrow is another day. Maybe I'll improve on acquaintance. See you tomorrow, eh?" I laughed.

She said, "I don't know."

I kissed her and asked, "How's that?"

She said, "You're queer. I can't make you out."

It was long after dark when I reached home. I said, "Auntie, there's a swell lot of chaps at the school. You must come in on the train some day and meet some of them. We'll have lunch together." I had my books under my arm and added, "Don't worry about girls, Auntie. I'm too busy for foolishness this time."

Next day it rained, so Maggie and I couldn't go lie in the primroses. We sat on the pier, me with an arm about her. "Hold me tighter," she said.

I said, "Bold bad girl!"

"Oh, you think I'm bad, do you?" she asked.

"Steady your helm. Never get excited. Keep cool." I laughed.

She said, "Cool!—Good Lord!"

And then one of the chaps from the school came along with a girl. They sat down with us and when we rose to go he went with Maggie and I with his girl.

Daisy Fenn was tall and clipper-built. She looked at me and asked, "Are all you sailors alike?"

"Thunder no! I'm eldest apprentice in the smartest clipper out of Liverpool," I replied.

"How do you like Maggie Cuddeford?" she asked.

I replied, "Any port in a storm. I like you heaps better. She's a bit too bluff in the bows, and square in the counter. You're clipper-built."

She laughed and said, "I don't know what that means, but I'm glad you don't like Maggie Cuddeford. I think she'll suit your friend lots better."

Next day was sun-bright with April clouds drifting over blue sky. Daisy Fenn and I sat in the primroses. I picked one and tickled her chin. She laughed, picked one, and tickled mine.

198

"How about a kiss?" I asked.

She pursed her lips to me. I kissed them. "I know why Maggie Cuddeford doesn't like you," she said.

"Why?" I asked.

"'Cause of the way you kiss," she replied.

"Don't you like my kisses?" I asked.

She said, "Silly, give me another."

In two weeks I was at Auntie Clarissa's again, on my way back to the ship. Dolly was there, but not Ede. I liked to just sit and watch her. I didn't have to hear her voice. I thought of the night she'd read me *Pilgrim's Progress*. I worshipped her, she unaware of my worship. An altar with a snow-white altar cloth. I remembered Billings and Thornton. What a puzzling world! You stain an altar cloth, and can you ever wash the stain away? Suppose you hadn't meant to stain it?"

"Tell me about your chum," Dolly said. I told her of the violets I'd bought. She laughed, and said, "Tell me more about him."

I replied, "Oh, there's nothing much to tell. I just loved him."

When I left next morning to join my ship she gave me a little package. "Open it when you're at sea," she said.

Pat O'Brien was there, and Alphonse, and five green apprentices. You would have thought I was at least an admiral, the way those green kids looked at me. The farmer's son had swallowed the anchor; left the sea and gone back to his pigs and cows.

"Come on! Let's go up town," I said to Pat and Alphonse, and to the green kids, "You kids, too. You'll soon be at sea. Make the best of your time. God help you!"

We rode up town on top of a tram. Alphonse told me he had 'anuzzer meestrees'. Pat O'Brien had kissed his first girl. The green kids stared at them, and blushed. We entered a pub, where were some apprentices from other ships.

"Tarpaulin muster," I said, and took off my cap and passed it round. Everyone chucked into it some money for drinks for the gang, and then the door opened, and in came a square-shouldered man of medium height, with black hair and sharp brown eyes.

"Where's the third mate of the *Silberhorn*?" he asked. No one replied.

"By God, where's the eldest apprentice of the *Silberhorn*?" he asked.

I said, "That's me, sir."

He asked, "Why in hell didn't you say so? Six times round the Horn you've been, by God! I've heard of you. You're going to do my work for me. Think I'm going to waste a fellow your size?"

"Suits me, sir," said I. And was I gay? Third mate! Live in the second's cabin and eat at the saloon table! No more maggoty hard-tack, rotten pork.

"Fill these lads' glasses. They're sailors, by God!" said the mate to the barmaid. He took my cap, passed it round, and said, "Take your money. The drinks are on me."

"Here's to ninety days to 'Frisco, and a fair wind round the Horn, boys!" he said, lifting his glass. We drank the toast, the green kids' faces awed.

He continued, "My name's John Martin and I'm tough as the old bull whale that had fifty cows in his harem and twins by each. Do your duty and you'll find me square. Don't do it, and God help you!" Then, looking at me, he added, "I'm not talking to *you*."

And was I gay-hearted when I rolled into my bunk that night! My last night in the half-deck! Tomorrow I'd sleep in the second mate's cabin.

Morning came and I gave my first order. "Wash the decks down!" The second mate was not yet aboard. What a sorry sight the old girl was! Her big belly was full of coke, coal, cement, railroad steel, fire bricks, pig iron for 'Frisco. Grime on her teak wood, on her paint. Her ropes, her gear, all thick with harbour grime. It would take a lot more than one washing to even begin to get the grime away. I could see the aching of the green kids' arms. All fore-noon I kept them busy hauling at her gear. The Old Man came aboard during the afternoon. The mate said, "I'm going to tell him I want you third mate." And off he went, and soon came back.

"All right," said John Martin, "You're third mate. The Old Man says you're the only apprentice he never heard answer an officer back. He says you'll make a good third mate." Remembering the night I'd cursed the Old Man from the mizzen topgallant yard, I grinned. Had

72. *DUCHALBURN at Seattle.*

he forgotten? Or was it that he liked a chap to show a bit of spunk?

Then the mate added, "You're to live in the half-deck still. The Old Man says you're so big it'd cost too much to feed you in the saloon."

And *was* I disgusted! For over three years I'd served the ship, served that fat-jowled owner, and now—I was to act third mate and, drawing no pay of course, to still live in the half-deck. Oh, well! Being big makes trouble for a fellow sometimes!

The mate said, "Let 'em knock off. Tomorrow we go out."

I went up town alone, too disgusted to want any company, and in a little park that overlooked the sea I saw a girl sitting alone. She was something new in the girl line. About eighteen, maybe. Hair black as the Horn midnight. Rather tall. Slim as a royal mast, and eyes— like Naples Bay in summer time. Her face was—swarthy might be the word. I passed on, and coming round a corner saw two apprentices from the *Duchalburn* sitting with two girls. I sat down by them.

201

"I need a tow boat's line. There's a dandy little clipper sitting all by herself behind that clump of trees. Couldn't you girls rig me up an introduction?" I asked.

The girls laughed and rose. "You stay here a bit, then come along," said one of them.

So I sat down with the *Duchalburn* chaps for a bit; and then we rose and strolled toward the bench where that girl was. In a minute the two girls were introducing us to that black-haired girl, and then they went off with the *Duchalburn* chaps and I was alone with her.

Nell Demotrokopolos, her name was: a Greek, with an Irish mother who was dead. Her father owned and was captain of a vessel in dock not far away. I said, "I've never seen a Grecian ship. I'd like to see one."

"I'll show her to you," answered Nell Demotrokopolos.

"What about your father? Won't he mind my being with you?" I asked.

She replied, "Why, no! Of course not! I've sailed with him ever since my mother died."

Not yet woman, she was, and yet, she was not child. Unsophisticated.

We came to the dock and I had to smile; so little the vessel was after my old Cape Horner. A brig. A small white wooden brig. Two masts. I crossed her gangway, and stepped to her topgallant halliards. I reached up and took a Cape Horner's long slow pull on them, and the topgallant yard started up! I exclaimed, "Good Lord! With two good men to help me I could handle this little packet." It took seven good men to hoist my old girl's topgallants. The brig was like a toy, after my old Cape Horner!

Nell Demotrokopolos was looking at me from wide admiring eyes when the cabin door opened and a man with grey hair and a wrinkled face looked out. Nell said, "There's father." And she took me to him.

"He's mate of one of the big English ships, father. He wanted to see our ship," explained Nell. So Captain Demotrokopolos took me into his saloon and brought out a box of cigars and a bottle of wine. Speaking English brokenly, but well enough for me to understand, he

202

73.   Danish brig MEDOR in the Avon.

asked me how we handled our great clippers. He told me he was from
Corinth.

   "Seex time you haff round zee Cape Horn been, eh?" he said.
And then he spoke of the Levantine seas, and I saw cargoes of currants,
figs, nuts, wines, and cargoes of marble. Names came to me. Corinth,
Chios, Sicily, Jaffa, Cyprus, Crete, and I thought of Ulysses and
Aeneas, of whom I'd read at school. Then Captain Demotrokopolos
continued, "I lose my mate. He an old man vos, and at Geebraltar
was seek. We leave him zere." He looked hard at me, and then he
asked, "Ow would you like to coom miz me, an' be my sheep's mate?"

   I saw Nell's Naples Bay eyes shining, from behind him. My
breath caught. Those Mediterranean peoples are less fussy about a
mate having a ticket. They don't have the strictness of the Northern
countries. Oh, I could handle that job very well! No more ice on the
gear. No more rotten pork and maggoty hard-tack. Why, that little

203

brig smelt of the sunny seas she came from! Smell of currants, figs, nuts, wines.

I replied, "I'll think it over, Captain. And thank you very much."

He said, "Oh, don't tanks! I like ver mooch you coom. My daughter ees half Ireesh. She mees her own peoples."

I said, "I'm half Irish too, sir. I'll let you know soon, Captain."

I thought, "By gad, I'll go fetch my sea chest, and skip the damned old bitch!"

Nell showed me to the deck. At the outer door she asked, "You're coming, aren't you?"

"I think so, maybe," I answered her.

"Oh, please do come!" she urged.

Away I went to my ship. Coal dust, coke dust, cement dust, brick dust. Grime everywhere, from stem to stern. The other apprentices and the mates were ashore. I sat alone on a hatch, and looked up to her towering poles, and along the wide spars whereon so often I had fought the vertigo and the hurricanes. Now—I could be done with all that! Some day Captain Demotrokopolos would die, and then—I'd have that trim little brig!—And, well!—I had a dream of old Troy town. A dream of Trojan Helen.—*Corinth Helen!*—Sure it was that Trojan Helen was no fairer!—Corinth Helen—and cargoes of currants, figs, nuts, wines and marble!

Of a sudden, I heard my father's voice saying, "You'll find it a hard life, my son."

And then I was sitting on Plymouth Hoe, and behind me was Francis Drake with a bowl in his hands; his eyes on the rim of the sea.

"I'll finish my game," said I to myself. And that was that.

CHAPTER XI

GOODBYE, CAPE STIFF

Douglas, who'd been third mate last voyage, had been a little bit of a chap. Hickley, who'd been third mate before Douglas, had been nowhere near my size. They'd both eaten at the saloon table, and shared the second mate's cabin. But they'd neither of them been any more than just fetchers and carriers for the mate. They had been given no responsibility at all. Neither sailors nor apprentices had bothered to address them with a 'sir'. The third mate of a sailing ship was pretty much of a nobody. Being still an apprentice he drew no pay. He was made third mate so that the owner could get an extra apprentice into the half-deck, but here was I, to be third mate and not even eat in the saloon! If ever there was a nobody, I was that nobody.

The second mate appeared. A big man, bigger than myself, he smelt of drink. Black-haired, black-eyed, muscular he was a big bull of a man. The minute he spoke I knew him for a Geordie. A native of the North Sea coast thereabout.

"Wot sort o' bloodie 'ooker is the bitch?" he asked.

Will Clegg could have asked me that when first we met, and I'd have replied, "She's a regular old bitch of a hooker, sir." But, looking Alwyn in the face, I replied, quietly, "When she's handled by the right man she can travel, sir."

"Oi'll 'andle the bloodie bitch," he grunted, and spat, and went off.

Alone, I sat looking at my old girl again. *My* old girl! That was what she was! It came to me now that while that sleek owner in

Liverpool ordered her goings and comings, really she did not belong to him at all. When had *he* ever steered her through a southerly buster in the night's roaring blackness?

The crew came aboard after dark that night. We pulled out early next morning. A grey day. Sea and sky sombre and chill. Five of her crew had failed to show up. So, as we glided past the pier-head, whereon stood a crowd of loafers, Martin called, "Who wants to make a voyage in a good ship? Five good men here!" At that, five of those fellows jumped to her deck. Pier-head jumps we called such men. Often amongst pier-head jumps were rattling good sailors, but those five didn't look like much to me.

The tug boat dropped us as soon as we had the lower topsails set, and what a job it was, getting the upper topsails hoisted! The crew didn't even know how to pull together. There wasn't a chantey-man in the lot of them. Many did not even know the ropes. Never had I seen such a crowd of wasters. There was but one man who was fit to call a sailor; a short stumpy Dane named Pedersen, and he was a stolid sort, not a leader at all.

Martin said to me, "By God, what a hurrah's nest! You'll have to make 'em into sailors!"

Oh well, I thought that maybe it was that the booze wasn't out of them yet. Once they were sobered up, perhaps things would be all right. Yet I knew that Tom Swift or Bloody Quayle, or any real sailor, could loose and hoist sails when roaring drunk.

Getting all sail on her, I pulled my arms out, trying by example to get some life into the mob. I heaved, and hauled, and shouted. No response. Alwyn damned and swore at them, but I noted that he didn't do any pulling his arms out.

Everything seemed wrong. And the old girl had a feel in her as though she herself was aware of that wrongness. A ship knows. Ask any sailor. I thought of the time that Chink, Polly and the rest of our half-deck crowd had handled the old girl when that Liverpool Irish crew had refused duty. What a change!

Somehow the day dragged by, and lordy, how tired I was! A little after dark a squall came along and Martin told me to "Go get the pocket handkerchiefs off her." So I called out the watch and hauled

74.   *COMBERMERE, when under the Italian flag.*

down the jib topsail, jigger topmast staysail, and gaff topsail. "Aloft
and make them fast!" I ordered.   While Pat O'Brien went out to the
boom end to furl the jib topsail I stood on the forecastle head, looking
over the dark sea to where England lay hid.   When Pat came in I still
stayed there a bit, listening to his chatter about the first girl he'd kissed.
It was maybe twenty minutes ere I walked back toward the bridge,
and, looking up, I saw the jigger topmast staysail flapping about.
I could just make out two dim figures struggling with the little sail.
I supposed they were two green apprentices, for a lad who has been a
week at sea should be able to furl that sail in two or three minutes.   So
up I went, to show the green kids how, but when I came to the sail,
good Lord, I found two supposedly able seamen up there.   "Get to
hell down!" I ordered, and furled the sail myself.   When I went back

207

to Martin and told him about it he said, quite calmly, "You've got a nice little job on your hands. You've got to make the swabs into *sailors* before we get to the Horn." And I'll tell you that those words *'The Horn'* sent a shiver down my spine! We'd be down there in the winter and the old girl undermanned! I'd a feeling of foreboding.

Morning came and the old girl was slipping through Dover straits. Dim in thin rain, I saw the high white cliffs. Cold cliffs, cold sky, cold sea. All frowning. I'd no time now to think of Hengist and Horsa; nor later when we passed that place where Norman William landed, of Harold with the arrow in his eye. I was third mate of a Cape Horner, and there wasn't a sailor aboard her, and the second mate was a louse. That feeling of foreboding was heavy upon me. Once I thought of that Greek brig, but I put the thought away.

A homeward-bound clipper came by, and her merry crew climbed to her rigging and gave us three high cheers, but, Lord, that spiritless mob didn't even give her back her cheers. Only Pat and Alphonse cheered her; the green kids raising a sort of feeble shy wail.

I turned and gave one of the mob an order, whereupon he said, "Aye, aye." So then I saw red, and strode up to him. "You'll tack a 'sir' on when you speak to me," I said.

Seeing my clenched fist, the fellow mumbled, "Aye, aye, sir."

Martin, who'd overhead, said to me, "Sail into the bastards, Bill! Make 'em toe the line."

In the half-deck later, Pat O'Brien said to me, "A bum crew, eh, sir?"

"Pat, you damned fool, keep that 'sir' stuff for when we're on deck," I replied.

But when a green kid spoke to me, calling me 'Bill', I said, "It's 'sir' to you."

He blushed and stammered, "I beg your pardon, sir."

I said, "Forget it. Remember next time."

The night was misty, but soon after dawn the mist lifted and— right ahead of the old girl were the black Cornish rocks! There was just time to brace her up and haul her away. "A close shave, by God!" grunted Martin. Once again I had that feeling of foreboding.

We had not been a week at sea when the Old Man reduced five

75. *The Norwegian SIAM. (Having just made sail, the buntlines are not yet over-hauled.)*

of the crew from 'able' to 'ordinary' seamen; cutting their wages from fifty to thirty-five shillings a month. One of the pier-head jumps was lately out of jail for robbery. Another was wanted for cutting a man with a knife. The knifer's name was Andersen. One jump had come across from Norway as cook in a fishing boat. That was all the sea experience he had had. There was a hulking great man named Nicholson, who vowed he was an able seaman and had discharge papers to prove it. He'd stolen them, of course, from some drunken sailor whose name he'd taken. He'd been a pugilist. The other jump was a poor little devil of a negro from Jamaica.

Alwyn was always cursing his watch. I didn't curse my mob, but tried the gentler way. "Look here," I'd say, and show one or other how to do some sailor job. But, Lord, there was no response. There wasn't a pennyworth of pride in the lot of them. Only in that Dane, Pedersen.

We'd been but a little while at sea when Alwyn began to suck up to me, trying to make friends. He came and sat by me on the hatch one evening.

"Wot koind o' bloodie luck d'ye 'ave wi' the girls, Bill?" he asked.

I replied, "I'm wondering what kind of luck we're going to have with this old girl, sir."

"The bloodie owld bitch," he sneered, and went to talking of his last ship and of what a much finer one she was. There was a sort of sliminess in his voice. He came into the half-deck one evening while I was talking to Pat O'Brien. The minute he entered the door I quit talking to Pat and began to talk French with Alphonse. Alphonse caught on, and while we jabbered in French Alwyn stood scowling. He soon went muttering off. From that evening he tried to pick on me, to find fault with the way I did things. I paid no attention until one day, when I came on duty, he strode up to me and shouted, "I ain't afraid o' no bloodie mon, if 'e's as big as the bloodie mainmast!"

I looked him in the eyes and said, "That's good, sir. We'll need all the guts we've got when we get down to the Horn." Pat O'Brien tittered behind me, and Alwyn went off mumbling about a son of a bitch of a bloodie third mate who thought he was somebody.

With a good crew, you carry sail on a ship till the last minute.

You drive her for all she's worth, and when that last minute comes you clew up sail in a rush, and go up and furl it in a rush. But, with the crew we had, we had to take sail off long before the ship was feeling it too much. To have tried to carry on with a crew who were so slow at everything would have been to have risked losing sails and spars.

It was right enough while we were running down the steady trade winds, where you carry full sail all day, day after day. There the old girl overhauled and passed other ships in the usual fashion. I kept Pedersen and Alphonse at work in the rigging; getting things into shape for the wild weather we'd meet by and by. The rest I kept scouring the paint-work, polishing the brass, holy-stoning the deck. They were good for naught else. Always I worked in the rigging myself, working my fastest.

"Alphonse, if you ever want to see a mistress again, by God, do your job right!" I'd say. And the little Frog's eyes would shine as he would answer me:

"Vee sees der sheep through, my vrend!"

And by and by we came out of the tropics, out from the trade winds, into the windy regions of the south. Then the Old Man, seeing other clippers pass us by because we dared not carry sail, was like an ancient bull whale that has been run out of the pod by younger bulls.

John Martin was ever philosophical. I liked him more and more, and on the bridge one night he told me something that tied me to him for good and all. He said, "I'd meant to have taken a good long holiday ashore. I was just in from a Calcutta voyage, and was fed up with the sea. There's a widow in Hull, a grand woman, passionate as they come. Then one day I was taking a stroll along the docks, and I saw this ship of yours. I said to myself, 'By God, she's a beauty! I'd like to go mate of her.' And here I am. The widow gave me hell for chucking her for a ship."

One dawn we saw a rival clipper on our beam. The wind was fresh and the barometer falling, but the Old Man could not bear to let that clipper run away from him. So we kept sail on her, and she ran like the good old girl she was. She felt herself again. You could tell that she did, and after a while I ordered my mob to the braces, to trim the sails a little; that they might better catch and hold each least last

211

breath of that fine bully wind. Seeing them hauling in that spiritless fashion, I got woolly. "Lay back! Lay back and haul! What in hell's the matter with you all?" I shouted.

Then that fellow Andersen let go the rope and drew his knife, and came right for me. I was too quick for him. John Martin came and looked at him, lying bruised in the scuppers. "Make 'em into sailors, Bill!" he said. After that the mob did a little better. There are some men you have to man-handle. It's all they understand, yet, it leaves a sort of nasty feeling in a way. That night again I heard Alwyn muttering about a third mate who thought he was somebody.

It was next day that the steward drew a knife on Martin. He'd spilt some soup in the alleyway outside Martin's cabin door, and left it there, so Martin said, "Get that damned filth cleaned up. What d'ye think this is? A pig pen?" The mate grasped the knife blade only just in time. His palm was badly cut. He said to me, "I'd have killed that yellow-bellied bastard of a Jap if the Old Man hadn't come just when he did."

There was a nasty feeling all about the ship. You never know when you'd get a knife in your ribs in the dark.

In this wise we took the old girl southward, the weather growing colder daily; the sea, the sky, ever more sombre. Alwyn forever cursing his mob, and I still trying to get a little sailor pride into mine. Pat O'Brien and Alphonse, caring not a cuss for anything, were yarning each evening in the half-deck about the Horn to the green kids; and, of course, making the Horn even worse than it was. So there was a little fun after all. Oh, you can always find something to grin about! Yet with me, there was always that feeling of foreboding that I could not be rid of.

There came a night when I was on the bridge with Martin. A bright night with a big round white moon high over the mizzen royal mast-head. You could see every rope and block and ratline. The wind was light. The sea soughed gently. Martin was talking of that widow woman when, glancing aloft, I saw a wisp of cloud no bigger than a handkerchief whip across the moon's orb swift as though fired from a gun. "Take a look at the sky, sir," I suggested. As he looked up another wisp of frayed cloud whipped over the moon's face. There

76. *DUMFRIESS-SHIRE—a three skysailyard, three-island four-master.*

was a sort of faint haze coming in the high sky. So Martin called the Old Man.

"All hands shorten sail!" roared the Old Man. Out came the watches. Alwyn came from his cabin

"Wot's the bloodie owld fool gettin' cold feet about now? 'E's got no bloodie guts, by Goad!" I heard Alwyn say. And, hearing him, some of the men began muttering about an Old Man who'd call all hands on deck to take sail in on such a fine bright night.

There was no fooling that night. Martin came down to the deck. We drove the mob. Carpenter, cook, steward and sailmaker were called, and Alwyn was oddly silent. Before we had the topgallant sails off the old girl, the sprays were driving over her full length in blinding

213

stinging sheets. We took in every sail save the main and mizzen lower topsails. It was round ten o'clock by then. The moon was hidden in a driving haze. There was no roar, no scream, no howl, no yell, to that wind. There was no roar nor thunder to that sea. There was only a long sibilant hiss. The wind was a solid thing, a wall that pushed its way, mercilessly, steady, never varying in pressure.

"Double lashings, Bill!" the mate yelled in my ear. I just could catch the words. I fetched out more gaskets and led the mob aloft, and we put double lashings round each and every sail. I don't know where Alwyn was. I didn't for a time at least. And all that night, despite the double lashings, the sails kept working free. You'd see a tiny scrap of a sail start from beneath its gaskets, and in a minute half the sail would have worked loose—and sails cost lots of money. So up I went, and down I came, and went up again leading the mob. I mind I had to mash my fist into the face of one fellow who hung back, afraid of the mast. You can't spare men in times such as that. I mind that in the moon's wan light I saw one rope that had got loose from its pin on the deck in the fore rigging. The longest rope aboard, the jib topsail halliards. It goes from the rail to the royal mast-head, maybe a hundred and eighty feet from the deck. It's as thick and half as thick again as a large man's thumb, and that rope stood straight out, stiff as a rigid steel rod, stretching upon the air, from the royal mast-head, without a quiver in its length, until its end began to fray. Then in a few moments there was no rope there. It was all frayed away, and maybe blown half across South America.

At some time after midnight I went to look for Alwyn. I hadn't seen him for some time and thought maybe he was gone overboard. I saw a light in his cabin, and there he was; sitting on his settee, his head bowed in his hands, his face hidden. Moaning, I guess; though had a million cowards moaned that night, or bawled their heads off, you'd not have heard a whimper.

Day came at last. It always does, though you may think it never will again. All that day I led the mob and pointed, and shook my fist in faces, and tried like a fool to make my voice heard.

It was about mid-morning when, looking aloft, I saw the windward half of the fore topgallant sail was all worked loose. It was a tight

214

balloon, without flap or shiver. I drove three men up, and followed them, and Alphonse followed me. In the rigging you could not budge at all when the ship lurched to windward or lay still. The wind held you; flattening you to the shrouds. And then she'd give a horrid lifeless lurch to leeward, and you'd dash a little way till, as she came lifelessly to windward again, you were flattened once more. We came to the top-gallant at last and walked out along its footrope. Five of us. Ten fists, and, all beating on the canvas together, we could not make a tiny dent. All the time the yard kept clacking—clacking. I knew the mast must splinter and go, and then I thought of Alphonse beside me. What use letting Alphonse die? I beat my fist on his shoulder. He glanced at me, his wide blue eyes a question. I pointed down to the deck. Only there was no deck. You could not see the ship at all. All you could see was her masts, rising from a white hissing fury. You could not see the sea. There was no sea. All you could see was the whole ocean's surface flying on the air. A hissing haze of tortured spray. Finer than any spray, though. Atomized, the ocean's surface was. There was no sky. There was something low and whitish that went hissing past above your head.

So Alphonse started down, not knowing why I sent him down, and we four pounded bloody knuckles on the sail again. *Clack—clack—clack* the yard went on the mast. At any minute now the mast would go, but I was not afraid. Not one bit. There is a time when you forget all fear. There's no such thing. There's neither fear, nor joy, nor hope, nor thought of any sort. You know you're going to die. That's all.

Then I felt someone at my side whence Alphonse was gone. How long it was that he'd been gone I do not know. John Martin was come up. Our eyes met. His held no expression of any sort at all, and some-how we got that sail gathered up and lashed down, and down we went. All day that wind blew. No man had slept all night, and no man slept all day. No man had eaten. Night came again, and still the old girl lived, and still the same, on, on, and ever on.

Sometime a bit before the dawn the wind ceased. Ceased as though a door had been shut, and sound came back. Why, you could hear a voice again! And you could hear the ship groan as she lurched, with a lifeless, weary lurch. You heard her blocks squeak. Her royal masts, her poles, her trucks were white with salt. From truck to rails she was coated with salt. A grey ship, and the hurricane was done, and you were living! But——

John Martin called the Old Man from the chart room. He looked at the ship. And I knew what he'd say, and so did Martin. The ship was lying like a bird with a broken wing; far over to one side. She'd shifted cargo. Cargo had slipped. It must have slipped just at the last of the hurricane or she would have been gone. Saved by a tick.

The Old Man said, "All hands trim cargo!"

We let them eat hard-tack and swig some coffee down. Then out we herded them. Oh, a bleary-eyed, weary lot! We took the hatch off the sail locker before the foremast. Alwyn appeared. "By Goad, the bloodie bitch!" he growled. Oh, innocent as pie!

We dragged all her spare sails up and under the forecastle head, and so got down to the deck of the sail locker. Then we opened the hatches in that deck. Under them was coke. We shovelled coke into buckets, hoisted the buckets and dumped the coke to the sea. I was at the hoist. No arms so strong as mine. But lordy, was I tired! Well, you forget your tiredness with a ship to save. You shout "Yo—ho!—— Hi—leee-oh!" You shout "Oh, can't you get a move on there!"

I'd see the weary shovellers look up, their faces coky-black, their eye whites showing. They looked like sinners doomed to feed old Satan's fires. "Shovel, my bullies!" John Martin said, and Alwyn shovelled too. *He* wasn't quite so weary. He yelled, "By Goad! Wot t'ell's the bloodie matter? Can't ye bloodie move?"

When they had dug down to the bottom of the coke they came to pig iron. So then they hoisted pig iron, and bore it, pig by pig, two men needed to lift a pig, and weight a-plenty for two men, to the old girl's higher side. Good heavy stuff pig iron is, to straighten a ship up. We shifted pigs all morning. And when we'd let the mob go nibble at some pork and gulp some pea soup down, we put the hatches on at the bottom of the sail locker; then led them to the quarter-deck and opened the after hatch. All afternoon we toiled in murky lantern light, shifting great crates, and moving railroad steel. And talk about tired!

It was at some time far into the night we had the old girl riding on

216

77. *Andrew Weir's ELLISLAND off 'Frisco. The fidded jigger topgallant-mast indicates she was once a full-rigger, (then owned by J. Houston of Liverpool).*

an even keel at last. We put the after hatch on, went forward and dragged her sails back to the sail locker. Then I went to Martin on the bridge. And talk about rejoicing! I did not have a care left. Lordy, but I was gay! For Martin said, "The Old Man's got cold feet, Bill. He's going to take her to Port Stanley and put these swabs ashore and get a new crew to take her round the Horn."

Oh, boys and girls on little Shetland ponies! They never were so carefree and so gay as I was then. Goodbye at last to all forebodings! Port Stanley, in the Falkland islands. Maybe a hundred miles or so in the southeast. A little breeze had risen. The old girl was heading for Port Stanley when I went off duty.

Later I joined John Martin on the bridge again. He didn't speak and I, looking up at the stars—I asked, "My God, sir, what's the joke?" For I could tell that she was heading south.

John Martin answered me, "A fair wind for the Horn, Bill. The Old Man couldn't bear to waste it." At that, my heart was down at the bottom of my sea boots. I was cold ice all over.

John Martin said, "She's a grand woman, Bill, and passionate as they come. By God, she gave me hell for chucking her for a ship!"

Oh, well, when you are face to face with death on a topgallant yard and know your time is come you don't give it a thought. But when you're sailing slowly to your death, when death is coming hourly closer, mile on mile, it's different. You think of things. How will it feel to have the cold old sea close over you? And will you try to swim? And will you struggle much? What will it look like as the ship goes down? How'll Pat O'Brien take it? Will he still have a joke? And will you, maybe, later, float? And will an albatross come and pick out your eyes? You think of girls you've kissed. Who's kissing her now? Some clerk? To hell with clerks! You're a *sailor!* Oh, you think of lots of things!

After I went off duty again I went to look for something in my sea chest. I don't remember what, but there I saw that little package Dolly'd given me when I left Aunt Clarissa's. I'd opened it long since, then dropped and never looked at it again. A little book, in red Morocco leather, with a verse of the Scriptures for each day of the year. The Scriptures, eh? God, and all that sort of thing.

218

They pray to God ashore. The church bells ring. A sailor doesn't pray. He does his job, brings his old girl in, and lets it go at that. And all the bells he hears are ship's bells clanging.

Oh, well, I did pick up the little book. I'd never opened it till now, and now I did. I remember thinking, "I wonder what good such things are to a sailor?" I looked up the day, the date. A winter day, and Cape Horn coming closer hour by hour. And this is what I read,

"When thou goest through the waters, I will be with thee; and through the deep waters, they shall not overflow thee."

Call it coincidence, eh? Oh, well, go on, and call it what you will! Call it, if so you care, an altar, with a snow-white altar cloth. A woman, far away, upon her knees maybe—and praying for a sailor! Aye, call it what you will! I don't know what I called it. I put the little book away, and rolled into my bunk.

There's no explaining some things in this life. The wise ones say there is. They sit and think and figure. They say that two and two make four, and you can't get away from it. Well, two times two does. But I have often thought there's something hid. Something the wise ones never will find out about. You get to think that way when you stand looking at the stars by night, alone, with no land nigh. A sort of star, this world; swinging midst other stars. Who fixed things so?

Oh, well, you don't do too much heavy thinking. You wake, and drag your stiff cold oilskins on, and chew some hard-tack, and swig some bitter coffee. And you say, "By God, *I'm her third mate.* Maybe we'll get the old girl round all right. By God, *we'll try!"* and you grin up your sleeve, maybe, thinking of sunny seas, more fragrant cargoes. Maybe you hear your father say, "You'll find it a hard life, my son."

And then you, maybe, say, *"I'll finish my game!"* You don't say it with too much conceit. Just with a bit of pride, tucked away down in your secret self. *Oh, sailor, sailor, sailor!*

Two nights later I stood with Martin on the bridge. It was dark, but not pitch dark. There were no stars. I could just make out the dim shape of the mizzen mast maybe some twenty feet before me. The wind was on her port quarter, and she was running under topgallant sails at a good clip—maybe at fourteen knots. Running for the Horn! A fair wind! Glory! We'd passed, without seeing it, the corner of

219

Staten Land. The seas rolled high, lifted, and dropped her; cried noisily after her, trying to leap over her railing but not quite able to do so with her running so gaily away from them. With that wind from the east laying its lash on her fearless heel, the old girl was laughing to herself. You could sense the joy in her.

Martin was saying to me, "She's a grand woman, Bill. She's Swedish. Comes from—what the devil's the name of that place?—By gad, the name of the place that widow comes from has slipped me. Wait a bit—I'll get it directly."

Then came a cry from the look-out man on the forecastle head, "Light right ahead, sir!"

The Old Man came from the chart room, and, seeing the light, said "A steamer coming home round the Horn."

I thought—Oh, I didn't *think* exactly, it was too swift for thought —that it was odd for a steamer to be coming home round the Horn, for steamers go through Magellan straits always. Somehow there came on me again that sense of foreboding, and I dropped from the bridge and ran forward and up the forecastle head. I was no sooner there than I was racing back, shouting at the top of my voice, but I need not have shouted, for the Old Man had seen by then what I had seen.

There is, or was in those days, on the east corner of Staten Land, a small lighthouse. Chileans who herded sheep on Staten Land tended it. If their ewes were lambing and they were busy they'd not light it. Only when all was well with their flocks was it lit, and it was a poor feeble sort of light at best, set above the murderous foreshore rocks at the east end of Staten Land. Now the old girl was driving hell for leather, under her bellied topgallants, straight for those night-hid murderous rocks.

"Down helm!—Let go weather braces!—Lower away topgallant sails! All hands on deck!" roared the Old Man.

Martin dropped from the bridge to the quarter-deck and ran, and I ran after him. As the helmsman hove the wheel down*, and brought the ship rushing up toward the wind, and meeting that high wild quartering sea, the seas came crashing over the full length of her railing in a thunderous shoulder-high cataract. Martin, just ahead of me, was

---

*i.e. Old helm orders—wheel up—helm down! [Ed.]

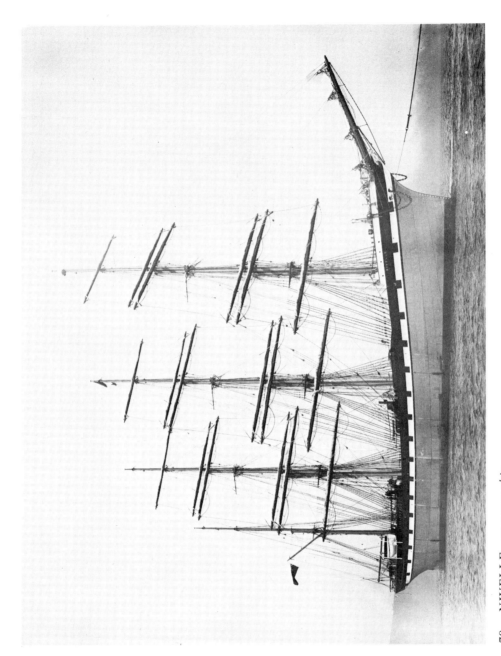

78. *NIVELLE—as a new ship.*

swept from his feet and vanished from my sight, but, grasping a shroud, I held fast till that first crash of water was gone. The second mate's watch were rushing to the deck; their eyes useless as yet because of the lamp light they'd come from. I heard a cry of alarm from Alwyn, and then I was throwing the ropes from their pins, to let the sails swing up. With water tearing at my thighs, I rushed from rope to rope, and Martin, on his feet again, raced too; both of us bawling orders. Added to the thunder of wind and sea, came the sharp running rattle of halliard blocks, and the thresh of the lowered topgallants high in the dark. You could feel the masts straining, feel the tension of the rigging—you could sense the old girl's sudden fear, and then, I saw, down to leeward in the darkness, a long blackness—and, between that blackness and the ship, the ghostly white of the breakers hurling themselves high on the murderous rocks. At the very edge of the breakers, the old girl was. Then I heard young Pat O'Brien's voice, Pat, hauling at the ropes with the crew.

"Alphonse, by God, we'll be taking a walk ashore in a minute," he said, cool as though we were bringing the ship to moorings in port, and I heard a laugh from Alphonse. Oh, there's always laughter where youth is!

Almost immediately, in a minute, all was well; and the old girl was running away from those rock teeth that had waited her swift keel's coming. She must well nigh have scraped the seaweed from those waiting rocks!

Then we hauled her braces tight, and hoisted the gallants again, and that fellow Pedersen sang,

> It's away down south where I was born,
> Oh, roll the cotton down!
> Amongst the fields of yellow yellow corn,
> Oh, roll the cotton down!

The mob was getting to be fair now at rousing a chantey chorus. They were learning the way of a sailor, at last.

The second mate and his watch went below again, and to my mob I called, "All right, boys! Get the ropes coiled!" and I passed here and there amongst them, to see that all was rightly done. Then, with things as they should be, I sauntered into the half-deck. Pat was lighting his pipe. Alphonse, leaning on the edge of his bunk, was looking at the photograph of his mistress, and a little first voyage lad, not yet fifteen, Bryant his name was, was on his knees by his sea chest. Every night since the old girl had pulled out to sea, he had said his prayers by his sea chest. A mother's boy. A nice little kid, and, of course, never once had Pat or Alphonse so much as smiled to see him praying. All the other green kids were sitting on their sea chests, looking a bit breathless; aware that there had been dangers, but unware of what a close squeak it had been.

"Give me a fill of 'baccy, Pat," I said, and as he handed me his 'baccy pouch John Martin's face appeared at an open port hole. Framed by the port, his face was; so that it seemed almost as though he were the picture of a man rather than an actual man. His hair was dripping with water. His cap was gone. He was soaked to the bone, of course. He looked at me, and he said, "Uppsala!—That's it!—I got it, by gad!—She comes from Uppsala!"

In a moment Martin was gone, and little Bryant rose from his knees, to blink a bit at the lamplight shining in his eyes. I set a hand on his shoulder, and said, "Fair wind for the Horn, son! Isn't that dandy, eh?" And he looked up at me, and smiled; thinking, maybe, that Jesus had answered his prayer. When I came on duty at eight next morning, there was the Horn a few miles away in the north. Black old Cape Stiff, staring at the old girl, seeming to say, "So—you come my way again, do you? All right. Watch out!" Snow on the summit of Cape Stiff. Snow on the highlands behind it. Snow everywhere. And the wind was fallen quite away, and the sea was flat. The ship lay erect, motionless, on a cold grey sea beneath a cold grey sky, with a million sea birds round her, resting on the lifeless water, and presently thin snow began to fall, half hiding the Horn. Presently the snow came thicker.

"Goodbye, Cape Stiff! Goodbye!" I said, as the Horn was lost in the snow. Aye—I said, *"Goodbye, Cape Stiff!"*

Ah, sometimes when you say a thing, you do not know just what it is that you are saying, eh?

All morning it snowed, great flakes slow-falling. On into the afternoon the great flakes fell. Not a sound. Not a motion. Just the great flakes falling, and toward evening John Martin said, "Best have 'em shovel the snow off her, Bill. It'll warm their blood." So I called out my mob and they went to shovelling the snow off her. So thick it fell, you could not see her deck's length. After a bit, I missed that big hulking fellow Nicholson, so I called him, and had no answer. Again I called. No answer. And then, in a minute, I found him skulking under the forecastle head. Well, the forecastle head beams were but six feet from the deck, and I was six feet three. He was yet a bit taller than I. So I said, "Come out on deck. I want to speak to you, and there's no room here." He followed me out to the deck, to where the mob was shovelling.

"Why didn't you come when I called you?" I asked.

"I didn't hear you," he answered; lying—and without a 'sir'.

And then I thought, "Somebody's going to get a hell of a licking and it may be me." I clicked my right fist to his jaw. Instantly he was at me, and all the mob quit shovelling to watch.

Well, it was all right. Had we been ashore he could have whipped me, but we were at sea, and I was fighting for my old girl. You have to have discipline if you're to bring a ship safe in.

"Go get a shovel and shovel the snow off her!" I ordered.

"Aye, aye, sir," he replied, and went to work; one of his eyes closed, and his lips bloody.

Dark fell. A long uneasy swell arose, from the westerly. The ship began to roll and to pitch. The snow ceased. Freezing, it was, and as the swell rose higher and higher, she rolled ever more heavily. Presently her bells began to clang. A clang every now and then. *Clang—clang—clang*. And somehow it reminded me of funerals ashore. And again I had that sense of foreboding.

"By God, Bill, we're going to get it, eh?" John Martin said to me.

And I replied, "I guess we are, sir."

So I called out my mob, and went to getting sail off her, and that chap Nicholson was a grand man! He led them all; first man into the rigging, last man down. I could scarce give an order but he was carrying it out almost ere it was given. And it wasn't through any fear of me. It was just that he wanted to show me he was a man. It's queer how you can whip a man and make a friend, eh?

We got it all right. In an hour or two it was yelling from the west, the grey backs were flooding all her length, and we had her stripped down to two lower topsails.

Ten days we were off the pitch of the Horn. The green apprentices were all sea-soaked, of course, from the first day, and all their palms were split. And all their knuckles were bloody. When I'd enter the half-deck they'd look at me as though I were an admiral at least. For the Horn was an old song and dance with me now. My palms were split, my knuckles bloody, and I'd no dry rag anywhere. What of it? Little Bryant would kneel and say his prayers, and Alphonse would talk about his meestrees. Pat would talk about that first girl he'd kissed, and there was a tall lad named Smith whose sea boots were too tight. So he wore bluchers* only, and ever had numb feet. I never once heard him complain, though his eyes were misery if I saw him when he didn't know I was looking at him. Two of the other green lads took things well, with youth's exasperated defiance. They cursed, of course, but what odds? Maybe when Jesus hears a sea-soaked hungry, bloody-knuckled green young sailor cursing, shouting his name in the midnight's dark, he smiles. The fifth green kid was a little pink-faced brat of fifteen. A liar. No one liked him. He'd suck up to the cook, for cabin scraps; and getting some would eat them all himself, hid in some secret place about the deck, instead of in the half-deck fashion of sharing things. He was in my watch, and never could I teach the young lubber anything. He wouldn't try to learn. So sometimes I was hard on him. Then he'd shed tears. A hard job, to handle such a kid you cannot trust, and if you try to trust him, he takes advantage of you. Somehow the young lubber stayed plump always, and kept his rosy cheeks. His name was Bain.

Oh, well, we drove the old girl hither and thither; wearing her round from one tack to the other again and again; sometimes piling the upper topsails on her for a brief while; then having to furl them in a big hurry because of the everlasting murderous wind from the black west. Ice on the rigging. Snow flying. Always the long decks flooded from end to end, and one night that fellow Pedersen got his right hand caught in a brace block and all his fingers mashed. He refused to lay up. With a bloody old rag round his mashed fingers, he stayed on duty.

* Wooden-pegged leather ankle-boots. [Ed.]

He'd go aloft and hang on somehow with his mashed hand, and work with the other. With him and Nicholson to lead them the mob did well enough. Even the little shivering negro from Jamaica, whimpering about how the sun shines there, did his poor best.

"By God, Bill, we'll have a crew yet, eh?" John Martin said to me one day, just as Alwyn went along the deck, and, looking at him, Martin shrugged his shoulders.

There came a day when I joined Martin on the bridge after breakfast. The old girl had six topsails set, and the foresail. Wind and sea were savage. All morning while we stood side by side, watching her fight, Martin never said one word of that widow woman. Trying to battle her way to the westward, the ship was, and she couldn't make it. Steadily, mocking, the wind drove her sideways—crab-fashion. 'Making leeway', we call it when a ship is in that fix. The wind wouldn't let her claw her way ahead at all, despite the six topsails and foresail. So at noon we took in the three upper topsails and the foresail. There was a yet darker darkness in the western sky. The wind was bringing up fresh battalions to mock her. When we had the sail off her, we wore her round; bringing her on to the other tack. It was a few minutes to four o'clock when we were finished that little job. The mate's watch, who should have gone off duty at noon, had missed their rest and their dinner too. Now we went for our dinner. There wasn't any dinner. A grey-back had swamped the galley, flooding the cook's stove. The little Malay cook sat on his coal locker, looking like a frozen tarantula. So we ate hard-tack. Taking the sail off her, and wearing her round, I'd shouted and yelled; trying to keep good heart in the mob. It's what a third mate's for, and was I fagged! Soaked to the hide, of course, just as everyone was, and now, since it was four o'clock, the mate's watch was on duty again. On duty till six. It was getting dark already, so I took up a few of my mob, to see that all was well aloft for the night ahead. I spent the whole two hours aloft. At six I should by rights have been off duty till eight. Two hours' blessed rest! Lordy, I wanted it! But John Martin came to me as the bells struck four bells, six o'clock, and he said, "You'll have to keep the bridge, Bill." I didn't ask him why. I knew. Alwyn was gone to pieces again.

Yes, we were getting close to death once more! The old girl was

226

a few miles to the westward of Hermite Island, which lies a bit west of the Horn, and the mocking wind was driving her down to leeward, toward the rocks of that Hermite Island that have taken so many good ships. So on the bridge I stayed till Martin came back at eight. Side by side we stood. Pitch dark. Dark as the middle of an ink bottle. Now and then the Old Man came from the chart room, stared to the pitchy night, and went back.

None of the mob were allowed to go below that night. We stretched a life-line along the poop, and ordered all hands to the poop. Men and apprentices, carpenter, sailmaker, steward and cook, stood behind the life-line, between it and the taffrail. Too scared to go to his cabin, too scared to stay on deck, Alwyn went moaning here and there about the poop.

An hour passed, and another. The old girl labouring in the mad seas. You could sense her fear. We'd hear the tinkle of her small bell in front of the wheel. We'd catch faint on the wind's roar, the deep *clang—clang—clang* of the great bronze bell upon her forecastle head. Like funeral bells, they were.

In the chart room sat the Old Man and his Old Woman with him. They held one another's hands. Grey-headed, they were. For thirty years they'd sailed the rolling seas together.

"She's going this time, Bill," John Martin said. "The jig is up."

Later, in the pitch darkness, I felt a hand that grasped my hand. I heard John Martin say, "She'll strike at eleven o'clock, Bill. The jig's up. Goodbye! *Good luck, shipmate!*"

And I said, "Good luck, sir! *Goodbye, shipmate!*" Ah, you don't know how much of meaning is in that word *shipmate* if you're not a sailor!

And I could see the chart room clock. *Tick, tick*—tick, tick——

You wonder how it will be, to go down in the utter dark. You'll not be able to see a comrade anywhere. But will you hear their screaming? And will *you* scream? You'll not see the old girl go. There'll be a sudden grinding deep under you. And then you'll feel her drop. You wonder if her masts will go crashing over when she strikes. Maybe a mast will fall upon and crush you. That might be merciful, perhaps. And, if not, how long will it take? You, and your comrades

227

in the utter dark. And, by and by, the day, and maybe killer whales and hungry albatross. Oh, well! *Sailor, sailor, sailor!*

It takes a lot of things to make a sailor, doesn't it? You learn to knot, and splice, and reef, and furl, and steer, and sing the good old 'Maid of Amsterdam', and take a landsman's girl away from him when you go strolling on the shore. Maybe you drink two glasses of shore beer, and you're drunk. Then the lubbers say, *"A drunken sailor,"* and look at you with scorn. Oh, well, you're sorry for them in a sort of way. Even tonight, deep down within, you do not envy them! The sea's the sea. A ship's a ship, and you are part of her, and she of you. The world's a sort of star swinging midst other stars. Who fixed things so? You do not pray. Maybe you shout Lord Jesus' name. Maybe a curse can be a prayer? Who knows?

Tick, tick—tick, tick—— And now it was a quarter to eleven.

And now there came a sudden little rain flurry, and often when it rains you get a shift of wind. So it was now.

Down I ran, and down John Martin ran, and all the mob behind us, to check her topsails in.

"Haul, lads!—Lay back and haul now, bullies!"

And from the weary mob a long-drawn "Yo–ho—ho–hi—lee—oh!"

For ten good minutes the wind blew from that new quarter, a thin rain falling. Then the rain let up, and that mad wind came back like all the demons hooting, but our old girl was safe. She'd needed but a mile or so more sea room. Now she had it.

So then the carpenter, and sailmaker, and steward and cook, and all the second mate's watch went below, and I stayed on the bridge with Martin. He said, "I'm going to marry that widow, if she'll have me; and I think she will. That passion business—well, that's quite all right. It ain't the whole works though, Bill. My God, we're human, ain't we?"

Midnight came, and then, as though frustrated, its venom spent, the mad wind fell. A new wind wakened. A waft from out the south. And we put sail on her. While setting the main upper topsail, that fellow with crushed fingers sang; hauling with one good hand:

228

> *So all you young sailors, take heed what I say,*
> > *Way, aye, blow the man down!*
> *Don't ever take heed of what pretty girls say,*
> > *Oh, give us some time to blow the man down.*

Because of ice on the gear, the topsail went up slowly. So to hoist the mizzen upper topsail we took the halliards to the quarter-deck capstan, and *tramp, tramp, tramp,* went the feet of all the weary mob. And *clank, clank, clank* went the capstan pawls. Falling from the frozen topsail, ice clittered on the deck, and Pat O'Brien sang,

> *Oh, who's been here since I've been gone?*
> *A Cape Horn sailor with his sea boots on!*
> > *Oh wake her! Shake her!*
> *Wake that girl with the blue dress on!*

And some man laughed, and then a ripple of laughter ran from man to man till all that weary mob was laughing in the pitchy dark. We toiled till almost two o'clock, piling the sail on her, our tired feet slipping on the rolling icy deck. Nicholson sang, and the sail flapped, and the sea lapped, and the blocks creaked, all in tune with his song,

> *The boys and the girls went a huckleberry hunting.*

And the little negro asked, "Wot's dem huckleberries?" And he added, "Boy, de sugar cane grow in Jamaica!"

As we gave her sail on sail, the old girl gathered speed, and when, at last, the mate's watch went below she had the bit in her teeth. "Fair wind for 'Frisco, bullies!" someone cried.

We'd beat Cape Horn once more. And turning into my bunk, I thought, "Next time I come this way I'll be second mate." But I'd not stay in the old ship. Not now, with Paddy gone. I'd find another ship to serve. And then sleep took me.

W.M. BIRCHALL.
1932

79. *COUNTY OF LINLITHGOW.*

CHAPTER XII

HERE GOES NOTHING

So the old girl started to climb the long hill from the Horn to the line once more, and she went away prancing. But she didn't prance for long, for the wind fell flat and we were becalmed again. All one long day she lay becalmed, east of the Horn. To have seen that flat dark sea, that unbroken dark sky, you'd have thought that so it was that things always had been. A picture of stillness, made by a god who, having made it, had said, "Ha! You can't beat that!" And the Old Man was dour-faced as the grandfather of all big and little crabs. Did he speak 'twas a bull terrier growling. Alwyn muttered about the bloodie owld bitch being an unlucky owld bitch. You'd have thought 'twas he had brought her round the Horn, with no hand to help him. But John Martin was just John Martin, unperturbed. He talked to me of his last voyage, mate of the *County of Linlithgow*. Racing she was, with the *Cromartyshire*, across the western ocean; the two of them going like stags through fog thick as the dirt on a tramp's toe nails. He said, "And a blasted good thing it was that the *Cromartyshire* was a few miles ahead of us, by gad, or maybe I'd never have met that widow from Uppsala, nor been mate of this barky of yours, Bill." Maybe you mind what happened? How the *Cromartyshire*, running like a frightened deer from the highlands of her Scotland, cut full into the French liner, *La Bourgogne*? Over two hundred people drowned, and most of them passengers; because the Frog sailors lost their heads. Maybe it's not for a sailing ship man to judge steamer people, be they foreigners or not. But the thing looked bad; seamen beating passengers from the boats with oars. After that Martin went to telling

231

80. *CROMARTYSHIRE towing down the Avon.*

81. s.s. *LA BOURGOGNE.*

me of his voyage before that one, mate of the *County of Roxburgh*. "By gad, we'd a crew of lice and 'twas make 'em into sailors somehow! So I was fined fifteen pounds by a blasted old judge in a woolly wig who said I was a brute in human guise; beating poor sailors. Before a man's allowed to be a judge where seafaring men are concerned, by gad, he ought to have to make a few voyages in a square rigger. To hell with the landsmen!" Then he looked away to the westward, and looked back at me with a wink. For the Old Man was looking westward too, and chewing his under lip. Two miles away lay the *Illawarra*, and, just beyond her our sister ship, the *Matterhorn*. Both 'Frisco-bound, they were. And did the new wind come out of the west, they'd get it before we did.

Night came, black as the Pope's best Sunday hat, and all we could see was the winking green sidelight of the *Illawarra*, and a faint far glimmer now and then of the *Matterhorn's*. But at a quarter to nine I woke. I mind looking at my watch, hung above my pillow. The chain sheets were clattering on the masts, and there was a flapping of canvas, and Alwyn was bellowing like a steer that smells blood on the butcher's pole axe. Knowing that a southerly buster was on her, I tumbled out and roused Alphonse and the two green kids. In a jiffy it was *"All hands shorten sail!"* By the time we hopped out to the deck the wind had her, and she was off for the north; going like all glory. I went to the wheel, anxious to see if the man at it was a fit man to be handling her in a buster, but he was not. So, taking the wheel over from him, I said, "Send Nicholson here and be damned quick about it!" But either he forgot or had the wits scared out of him, for no one came and there I was. It was just nine o'clock. The hands were clewing up the mainsail and cross-jack, in a big hurry, and the buster was yelling at her heels like all the demons out of hell. It wasn't long till I knew I must have a hand at the lee wheel to help me handle the old girl. I shouted, and the wind laughed at me. Sea and wind said to one another, "That young fool think's she's *his* ship. We'll show him something."

Well, I'd steered her maybe two hours when the binnacle light went out; the little oil light that, set in a sort of cup at the compass edge, gives the helmsman light to steer by. Pitch dark it was, and all the devils out of hell riding on the wind and laughing their fool heads off;

mocking a man at the wheel, left with no light to steer by. Well, what do you do in a case such as that? It takes a lot of tricks to make a *sailor*. There's but one thing you can do. You keep the wind blowing right square on the back of your neck. It's a good plan to take off your sou'wester. I did so. Snowing, it was, but what odds? And the old girl tore at me, bewitched by those bastardly wind demons. I strained, using every last ounce of the strength that fighting the sea through nigh four years had given me, "Steady you old bitch! Damn you, now, steady!" I'd say to her. Did she once begin to veer too far to one side of her course for the northward it'd be Davy Jones' locker for her. More bones for Davy Jones and his old Mother Carey to pick, down in their cave at the sea bottom. I shouted and I yelled, wanting a man at the lee wheel. Wind and sea jeered to hear me. So I quit my noise. "Save your breath, you damned fool!" I said.

After a bit, I was aware of someone beside me in the darkness. And I heard *"My God!"* The Old Man, it was, come to see who was holding her. And he could see neither me nor the compass. So, in a minute, he was back from the chart room, with the binnacle light lit. He set it in its place, and its glimmer shone on my face. "Can you hold her, boy?" he bawled.

And I bawled back, *"Yes, sir!"*

There's a thing called pride, and there's a thing called love that goes with it. And when you've been nigh four years in a ship, if you don't have them for her—then God help you! *Oh, sailor, sailor, sailor!*

So the Old Man went off, leaving me there, alone I stood; bare-headed, because the wind had long ago carried my sou-wester overboard and, lean though I was, there was sweat on my face. "Pull, you old bitch! You don't get away from me, damn you!" I muttered.

Two hours is a man's trick at the wheel, and I should have been relieved at ten o'clock. But when all hands are busy getting sail in, you leave the helmsman where he is till the job's done. Of course I knew that Martin would be leaving it to me to see that her wheel was being cared for by one of the best of the crew. Martin was aloft, with the mob.

Well, it was three hours and three-quarters that I held the old girl.

82. *COUNTY OF ROXBURGH.* (*Note her spencers.*)

Not till a quarter past midnight did Nicholson come to take the wheel over, and with him came another man, to take the lee wheel. Taking the wheel from me, Nicholson did a thing that a foremast sailor doesn't do to an officer. He took what would have been a liberty, had it been a liberty. He whanged a big hand on my shoulder and I heard him shout, *"By Jesus!"* Weary as I was, that whang almost knocked me down, despite the good nature of it. I tottered away from her wheel, and bumped into Martin. Alwyn and his watch were gone below, all being well now; the ship running under six topsails and foresail. Till four of the morning, I stood there with Martin on the old girls bridge. Not to this day does he know that I was three and three-quarter hours fighting all the devils out of hell to keep the old girl from Davy Jones. Not a thing could we see of the *Illawarra's* light, nor of the *Matterhorn's*. Later, when we came to port, we heard about them. Both ships lost a full suit of sail when that buster struck them, and *they* were said to have good crews. Whilst we, with that mob of wastrels we'd left port with—we never lost a stitch. We'd made 'em into sailors. By a week we beat the *Illawarra* to 'Frisco, and the *Matterhorn* by ten days; because they both had to heave-to and ride the buster out.

The buster died after some thirty-six hours and a stiff breeze came from a bit west of north. Once again the Old Man was dour as the grand-daddy of all the crabs. He'd been counting on getting a wind from west or south-west and, having run the old girl due north before she was much west of the Horn, he'd got her too close to the coast of Chile. He'd taken a chance and the cards had fallen wrong way up. We were on a lee shore. And when, black as thunder at taking her so far off her course, he decided to sail off to the south-west to get clear of Chile, the wind shifted and came from due west. So there she was, unable to go south-west. In irons. Three days we lay there, tacking ship every few hours; night and day. And by day we'd see, coming ever closer, the coast of Chile, barren and desolate. Let a gale blow up, and we'd be done for for sure. And John Martin said, "Bill, if I'd married that widow I'd not be in this damned fix. But what's a sailor to do when he falls head over flipper in love with a ship, eh?"

All the while, Alwyn went about the decks, mumbling, "There's bloodie cannibals on that there bloodie coast."

236

83. ILLAWARRA.

Little Bryant said his prayers to Jesus, and the green kids looked sort of glum. And Pat O'Brien said, "There must be a Jonah in the damned ship."

Alphonse asked me, "You beleefs in zee Jonah beesness, Beell?"

I replied, "By God, I don't know. It certainly looks damned funny."

Then Pat asked, "Where's that fat little bastard Bain?" So he and Alphonse went on deck to look for that pink-faced brat; and found him sitting in the lee of the deck-house eating a cold baked potato the cook had given him. I'd something to see to just then, and went about it, but in a few minutes I came to the half-deck again; and they had Bain face down on his sea chest. They had pulled down his pants, so that his fat little white bottom was bare, and were spanking his fat little white bottom with a piece of board dipped in tar, while he was blubbering like a little girl who's had her dolly stolen. I said, "Give

237

the young son of a bitch one for me too!" and Pat, and the Frog, and each of the green kids but little Bryant, larruped the little devil's bare white bottom, and each of them gave him an extra one for me. Then they made him pull up his pants, and buckle his belt, on top of the tar.

By gad, it worked! I'm not superstitious. I never was. But how do you explain it that inside a half-hour the wind hauled round and came out of the south-west; so that the old girl took the bit in her teeth, and ran away laughing? Queer things happen at sea. Ask any sailor.

Soon we were running up the south-east trade wind, with all sail on her; the ship lying down till her lee rail scooped blue water, day after day, night after night. I mind a night when, from horizon to horizon, all the ocean was a sheer flame of phosphorus. A dark night. Overhead, in a sky of dim indigo, the big and little lanterns of the swinging stars. All about her, pale green phosphorescent fire. Why, you could see her royals even, faint-lit by the sea flame. On her deck you could have read a book, had its print been of fair size. The wind thrummed in her rigging, and the sea soughed, and she rolled easily; and pitched like a horse cantering home to the stable with a feed of oats waiting in the manger. And I heard my father's words, "You'll find it a hard life, my son."

I replied to his spirit, "Hard it was at first, father: but this night pays for all." And I'd not have changed places with all the nabobs of the east, with their rubies, emeralds, pearls, and so forth. Pat and Alphonse and I stood by her rail, and gazed at the night. And Smith came out, and two other of the green kids. But not that little fat boy with the white bottom. Nor little Bryant, till Pat looked into the half-deck and said, half mocking, "Bryant, come look at the stars Jesus hung in the sky." He came out then, and he stared at our sky, and he took off his cap.

"Pretty swell to be a sailor, eh, kid?" I asked him.

He looked up at me and smiled and, by gad, I had to take off my cap, too. Who knows about it all? There's pride, and there's love— and there's the thing called reverence, and it's the greater part of them both. You'll find it in the faces of the roughest old world-wanderers. Wanderers, and wonderers too, they are. You do not know just what it is that makes you feel that way. You only know there's *something*.

238

It isn't only where the robed priests chant, and censers sway, and gentle women kneel and pray, and sweet bells ring, that God, or whoever it may be that set the swinging stars above our rolling sea, sees altars. Why, He can see an altar in a whore-house, sometimes, I think.

So we began to get the old girl into trim for port once more, smoothing the paint on, laying on the varnish. Making her brasswork shine till you could see a sailor's face in it. We came up to the line, and lay there on a windless day; a great, slow, long, high-sided swell swinging under her so that she rolled and pitched like an old washer-woman who's given birth to fourteen kids, and swilled down too much ale on Saturday night in the corner public-house. And that day I said to myself, "It's time the trucks were gilded."

I fetched out that same little pot that Will Clegg had given me a year or so ago, and into it put some gilt paint. And up I went, with a brush tied to my wrist. Clinging to the poles, one after another, I grinned at the thought of how I used to have that vertigo. *Oh, sailor, sailor, sailor!*

When I came down from the last mast, from the jigger, the Old Man was on the poop. He looked at me from his sharky grey eyes, and said, "What are *you* gilding the trucks for, eh? Why don't ye send up one of the hands? What d'ye think an officer's for, eh?" And I said devil a word.

Eldest apprentice. Third mate. Cock of the walk! I'd soon be a second mate now. Then soon, again, I'd be mate. And—ah—wait! Just wait a bit, eh! Oh, yes!—There'd come a day when little green apprentices, and elder ones, and wrinkled foremast sailors, would speak of me as the Old Man! I'd be skipper of the smartest clipper on the whole wide sea. If she wasn't smartest when I took command of her, then, by God, I'd make her so! You'll let a sailor have his bit of pride, eh? And will not judge his pride to be conceit?

Yet perhaps, at that, maybe I *was* a little cocky! It's natural, isn't it? When you are nigh to twenty-two, and all your life's before you?

There was no bickering now with any of the crew. She was a happy ship. At evening, in the dogwatch, sailors and apprentices gathered on the hatch and sang, and danced, and wrestled; and took their simple

239

sailor joys, and no one thought how Andersen had once been in a jail; nor how he'd tried to knife me. They called as I passed by one evening, asking me to come join them, and show them what a *sailor* was. So man by man I tried my strength against them. When we were done, Pat said to me, "By God, Bill, you *are* a beefy chap!" There wasn't anyone could come near handling me.

Next morning, just ere five o'clock, I said to that young fat pink-cheeked kid, "Go get the coffee." He came back with none.

"Where's the coffee?" I asked.

And that kid said, "The cook says you're a stuck up son of a bitch. The coffee isn't ready."

So I strolled out and went to the galley. The dinky Malay cook was there alone. I stepped in and took him gently by the throat. I said, shaking him not too roughly, "Doctor, you want to behave yourself." You call a ship's cook 'doctor'. And then I let him go, and instantly, before I knew what he was up to, his arms were round me underneath my armpits. His legs were tight-clasped round my hips. His teeth were fixed on my left breast. Tarantula!

There was no room with him so close to me. I just drew back my fist and tapped him on the forehead. He fell, spread-eagled on the galley deck. So then I turned to go; to step over the high door coaming. A coaming's what you'd call a sill ashore maybe. It keeps the water out. Two feet high perhaps. And, as I lifted a foot I heard a sort of sound behind me. And out of a quick eye corner I saw a hand up-lifted, with, tight-clutched and just above my skull, a broad meat cleaver. In his other hand he held a long bright butcher knife! And *did* I hop out to the deck, and turn and run! The cleaver whizzed past my head, hit on her trail and clattered to the deck. Then he was at my heels, that knife in his hand. A big full moon shone bright in the dim dawning's pearly sky. Not moonlight, yet not daylight.

Round the mizzen mast is a railing called the fife rail. Ropes from the mast come down and are made fast to it. It's maybe four feet from the mast. I came to it, and round and round I ran; that spider at my heels, while I heard John Martin on the bridge above, cackling like a whole coop of roosters. "Oh, ha, ha, ha! Oh, hee, hee, hee!" Well, maybe it did look funny. It didn't feel it. Me six foot three, and naught

240

84. *TAMAR.*

but bone and muscle. The doctor nearer three foot six and naught but
skin and bone. I ran away at last, along the deck, and he ran after me.
Then, suddenly, I dropped upon my hands and knees, all in a tick.
He catapulted over me. He lay, face down upon the deck as I leapt up.
The knife had fallen from his yellow claws and I picked it up. He rose
and faced me, hate in his yellow face, murder in his black eyes, while I
heard all the sailors laughing, and the apprentices.

   "Here's your knife, doctor," said I, and holding the blade's end
held the handle toward him. He gave a sort of start. "Sungofabish!"
he muttered, and took the knife, and went into his galley. Then I saw
that little fat white-bottomed boy. He wore a displeased look and then
I knew! The little lubber never had been to the galley. He'd just
invented the whole thing. I was quite shivery.

John Martin called me to the bridge. "Why didn't you half kill that yellow-bellied little bastard, Bill?" he asked, and then he started that cackling again; and shook and shivered with his damned merriment.

I said, "I hope, by gad, your widow's married to a grocer when you get back home, and that she's eight months gone." He only laughed the more.

That sort of thing is just what happens when you get a bit too cocky, and like as not it takes some little swab like that young kid to do it to you. All day the whole crew grinned, unless I happened to be looking at them, while Alwyn wore a most delighted look. "Scared of a yellow bastard," I once heard him mutter.

The trade wind falling ever lighter as we neared the line, we rambled up the South Pacific. Then came a day the trade wind left us. That day was windless and still. Infinite blue above and beneath, and now and again a black doldrum squall coming up from the glassy horizon to pass over the sky with its puff of wind and torrent of rain. Sooner or later one would come our way, and then another; and after a while we'd be borne into the steady north-east trade wind and go on our way again. The crew were holy-stoning the quarter-deck; all but Pedersen, who was painting the old girl's name fresh on the poop lifebuoys. He had them down under the break of the poop, lest a shower come.

The mate's watch went off duty at noon and Alwyn sent one of his men to do the last buoy. When I came back on deck at four o'clock I took a look at that buoy. Very particular the Old Man was, about having the lifebuoys neatly painted. The ship's name on the upper half circle, Liverpool at the lower, the red ensign to the right, and the company's house flag to the left. And the fellow who'd done the painting had done a bosh job. I called Martin to look at it. He said, "Have Pedersen get some oil and clean all that blasted mess off. He'll have just time enough to do a good job before dark."

But instead of calling Pedersen I thought I'd do it myself. Just as I was starting to clean off the mess Alwyn came from his cabin close by. He saw me at once, and he bawled, "Now wot's the bloodie matter? By Goad, look after yer own bloodie work an' oi'll look after moine!"

242

So, wanting no trouble, I rose to my feet. Silent. And then he bawled, "By Goad, I ain't afraid o' no bloodie mon, not if 'ee's as big as the bloodie mainmast!"

I had to laugh. I couldn't help it. Then his rage got the best of him, and he strode toward me; with a fist uplifted; knowing well that an apprentice could not strike an officer unless the officer first struck him. Knowing that the first blow would be his. Strong as a bull he was, in muscle.

At that moment John Martin appeared, at my side, and said quite calmly, "What's all the fuss about, Mr. Alwyn?"

That was when Alwyn made the mistake of his life. "You, blast you! You an' yer Goad-domned pet apprentice bastard!" he bawled.

Martin was plump, and soft-looking, with a very white skin. I'd seen him naked once, and there wasn't a hair on all his body, but never till now had I had any idea of how agile he could be. In less than an eye flick he stepped forward and, with a flat hand, struck Alwyn on his face. Smack. The men stopped their holy-stoning, rose to their knees, while Alwyn, like the poor ass he was, supposing that to smack with a flat hand was all Martin knew of fighting, aimed a savage blow at Martin's face. It didn't reach Martin's face. There was the quick click of a fist upon bone, and then another. Alwyn was beaten to his knees.

Looking up at the mate, Alwyn said, "Wot's all the bloodie fuss about, sir? I ain't a-lookin' fer no trouble.

And Martin said, "Get up, you dirty dog!"

With a hang-dog look in his eyes, and blood on his chin, Alwyn rose. And then again there was the quick click of a fist upon bone, and he was down again. And then he started to bawl, "Captain—Captain!"

The Old Man looked down from the poop rail just above.

"Get up!" said Martin again. Thinking that the Old Man would protect him, Alwyn rose, and then John Martin went to work on him in earnest; and drove him backward, till the cabin bulkhead was behind him so that he wouldn't fall, and rained blows on his face till his face was a sight to see.

Bawling like a stuck hog, Alwyn broke away, and started to run.

243

But the mate grasped his collar, from behind, and held him.

"You're too damned dirty to hit. You're only fit for kicking," said the mate, and began booting him.

Alwyn's watch, men and apprentices, had come running to the deck. The cook, the steward, the carpenter and sailmaker, all were come to look on, and then John Martin swung Alwyn round, facing him; and stepped back a little, and took one long strong Cape Horner's drive full at his jaw. Down he went, and lay still. Then Martin called to one of the crew, "Bring your bucket here! I've got to wash the slime off my knuckles." Cool as though he were washing out a handkerchief, he washed his hands. Having washed them, he picked up the bucket and slapped its contents into Alwyn's face. Then he looked up at the Old Man.

"I guess the third mate will have to take the second mate's watch for a time, sir," said Martin, and, without having spoken a word, the Old Man strolled off into the chart room.

Martin went to his cabin, and the men to their work; I to cleaning off the lifebuoy. And presently Alwyn climbed unsteadily to his feet and tottered into his cabin; his hands outstretched before him, feeling his way, because his eyes were both bunged up.

There was a pleasant, restful, clean sort of feeling about the ship when quitting time came that evening. All hands gathered on the hatch, and you should have heard them sing! Windless and still it was, and the sails all hanging flat from their spars. Voices rang clear. Presently that big chap Nicholson, standing out on the deck, where he could be seen by the Old Man and Martin and myself on the poop, sang, as though for our benefit, the old song about the ram of Derby:

> *As I was going to Derby, all on a market day,*
> *I met the finest ram, sir, that ever was fed on hay.*
> *Dinkey, dinkey, Derbyshire, dinkey, dinkey day!*
> *It was the finest ram, sir, that ever was fed on hay!*
>
> *That ram he did get drunk, sir, as drunk as drunk could be,*
> *And when he sobered up, sir, he was far away at sea!*
> *Dinkey, dinkey, Derbyshire, dinkey, dinkey day!*
> *It was the finest ram, sir, that ever was fed on hay!*

244

The butcher who killed that ram, sir, was up to his knees in blood,
And the boy who told the tale, sir, was carried away in the flood.
Dinkey, dinkey, Derbyshire, dinkey, dinkey day!
It was the finest ram, sir, that ever was fed on hay!

And then all hands hooted with laughter, and bent themselves double, and whanged one another on the back. And after a bit Nicholson cried, "Hold on, boys! Let's finish the song!" And he sang:

The crew of the Silberhorn, sir, are handsome, strong and brave,
The smartest lot of sailors that ever sailed over the wave.

The Old Man grinned and went into the chart room. Turning to me, Martin said, "They're a damned good lot of lads, Bill! By God, who'd ever have thought it that morning we pulled out to sea, eh?"

Presently the Old Man looked from the chart room, and called to the mate, "Tell those five men I disrated to come aft here, mister."

Along to the chart room came Nicholson, Andersen, the little Negro, and the two others who'd been disrated, and, by gad, the Old Man straightened it all out for them. "You'll get able seamen's wages from the day she sailed," he told them.

When the five men were gone merrily forward, John Martin said to me, "It's hell to be third mate, ain't it, Bill? You made those fellows into sailors and you don't get a damned penny at all."

As I looked along the old girl's white decks, I replied, "I don't give a tinker's damn, sir." For there's that thing called pride, and it has nothing at all to do with the damned dollars.

From eight to midnight I took the second mate's watch, the old girl in my care. Windless and still. Nothing to do but look at the stars, and think. Again at four in the morning I took charge of her. No wind. But toward five, just when I was about to call that fat kid to fetch me my coffee, I saw a doldrum squall coming. It struck her fair and away she went; her lee rail down to the sea. But it soon died away again, and, maybe a mile to windward, clear in the dawn's pearly light, was a north-bound clipper that it had brought up from under the rim of the sea. I fetched the telescope and read her name. A tall four-mast barque, and a flyer. The *Falls of Clyde*. I'd heard of that packet.

During the middle watch Martin had taken the royals off the ship. The *Falls of Clyde* had her royals furled too. I thought of Willie Clegg,

245

85. *FALLS OF CLYDE off Tampico.*

and knowing well what he would do were he in my shoes, I called Pat
and Alphonse and that tall first voyager Smith. "Hop up and loose the
royals!" I told them.

When I called the men out, I said, "Don't chantey the royals up.
If you hoist 'em with short chantey pulls they'll blow away in that new
squall that's coming. Grab the halliards and run 'em up quick!" As
Pat, Alphonse, and Smith went scuttering aloft I saw chaps going aloft
on the *Falls of Clyde* to loose her royals.

"All ready on the main," Pat called down in a minute.

"Walk her up, sons!" I shouted, and grabbed the halliards and
laid my weight on them. My lads grabbed them, and laid their weight
on them. In half a tick the main royal was set. Then, looking at the
Falls of Clyde, I grinned; for her chaps had tried chanteying her main
royal up and the sail was split from head to foot.

I got our three royals set all right, but the *Falls of Clyde* lost her
fore royal as well as her main, and you can't set a royal on the mizzen

246

only. Oh, we began to fairly walk away from her! The squall whooped harder and harder and my old girl lay over till you'd have thought she was going to capsize. I was half afraid one of her royal masts would splinter and come down in wreck. But I said, "Stand it, lady! What you can't carry you can damn well drag!"

Then I heard the Old Man's whistle shrill, and ran to the speaking tube. "What in God's name are you trying to do with the ship?" he called up the tube.

And, grinning up my sleeve, I replied, "Maybe you'd best come have a look, sir!"

So up the old boy came, in his pyjamas and carpet slippers; and the jiffy he stepped from the chart room and saw the old girl he shouted, "Get those royals off her! Look alive! My God!"

But I, pointing away to the *Falls of Clyde*, said, "She was abeam of us when I set the royals, sir."

And then old mister Shark Eye, seeing the *Falls of Clyde* for the first time, growled, "Leave the royals stand." So the old girl drove on, hell for leather, every sheet and halliard groaning; and things almost at the breaking strain, but not quite. And the *Falls of Clyde* dropped farther astern every moment. I could see some of her chaps aloft, sending her split royals down.

Those doldrum squalls never blow for long, and soon the wind eased away, and the clouds cleared, and the rain let up—and there we were, dancing along on a bright blue sea under a bright blue sky, the white caps gleaming from horizon to horizon in a steady north-east trade wind; and the *Falls of Clyde* almost hull down astern.

After a while, old mister Shark Eye looked at me, and asked, with a sort of veiled sneer on his sandpapery tongue, "You think you're pretty smart, sailor, don't you, eh?"

I looked Shark Eye full in his face, and replied, "Sir, I've served nearly four years in the smartest clipper out of Liverpool, under the smartest skipper ever came out of Windsor, Nova Scotia—they call them Blue Noses, sir, and no offence meant—and if I'm not a sailor, by God, I'd best jump over the side and say *'Here goes nobody'*."

Shark Eye sort of started when I said "They call them Blue Noses". Then there came to his leathery face the merest little suggestion of a

247

sort of red tinge, and then there came to his thin lips the merest suggestion of a little sort of grin. Without another word, he strode off, into the chart room, and below. I sang out, "Wash the decks down! Step along!"

For my part, I could almost feel Willie Clegg's hand on my shoulder and see his smile; and hear him saying, "That's the way, shipmate!" *Oh, sailor, sailor, sailor!*

For four days I had charge of the second mate's watch, living in the half-deck, eating the same old grub, and drawing devil a cent of any wages. Oh, well, what's wages? And then Alwyn came back to duty.

CHAPTER XIII

THREE CHEERS FOR THE HOMEWARD BOUND

Once more we shone the old girl up and made her sparkle. Brasswork and varnish all a-glitter. Rigging, well rubbed with tar and varnish, all a-glitter. Paint all bright. Nowhere a speck of rust or dirt on all her pretty length, and not one of those chaps who'd jumped aboard from Tyne Dock pier-head but had pride in his face. "Allee same heap pletty!" said the steward. That little Malay cook, looking from his galley door, nodded his head approvingly. And I said to Pat and Alphonse, "Well, you young beggars, she'll be yours next voyage. I hope you treat her well."

"You lucky devil, Bill! Out of your time now soon. By God, I envy you!" retorted Pat.

I looked back along the long four years since that night I'd sat in the Sailor's Home, and thought of Glynn and Wood. I heard Glynn say, "Don't go to sea. The sea's hell," and I smiled. I thought of Paddy, white bones deep down under. I gave Will Clegg a thought. "Tough luck, shipmate!" said I.

Simultaneously I thought, "The damned sea can't break me. She tried, and I fooled her. I'm too damned tough, by God!"

So one day we saw the land, the harbour heads. The Old Man was below, and I said to John Martin, "It's my last voyage in this packet, sir. I'd like to take her in looking her very best."

"Well, what d'ye want, by gad! Look at her! Ye can't do a thing more," replied Martin.

So I told him what I wanted to do, and he said, "Hop to it!"

249

I went to the flag locker and brought out the flags I fain would dress her in and with my own hands I hoisted them. At her gilded fore truck the long pennant, crimson-bordered, with on it her name in golden letters. At her main truck the prettiest house flag on all the wide sea. A snow-white flag with a pale blue border, and in the centre of the white a five-pointed blue star. I hoisted her great silk ensign, and at her lofty peak I flew her numbers; the four flags that represented her name in the Code book. J.H.L.N. her numbers were.

Thus my old girl sailed in, the air fragrant between the sunny harbour heads. I mind that a tiny humming-bird came hovering about her numbers, thinking them to be flowers because of their gay colouring.

As we went sweeping in with every wide wing wind-filled, we met a homeward-bounder going out to sea. And all our chaps climbed into the rigging, and Nicholson cried,

"Three cheers for the homeward bound!"

From headland to headland our cheering rang, and she gave us three cheers back. Then we gave her one cheer more, in the customary fashion.

We lowered her sails and let her anchor go. I mind the full-rigger *Sardomene* lay at anchor close by, all her people gathered on her rail to watch my old girl. Near us too lay the barque *Corunna*. Oh, there were many ships in 'Frisco bay that day, but none like the *Silberhorn*. It was early December. In February my apprenticeship would be up, and I'd be free. But despite my gladness there was on me something of a feeling of shadow; a gloom that I could not shake off for a while.

I thought, "If she's away to sea again before my time is up, by gad, the Old Man's got another guess coming if he thinks I'm going to act third mate and eat in the half-deck still. If I'm to be third mate, by gad, he'll feed me in the saloon. I'll live on in the half-deck, not with that swine Alwyn, but it's in the cabin I'll eat." After that I shook off my queer shadowy feeling of sadness.

Oh, yes! Once free I'd be able to lay down a bit of law to the Old Man. Cock of the walk I was.

Next day we docked her, and all we apprentices strolled ashore together but that pink-cheeked young lubber. We came to the corner

250

86.   *SARDOMENE.*

87.   *CORUNNA.*

of Pacific Street, and heard the pianos on the Barbary Coast. Alphonse said, "Let's go see zee girls!" And Pat O'Brien paused, half shy and half eager.

But I said, "Oh, cheese the girls! Let's go to the Institute." So we did, and that same lady was there, and the chaplain.

The chaplain said to me, aside, "You've got some youngsters in the ship this voyage, Bill. You'll do the right thing by them while you're in port, I hope. Where's your old chum Paddy?"

"Deep down, sir, in the South Atlantic. Lost overboard," I replied.

"In the midst of life we are in death," said he, and added, "There are only seven of you. Where's the eighth?"

Laughing, I replied, "Oh, he's a young waster. He'll never make a sailor."

We sat about, reading our letters sent to the Institute by our people. I'd one from Auntie Polly. "You'll not have anything to do with silly girls, I hope, dear." I laughed. She meant with whores, but 'silly girls' was as strong as she could put it.

Some chaps from other ships came in; chaps who'd known Chink, Polly, Paddy and the old lot. We old hands sat chatting of plans we had for the good days when we'd have won our officer's tickets, and life was mighty good. When, last thing, the chaplain went to the little chapel I went too, and took the green kids with me. Green kids will follow an old stager. Seeing me lead them in, the chaplain beamed. Pat and Alphonse came also. I sat in the rear seat where I'd sat that night when Paddy and the wild bunch had called to me, "Let's go see the motts!"

Thinking of that little red book, of "When thou goest through the waters I will be with thee," I bowed my head. I heard John Martin saying, "She'll strike at eleven, Bill. Goodbye, shipmate! Good luck!" I'd never looked in that little book again. Yet I saw Dolly's face.

When we went out to the street, Pat and Alphonse, with some of the older chaps, took the shortest way to sailor-town, but the green kids followed me. When we came to the foot of Pacific Street again I heard the pianos, and girls' voices. I paused. When you have been at

88.   *The 'Frisco waterfront.*

sea for over five long months—oh, well. And then, seeing the eyes of
little Bryant on me, I thought, "Well, not tonight." And I led the green
kids down to the ship.

Alwyn was singing, drunk on the quarter-deck, Martin ashore.
The little pink-cheeked lubber was ashore. I turned into my bunk.

At some time in the night I woke to hear Pat and Alphonse
talking. "Cut out your gab. You're too damned noisy. Let a fellow
sleep!" I grumbled.

Alphonse replied, "Beel, zees beeg night. Pat los' 'ee's maiden-
head."

And I saw roses in a woman's hand; a silver bracelet on a woman's
wrist.

253

Life's a queer deal, eh?

Next morning when the night-watchman roused us, that little pink-cheeked lubber was gone. He'd left his sea chest, but taken all his shore clothes. He'd skipped; swallowed the anchor, as we say. The watchman said, "I seen 'im go ashore wid a feller wot looked like some sort o' pimp."

That night I went ashore with John Martin. As we were walking past the old girl's bow—I mind I glanced up at her figurehead, that woman with a bare white bosom and with a long silver trumpet held to her lips—John Martin paused. "I've got something to tell you, shipmate," said he. "The Old Man was talking about you to me this afternoon."

"What was it, sir? What did the old devil have to say of me?" I asked, much wondering what Shark Eye'd said.

John Martin answered me, "The Old Man told me that you're the smartest officer he's ever had under him."

Oh, sailor, sailor, sailor!

God forbid that I should seem to blow. But a lad's allowed a bit of decent pride, eh?

So we walked on, with my blood a-tingle. Not yet quite twenty-two. Cock of the walk! The whole world mine! Soon we were at the foot of Pacific Street, and Martin paused and said, "I'm going up there, shipmate."

I was about to say, "All right! Suits me, sir!" And he spoke again.

"But I'm not taking you. I wouldn't take a decent chap like you. It's different for an old stager like me, shipmate."

Oh, well! So I was decent, eh? I didn't want to be just then, so very much. Six foot three, a hundred and eighty-seven pounds, stripped to the buff, and all my blood a-tingle!

"So-long, shipmate!" said Martin, and I went none too keenly to the Institute. The chaplain asked, "Where's that youngster who didn't come with you last night?"

"He's skipped, and a good thing too. He'd never make a sailor," I replied.

The chaplain said, "I had a sight of him once when I passed your

254

ship. Oh, God!"

"What's up, sir?" I asked.

"That little pink-faced lad! Oh, God! They look for such as he, the evil people. Oh, it makes me sick!" exclaimed the chaplain, and called to his assistant, "I've got to go and look for a poor little lad to save him from—you know—" And off he hurried.

"Why all the fuss?" I asked the assistant chaplain.

"Sodom was not only where the Dead Sea lies," he answered me. Then he asked me, "Were you too hard on him?"

I said, "If one kid shirks, another has to do the job he leaves undone. That's fact, sir, on the sea."

He muttered something about me being my brother's keeper. The kid was never found.

They emptied the cargo from the old girl's deep belly until she lay with but a few tons left in her, scarce enough to keep her upright did a stiff wind blow. She was moored down at the old sea wall that's gone today; her high side well above the level of the sea wall.

There came a night when, feeling a bit off colour, I did not go ashore. I turned in early. There was a sort of heaviness all over me. My throat was sore. A sailor often gets a touch of cold when he's in port, in from his clean open sea.

I woke to see the Old Man in the half-deck, lighting the lamp. A wild, high wind had risen. I heard the rain lash down. The Old Man said, "Get out! She's parted her forward moorings, all but one line. Get out and tie her up, or she'll spill over." Off he went, leaving the ship to me.

Out I ran, just as I was, pyjama-clad and barefoot, from my warm bunk. No hat. The mates were both ashore, and all the crew but three green kids and three of the foremast hands.

I climbed ashore, hand over hand, along the sole remaining forward mooring line; a monkey in the gale. A shivering monkey. I took a new line with me, slung about my shoulder, and made it fast ashore; and then climbed back. Bit by bit, with heave and haul and drag, I got the ship made fast again; quite safe from spilling over. Windy wet dawn it was by then, and very, very chill. John Martin came aboard.

The cook was in his galley, lighting his morning fire. Martin took

255

my arm and led me thither, saying, "First thing you know, by God, you'll be getting one of their damned shore sicknesses." I sat down on the galley coal locker, and he dragged off my pyjamas and rubbed me down with a dish rag. "Here, doctor! Shake a leg! Get the third mate some good hot boiling coffee!" he ordered.

After a bit I was warm in a sort of way, and went to the half-deck and got into my clothes; then started the gang at washing the decks down. I felt most miserable all day, but stuck it somehow. Next day I felt worse. But third mates don't lay up for a bit of silly shore sickness.

On the next day a tug took the ship over to lie in Sausalito creek to wait her charter for a homeward cargo. That day, when she'd her anchor down, I turned into my bunk too sick to keep the deck.

I've never known just what was the matter with me. I slept much by day, and at night was often delirious. I mind a night I called for water, and Alphonse went out to the rainy deck to fetch me a cold drink from the ship's pump. When he brought it to me, I mashed my fist into his face and knocked him down. I see him yet, risen to his feet, staring amazed at me. I see Pat, on his elbow in his bunk, looking at me from puzzled eyes. If during those first days the Old Man ever came to see me, I don't remember it. With the owner hounding him to get the ship a homeward charter, he was a worried skipper. If ever he did come to look at me, he doubtless thought, "You're needed on the deck! Look alive, boy, and get well." That was fair enough. A sailing skipper cannot be expected to recognize serious illness when he sees it, and he had other things to think of than a husky hundred and eighty pound third mate who was ailing. So the days passed till one morning I climbed from my bunk and dragged my clothes on, my limbs shaky, my voice a wheeze. That morning he came to the half-deck. "I guess I'd better send you to hospital," he said, in the tone in which he'd have said to the sailmaker, "Get a new cloth sewn in the main topsail." I was to Shark Eye a part of the ship, not a human being in misery. I don't mean that there was no heart in him. It was the sea's hard way. There's little room for softness where the tall ships go.

I don't recall the trip across the bay to 'Frisco and hospital. It was the same ramshackle old wooden building whither Will Clegg had gone a year ago: a dismal crowded place where went the city's paupers

89. *QUEEN MARGARET.*

—and sailors. My bed was the same bed that Will Clegg had lain in. Ward H, bed 5. The sailor's ward. In a corner lay the second mate of the barque *Falkland**, with a rubber tube in his lung. He'd sometimes talk. Sometimes, delirious, he'd sing a quavering song. Across from me, all bandage-swathed and still, his ribs caved in, his face a blotch with broken nose and jaw, was a foremast hand who'd been knocked down by a sea and swept to and fro across his ship's deck the day ere she came in. He was unconscious mostly. Next to me, a hip smashed by a falling spar, was an aged ship carpenter, beyond whom was a foreign sailor who never spoke; but often, with tears on his furrowed face, groaned with pain.

The doctor came next day. A short fat man with cold hard sneering eyes and the voice of a cattle tender who despises his cattle. I'd heard that he got forty dollars for every limejuice ship that came to 'Frisco. If anyone was sick aboard a limejuice ship, he did the doctoring, and got no more than forty dollars: no matter how sick the man, or how many men were sick. If a ship had no sick men he drew his forty dollars just the same. The chaplain had spoken to me of him, saying, "He loves to buttonhole me on the waterfront if he meets me there, and always tries to tell me some vile tale. His favourite tale's of how when he was a boy his father gave him money to hire a woman, and of how he kept the money and seduced his father's servant girl."

The doctor set a rubber tube to my chest, listened, and grunted.

"When can I go aboard my ship again?" I asked.

"Never," he replied.

"Oh, well——"

And then he went, and I lay staring at the ceiling. The pretty nurse came in to quiet the *Falkland's* second mate who'd started his customary song,

> *Oh, blow today and blow tomorrow,*
> *Blow boys, blow!*
> *Oh, blow for all poor tars in sorrow,*
> *Oh, blow my bully boys, blow!*

He never sang again. He died that night.

"Doctor, what's wrong with me?" I asked next morning, calling to him as, without having paused at all beside me, without having

---

* The *Falkland* capsized and foundered off the Bishops Rock later in the year. [Ed.]

90. *FALKLAND in dry-dock*.

glanced at me even, he left the ward. He didn't stop, nor call an answer.
Again next day I asked, "Doctor, what's wrong with me?" Frowning,
he turned upon me and gruffly said, "I've told you that you can't go
back to sea." His tones implied, "Be damned to you! Your goose is
cooked. Don't bother me." So, day by day, through two long weeks,
he came, and went, and never paused at all to look at me. Hard as a
stone he seemed. And I was dazed, incredulous, too stunned to think
or try to think.

Sometimes the chaplain came and sat a while. "The sea's not all.

259

There will be other things for you to do," he'd say. His words meant naught to me. What could there be, save ships?

Often I'd think, "The doctor must be wrong. Of course he's wrong." And yet I was so weak. Often I felt faint. I'd waken in the night, and, with a horror on me, sit up; unable to sit up quickly enough, suffocating, feeling as one who drowns must feel when for the last time the sea rolls over him. I wrote one day to Dolly. Writing to her helped, made me feel less alone, brought me a sort of feeling of security. The thought of her quiet eyes was to me as it is when fogbound sailors see a lighthouse gleaming through dense fog. I didn't write to Auntie Polly. I'd rather keep my troubles to myself than read of loving Jesus from her answering pen.

Finally, one day, instead of passing by my bed when he came to the ward, the doctor came straight to it. It was many days since he had said a word to me. Silent, afraid to speak since all speech was useless, knowing too well the verdict he had stressed so surely, I looked up at him. Then he spoke, and said quite casually.

"You're all right now. You can go back aboard," he said.

Oh, boys and girls on little Shetland ponies! Now I'd be a sailor, as I'd sailor been! I understood at last. The doctor'd had a joke with me: had wanted perhaps to scare me into doing as the nurse desired. Those other chaps were always worrying her. Bitter though his joke had been I didn't care now in the least. So, with the doctor gone, I gaily called "Hey, pretty! Bring my clothes and step along!" Waiting for the nurse to come with them, I sat erect for the first time since I'd come to hospital. At once my limbs began to tremble. At once my heart became a hammer on my ribs. She brought my clothes, saw me all trembly, and took my arm. I pushed her hand away. "Poor boy!" she said.

But I said, "Keep your sympathy, pretty! By God, I'm man, not boy! And you can tack *sailor* on before the man. Sailorman, see?"

Smiling, she replied, "I know you're a sailor, and that sailors are never sick. I'm a nurse. Did you ever know that nurses have to obey orders too?" Then, called to another ward, she was gone. And something in the way she smiled, something in those words of hers, sort of puzzled me.

260

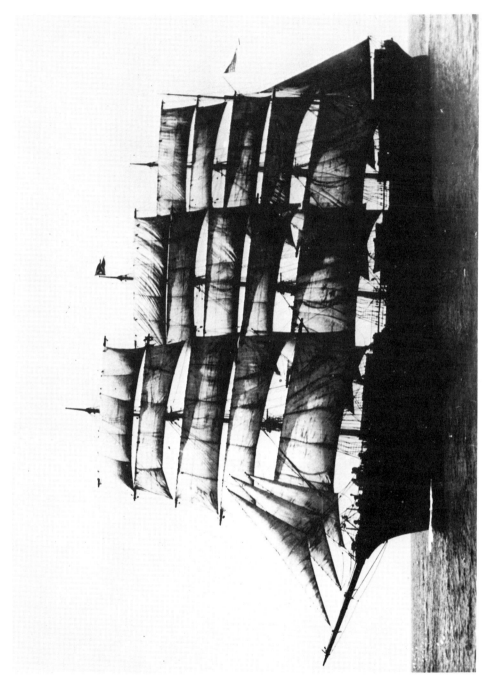

91. *STAR OF ZEALAND, built as the ATLAS, then with royals crossed.*

While I was fumbling with my clothes, I heard that old carpenter mutter, "Sons of bitches!" And then he called to me, "Yer about out of yer apprenticeship, ain't ye?"

"I'll be out very soon," I replied.

"Dirty bastards! Sailors an' dogs all one to a bloody ship owner!" said he. "There was a first voyage kid in the next bed to yer when ye came here. They took his appendix out one morning an' packed him down to his ship that evening. She sailed next day. Ye know wot come of him."

"The doctor says that I'm all right," said I.

"They told the kid as he'd be all right," retorted the carpenter.

"Why would they send me aboard if I'm not fit?" I asked.

"Yer too bloody innercent, son! Dollars comes afore dogs. Ye've been here just two weeks. Time enough for yer skipper to get a letter to yer owner, saying ye're in hospital, and time enough for yer owner to cable the doctor to give ye a clean bill of health and send ye back aboard. D'ye feel any better'n w'en ye come here? Ye know damn well ye don't! If they have ye aboard yer ship an' seemin' well w'en yer apprenticeship's done they'll have no responsibility. If ye was ashore sick they'd have to pay yer way home. Look at ye, by God! Weak as a louse!" he answered.

"What do you expect when I've been in bed two weeks?" I laughed. "Why, you damned old sea lawyer, you're making a howl about nothing. I'll be *all-Sir-Garney-oh* aboard." I bade him a cheery goodbye, and, trying to shake off my stupid weakness went down the long corridor and out to the street.

On the street I came face to face with the chaplain. "What in the world are you doing, out of bed?" he asked, amazed. When I replied that the doctor had told me I was all right and could go aboard, he looked grave and said, "I wish you could see a doctor who isn't connected with any ship owner."

"All I need's a good long whiff of Stockholm tar. Once aboard, I'll be *all-Sir-Garney-oh*," I laughed.

"It'd be murder to let you go to sea in the ship. You're not fit to be aboard her. If only your apprenticeship were done I'd take you to a doctor who's a good friend of mine. The best doctor in 'Frisco. But

262

I can't interfere between an owner and his bound apprentice," he replied.

"Don't bother about me. You've troubles enough," said I, and true it was that he'd plenty of trouble. He was forever fighting the crimps who sold foremast sailors to skippers, just as cattle are sold, and skippers, who could get men only through the crimps, had scant patience with his interference. The shanghaiing of sailors was established custom, very useful to skippers in a hurry to get to sea. If the chaplain were to try to interfere on behalf of an apprentice he'd gain the ill-will of every skipper in port, and without some good-will from skippers the Institute might as well close; for skippers could forbid their apprentices to go to it.

"God grant your apprenticeship is done before your ship goes to sea! You must promise to come to me at once if it is," answered the chaplain. So I promised to do so, but laughingly assured him that I'd be all right once aboard and, feeling groggy but determined to shake away my weakness, I went on my way.

"Wait till I see Martin! I'll be *all-Sir-Garney-oh* then. To hell with silly shore sickness! He'll laugh it all out of me," I thought. Very soon I was climbing the old girl's gangway. When I came to her rail, there was Martin.

Staggering as I stepped to her deck, I clutched the rail to steady myself.

"What's up? How d'ye feel? You look a damn sight worse than when you went away," said Martin, and his words gave me a feeling of foreboding. But I shook it away. Impatient I was with them all— the gloomy old carpenter, the nurse with her infernal sympathy, the chaplain with his sob stuff, and now even Martin.

"What in hell do you expect, sir, when they've had me laid on my beam ends in bed for two weeks? If this old packet don't make a damned fine run home it won't be my fault," I retorted. Then, going suddenly faint, I grabbed his arm.

"Best go roll in your bunk for a bit. You look like a bloody spook," said Martin. Feeling like a bloody spook, I went to my bunk; but called back to him, "I'll have my sea legs in no time, sir!"

Pat and Alphonse came to the half-deck. "Pretty damned soft

263

for you, Bill! Two weeks eating shore grub, by God! Jesus, I bet you had a corking time with the night nurse!" laughed Pat.

Putting on a face, I replied, "If you young beggars don't step lively when I tell you to on the run home—look out for yourselves!"

"Beel, ee's 'ard case son of beesh!" laughed Alphonse, and one of the young kids brought the dinner in. I turned out and sat at the table, but everything went suddenly blurry, and that foreboding came on me again. Once again I shook it away, and I ate the ship's coarse fare.

For some days I pottered about the deck, trying to work; but with no strength at all. At night I'd wake suddenly, sit up and fight for breath, and have that horror on me. So one morning I went to see Shark Eye in the cabin. "I don't feel right, sir. I'm no good on deck. I thought maybe I'd best go back to hospital for a bit, sir," I told him.

"The doctor says you're all right. Why d'ye mean? Trying to soldier on your job, are you?" Shark Eye replied.

"By God, sir, not you or anyone else can say I ever soldiered on my job!" I shouted. And that was the end of that. Out of the cabin I swung, muttering under my breath, "You old son of a whore, I'll show you something on the run home, by God!"

That day the ship went to her loading berth on the Sacramento river. Then, day by day, I sat in a drafty warehouse tallying wheat sacks into her big belly, but all the time I felt like a bit of chewed string. At night when the cold fogs rolled up the river, I'd wake with that horror on me and sit up and fight for breath.

After dusk on the tenth day the last sack slid into her hold. I closed my tally book. She was loaded. At midnight my apprenticeship would be over at last! Two more days and she'd be at sea. Once at sea, I'd be myself again. Doctors and shore sickness could go to hell. But, walking the gangway, I staggered, and, taking my arm, Martin asked, "What's up, Bill?"

"Haven't quite got my strength yet, sir. I'll be *all-Sir-Garney-oh* once we're at sea," I replied.

"Wait till I meet that Uppsala woman, by gad. I'll be *all-Sir-Garney-oh* then too," said Martin.

That night Pat and Alphonse sat up late, talking about girls, and because I had a sort of dread of my bunk I sat up late too. It was close

264

to midnight when we turned in, my last thought ere I dropped off that at midnight I'd be out of my apprenticeship.

Then in the cold dark Pat was asking, "By God, what's the matter?" Alphonse had lit the lamp. I was sitting up in my bunk, throwing my arms about crying, *"Dolly! Dolly!"*

"Douse the glim. I'm all right. Had a damned nightmare," I said in a minute. Pat blew out the glim. Alphonse grumbled, "Vot you means, big son of beesh, vakin' faller oop?"

For a while I lay shuddering in the dark, and then the bell clanged high and clear; the watchman striking midnight. *My apprenticeship was done!* And to sleep I went, thinking how on the run home I'd eat at the cabin table. To hell with doctors and shore sicknesses!

I slept well the rest of the night, and woke feeling gay. Tomorrow I'd be at sea. Meantime I was free, for the first time in four years. No need for me to so much as think of any work. I'd take the day off and Shark Eye couldn't kick, by God! Then Martin told one of the kids to hoist the burgee, the flag that signifies that the skipper wanted a launch to come off and take him ashore. I said to myself, "Damned if I don't go ashore too! I'll come aboard tomorrow, just before she sails." I'd go to see the chaplain, and tell him I was *all-Sir-Garney-oh.* If he was still all fussed up about me and wanted to do so, maybe I'd let him take me to see the doctor; just to set his mind at rest. A good sort, the chaplain! Perhaps, too, it'd not be such a bad idea to have the doctor look me over. I'd be all right at sea, of course; but maybe the doctor could give me something to hurry things along.

"What's this?" demanded Shark Eye, coming down to the launch and finding me in her.

"I'm out of my time and going ashore, sir," I replied.

You should have seen the Old Man start. "You're coming home in the ship, ain't you?" he queried.

"If I eat at the cabin table and draw wages," said I, and added, looking him squarely in the eye, "Unless you don't want a man who soldiers on his job."

A grin came to his leathery face, and I grinned too.

"I don't want to lose a good man, and I thought for a time I was going to," said Shark Eye. "You've been a long time in the ship, and

265

92. *BRACADALE, one of the Grain fleet off 'Frisco. (Note method of painting her ports.)*

getting sick's no way to leave her. I can take you on second mate next voyage and mate the voyage after. One of these days I'll be retiring. A word from me, and maybe you could be master of her."

At that, by gad, I forgot all about having been laid on my beam ends. It didn't matter now. Master of my Old Girl, eh? And then Shark Eye said, "The mate was worried about you, thinking you a lot sicker than you were; and he got me a bit worried. There'll be a new crew to lick into shape when we go to sea, and it'll be your job to do it. I've been counting on you."

"You can count on me, sir," said I, "And I don't care how tough the swabs are. I'll make 'em into sailors. There'll be no soldiers amongst 'em. They'll know their job."

"Be aboard by ten in the morning, boy," the Old Man ordered as we stepped ashore. 'Boy'—I was still 'boy' to him. And I liked it well.

266

So off I went toward the Institute, feeling a bit groggy, but sure I'd be all right once the doctor had looked me over—and I was at sea again.

"Thank God! I've been counting the days till your apprenticeship was done. I'll take you to the doctor at once," said the chaplain the minute he saw me.

"I'm ashore till tomorrow. We pull out in the fore-noon, sir," said I. And as I said it went a bit faint, and felt my face go pale.

"Forget that nonsense," replied the chaplain, and went to the telephone. While he spoke to the doctor that faintness grew worse. I felt weak as a cat. Dizzy I was, with all things a blur before me. But when the chaplain called to me, "Come along. He'll see you at once," I took heart. The doctor would give me something to fix all that damned silly feeling.

The doctor bade me strip, and for a long time set tubes at my chest and back, and listened; asking me many things about the sea and the life of a sailor. Then he bade me dress, and while I dressed talked aside with the chaplain. Knowing that he was going to fix me up all right, I felt chipper enough though none too chipper. Then he sat down, face to face with me, and said, "You can never go back to sea, my boy. Hard work of any sort would kill you. Any sudden shock would be your death. Your heart's in a bad way, and your windpipes are choked with asthma. What you need is a long rest and good food."

"You can never go back to sea—"

Oh, well, I didn't hear the rest of what he said: talking about this thing and that thing amiss with me. He talked for a longish time, I know. I just sat staring at him, without really seeing him; or hearing more than the steady flow of his words.

At last the chaplain's hand was on my arm, guiding me from the office, and the doctor was calling after me, "I'll see you tomorrow." Then the chaplain was telling me that the doctor owned a private hospital and that I was to go there as his guest till I was fit to be sent home. I didn't take any of it in. All I knew was that the ship was going to sea tomorrow, and that I was not going with her.

Down to the water-front the chaplain took me, and hired a boat that I might go aboard and fetch my sea chest. It was the noon hour when I entered the half-deck. Pat and Alphonse were surprised to see me back so soon. When, without a word, I began to throw my things into my chest, they were the more surprised.

"Yes, I'm leaving the old bitch. I've changed my mind," said I, replying to their questions. I didn't tell them why I'd changed my mind. My pride was too hard hit for that.

"We'll miss you when we furl the topsails, Bill," said Pat. Knowing I'd not furl a topsail ever again I had to grit my teeth.

"What's up? You're not going back on us, Bill?" asked Martin, looking in.

"Four years in a ship's enough, sir," said I, avoiding his eyes and, while I packed and lashed my sea chest, I was aware of him watching me.

Soon I was lowering my sea chest into the boat, with Martin and the apprentices all gathered at the railing above her, and the foremast hands looking on from nearby. I went to the half-deck then and wrote Shark Eye a note, telling him that I had changed my mind and asking him to send me a reference to the hospital. Then I went back to where stood Martin and the others, and gave Martin the note; asking him to see that it reached Shark Eye. As I started down to the boat Martin gripped my hand.

"Tough luck, shipmate," said he, and I knew that alone of them all he understood.

"Good-luck, shipmate. Fair winds homeward!" said I, trying to grin and not making a very good showing.

As the boat pulled away from the ship I saw Nicholson and Andersen and the little Negro, those few who hadn't deserted her when she came in, and the apprentices, climb into her rigging. Then Nicholson took off his hat, and waving it called, "Three cheers for Bill Adams and a damned good shipmate!"

I took off my hat, and held it high, a lump in my throat. And I still hear their cheering.

Leaving me in hospital that night, the chaplain said, "The sea's not all. There will be other things for you to do. God hasn't forgotten you."

"Damn God," said I.

Oh, well!—Sometimes when you say a thing you do not know

268

what you are saying, eh?

A nurse gave me something to make me sleep. I woke late next morning and looked from the window opposite my bed out to 'Frisco bay, with the sun bright on its green water. Shining in the sun in full view, was my Old Girl, with her great silk ensign fluttering at her peak. Ahead of her was a tug boat, and I knew that they were heaving her anchor in. Well, oh very well, I knew that song that they were singing:

A'rovin', a'rovin',
Oh, rovin's been my ru–i–in,
We'll go no more a'ro–o–vin' with you—fair—maid!

Though forbidden to move, I sat erect in my bed till a hand touched my shoulder and the nurse's voice said, "Come! You must lie down at once!" I turned to her and she put into my hand a letter; at the same time pushing me down from my sitting posture.

"This is to certify that the bearer, B. M. Adams, has served his four-year apprenticeship in the ship *Silberhorn*, under my command. I have always found him strictly honest, sober and attentive to his duties. It is with pleasure that I recommend him as an excellent officer to any shipmaster."

There ends the yarn of a sailor. There were no more ships for me.

Weary the days that I lay there, and lone beyond all telling. Nothing to do but gaze from the window, out to the bay where ships came and went, and on beyond the bay and its ships to the California hills. I must forget ships. Ships were nothing to me now, and the California hills were nothing, worse than nothing to me. A stranger in a strange land, I felt for them the hate the prisoner feels for his prison bars.

I'd think of Glynn and Paddy, and envy them mightily. Far better to be dead than as I was.

I'd think of Dolly, see her at my bedside, soft-eyed in the midnight, her loose hair glossy in the candle's yellow light, reading from *Pilgrim's Progress* to a child frightened in the lone dark. I'd see the snow of her pillow, at Aunt Clarissa's, her Bible on the chair beside it; see her handing me a gold ring set with pearls; hear her say, "It was your mother's, dear." I'd remember how she had kissed me goodbye on

269

the following day. Different to all other girls she ever had been. No kiss as was her kiss. Always in her presence there was peace and awareness of beauty. An altar, with a pure white altar cloth. Then I'd think of the little red book that she had given me ere I sailed on my last voyage—my last voyage! No more voyaging for me! "Read it when you're at sea," I'd hear her say.

When thou goest through the waters I will be with thee ; and through the deep waters, they shall not overflow thee. I'd wish then that the ship had crashed in that black midnight upon the stark rocks of Hermite. *Damn God,* I'd think ; flat on my back, staring at the blankness of the ceiling.

A good sort the chaplain was, and the doctor too. I've not forgotten them, nor ever will forget. They had me homeward-bound at a month's end, and came to see me off, the two of them ; my fare across the continent and on by steamer to Liverpool paid by the Institute. I'd never written to Aunt Polly ; nor said a word about her to the chaplain save to tell him, "I've got an old maid aunt, and no one else."

"She's poor?" the chaplain asked.

"She says she is," I answered, knowing full well that she would never foot the bill to pay my way to England. "I'll see you get paid back some day," I told him. He said, "Forget it, Bill."

As my train pulled out the doctor called, "No baccy now, remember!" I'd a quick vision of a little rust-stained half-deck full of apprentices, their faces misty in the thick tobacco smoke. Then the bay of 'Frisco soon passed from my view. "Goodbye!" said I, "Goodbye, and damn you!" And to the hills and valleys of California as I passed through them I said the same. Oh, little then I knew! Little I knew the day would come when every hill and valley would be known to me as well as, aye, and better than, the hills and valleys of my boyhood land. Bitter my heart was then. I did not know that hate can turn to love, and curses turn to blessing.

No need to tell of that slow train across the continent. Mutely I sat each day, speaking to no one: nor answering did any speak to me. A hurt dog homing to the kennel, with only growls in its throat for as, reading its silent hurt, would give its homeward yearning kindly interruption. All the way across by sea to Liverpool I wheezed,

93. *Once a German nitrate ship, the PONAPE, built in Italy, was Finnish when this picture was taken of her making 12 knots off the Fastnet.*

fighting for breath. Only one day I went up to the deck. A day of sun, and swiftly scudding cloud. Wind from the northerly, and a fine high sea that kept all other passengers below. I stood alone, to watch a lofty clipper under every sail drive by. She was the last tall ship I was ever to see under sail. Proudly she came, flinging the greening combers from her plunging bow; sun on her canvas now, now shadow. Rolling she was, and her low sails all dripped with drenching sprays that flew in sheets across her. She passed close by, and on her deck I saw men of the breed to which I once belonged. They waved, and clear their cheering came across the windy sea. "Damn God!" said I.

I mind that changing trains from Liverpool to Devon, where Aunt Polly was, I waited for my train in Bristol station. A mile or two away was Albert Villas. Near me was that old dock where long ago had lain the tall *Tythonus*; near me the river where I'd seen the *Beatrice* fast on the mud, and near me, too, was that high cliff whence long ago I'd seen for the first time the sea and a ship.

As I stood there, shivering in the crisp March wind, I saw approaching me, hurrying along the platform, a young lad rigged in the gay brass buttons of a first voyage apprentice. Pink-faced he was, and very bright of eye. On one side walked his father, his mother on the other, and I could see how proud they were of their young sailor son.

I stepped forward, and laid my hand on that young lad's tender shoulder. He stopped, and gazed up at me in my rags; my face un-shaven since I'd left the hospital. His father and his mother gazed at me, as though to ask, "What to you mean, laying your dirty hand upon our son?"

"Going to sea?" I asked that hopeful kid.

"Yes," he replied, and for some reason, maybe because he sensed the knowledge in my eyes and old authority, added a 'sir'.

On impulse I said, "Don't go to sea. The sea's hell!"

For a moment we stood there, we four. Just for a moment. Then they were gone; that young lad with his face a little flushed, but in his eyes defiant eagerness; his parents' faces scornful of the platform's ragged tramp, while I saw that long bench before the fireplace in the sailors' home, where I had sat on that last night ere I, a green appren-tice, went forth to the sea. Then I saw Wood and Glynn. I heard

Glynn say to me those age-old words so many sea-wise sailormen have said to those unwise. And then I heard upon the midnight's dark, *"Man overboard!"* I saw it all. Sun on the sea, and gentle little white caps softly breaking. Ice on the sea, and chaos. Chaos in the air. Thinking thus, I muttered "You poor little ignorant son of a bitch, good luck to you!"

It was long after dark when I reached Aunt Polly's, and went to her back door, and found the kitchen lit and Polly Dobbins there. Her mouth fell open when I entered without knocking. Staring at me from big concerned eyes she cried, "W'y, maister, 'ow you'm changed!"

The dining room door opened, and in the doorway appeared Aunt Polly, her fat pug in her arms. There was a frown on her face, while with one thin hand she fondled the fat pug.

"Where do you come from? Your ship's not due for months."

"I've been ill. Still am ill. I've had to leave the sea," I replied, and briefly told her my tale.

"I paid out thirty pounds for you to go to sea," she said when I was done. Bitterly, I thought of the fortune she'd paid out for Uncle Robert to fritter away on his women.

"I hoped you'd be on your own feet by now," she continued. "I've done my utmost for you so long. It can't go on, and on."

And of a sudden there came to me a quick memory of a basket of grapes that the girls of the 'Golden Eagle' had sent me that time when I was ill in Portland. I laughed aloud, and the fat pug barked at my laughter.

"I was a poor damn fool to take the chaplain's advice," I said bitterly. "Far better to have stayed with the ship and have died, or to have hung around the waterfront where at least the sailor-town whores have a heart for a chap who's down."

Horrified she exclaimed, "You're coarsened by the sea! All the religious upbringing I gave you's forgotten, is it? Put your trust in the sweet Jesus. He will take care of you."

"Oh, damn your sweet Jesus!" I burst out.

Aghast, she started a stern reproof for my blasphemy. I don't know just what she said, for I'd gone suddenly dizzy. Everything went black. I no longer saw the plump pug clutched to her flat bosom.

273

I only heard her voice going on, and on. And somehow its cold tones reminded me of the pounding of the sea on the Ramirez rocks, while from somewhere there came to me a vestige of the sailor pride that once had been mine, and, breaking in on her sharply, before that blackness should overwhelm me and I crumple into unconsciousness, I said, "I'm really very tired. Can I have a bed for tonight? I'll be moving on in the morning."

Curtly she told Polly Dobbins to make up a bed for me and off to her own she went. And Polly made up a bed, and put in it a hot water bottle, and lighted a fire in the cold room; and, having brought me a cup of hot tea and some food after I was abed, asked sorrowing, "Young maister, be there owt else as I can do for 'ee?"

I had some sleep that night, and rose when I heard Polly Dobbins descending the stairs at five o'clock. "Fix me some coffee and a bite, Polly, and I'll get out of here," I said, adding: "Quit your blubbering, there's a good girl."

Not yet dawn it was when I left Aunt Polly's door. The railway station was not far, and, with the March wind whining over the sere hawthorn hedges and the rain whipping down, I made my way thither; weak as a half-drowned kitten.

'Twas Dolly opened the door to me when, at a bit past dark, I came to Aunt Clarissa's. I'd written to her last from the hospital, saying, "I'll be leaving for England soon." As she stood framed in the lamp-lit doorway there was in her face neither surprise nor any worry. Fully serene her grey eyes were, and her smile was as the breaking of the dawn when the wind lulls and the black storm is spent at last after night's dark fury. Calm her face was as though she had asked me a few moments ago to step out of the house for something needed, and I were now returned to her. She closed the door behind me, on the wind and the rain. She lifted her face and she kissed me.

"I hoped you'd come to me, dear," she said. And I broke down and cried like a kid.

"Don't cry, dear. Everything will be all right," she said, whereupon, as a young apprentice on a gale-ravaged deck gives over his fear when he finds his strong chief mate nearby, and hears his chief mate's steady tones, I quit my crying. Peace came to me then, at last.

274

Peace such as that peace had come when on my last voyage we'd weathered the grim rocks on Hermite, had beaten the Horn at last.

That night I went to sleep once again to the sound of her voice reading to me. What it was that she read I know not, save that it was from her Bible. I heard no word; lay gazing at and worshipping her till, aware of her lips on my cheek, I drifted into sleep.

She nursed me back to health: to health enough: new courage and new pride. The doctor came and went, and ever said the same. If I was to live, I must seek a dry climate. "Australia would be the place for you," he said.

Gradually I began to think of that land of my last port, the land that had seen my undoing. I'd heard in hospital men talk of valleys inland, where a warm sun shone ever in a cloudless sky. Often we in the half-deck had longed to go, instead of round the eternal Horn, to Australia; and ever had been denied. Then I'd not go there now. I'd go back to the land of my undoing, fight things out there somehow. And not alone would I go. My grey-eyed comrade would come with me. I didn't ask her. I said, "We'll go together." As if expecting it, she answered "Yes, of course, dear."

I've told a sailor's tale, plain and simple. Maybe someday I'll tell the landsman's tale; of things I found to do ashore; plain things and simple too, with a comrade ever nigh.

No matter how weary I was in the new land, and weary I often was, I had also my memories. I'd talk of them at times. I mind well a time when as I talked of my rolling sea a landsman cried, "My God, man, you've got no business shovelling concrete for a living." And I replied, "A man has to take what comes. Maybe I'll not always be shovelling concrete."

So we battled along together, and if at times my courage faltered, hers never did. Her way was hard, aye, harder, I think, than mine.

Sometimes she'd say to me, "Someday you'll write."

"Write what?" I'd ask.

"Just write," she'd answer me. "When the time comes you'll write." It was the same notion that that chap had had who'd cried, "My God, man, you've got no business shovelling concrete!"

Often, working in a packing house with the sun pouring in on the

94. *DIMSDALE.*

golden fruit, the machinery clanking, the packers calling one to another, the hame bells on the mule teams jingling at the wide door on one side of the building and a switch engine puffing at the other, I'd be seeing that white clipper racing past Pitcairn and the islanders throwing their fruit to the sea. Or I'd see the bergs off the Horn. Whether I was digging a ditch, milking thirty cows at two of the morning, pruning an orchard or walking my long beat as a policeman, I'd be thinking of Paddy and Tom Swift, of my Old Man, and of my Old Girl and the white sails of rivals lifting from the mid-ocean horizon. And a hunger to set it down on paper would bite at me. I'd be wanting to tell of the beauty I'd known.

And so the years passed until came a day when, because of the yearning that was on me, I took paper and wrote. Lifted out of myself I was. And the sea lapped and the sails flapped and the wind thrummed in the rigging. I was at sea again, the intervening years forgotten. Again my hands felt the cold of the snow on them, the sting of the spray. My oilskins dripped, and the ship rolled, and the sea stars shone. *Oh, sailor, sailor, sailor!*

I'd fooled the doctors. The heart they said could never stand a strain had stood some fourteen years of gruelling labour under the baking sun of the San Joaquin. "You can never go back to sea," they'd said. *I'd never left the sea.* Roving with my Old Girl I was again. The Maid of Amsterdam had never died.

And had I really been able to stay at sea, 'twould not have been so good. For ships were gone ere I began to write, and steamers had our sea. Aye, steamers have our sea, and sailing days are done. But never done for me. Still battling the wild gales, the tall Cape Horners fight toward the roaring west. Stern mates bawl orders in the murderous dark, and young apprentices leap from their sodden bunks to climb the reeling masts and sway, spider-like, high up above the raging waters far below; gathering ice-sheathed canvas under their cold breasts. And I've had letters from men of the breed to which I once belonged, and yet, and ever shall, belong. Letters from lads I knew that other day. Letters from landsmen too, asking, "How did you fellows manage to survive?" And I reply as all sailors do. "It was a dog's life, but it was a man's life."

I hear my father saying, "You'll find it a hard life, my son."

Who'd ask it easy?

I like to think that the unconquered old soldier would approve perhaps of the way I'm finishing my game. A man has right to a bit of decent pride, eh?

And best of all I'd realized my comrade's faith in me. I had the satisfaction of knowing that because of my writing I was able to make life a little easier for the comrade who'd toiled uncomplainingly through the hard years beside me. We were able to leave the torrid valleys where I'd had to toil as a labourer for a home in the mountains. I was able to give her the happiest home she'd ever known. It was by chance that we found the village, tucked away and forgotten in the Sierras. A ghost town* of the old mining days of California. And the moment we saw it I knew, and she knew, that here was the place we had longed for through many a year. The trees of the forest all round it, and streams flowing by. Red earth, and a sky of limitless blue.

* Dutch Flat. [Ed.]

Bird song and wild flowers, and soft clouds gently drifting, in spring time. In autumn gold's glory on poplar and oak, crimson on dogwood and cherry and maple. All the long night sheer silence save for howl of coyotes, cry of night hawk and whip-poor-will. In winter the snow flying, and crisp air sweet with the fragrance of wood smoke.

Four years ago I buried Dolly on a hill side across the ravine from my home. It was her wish that no flowers be ever laid there, and save by the flowers of the forest her grave in unmarked. But on Easter Eve, Christmas Eve, and the eve of her birthday, her daughter and I go across the ravine, up the hill to our Holy Land, to light candles on the resting place of the one who was ever my Altar. Till far in the night, till they flicker and fade in the stillness, we watch them from the porch of home.

It was hard to see her go. For thirty years we'd played the game together. Everlastingly, still there's pride, and love and reverence which is the greater part of both.

Dying, she smiled to me, as ever she had smiled; entering with no fear the deep waters.

On her last conscious day she beckoned to me. "Your best story isn't written yet. Someday you'll write it," she murmured.

So now I've tried to do it.

W M BIRCHALL
1931.

TEA SHIP

Drear dusk falling. Wild wind howling. Seas rage over the rolling rail.
    Skipper and mates are grimly scowling,
Stern eyes watching each straining sail.

Down she dips to the mad sea's thunder,
    Flinging the sprays to her leeches high;
Deeper she dives, till her boom goes under—
    The wind is a wolf-pack in the sky.

The tall masts strain. The backstays shiver.
    Chill in the gloom whirls driving snow.
From stem to stern she flies a'quiver,
    Lashed by the roaring forties' blow.

"All hands handy."—The order echoes above the weather's roar.
    Hid in the gloom, a sailor's singing
"I love your daughter, Shenandoah!"

Foochow port lies far behind her.
    Norrard lies Agulhas cape.
Only the speeding whales may find her,
    Only the sea-birds glimpse her shape.

Snug the hearths of London city,
    Fair the girls of London be;
Maid, and matron, gallant, witty,
    Wait the ship with China tea.

Lord have mercy! Lord have pity!
Bergs are on a hidden sea!

BILL ADAMS

279

WMBIRCHALL ·1928·

MEMORIES

DEEP-SEA AND LONGSHORE

With the exception of No. XXV, *The Helmsman of the 'Star'*, and the Poem *'Flower Child'*, the following articles all appeared originally in that excellent magazine *The Blue Peter*.

95. *Bill Adams—when he wrote his "Memories".*

CHAPTER I

FLAMES OVER THE SEA

Strange how things happen, isn't it? Queer how the solemn moments of life come to us suddenly, all unexpectedly, and, torturing us a while, leave when they are gone a light of promise softer than the rainbow light?

The other hired man and Big Nig, Little Nig, and I were hauling rock with the dump-wagon. We were clearing a piece of land in the fall of the year; ready for seeding when the rains came—or before they came, for that matter, if they came late.

Big Nig and Little Nig didn't know much about me beyond that I curried them, and wouldn't let them drink or have their barley while they were very hot. Wet days in winter they'd see me and the other hired man greasing their harness, maybe, and hear us talking; but they'd not know what we talked about, though they'd watch us with great big, interested gentle eyes, their black ears tipped forward.

Shirty knew I was a sailor.

It was a hot fall, the air still as—still as what?—I don't know. The close approach of death, maybe; or the moment before a big rain bursts in October to tell you summer's done.

Shirty sweated. I was too lean to sweat at the end of summer. I was dried out, a bit dispirited. The earth was dusty and the rocks heavy. It took the two of us to lift them to the wagon bed. Big Nig and Little Nig were sleepy. Working for wages isn't all a picnic, I can tell you. A fellow gets the dumps. There's nothing ahead—just wages, work, more work, and wages. The dust settles thick from ear to ankle, gritting all your skin. Your shoes are hard. Cheap socks get stiff. There's a raw spot on your hip where your belt chafes. You wait for quitting time, so you can go play with the kid a while; or, if you're dead tired, just flop on the bed and sleep without undressing or even eating any supper. Maybe you wake at midnight, and, looking down at the kid's dear head, say: "Poor little kid! God help you and me!" Then you undress and lie down again, and toss about, perhaps, and, looking out of the window at Sarah I Mew, wonder whether her calf will be a heifer you'll be able to sell for fifteen dollars, or a bull you'll only get a dollar for from the butcher.

It's not always that way. But that's some of it.

That's about how it was that day when the two Nigs and me and Shirty were hauling rock with the dump-wagon, preparing stony soil for a harvest.

Shirty rolled a fag and struck a match.

"What's the name o' that ship I've heard you tell about?" asked Shirty.

I told him the name, the musical name, of the ship of youth's ambition—my first ship; the ship I'd sailed with for four full clean years.

"I seen sum'thin' about it in the paper this noon," said Shirty.

"What?" said I.

"Why," said Shirty, puffing his fag and stroking Big Nig's flank, "it's got lost or sum'thin'."

It was quitting time, and I left Shirty to take the two Nigs down to the horse barn, while I went to the ranch house to ask for a look at the paper.

That evening I didn't hear 'Silk Hat Harry, the Dressmaker' or any other of the eleven cats purring; or the pleasant 'swiss, swiss, swiss, swiss' as Sarah I Mew's milk poured down into its snowy foam.

I didn't hear the music of the head-stall chains jingling over the crick at the horse barn, or know if the coyote howled the whole woe of that mountain valley.

The kid and I kissed each other goodnight. Then I walked away, far up and over a ridge-top, through mountain lilac and chaparral, and sat by and by in the moonshine, the letters of the newspaper before my eyes, the hiss of fire in my ears, smoke and a wet, salty scent in my nostrils.

I was not where the mountain lilies grew, or deer browsed in the greasewood clearings, or doves cooed in sycamores.

"Sighted burning and abandoned. Lost with all hands."

My old ship!

Crested combers rolled and great white albatross flew by.

We sat together in her half-deck, singing the song of youth.

"What'll you do when you've got your master's ticket?" a comrade, bright-eyed, asked me.

Queer how things happen, isn't it?

Good to have the promise of the rainbow; soft lights that arch from birth to death and mingle earth with heaven; bringing from torture gladness, wakening hope from fear.

W·M·BIRCHALL
1928

96. *RED ROCK—one of the slow-coaches of the 'Frisco grain fleet.*

CHAPTER II

LONGSHORE REFLECTIONS

I ,was sitting on my back step listening to the song of a golden oriole in the cotton-wood tree near by, when of a sudden there came to me a vision of Belliver Tor. From Belliver my dreaming went by way of Longford Tor and down to Wisman's Wood. I wonder, does the bracken grow there yet; do fox-cubs play above the bubbling Blackabrook? Long ago there were red squirrels in the trees by Yelverton. Plymbridge in the moonlight was a lovely place. Dartmeet by starshine was all glamorous.

This morning I found the first eggs of the red-wing blackbird. In England is no bird like the red-wing. Jet-black elsewhere, he has upon each wing a broad patch of flame. I know no red quite like it— it is not orange-red, nor yet scarlet, nor crimson; just red-wing red. His hen is modest brown. His nest is found interwoven amidst the tule stems (bulrushes you would call them), or in the willows or the golden-rod; in any plant that grows in, or close beside the water. The one I found this morning is in a wild blackberry-bush, the bottom of the nest all but touching the water. Within a dozen feet of it is the nest of a mocking-bird that clears the water by but an inch or two. A little way up the stream is another mocker's nest, six feet from the ground, in an almond tree; and a quarter of a mile away is yet another mocker's nest, forty feet from the ground, in a blue gum. The golden oriole builds in gum trees, his nest interwoven amidst close-hanging leaves.

We have no skylark, but meadow larks were singing everywhere at dawn this morning. Our meadow lark is almost as large as an

287

English thrush; his head and bill are large, his tail stumpy and square. Except for his breast, his plumage is brown; his breast is brilliant deep lemon-yellow. Perched on the top of a fence post, a power pole, or a vineyard stake, or on the topmost twig of a fruit tree, he sits singing hour after hour, his song most gloriously liquid and sweet. After singing his brief, clear song he seems to listen till it is repeated by a rival singer, near or far; then sings again, and so on, and on, and on. His mate's nest is very hard to find, for nesting on the ground beneath a clump of grass she, when disturbed, runs, crouching low to the earth, for a considerable distance ere she takes to wing. In spite of many foes—skunk, snake, blue jay, butcher-bird, crow, ground squirrel, hawk and prowling cat—she holds her own by laying large clutches of eggs and bringing off two broods in a season. Whether meadow lark or the jubilant mocker is the sweeter singer I can never quite determine. The verdict goes now to one, now to the other. The mocking-bird is a merry, impudent little fellow with a soft brown back, a soft grey breast, and white bars upon his wings. He mimics every bird, almost. Morning by morning I hear one echoing the dawn-time chatter of some young pullets that live at the rear of a neighbour's house. Hearing the song of the golden oriole yesterday morning, I thought at first that it was a mocker singing.

But this morning I both heard and saw an oriole. So the oriole is back with us again, a beautiful, flashing, sunny, golden singer. The swallows that went south on September 6th came back on March 18th and are already building beneath the weir where I take my morning swim. They've been to Mexico, to Panama, to South America, perhaps; while I've been here. Lucky travellers! Under the weir, too, is the nest of a black phœbe, a small brown bird with a slightly crested black head and a pale grey breast. Nesting always beneath a bridge or weir, the phœbe brings off two broods a year; four delicate white eggs to a clutch. In an apricot orchard close by, many pairs of red-breasted linnets are nesting; mischievous, fruit-eating birds, disliked by the farmer. Mourning doves nest there too. Mourning doves nest every-where—in peach, almond, apricot, gum, cotton-wood, orange, pomegranate—wherever a tree is, the nest a crude platform of twigs with a few dry grasses for two round white eggs to rest upon. From

288

March till September one is rarely without sound of their low, continual 'coo-coo, coo-coo'. Though a good friend to the farmer, a devourer of weed seeds innumerable, the mourning dove is slaughtered unmercifully autumn by autumn; slaughtered to make 'sport' and to furnish 'dove stew'. A tiny bird, with but a mouthful upon him. And always when the 'open season for doves' begins and the gunners go forth, there are fledgelings in the nests, for the dove broods continuously from spring into autumn.

Through the winter months kingfishers frequent my swimming-pool. Quite unlike the English kingfisher, they are modestly coloured in soft blue with a broad, conspicuous band of white about the neck. In the early morning the sand-hill crane, great blue heron and little heron visit my pool. On a sunny evening a few weeks ago there was a great white heron there, a lovely wader of snow-white plumage throughout. This is the egret, whose crests have been so long sought by market hunters for the decoration of womankind. The law protects him now. Taking not the least heed of me, he fished for minnows within thirty feet of where I stood. Stalking slowly through rank water-side grasses he now and then came to a standstill and, neck outstretched, eye down-turned, watched his chosen victim until, with a dart so swift that to follow it was almost impossible, he transfixed it with long spear-like bill. On the following morning he was in company with a great blue heron. Lying prone in the grasses, I was able to watch them for a long time while they fished within a few feet of me.

There is always something of interest in my swimming-pool. While swimming, I noticed one day a large frog seated upon a piece of driftwood that was caught in an eddy. Seeing that he had something in his mouth I swam up to him to see what it might be, and at first took it to be a large caterpillar that, held by its centre, extended outwards at right angles to the feaster's head. But, seeing that the frog appeared to be having trouble in swallowing his meal, I presently took him in my hand to have a closer look. What I had taken for a caterpillar proved to be the two stiffened legs of a smaller frog. Holding the would-be diner in one hand, I took one of his victim's legs in the other and pulled. Out came an entire frog. How long he had been half-way down the throat of the bully I do not know, but his close imprisonment had done him no harm, for when I set him beside his captor he hopped into the stream and swam off without so much as a 'thank you' to me or a wave to his aggressor. When I had had my swim I went on my way up the stream's side, and on my return stopped to see if the big frog was still on the eddy-caught driftwood. He was gone. Where he had been was a coiled snake, one of the harmless black and yellow snakes that are common by the water's side. Had I not rescued the smaller frog, the snake would have had an even more satisfying meal.

Though rattlesnakes are plentiful in the foot-hills and mountains, we have no harmful snakes in the valley. Commonest of the harmless ones is the gopher-snake, which feeds upon small rodents and often takes ground birds' eggs; sometimes an egg from a hen's nest. Because he accounts for many gophers he is looked upon as a public benefactor; for the gopher, a burrower, who does great damage in alfalfa-fields and orchards, is a costly nuisance everywhere. I have known one gopher to take the bark from around the trunks of three mature orange trees in one night, thus killing the trees; a loss that may be set down at fully a hundred and fifty dollars. Like the English mole, the gopher throws up large mounds of earth. But he is much larger than the mole and a vegetarian. Grasses and flowers, bark, from both the low trunks and the roots of trees, alfalfa and hay of every sort, form his diet. Though preyed upon by snake, weasel, cat, hawk, owl and sometimes by coyote, he multiplies rapidly if food is plentiful and if mankind does not bother him. I have often dug out a nest containing from ten to fourteen young.

Owing to unusually early warm weather snakes appeared at an earlier date than usual this spring. Rattlers have been plentiful in the hills, and, because unexpected, dangerous. Some years ago when in the hills I twice stepped upon a rattler and was lucky enough to escape unharmed. In each instance the snake gave no warning of its presence. Both had recently dined, and so were in a sluggish condition. I know of no sound more alarming than the sudden angry whirr of the rattler. He is a devil in the dry grass. Thanks to the fact that he invariably gives warning, it is very rarely that there is a fatal accident. In twenty-five years I have heard of but four or five people being fatally bitten.

If taken in time the poison of his fangs can be counteracted. A week ago a man who was bitten was saved by being hurried by aeroplane to a city some sixty miles from the scene of his mishap.

The first gopher-snake I ever saw was shown to me by a blue jay who was scolding him from the top of a fence post. Not at that time aware of the harmlessness of the reptile, I killed it. It measured rather over five feet in length and on cutting it open I found within it eleven eggs. But for the blue jay and my ignorance, there would shortly have been eleven more gopher-snakes to combat the gopher! I once lost a job through the agency of a gopher-snake. It was discovered one morning in the bedroom of my employer's sister-in-law, a very nervous woman. Though I protested that any man who would place a snake in the room of a woman and thereby risk throwing her into hysterics and perhaps endangering her health, if not her life, would be both a fool and a villain; although I tried to explain that the gopher-snake is given to climbing up between the outer and inner walls of our California houses, in his search for mice, my protestations were of no avail. My employer's wife was adamant, sure that I had been guilty of a practical joke. I was fired.

The California blue jay is a common scold, like his more gaily feathered English cousin. Garbed in blue and grey, he is a robber of hens' nests and of the nests of whatever wild birds he can find. He helps himself liberally to almonds from the almond orchards. Always regarded as something of a nuisance, he is now more than ever frowned upon, for, of late, pheasants have been introduced into several sections of the State and the blue jay likes pheasants' eggs. The sportsmen are after him. What with racoon, skunk, weasel, hawk, owl, coyote, ground squirrel and blue jay, let alone the frequent flooding by irrigation of much of the land, I very much doubt if the pheasant will be able to hold his own in this part of the State; and I am quite sure that without the waging of a steady and relentless warfare, the blue jay will survive, for he is a merry thief, whose motto is, "I care for nobody, and nobody cares for me". You'll hear him scolding half a mile away, long before you come near him; unless you chance to be approaching his nest, when he at once becomes silent.

Our butcher-bird is also under a ban, but in his case it is unmerited.

291

Though he may help himself to an occasional quail or pheasant egg, he does much toward keeping down the orchard-robbing linnet. Sometimes you'll come upon his larder, mouse or fledgeling spiked upon a thorn. Such small damage as he does is more than offset by the numbers of injurious insects he devours.

One bird we have in California is, I think, found in no other part of the world. There are but a few colonies of him, one of them not far from my home. Owing to an unwarranted prejudice, he is in some danger of extinction. England has his near relative, but England's magpie is a less gaudy bird. Ours wears a marvellous bright yellow bill. There is not a more striking bird in the State.

Three days ago I saw in my garden the first humming-bird. Soon there will be many. Day by day, all summer long, they hover over Canterbury-bell, larkspur, hollyhock, sweet-pea and honeysuckle. By keeping utterly still one may have them come within a few inches of one's face. At the slightest motion they are gone, swift as the sun-rays; their darting flight scarce visible. To find their tiny nests takes long and careful searching.

All night the mockers sing; all day the meadow larks, the golden orioles. All day the mourning dove coo-coos. All day the bees hum in the orange and the lemon blooms. Evening by evening the humming-bird moths come out to dart from flower to flower. No chill wind blows; no cold rain ever falls. We set a date a month, two months ahead for picnicking and picnic when the day comes.

In Devon hedges there are yellow-hammers. In Devon hedges pale blue eggs of hedge-sparrows are found. In the old elms close by a little tree-hid church the jackdaws build. And in the copse nest six grasshopper-warblers, white-throats, bullfinches. On Devon hills the skylark sings. I haven't seen a rookery for years, nor heard a rook. Nor have I seen the hungry thrush break breakfast-snails upon a stone, nor the blackbird in an ivy-covered wall. And how I'd like to see a tom-tit once again! A great tit, and a long-tailed tit (we called him 'mumruffin').

Do fox-cubs romp by Blackabrook today? Is Wisman's Wood the same? Does purple heather bloom on slopes of Belliver? And is the moor mist still a gentle, friendly thing, and driving rain a comrade

292

on the tors?

I'll trade you red blooms of the pomegranate for Dartmoor heathers and orange blooms for golden English gorse. And cowslips? Wild gaudy Mariposa lilies you shall have for cowslips—and trees or say mimosa for a Devon bluebell!

I know a high round hill the side of which is full a hundred acres. In April's month one-half that sunny slope is solid flame of fiery California poppy; the other half is all deep purple Indian paint-brush. You may see the hill from far, morning, noon and eve—a sort of holy hill, a place for prayer and praise. . . . I'll let you have it for a primrose-bunch, picked in a Devon lane!

Old memories are sweet.

W.M. BIRCHALL.
1920

WM BIRCHALL. 1928

CHAPTER III

A PASSING SHIP

We were bound from Oregon to Antwerp with barley. No—it was wheat. I remember, because we ran short of stores on the passage and lived upon gruel and coarse bread made out of cargo.*

We sailed down the North Pacific, crossed the line, stopped at Pitcairn Island for fruit, and rounded the Horn, without once seeing another sail. That was unusual. Often we'd see a ship every ten days or so. Sometimes we'd sight two or three every day for a week at a time.

In the South Atlantic we remained solitary, and the sense of loneliness crept in. We began to hunger in earnest for companionship. We came into the forties, still alone. We reached the thirties, and it was as though the end of the world had come since we left Oregon— as though God had left only ourselves and the sea.

We grew oppressed, exasperated, by magnitude of universe and littleness of man.

In the apprentices' quarters we had swapped our girls' pictures till each girl had made the rounds, had hung above every pillow, several times.

We entered the tropics again, and morning by morning the mate sent a hand to the masthead to scan the horizon. The skipper walked his poop with a telescope beneath his arm. The sea was deserted.

The tropics blazed, the trade-winds were very light. Passing whales but added to our exasperation. They could speed whither they willed. Antwerp, our port, might as well have been in the moon.

---

* Old men forget! This reminiscence probably refers to his first voyage, bound to Liverpool with canned salmon! [Ed.]

We crossed the line, and, creeping into the North Atlantic, saw, far in the eastward, black on the blue sea of mid afternoon, the pinnacle summits of St. Paul's rocks.

A sailor went aloft, listlessly, ignored by all.

"Sail ho!"

Men, boys, and mates, master and carpenter, steward and sail-maker and cook, ran to the railing. There was nothing to be seen from deck but the blue sea, the blue sky, the far-away clear, lifeless pinnacles.

The man aloft pointed, and the skipper spoke to the mate. Our course was altered to bring us toward our invisible sister. As the sun dipped to a cloudless horizon, while from a fiery sky red faded to pink and pink to warm saffron, while blue water became indigo, we saw and impatiently approached the distant white dot of her canvas. At the expectant moment, ere the appearance of the first of night's stars, we watched her flags flutter to her masthead, replying to our own.

Light faded, as the passing of a cloud in April. Above us a star winked. The name of the ship, and nothing more, was ours. Whether she were from Africa or from the Indies, from China or Taltal, we could not know; nor whither she was bound. Through the night we watched for a glimpse of her lights, but saw none. At dawn she was gone. Men of our crew who had known her discussed her—the *Loch Linnhe*, of Glasgow.

Port was become again a possibility. We were not alone.

Fifteen years passed.

I leaned on my gate, athirst for cool wind, parched with mid-August heat, at the close of a day when I had been too dispirited to work. There was no sound but the occasional call of a child or the wail of a heat-distressed baby. From the bare land over the road came the scent of desert weeds. Beside the bare land orange orchards, the trees limp from drought, bided the coming of night to revive their blue-green foliage. The well-to-do were long ago gone to the coast or the mountains. None but working folk remained in the valley village.

The sun sank as, turning to enter my shanty, I saw a man come down the street. I sat on my doorstep and watched as he went from house to house, pausing at each but a moment.

When he approached my gate, I rose to meet him. Over his

97. *LOCH LINNHE, originally full-rigged, in later life as a Finn.*

shoulder he carried a carpet-sweeper. I was too poor to afford carpets, and told him so. He sat at my side on my doorstep and searched me with a long look.

"What ship did you serve your time with?" he asked.

I told him, and asked, "Where did you?"

"The *Loch Linnhe*," he answered.

I said, "I met the *Loch Linnhe* once," and looked to the sky, where, faint above us, the first of night's stars winked dim.

We were silent a moment. Then the man with the carpet-sweeper spoke.

"Off St. Paul's rocks."

Whence we were come, whither we would go, neither spoke of. We talked of the sea.

Port was become again a possibility. We were not alone.

297

98. GALGATE.

CHAPTER IV

DAYS OF MY YOUTH

I was very much interested to see old *Galgate* spoken of some time ago in 'The Blue Peter' and particularly interested to hear that she had once made a smart passage—Shanghai to Astoria in twenty-eight days—I didn't suppose that she had the makings of a passage in her. I remember the big four-masted barque very well. She lay astern of me once in Portland, Oregon. Her sister ship, *Lydgate*, lay just ahead. I think that they were of two thousand seven hundred tons net register. Between them, my own ship, one thousand seven hundred and seventy-four tons, had the appearance of a regular little fly-away. I was an apprentice then and knew their apprentices very well indeed. Both were 'high-living' ships—my ship was not. In fact, she had the name of being a very hungry ship, indeed. Every night after quitting time, my shipmates and I used to invade the half-decks of the two big vessels, where we devoured all such scraps as their apprentices had left from supper.

There were great numbers of square-riggers in Portland in those days. I remember *Hougomont* and *Nivelle*, big new four-mast barques, both of them making their maiden voyage. They had painted ports, and I recall that they had donkey boilers wherewith to hoist topsails in heavy weather;* also on their bulwarks were little winches where-with to haul the braces tight. We apprentices of the older style ships looked upon them as lubberly, new-fangled tubs. I remember also *Euphrosyne*. I never saw a prettier ship. A main skysail, her masts and yards all painted white, her sides a handsome green with white ports. She lay just over the river from my ship. Then, too, there were

---

* Usually only used to set sail on leaving port, when the donkey boiler had been used to heave up the anchor. [Ed.]

99. *LYDGATE in Carrick Roads, Falmouth.*

Patriarch, the old clipper, and *City of Athens*. *City of Athens* tied up alongside us. She had had a rather interesting time of it getting out to Portland. Off the River Plate a pampero gave her a severe buffeting. Her apprentices were all first voyagers; I think there were five of them. During the pampero their half-deck was completely gutted; everything they possessed went over the side; the door was carried away. When the ship arrived in Portland, they were wearing suits made by the sail-maker from old canvas. They were sleeping on the deck—for some reason no new bunks had been built in the half-deck. Their only light was provided by a canvas wick stuck into the spout of an old coffee pot—just such a light as one used to see at country fairs in the old days. After bringing his ship through the pampero safely, the skipper had a tough time of it off the Horn. Eventually, he gave up trying to get her

300

100. FORTHBANK.

round the Horn and came out to Portland by way of the back door, as it were, round the Cape. I do not remember the length of her passage. But one thing struck me very forcibly about her apprentices— I never heard a grouch from them.

City of Athens was so old at that time that they did not dare to use chipping hammers on her sides—they scoured her with sand and canvas. I remember that she had spare spars lashed all along each side of her deck. I never saw a ship so amply provided with spare spars. She left the Columbia a day or two after we did, and made a good passage home.

I remember a little barque that came in to Portland two hundred and ten days out from Genoa—the *Forthbank*. She had been given up, if I remember aright. Her cargo consisted of sulphur. Her second

301

101. *MOOLTAN.*

mate used to go round with a clipper-built girl, who made a living by painting pictures of the ships that came to Oregon.

In Portland at that time were also the *Lady Isobel, Mooltan, Wiscombe Park, Lord Shaftesbury, Inverurie, Eulomene, Sardomene, Cambrian Hills* and a little barque of four hundred and forty tons— the *Lord Kinnaird*—besides many others I have forgotten.

Apprentices used to have great times in Portland in those days. I think that about the finest bit of luck that ever came to any apprentice happened to those of the *Cambrian Hills*. While returning to their ship after having taken the Old Man ashore in the gig at Astoria, they found a dead body floating in the river. They took it ashore and to their joy discovered that it was the body of a man for whom a reward of one hundred dollars had been offered. They collected the hundred dollars. I remember our sorrow that we were going to sea and so were

102. *LORD KINNAIRD in Penzance.*

unable to help them with the spending of it.

Probably a good many sailors who knew Portland in those days recall the old 'Seaman's Bethel'. It was managed by a kind-hearted old white-whiskered fellow by the name of Fletcher. He knew very little about salt-water Jacks; but he meant first-rate. What a time he and the several well-meaning ladies who assisted him used to have, trying to save the souls of young sailors! Good old man! Many the doughnut with which he fed me; many the cup of good coffee. On the wall of his establishment was a notice that never failed to rile apprentices: "Gentlemen will not, others must not, spit upon the floor". No doubt he did a lot of good; I remember one night seeing him dissuade a number of young first-voyage boys of the ship *Clackmannanshire* from entering one of the toughest joints on the whole Pacific coast.

303

103.   WISCOMBE PARK with wind right aft.

It was while we were in Portland that Larry Sullivan, the boarding-master, shipped a dead man's body on the *Wiscombe Park*. Sullivan was about as hard a case as you would find. So, too, was his runner, a fellow named Grant. When last I heard of Larry Sullivan he was serving a term in the Nevada state penitentiary. And I have no doubt that he deserved it and I hope that it was a long term and that they kept him breaking rock. In three years in Portland, Sullivan cleaned up eighty thousand dollars by shanghai-ing sailors.

It was a wonder that apprentices did not get into more trouble than they did. We used to pull off a good deal of devilment—a sky-larking crowd. I recall especially a certain evening on the morrow of which three homeward-bounders were going downstream. Their apprentices foregathered in a good-class restaurant on the principal street for a last shore feed; there were a dozen of them, all told, all big, husky old hands, who had been at sea for several years. Naturally, they wished to sit all together, so they crowded into a little side room,

304

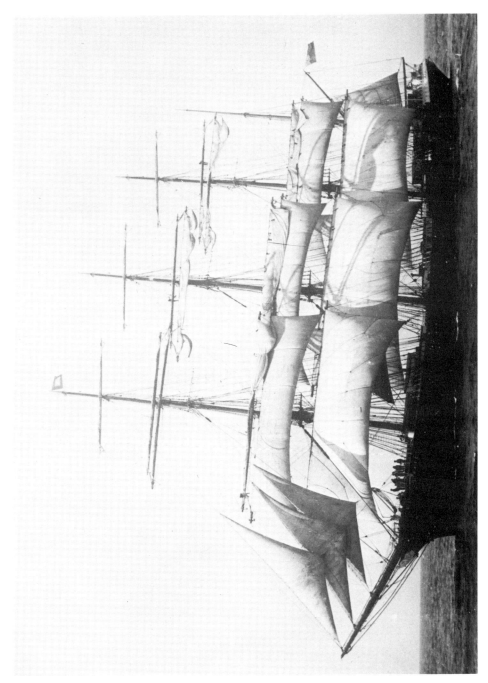

104. *GOLDEN GATE, formerly the LORD SHAFTESBURY, making sail.*

in which were chairs for only six. The proprietor came and being, apparently, one of those peculiar people who imagine that no sailor is a gentleman, ordered them to be quieter and to disperse. One after another, the six for whom there was not room in the cubby-hole, grasped the edge of the partition and swung themselves cheerily over it and into the cubby-hole adjoining. One of them happened to land on the table; it gave way with a crash. The proprietor immediately called all his waiters and, bidding them to see that none of the salt-water Jacks made his escape, hurried off to call the police. The apprentices made for the door; it was blocked by waiters. So the apprentices picked up a table, grasped it by the legs, and pushing it bodily, like a shield, before them, made their exit through a plate-glass window. Leaving the table amidst broken glass, they made their get-away down the street. How it happened that none of them was apprehended, I have never been able to think. Every one made his escape. Later in the evening they feasted in another restaurant.

Many 'Blue Peter' readers no doubt remember the burning of the ship *Pyrenees*.* One morning when they were washing her decks down in the South Pacific, one of the men happened to lay a hand on the main hatch. The hatch was hot. He called the mate and the mate called the Old Man. They battened her down, closed the ventilators and headed for Pitcairn Island. Long before they came to Pitcairn the only way in which they could obtain stores from the lazarette was by lowering a man with a rope round him. For food they had to make out as best they could with coarse cakes made from the wheat with which she was loaded. When the ship reached Pitcairn she was in a very bad way. Her skipper had hoped to beach her at Pitcairn. But Bounty Bay is, of course, no place to beach a ship. And thanks to a fresh breeze, the sea was considerable. The islanders came out and informed the skipper that to beach her would be quite impossible. So, instead of abandoning her, as they might very well have done, they sailed her away for Manga Reva, some three hundred miles distant. Manga Reva has a low, sandy beach, and there they ran her ashore. On landing, they found that the natives of Manga Reva were short of food and living upon nothing but a little bread-fruit and unripe bananas. In a few days' time, however, a small trading schooner

* November 1900. [Ed.]

105. LADY ISOBEL.

appeared and took off the company of the *Pyrenees*. Their lot aboard the schooner was very little better. She was so crowded that it was almost impossible for them to find room to lie down. Eventually they were picked up by an Oceanic liner and brought by her to San Francisco. Some of them shipped with the vessel in which I was an apprentice. And thereby hangs a rather curious tale.

Many years after I had left the sea, I was in the police force of a little city in Central California. My beat was from 6 p.m. to 6 a.m. It was the winter season, and orange packing being then in full swing, the town was crowded with itinerant labourers. To find a place to sleep in, in that particular town, is just about impossible, once the fruit workers have arrived for the handling of the orange crop. Every house is crammed to its utmost capacity. It constantly happened that men who could find no place to sleep, came to me for assistance.

I was standing alone at a street corner late one wet and windy night, when a voice at my shoulder asked, "Mister could a fellow sleep in the station?"

307

Though the railway station of an American town is always spoken of as the 'depot' and never as the 'station', I supposed at first that my questioner was referring to the 'depot'. For it was easy to see that he was not an American. In a moment, however, I realized that it was to the jail that he was referring. So, the jail being at that time empty, I took him to it. It was a dirty little hole, with but two tiny rooms, an iron cot in each—a trivial affair, built of two-by-four timbers spiked one on top of another. Throwing open the door, I said, "I'm sorry the accommodation is so poor". Imagine my astonishment when the fellow replied, "Well, it beats a fo'c'sle off the Horn, anyway".

"When were you in a fo'c'sle off the Horn?" I asked, and taking for the first time a good look at him, saw at once that he was of the old sea breed.

"Last time I was off the Horn, I didn't get so far as the Horn," he somewhat ambiguously replied.

"How so?" I enquired.

"The old hooker took fire and we had to beach her," said he.

Charley, which is the only name I ever knew him by, had been an A.B. in the old *Pyrenees*!

"Well," said I, "this is no place for any salt-water Jack," and leaving my beat to look after itself, took him home with me. Next morning I interviewed the proprietor of the one hotel on his behalf. He was set to work as a dish-washer. But he did not stay long at dish-washing. The hotel-keeper very soon discovered that he was a man who could turn a hand to anything that came along. Charley became a sort of major-domo. All went well for a time; then one evening I found my salt-water Jack half-drunk, singing, "Poor old Reuben Ranzo" in a genuine deep-water voice in front of a pool hall. He had a crowd round him. Also my fellow-policeman had him by the arm. The judge in that particular town had no mercy at all for drunks, It was a 'dry town', though nation-wide prohibition was not yet the law. I rescued my Jack from my fellow-cop, saw him safely to his room and read him a lecture—just such a lecture as a skipper of the old days would sometimes give to an erring apprentice. For a few more weeks the old *Pyrenees* A.B. behaved like any landsman and

106. *PYRENEES being converted to the MANGA REVA.*

gave no trouble at all. But, by and by, the orange season being over, his boss gave him a screwdriver and told him to unship a row of some two dozen little revolving stools that stood before the counter of a quick-lunch room adjacent to the hotel. Left to himself, Charley unshipped a few stools in good order. It appears, however, that he had in his pocket a bottle of 'dry town' liquor. He rested awhile and refreshed himself. Having refreshed himself, he returned to work. Unscrewing the remaining stools was too slow—he took them one by one in his powerful hands, and one by one he snapped their stems short off! That was too much for the hotel man—Charley lost his job. When last I saw him he was cheerily heading away down the railway track, bound for who knows where? The sea, I presume. I never heard of him again.

But foolish though he was, Charley was of a very different type from most of those who at various times appealed to me for help.

309

On the first night we met, I put a ten-dollar gold-piece into his horny fist, for he was, of course, broke. Just as soon as there was that sum due to him from the hotel man, he drew it and hurried to me. "Here's your money, captain," said he. "Keep it," said I, "I don't run across an old square-rigger man every day; you're mighty welcome." But Charley frowned. "I ain't that sort of a Dick," said he; "here's your money, captain." And I had to take my ten dollars back.

*   *   *   *   *   *

The *Pyrenees* burned herself out on the Manga Reva beach. Her hull was later sold to a San Francisco firm, who floated and refitted her.* I saw her a year or two later alongside the Howard Street wharf, San Francisco. She was painted a sort of wine-red and her name was changed from *Pyrenees* to *Manga Reva*. What eventually became of her I do not know.

*   *   *   *   *   *

I recall a voyage in the *Silberhorn*, which made the passage from Antwerp to 'Frisco in one hundred and ten days. She was fifty-three days to the Horn. When abeam of the Horn, with a grand northerly wind to whoop her along, we took in the royals. I furled the main royal. We were close to the land, and while I have, in my day, seen many glorious sights, I have seen nothing so magnificent as the scene that I looked upon from the royal yard. Immense rollers coming up on the starboard quarter; monstrous white breaking combers, upon which there now and again came for a few moments a burst of wintry sunshine. Huge white clouds sweeping overhead. Albatross, mollymawks and Cape pigeons flying in countless thousands all about us. The sea a sheer emerald in the hollows. The foreshore frowning black, with, behind it, mighty, snow-covered mountains. When I came down, I was called to the poop, and there I heard a remark that has stayed with me through long years. The Old Man, a Nova Scotia blue-nose, stood by the taffrail, looking forward the land. Hard case though he was, there was a strange expression in his furrowed face. His wrinkled eyes were lit with a light that I had never before seen in them.

"Boy," said the Old Man, turning to me, where I coiled a rope close by, "See there!" From beside my oft-hated old skipper, I looked toward the wondrous beauty of the snow-white hills of Tierra del

* In 1902. [Ed.]

107. *SILBERHORN.*

Fuego. Unconscious of me now, his stern lips moved. I heard his words, as words from the lips of a man all new to me.

"The new Jerusalem! The new Jerusalem!" murmured the Old Man.

From the Horn we were twenty-two days to the Line in the Pacific. All the way from the Horn to the Line we never started a sheet. She boomed on steadily with her three royals set. In the south-east trades her lee-rail lay almost level with the water day after day, night after night. Often her deck was flooded with lee-water. From the south-east to the north-east trades, we ran without a pause. Day after day of warm sun, warm wind, warm water.

Some say that every sailor is a liar. And so I hesitate to tell the tale of the rest of that passage, which, to all appearances, was to have been a record. Yet, since the tale is true, I'll tell it.

311

On a fine bright evening, while we sat yarning round the fore-hatch, the booby birds appeared and, as was their common custom, settled, as darkness fell, on our yards to roost.

We had with us in the half-deck a young first-voyage apprentice from Worcestershire. He never should have gone to sea. He was a farmer, first and last. Not a sea instinct anywhere in him. (Once when he was not relieved promptly at the wheel he left it untended and started forward!) Shortly after dusk had fallen, this young lad went aloft on the fore, and brought down a booby. One could always take hold of a booby. They were unafraid of man. Before any of us, his fellow apprentices, had seen what he was up to, he wrung the bird's neck. He wanted its skin to "take home to my sister". I've often read of sailors killing sea-birds; I have never, save on that one occasion, seen it done.

Within half an hour of the destruction of the booby the wind left us; a bank of cloud appeared in the north. By eight bells, the yards were jammed hard on the port backstays. Our luck was gone.

To punish the young farmer we sent him to Coventry. Day after day went by and no one spoke to him. He took to going to the galley in the dog-watches, to talk with the cook. We kicked him from the galley door. He had become a very leper to us and we let him know it. One night we found him stretched face down on the main hatch, his shoulders shaking. He was crying like a baby! After that, we forgave the young blackguard. Or at least, we let him out of Coventry. But no one was sorry when, on the start of a new voyage, he failed to put in an appearance. Our Old Man had told the owners that he would not have the boy in his ship!

I'm not superstitious; but I've been to sea; I know the ways of the sea. And, foolish as it may seem to such as do not know the sea, I do yet believe, in fact, I know, that but for the killing of that white booby bird, we should have piled up a record to Oregon. Call me fool, if you will!

> *They call me Hanging Johnnie!*
> *Hang, boys, hang!*
> *I never hung nobody!*
> *Hang, boys, hang!*

312

CHAPTER V

SINGERS OF THE SEA

Did you ever hear this sailor chantey?

When whaling Johnnie went to sea,
Whaling Johnnie, hi-hoh!
A randy dandy lad was he,
All bound away to Hilo.

But whaling John, when he came back,
Whaling Johnnie, hi-hoh!
He'd shell-fish growing down his back,
All bound away to Hilo.

His gal had wed a tailor bold,
Whaling Johnnie, hi-hoh!
Young whaling Johnnie's heart was cold,
All bound away to Hilo.

Of rum he drank a steaming dram,
Whaling Johnnie, hi-hoh!
Said he, "I'll go and fish, by damn!"
All bound away to Hilo.

And still he wanders there and back,
Whaling Johnnie, hi-hoh!
With shell-fish growing down his back,
All bound away to Hilo.

It was at midnight in 60° South that I heard it, sung not on my own ship, but on an unseen ship that passed close by.

We were almost becalmed, after a buster, and bound to the

313

108. *SCOTTISH MOORS—at the end of a voyage.*

westward. The other ship, eastbound, was setting her topgallant sails.
We could hear the rattle of her sheaves and the squeal of her brace
blocks. As she passed away, and we saw for a moment the glim of
her binnacle light, the last stanza came over the rollers:

> *And he still wanders there and back,*
> *Whaling Johnnie, hi-hoh!*
> *With shell-fish growing down his back,*
> *All bound away to Hilo.*

One of the best sea singers that ever I heard was a red-bearded
sailmaker. We were creeping one evening past the Diego Ramirez.
The sea was smooth. The horizons were clear. The clouds were high.
There was no sky. Sea-soaked clothing hung on lines stretched from
stay to stay. Dungarees, much patched shirts, and oil-skins drooped
in the rigging. The canvas was barely full to a breeze from the east-

314

ward. Storm sails were yellow. Rails were rusty.

The sailmaker came from the forecastle and stood by the rail, staring at the bleak Diegos. His voice broke the silence:*

> *Good-bye and farewell to you, fair Spanish ladies;*
> *Good-bye and farewell to you, ladies of Spain;*
> *For we've received orders to sail for old England,*
> *But we hope very soon we shall see you again.*

We'd been down there for three or four weeks, trying to get round the corner. It was midwinter.

I remember a midsummer evening in those latitudes. She was eastbound. Squalls, wild from the westerly, struck her in quick succession. Daylight lasted till far into the night. During the morning we had shovelled snow from her decks in a calm. During the afternoon we had shortened her down from full sail to six topsails and a main topgallant sail. She was booming, her decks dry but for an occasional sea. Crests of emerald rollers seethed along her sides. Very small amid the foamy valleys, she leaped as the squalls smote her. It was Christmas day, and we had celebrated with boiled beans and rice with raisins in it.

When supper was done, all hands came to the deck to watch her go.

We had a fine chantey-man in both port and starboard watch and a fine crew.

The chantey-men started a song, singing together.

All hands came in on the chorus. It rose above the music of the westerlies. It rose above the roaring of the sea:

> *Noel, Noel,*
> *Noel, Noel,*
> *A King is born in Israel*

---

*Compare p. 70, ref. the *Aladdin*. Old men forget! [Ed.]

315

W.M. BIRCHALL
1937

CHAPTER VI

TIMES REMEMBERED

I must thank you for the New Year card that came yesterday. It is far and away the best card that I have had this year. Looking at that fine homeward-winging ship, I feel and scent the sea. "Homeward Bound—the Old Way."

If I shall never more go home that good old way, neither will any other man. Those days are done. I'm glad that I was born in time to know them. I can think of no era that I would have lived in rather than in this era that has seen the last of the great days of sail. Not to have known the glory of the square-rigger would have been a vast misfortune. I cannot imagine my life without in it, from earliest youth, a consciousness of the nearness of ships and the sea. In the earliest recollections of my childhood, I see Atlantic rollers. I see, and I scent, ships. There is no scent to compare with the scent of a ship. Once the scent of a ship, scent of timber, scent of sail, scent of cordage and of cargo, has seeped into a lad he'll have something to make his blood tingle through the whole of his life. The days, murky or bright, when as a little lad I watched the tow-boats bringing ships up a winding, narrow river from the sea, are amongst my most cherished memories. I'd hear the voices of their sailors, see the rust upon their hulls, the stains upon their figure-heads. How a lad would envy those brown-faced, nimble men, who threw their heaving lines so cleverly! And, by night, I'd awaken to lie and listen to the hoarse, far-off blasts of the tow-boats at high-water.

If a man has spent his boyhood by the sea and the best of his years upon it, he'll have a grand picture gallery to wander in when he's old, when he's waiting till his pilot comes.

109.   Wreck of the LIVERPOOL.

Pictures of rivers, harbours, headlands, lighthouses, of ships in storm and calm, hang on the walls of an old sailor's memory—*Beatrice, Dumbrody, Yarana*—dozens more. There was the *Liverpool*, four-mast full-rigger; the biggest full-rigged ship of her day. We met her as we came toward the channel, homeward bound. Under full sail she was, upon a level sea, with barely any breeze, a great, proud-looking ship. One of our young apprentices, seeing them all tight, said that her buntlines needed overhauling. She signalled us and slowly passed from view. Two years later, I heard of her again—lying with broken back upon the rocks of Alderney.*

Pictures hung upon the walls of an old sailor's memory!

"Homeward Bound—the Old Way." The Best Way—the sailor's way.

---

*The *Liverpool* was wrecked in fog on February 2nd, 1902. [Ed.]

CHAPTER VII

SEAS OF MEMORY

Ask an old sailor, a fellow who went to sea when he was a lad, what was the best time that ever he had, and he'll probably have a hard time finding an answer that just suits him. It's so with me.

Looking back to the old days, I have an idea that perhaps the best time of all was when you joined your ship for a new voyage. You'd get out of the train at Lime Street Station, maybe, and hire a cabby to take you and your sea-chest and sea-bag down to the ship. "She's in Salthouse Dock," you'd say; and pretty soon the cabby would pull up and you'd see the lamplight shining through the rain on a ships name. "There y'are, captain," says the cabby. "No, no! That's the *Aberfoyle*," you'd answer. "Drive on a bit." (What a bluff old brute the ship *Aberfoyle* was!) Presently you'd see your own ship's name, and, not bothering to go aft to the gangway, jump over the rail and make for the half-deck door. The man who has never seen a gang of brassbounders sitting in the lamplight on the last night in port has missed a picture for sure. There was comradeship in those good days!

"Where's she bound?" you ask. And *there you are!* I'm not sure that the best time in a young sailor's life was not that moment when he heard that his ship was bound for some port to which he'd never yet been. It'd be, "The Colonies," maybe; or it'd be, "The West Coast"; or it'd be, "'Frisco"; or—ah, what's the good of talking about it? Before dawn, like as not, she'd pull out, with one of the big Joliffe tugs ahead, bound across to New York in ballast to load case-oil

319

110. *The Salthouse Dock. ANGERONA (later Norwegian HIPPEN) in fore-ground.*

for China, or bound round the Horn with coal for the West Coast, or with general for California, Oregon, or B.C.

There'd be a new mate, maybe, and you were pretty sure to have a new second. You'd keep a mighty close eye on both of them to see which of the two you liked best, hoping that you'd have the good luck to be in his watch. You'd size up the hands, wondering what sort of a crew the old hooker was going to have when it came to beating round the Horn in June; and you'd more than likely see a mighty rummy assortment. I mind a voyage on which, with the exception of a couple of Swedes, there were no two men of the same nationality in the fo'c'sle. The only 'white man' was a New Zealander. (None but Yankees and Britishers were 'white men' in the eyes of the half-deck.) When he heard some fellow jabbering in a foreign tongue, the eldest apprentice walked up and kicked him. "English aboard of an English ship!" said he. A great passage we had that time! How *was*

111.   ABERFOYLE.

it that some of those old ships ever did get round the Horn, or, for that matter, even through Biscay? On that passage, if it hadn't been for the apprentices there'd have been no one aboard who could have sung a chantey! But we made it out to B.C. all right, and the first night we got ashore the eight of us walked into a restaurant and ordered "Ham and eggs for three, on one plate."

"What's that, sir?" says the waitress.

"Ham and eggs for three on one plate for each of us, barring Tattersall," replied the eldest apprentice.

I wonder, is Tattersall alive yet? He was a grand young sailor, tough as teak-wood. But there was one queer thing about him—when we got ashore his order was always the same. "Two eggs and a glass of milk," he'd say. After he'd finished the two eggs and the glass of milk he'd have the same again; then he'd have it a third time. He was a temperate sort of chap—couldn't get him to vary that glass of milk!

321

112. ARISTIDES.

I mind a last night ashore when he and I went to a theatre together. It was 'Iolanthe' we saw. On the way down to the ship I led him into a pub; "What's yours, Tattersall?" I asked. "A glass of milk," said he. I can see the face of that Liverpool barmaid yet! But Tattersall was a rattling good shipmate. He was the worst grouch in the half-deck, but he was always the first man aloft. He passed for second mate before Captain Saul. Many a 'The Blue Peter' reader remembers Captain Saul. "Whatever you do, don't go up before Captain Saul!" we used to say; but Tattersall did it, and passed.

Just how it happened I never knew, but Tattersall must have gone back on the glass of milk at last. He went into Portland, mate of the old *Aristides*, and a few days later he woke up in the fo'c'sle of a homeward-bounder at sea—shanghaied! I'd like to have seen his face! But I'll bet he was cock of the fo'c'sle.

I don't know whether perhaps the best time in a sailor's life was not when he sat down to his first shore feed after a long passage. But then, again, there was the day when you hauled in the mooring chains and towed to sea *homeward bound*. And then, too, there was the dark night on which you *picked up Fastnet Light after a hundred and fifty days out.*

Speaking of Captain Saul, I know one chap who never would have passed before Captain Saul. He was level headed enough at sea, but in doing his chart work, while up for second mate, he got rattled and worked his course from B to A, instead of from A to B. The answer was the exact reverse of what it should have been, of course. Just as he came to the examiner's desk he saw what he'd done, and his heart went cold. "What's the matter?" asked the examiner, noticing the look on his face. The examiner let him go back to his seat and look his chart work over. Maybe, after all, the best time in a sailor's life was *when he took the little blue slip from the hand of the examiner.*

I mind a time when my ship was in 'Frisco for Thanksgiving Day. In those days there were a lot of good people in 'Frisco who, thanks to the efforts of the London Missions to Seamen (The Flying Angel), took an interest in young sailors. A certain lady, who had two charming daughters, invited two apprentices to her home for Thanksgiving dinner. They showed up at her house a few minutes before noon. There was no sign of any dinner, no vaguest scent of roasting turkey! And the lady and her daughters wore rather puzzled looks. The lady had meant a seven o'clock dinner; the apprentices had supposed dinner to be a noon meal. A little diplomacy straightened matters out. After a light lunch, the boys were consigned to the care of the two daughters, who took them out and showed them the sights of 'Frisco. Looking backward a matter of thirty years or more, one of those boys remembers that day as one of his very best.

Then again, what of the time when we pulled the Old Man ashore in the gig when the ship was at anchor between Goat Island and the Ferries, waiting a berth? "I'll be back in half an hour," said the Old Man, "you can wait for me." And while forgetting all about us, the Old Man stayed ashore till supper-time. We passed away a happy afternoon loafing about Meiggs Wharf, while our envious comrades, seated on stages slung over the side, chipped the rust from the old hooker.

And there was the time when the Old Man said, "You can go ashore if you want to; be back at the boat at four sharp." On that occasion he, for some unknown reason, opened his heart and gave each boy half-a-dollar. That was the day when, after tossing to see who stayed with the boat, four apprentices, dressed in dungaree shirts, and with dungaree pants rolled to their knees, with tam-o'-shanters on their heads and sheath-knives in their belts, walked barefoot up Market Street, and, quite unconscious of the stares of the 'Frisco people, went to feast on strawberry shortcake at Clark's on Kearney Street. *Was ever a better day?*

Well, let's see! The old ship's moored in Salthouse Dock once more. We're heaving a line tight on the quarter-deck capstan. Someone's singing:

> *Leave her, Johnnie, leave her like a man,*
> *Leave her, Johnnie, leave her!*

The chantey dies. The mate says, *"That'll do!"*

Or maybe you leave the old ship in Hamburg; or over at Antwerp, in the African Dock. She's tied at the mooring buoys out in the middle of the dock, perhaps. As a boat-load of apprentices, with their sea-chests and sea-bags, pulls for the landing-steps you glance round. Her sides are scarred and rusty; long rust streaks run down from the letters of her name. But there's a grand harbour stow on her sails. She shines from boom end to half round. The sun strikes her brass-work and her varnished teak, glitters on the serving of her standing rigging that a few days ago you rubbed down with a mixture of tar and varnish. The Old Man is walking slowly up and down her poop, his hands behind his back. And in the whole of your being there isn't a memory of hunger, of maggoty hard-tack, of thin, over-salt pea-soup, of bloody knuckles and frozen feet. She's the prettiest ship in the dock. *And she's yours!* Just for an instant, starting for home though you be, there's a queer wild joy in your soul that has nothing to do with home. You're a sailor, and—*there's no other life for you!*

You're down at the ticket office, buying a ticket by the Harwich boat, the eight of you from the old hooker; and as you come from the office you meet the apprentices of the *Gulf Stream*. She left 'Frisco ten days before you did. You spoke her once, down in the south-east trades. And along behind the boys of the *Gulf Stream* come the boys of the *Jessie Thomas*. The *Jessie* is just in from the Colonies. You met her south and west of the Western Islands, and for three full days you sailed neck and neck with her. Then, just after daybreak, your jigger topmast staysail halyards carried away, and before you could reeve off new ones, she crept ahead a few feet. But you beat her at last—she docked an hour after you did.

It's night, and we're all aboard the Harwich boat. She's slipping along at twenty-two knots. We're travelling second cabin, of course, and down in the second cabin accommodation above the rudder there's a crowd of Germans, Dutchmen and Belgians. The bunks are arranged in two tiers, one tier above the other, and in the top tier the bunks are arranged four wide. You have one of the farthest-in bunks, against the ship's plates. To get in, or to get out, you have to climb over three perturbed fellows who are trying hard to get a little sleep, and who can't speak a word of English; and you spend the night crawling to and fro. For a time you lie in your bunk and shout to one of the *Jessie's* boys in a bunk beneath you. As he and you decide to get up and go and walk the deck a while, a gang of the other apprentices come below to turn-in. You all stand in a crowd, talking and laughing. You've all got good shore 'baccy. At sea, because the Old Man's slop-chest was empty, you've been smoking dried tea-leaves for three weeks past. One of the *Gulf Stream* boys has found three bottles of wine in the bunk of one of the foreigners, and has appropriated it. The foreigners can't make you out at all; think you belong to the ship, and believe you when you explain to them that passengers are not allowed to have wine with them. *Was ever a better night?*

Morning comes. The Harwich boat docks, and you scatter. "So-long!" *Was ever a better morning?*

So-long! Meet me off the Western Islands, and we'll roll up the Channel together!

W.M.BIRCHALL. 1929.

CHAPTER VIII

HAIL AND FAREWELL

Last night the wind blew in from the sea. At two this morning, snug in bed, I heard it roaring over the hills. In the dark of my bedroom I could taste the sea fog. The old oaks on the hill ridges behind my home lean far over to the east, blown through long years by the winds that come in from the sea.

The old trees from whose acorns they sprung leaned as they now lean when Drake dropped his anchor in the small bay a few miles to the north of the Golden Gate. A chill climate, Drake said it was, and with "a stinking great fog." Where my roof rises the sea fog seldom comes. It rolls along the ridges a mile away, coming usually no lower. But this morning, detached by the roaring wind, great wisps of it whirl over my roof tree.

And watching it drive by I think of Drake, and the sea roads that lie beyond the hills, and of old comrades of the days when I followed those sea roads.

There comes to me a memory of the man who was mate on my first voyage. He is dead long since, buried in the dark deeps far down beneath the upper azure. A small square man with a quiet voice, and brown eyes in which was never any trace of excitement or of any wrath, no matter how suddenly a squall might heel the ship down, and blow topsails and courses out of their bolt-ropes; no matter what cause for wrath a loafing apprentice might give him.

There was in his quiet voice a scorn far more cutting than any anger ever could have been. "Hop along!" I hear his quiet voice say, "Hop along, and overhaul that mizen royal bunt-line!"

As though to climb to a royal swaying through an arc of nigh eighty degrees, to a racking spar just discernible against the stars, was no more than to pick up a lady's handkerchief!

But it is the freeing ports that come most often to my mind when I think of the mate of my first voyage. It was always I whom he called on those Plutonic nights when they must be lashed wide open to let the water flow from the swamped decks. We four apprentices of his watch would be sitting in our half-deck, in oilskins and sea-boots, listening to the rage of wind and water without; the ship staggering under a main topgallantsail perhaps, or shortened down to topsails and foresail; the wind steadily freshening.

Or perhaps we would be out on deck, huddled together in the lee of the midship house, mute and shivering, cursing ourselves for fools for having come to sea. A whistle shrills from the darkness close by. My name is called. I hurry from my comrades. "Aye, aye, sir!" I cry, and perhaps bump into the invisible mate as I speak. "Get a chain hook and come aft!" he orders, and I run through the inky night to the locker under the fo'c'sle head where the chain hooks are kept, and thence to the quarterdeck where the mate awaits me.

With the chain hook in his hand, the mate kneels on the topgallant rail while I push open the first freeing port, thrusting out the bight of its lanyard that he may grapple it. "Make it fast!" he shouts, as I rise to my feet and take the lanyard from him. While he hurries on to the next freeing port I lash the first wide open. I am soaked to the hide, of course, already. Darkness is absolute. Rain falls in stinging sheets, mingles with the hissing sprays, smites my down-bent face.

From the break of the poop to the break of the fo'c'sle head I go, till each of the six freeing ports is lashed. But was it only six? Or was it a hundred? At each I must push out the lanyard for the mate to grapple. The sea washes high about me as I kneel in the scuppers. It comes to, comes above, my shoulders often. It chokes me at times, so that I am forced to let go the heavy iron freeing port, which, unless I withdraw it quickly, falls upon and bruises my arm, or my hand. Save to shout "Make it fast!" the mate never speaks.

He shouts that at the first port only. It is as though he were an automaton, without feeling. As he is, so must I be. But at last, with

328

113. No weather for securing wash-ports! The ELGINSHIRE.

all the ports open, I hear his voice again. "All right! Put the chain hook away!" I feel for the chain hook that he is handing me, moving my hand, the knuckles of which are broken and bloody, from side to side in the pitchy dark. My hand touches his. There is no warmth in his hand. It is like an iron hand, cold, hard as the iron of the freeing ports.

Never does he say "A nasty job, boy!" or say anything at all. I do not expect him to, and yet—did he do so—it would make the night, if not warm, at least a little less bitter cold.

In bad weather I always stayed on the poop when it was my turn to "keep the time"; to watch the chart-room clock and strike the bell at each half-hour. Save to say "Go fill my pipe," he never spoke to me.

Then I would go down to his cabin, find his plug of black tobacco,

329

and with my sheath knife cut enough to fill his old black, evil-smelling pipe. The first time I did so I took the pipe back to him unlighted.

Only on that one occasion did I ever hear any trace of impatience in his voice. Thenceforth I always lit it for him, and kept it drawing well till I put it into his hand. He never said "Thank you." I did not expect him to. Yet had he done so it would have made the cold night a little different.

It was as though the opening of freeing ports and lighting of a pipe so strong that it made my head reel were matters too inconsequential for any mention.

On fine nights I often kept my time on the poop also. Throughout my two hours I would see his short, square form pacing to and fro, to and fro, to and fro, pausing now and again to look at the compass, or up to the dimly visible leech of the mizen royal.

Only once in the thirteen months that I sailed with him did he speak to me save to give me an order, or quietly to berate me for work ill done. That once was on a night when the ship lay on a sea as level as a dance floor, her sails flat and lifeless, no motion of any sort in sky, air or water.

He said then, in a tone so low that I did not catch his words, something about a woman, and I knew that he spoke of his wife ten thousand miles away. He had never told any of us apprentices that he had a wife. We had come to know it through some other channel, and that he had also a very small son.

Only on that one occasion in more than a year did he give any sign of being other than an automaton. In the darkness of that night it seemed to me that in his low voice, so low that words were indistinguishable to me, there was very great tenderness.

During that voyage of thirteen months he came thrice into our half-deck. The first time that he did so the ship was somewhere in the South Pacific. Two weeks ago we had at last, after a full month of savage gales, rounded the Horn.

Now, with a fine fair wind driving her, she was going at a fast clip under full sail. With an atlas open on our small table we were trying to figure out her probable whereabouts. Not once since she sailed had we known her position.

A ship's crew very seldom knew where their ship was. Only the skipper and mates knew. Hearing someone enter our door, we turned to see the mate. "Who's got a match?" he asked. Given a match, he stood drawing at his old black pipe, his expressionless eyes upon the atlas before us.

"Whereabouts are we, sir?" asked the eldest apprentice. He had just got his pipe to draw well. He glanced casually at the atlas, and seemed to be about to turn and leave us. Then, as though suddenly changing his mind, he leaned over the atlas, studied it for a moment, and, taking his pipe from his lips, set the end of his pipe stem upon that part of the South Pacific where the ship was. And then, without a word, he was gone.

The second time he entered our quarters was at close to midnight of a black squally night in the North Pacific. A few minutes ago he had brought the boat back to the ship after having for two hours in a rough sea sought in vain for an ordinary seaman gone overboard from the fore royal yard a hundred and sixty feet or so up in the darkness. "Who's got a match?" he asked. Given a match, he stood drawing at his old black pipe, expressionless eyes upon us where we sat heavy-hearted on our sea-chests. When the pipe was drawing well he took it from his lips. "Hold on well when you're aloft!" he said, and turned and was gone. It was an order. To hold on well when aloft was part of a sailor's job, and must not be neglected.

The third time he visited us was when the ship was well up in the North Atlantic, some seven months later. We should be home soon now. But how soon? Would it be a month, weeks, or days? "How many more days will it be, sir, till we sight land?" asked the eldest apprentice, when the mate had been given a match and had his old pipe drawing well. Without a word, with a scarce perceptible shrug of his shoulders, he turned and was gone.

His personality seemed always to imply that in his mind was but one thought—"Do your job. No talk." And somehow, despite his seeming indifference to the longings of our youth, we all liked him. We felt something of pride in learning under him what was described in our apprentice indentures as "the business of a seaman."

Did our old Blue Nose skipper berate us, as he not seldom did

331

in no uncertain tones, we jested about it later in our quarters. Did the second mate, a big blustering Geordie, swear at us for a lot of useless young lubbers, we felt merely a cool contempt for him.

But did our little mate voice for any one of us a quiet scorn, that one felt humbled for a long time afterwards. To hope to win from him a word of approval was useless, we knew. So it was that he trained us, his callow charges, by precedent, without speech.

When the ship came to port and we joyously left her to go to our homes not one of us bade him good-bye, or had from him a good-bye. At my last sight of him, when I turned to look back to the ship, he was standing on her deck, looking aloft and calling a quiet order to a rigger calm as though there were no such thing as a home port, collected as though there were not on earth any other thing beyond the attending to of duties.

Close to him the skipper stood in excited conversation with the owner, who was equally animated. Flags whipped on a brisk wind. Tugs taking ships seaward, or bringing in, hooted impatiently. The morning reverberated with the sirens of liners bound in or out. From streets near by came the clatter of wagon wheels over cobble-stones.

From warehouses stevedores hastily trucked bales and boxes of cargo for all the ports of the world. Winches whined and shrieked. Blocks rattled. The little mate saw nothing, save the matter about which he called to the rigger up the mast. But in that last momentary glimpse of him I remembered that night when, with the ship becalmed upon a motionless ocean upon the world's other side, he had spoken of a woman. Would he unbend when he met her? I knew that he would. But I did not picture him so doing. I did not try to. Only I remembered the tenderness which for that one brief moment I had caught in his indistinguishable words upon that far-off sea.

When I joined my ship for another voyage our little mate was gone. If, for the first day or two, we missed him, we soon forgot him. He became but a memory. Somewhere at sea was a ship, with him for her mate. We were at sea in a ship, and to-day was to-day. In all probability no one of us would ever again set eyes upon or hear of him.

Years passed. There were bitter winters off the Horn, parching calms on the line. Between the Horn and the line the trade winds blew balmily. Always there was a port waiting us at voyage's ending. A sailor's first voyage becomes a faded picture, hung away on a far dim corner of the hall of memory.

Voyage by voyage when the ship came home older comrades left her. By and by my turn came. My apprenticeship was done at last. Four stern years of it. Now to win my ticket! There was no other candidate the week I took my exam. The examiner, an old grey-headed retired clipper captain, had me all to himself. Nervous work it was for me!

The old grey head had a reputation for laying himself out to trip candidates. A man of the older school, with something of contempt for the youth of today! Every fibre of my being was alert and at last it was over. I'd won. But then, when I thought that every question had been asked, the grey head called me back. "What," he asked, his solemn eyes searching my face, "is your opinion of the sort of man a mate should be?"

I was staggered. Here was something totally unlooked for! Suppose I made the wrong answer? Would the examiner fail me?

And then there came to me a sudden memory of the little mate of my first voyage. Instantly I replied, "Do your job. No talk."

"Very good," murmured the old grey-headed captain, with the hint of a smile about his wrinkled lips.

It was some three years later. I was at Santa Cruz de Tenerife. The volcano of Tenerife stood distinct in the clear tropic air as my ship steamed into the harbour. Heliotrope, bougainvillaea, jasmine and roses trailed high over the flat-roofed houses of Santa Cruz, houses of red, of blue, of pink, green, ochre and white. The bright morning sun gleamed upon the shining foliage of palm and of pepper, of orange, lemon, frangipani and banana. No ripple stirred the peace of the deep azure water, no least cloud marred the ineffable azure of the sky.

Our anchor dropped to the sea bottom. The ship lay still. Thralled by the morning's beauty, her seamen, master, and mates and men, stood silent at her rail. And then, as a white boat with oar blades flashing in the sun drew under her side, a paean of bells burst forth from the dark cathedral tower of the little fairy-like city.

A newspaper tossed from the boat fell at our captain's feet.

And then it was that I heard of the little mate of my first voyage again. Three days ago it had happened. Three days ago they had buried him, at the other side of the sea, to the south and the westward, in the blue deeps nigh to Martinique.

I could see him plainly, could hear his quiet voice, as, with Mont Pelée in sudden eruption, with fiery ashes and cinders and hot rock falling in terrible showers upon his vessel's deck, he ordered her crew below to safety, and himself took her wheel to steer her seaward from the harbour of St. Pierre's doomed city.

It was by chance that later, in Port Natal's harbour, I met one who had been with him. "Roasted alive on his feet, he was, saving his crew and his ship."

WMBirchall 1925

CHAPTER IX

LIFE IN THE GOLDEN WEST

(Extracted from a letter to the Editor of 'The Blue Peter')

It is sad to see the old sailing ships rotting at their moorings. It is good to have known them in their hey-day. Since I knew them I have known the mountains and the deserts—and there is still no loveliness that can compare with the loveliness of the sea. It is good to think upon the watery prairies where the trade-winds blow; good to think upon the thunderous waters about the Ramirez and the Crozets. One may yet feel the swing and hear the roar of them. It is good to know that they are unchanged, beautiful as ever; though empty of ships to-day. It is strange to think of the old sailing tracks as deserted. Never a sail goes by, never a side-light glimmers; never an albatross dips to the wave-crest to seize upon scraps from the sea-cook's galley. Our sea rolls on and on. There still are nights when phosphorus gleams from horizon to horizon, when all the ocean seems aflame with green fire. There still are the moon-bows. There still are calm, and gentle breeze, and furious hurricanes. But now no weary sailor comes creeping down the rigging with knuckles bloody from furling ice-stiffened sails. No sailor moans, with lips thirst-swollen. And no man asks another, "How many days do you give her to make the passage in?" To-day men go to and fro upon schedule. They judge the sea tamed. But now and then, when it so decides, the sea will take its way with men. Mountain may be tamed by high-way and by tunnel. Deserts may be irrigated, tamed utterly, made into gardens. They'll never tame our old sea; for when He fashioned the sea, God said, "This I keep for My own. Here shall ever echo the sound of My 'I AM'."

335

That is how I feel about the sea. Man's footprint may not soil it.

It is but a few years ago that the plains of Stanislaus were a desert, or well-nigh a desert. In the early years of California no one paused to consider the plains. Men made all haste from the sea to the Sierran foot-hills, where the world was gone mad over gold. Galloping stages took the shortest cuts from the sea to the gold-country. Men hurried on horseback, or afoot, if they were too poor to afford four feet beneath them. The hills were upturned with pick, shovel, and dynamite. It was not till the height of the fever passed—when it became apparent that the hills were not all gold—that men began to eye the wide plain. Then for many years, because nothing but stock was raised on the plains, the little mining towns supplied the valley settlers with much of what they needed. If the settlers on the plains bought fruit, the fruit came from the foot-hills. "The plains will never be fit for anything but cattle country"; and at that there were dry years, years of scant rainfall, when stock wandered hungry.

When someone discovered that grain could be grown on the plains, a change took place. Wheat and barley began to take the place of herds; ships began to come from Europe. As more and more acreage went under the plough, more and more ships came to San Francisco, and to the wharves along the Sacramento River. And in time the plains of Stanislaus were a vast grain field. "The plains will never be fit for anything but cattle and grain"; and by that time the days of gold-fever were done, and the old hill-towns were grown sleepy. The rivers were busy with flat-bottomed stern-wheelers that came to take the grain to where deep-water ships could load it. Little cities sprung up on the plain; cities without very much hope, because but for the water of the rivers, there was scant water, and without water no city may thrive.

In the 'seventies the railway came down the plains of Stanislaus. It came towards Toulumne and Paradise cities, little settlements that stood beside the Tuolumne River. The railway people asked the people of Paradise to give them a right-of-way through their town; and the Paradise people refused, being quite without vision. Then the railway people bought land and set out a new town-site for themselves. When the town of Modesto began to rise like a mushroom the people of Paradise and Tuolumne realized that they had made a mistake; realized that no town on the open plain could hope to compete with a town through which ran a railway. So they jacked up their store-buildings and their residences, hitched great teams of mules and of horses to them, and dragged them over the dusty road to Modesto.

It was not many years after the birth of Modesto that here and there men began to speak of water—water from the hills; water to be had by damming the rivers where they flowed out through the Sierran foot-hills. Other people laughed at these, saying that it was a fool's dream; that the plains were doing as well as ever they could hope to do in raising wheat and barley.

It was only after many years of hard fighting that the dreamers won their way. There were endless lawsuits; there was endless bitter-ness. But at last a dam was built at the old mining town of Le Grange, thirty-two miles from Modesto, in the foot-hills. And after that the face of the plains began to alter.

It was not till five years ago that a second dam was finished where the tiny town of Don Pedro stood. That dam backs up the water of the Tuolumne River, and forms a lake fifteen miles in length. Beneath the lake lies the old town of Don Pedro. At the foot of the dam is a power-house. Eight miles down-river is the older dam, the diverting dam, at Le Grange. From it canals carry the water out to the plains of Stanislaus. When the river runs low in late summer the gates of Don Pedro are opened and the lake is drawn from to irrigate the plains.

To-day Modesto, with, in its very heart, one of the old buildings brought from Paradise city, has fifteen thousand people. For miles on all sides of it are orchards of peach, apricot, fig, and almond. Amongst the orchards are vineyards of table, and of wine, and raisin grapes. There are over fifty thousand head of dairy cattle in Stanislaus county. Such little grain as is still grown is grown along the lower foot-hill slopes. Such beef cattle as are raised graze along the grassy hills. Where Paradise and Tuolumne cities once stood there is no sign of any city; there are vineyards and orchards there. No stern-wheelers come up the rivers to-day.

Even in Stanislaus county few people have ever heard of Estanislao. Estanislao was an Indian of California's early days, a convert of the

337

Franciscan fathers at Mission San José beyond the coast range. Having grown weary of the peaceful ways of the fathers, he made his escape and found his way through the ranges into the open interior plains. There he took to raiding what few settlers there were. The Spaniards sent a force after him; he defeated it. They sent another; he gave battle in the willows and bullrushes of the river-bed. The Spaniards set fire to the bullrushes, and his small following was conquered. Having escaped himself, he later returned to the Mission and became a "good Indian" once more. Now and again a farmer ploughs up a skull or a broken weapon on the site of Estanislao's last fight. From Estanislao, Stanislaus county gets its name.

Shortly after the war, two unscrupulous Englishmen, who had long resided in California, advertised a worthless section of the interior valley and brought out from England some forty families. They sold, to these their fellow-countrymen, land that was practically valueless, owing to lack of water. To-day not one of those forty families is left— one poor fellow killed himself; the rest are gone, impoverished and doubtless in despair. The rascals who robbed their fellow-countrymen have left the country; their names are a byword.

All land in California is not good land. There is waterless land, and there is some alkali land. Even in the best sections of the State farming calls for skill to-day. The man who buys before he has stayed to make a careful investigation is foolish, in whatever section he buys.

It is the river-water that has made Stanislaus county. There is irrigation for every farmer in turn, all summer long. The irrigation season usually starts in late March, after the rains are over. The water is turned out of the canals and back to the river-bed in October, when all need of water is over at the end of harvest. The rains usually begin in November, sometimes in October, and sometimes not till December. The rainfall is usually about fifteen inches, sometimes more, sometimes less. The more rain, the more snow on the Sierras. It is the snow on the Sierras that makes the summer irrigation-water for the plains. Grass grows all winter long, for there are not many nights of frost. Once in a great while there is a slight flurry of snow, that melts within a few hours of falling. But though not a country of frost or snow, the cold of Stanislaus is penetrating. Orange and lemon and pomegranate

338

trees thrive. None the less, on winter days, people are comfortable in a heavy overcoat. In summer, there is, almost always, a pleasant north-west trade-wind all day. At times there are 'hot spells,' when the thermometer climbs to 100° or 110° in the shade. Once in a long while it goes as high as 115°. But a hot spell never lasts for more than three days. The average summer heat is around 90° in the shade, and the air, being dry, is not oppressive. There is good swimming in deep canals, and in the rivers. In the rivers, too, black and striped bass are plentiful. Deer and bear are plentiful in the mountains. And in the mountain streams are plenty of trout. Mocking-birds sing all night through spring and early summer. Orioles nest in the blue gum groves. In winter many migratory birds make their homes on the plains. All the year the great blue heron fishes in the rivers and canals. San Francisco Bay is eighty miles away. One can leave home in the morning, spend the summer day in sea-fog, and be home by night.

In the foot-hills fifty miles away the old gold-mining towns lie dead. Columbia, that once had a population of over thirty thousand, is deserted. The sites of some of Bret Harte's mining towns are represented to-day by but a few tumble-down dwellings. The ships that used to come for wheat and barley come no longer; big Liverpool steamers load cargoes of canned fruit from Stanislaus plains to-day.

By the way, English may grows well here. Not as well as in Gloucester, Somerset, or Devon, but it grows; it does well round the bay. My garden is full of old English flowers—sweet william, stocks, wallflowers, Canterbury bells, etc. Roses are a glory here in spring. To-day (November 17th) I have a house full of chrysanthemums. But any night now we shall have our first frost; 25° or 26° above zero is about as low as we get. Once in a while it drops lower; once in a while we have a practically frostless winter.

W M BIRCHALL 1935.

114. *Old sailing ships rotting at their moorings in 'Frisco.*

CHAPTER X

CALM

W̶e were bound from the Columbia River for Falmouth with a cargo of wheat. One morning, when we were a few miles north of the Line in the Atlantic, the last faint airs of the south-east trade-wind died away. A windless, unrippled sea rolled up from south-east in long, smooth, blue swells. With no wind to steady her, the ship rolled and pitched with a motion so sharp and jerky that, unless one held to hand-rail or bulwark, to walk her decks was impossible. The parrals clacked. Chains slatted against the masts. Sails flapped heavily against the rigging. Bubbling in at the scupper holes, water flowed in lazy trickles from side to side of the main-deck. Presently the skipper came up from breakfast. He gazed round the horizon. There was no cloud, no vestige of any cloud, in all the sky. He scowled, and called an order to the mate.

One by one, to save them from chafing, we clewed up the square-sails till courses, topsails, topgallant sails and royals hung idly drooping in their gear. We brailed in the spanker. We hauled down the gaff topsail, the staysails and jibs.

Without an inch of canvas set, the ship tossed lifelessly on water so limpid that if one dropped anything overboard it could be seen till it was far below her twenty-three-feet-deep keel.

It was March, and the sun was overhead. The heat was intolerable.

A Norwegian sailor went to the carpenter's shop for the shark hook. From the carpenter he went to the cook to ask for a piece of salt pork. The bait was no sooner in the water than a number of pilot-fish came to investigate. They were still swimming about it when the

341

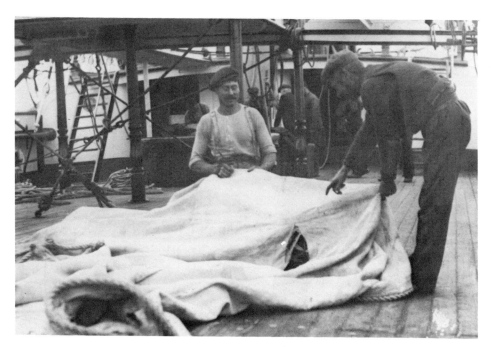

115. Repairing sail on deck aboard the German FAHRWOHL.

shark arrived. He dived, turned over, and rose with his white belly uppermost, and his great semi-circular jaws wide open. Another moment, and, assisted by four of his comrades, the Norwegian was hauling him aboard.

A sailor fetched a capstan bar from the rack—a hardwood bar some seven feet long, squared at one end and bluntly pointed at the other. They placed the pointed end between his jaws and thrust it well into his throat. "Bite on that, ye sailor eatin' devil!" they jeered. He gnashed it savagely. They drove sheath knives deep in his brain; one cut his tail off. When, after a long time, he began to weaken, they cut his head off. An apprentice cut out his backbone to fashion it into a walking stick. Another took some of his teeth to have them made into tie-pins when the ship reached port. At supper that evening the Scandinavian and the German and Finnish sailors feasted. But the English sailors and apprentices preferred to sup upon the customary hard-tack and thin tea.

Day passed, oven hot, with the pitch bubbling from the seams, and the deck too sun-heated to walk upon barefoot. After sunset we slapped sea-water over the deck's length to soak and tighten the scorched planks.

By sunset the swell had died down. After the decks were wetted, the sailors and apprentices gathered on the main hatch. The Norwegian who had caught the shark fetched his concertina. Twenty sailors danced, barefoot. Chips, the carpenter, sat on the bulwark to watch. The Chinese cook stood grinning in his door. The two mates walked the quarter-deck together. The skipper moodily paced his poop.

Eight bells went. The sailors of the watch on deck and those of the watch below, and the apprentices of both watches, lay down on the hatches to sleep the night away. Lest they be struck moonblind, all slept with covered faces.

While the man at the wheel stood motionless in the bright moon-light, while the man on look-out on the forecastle head stood statue still, the mate leaned on the taffrail and softly whistled for a wind. Shadows of mast and spar, of standing and of running rigging, lay clear cut upon the long white decks. No motion. No sound. From the open port of the cook's room, on the deck of which lay the pig-tailed cook and his compatriot, the steward, a heavy odour of opium pervaded the becalmed ship.

Morning came. The sun leapt from beneath the sea rim. As we finished scrubbing the spotless decks from end to end the skipper appeared. Scowling, he looked round the cloudless horizon.

Day passed, the ship utterly motionless upon an utterly motionless ocean. During the afternoon dolphins appeared, long blunt-nosed tapering beauties, some of them five and six feet long. While swimming in the sunlit water they were of scintillant emerald. When they swam close in, under the ship's shadow, they turned to scintillant purple and violet.

His hook baited with a scrap of red and white rag, an apprentice sat on the boom end fishing. That evening at supper the apprentices ate dolphin. The foremast sailors refused it. "It'll poison a feller,"

343

they said. The boys laughed at them, but within a few hours of supper the apprentices' heads felt swollen and puffy.

Night passed as the preceding night had passed, save that sheet lightning played incessantly all round the moonlit horizon. All night the mate or second mate softly whistled for a wind. Now and again the skipper appeared, to gaze round the horizon for a time and return scowling below.

Another day came. Another night came. Not an air, no cat's-paw on the water, no motion. By day the blazing sun, by night the flashing lightning. It was then discovered, when one fresh water tank was almost empty, that the other was contaminated, and we were put on short rations.

Morning by morning we scrubbed the decks. Evening by evening we wetted them down again. During the day we worked in the blazing sun—some making spunyarn from old rope, some tarring the standing rigging, some chipping iron rust from the bulwarks, some painting. We no longer danced in the dog-watch. We no longer sang. At breakfast and at supper we munched sea-biscuit, hard-tack that, having voyaged from Liverpool to 'Frisco, from 'Frisco home and out to Oregon again, had grown soft. It was full of long, white maggots. At dinner we swallowed pea or bean soup, and chewed old tough salt pork—the soup always over-salty from the pork that had been boiled in it. Night by night we gathered by the big wash deck tub, and, having pumped it full, slapped sea-water over one another's naked bodies. We took turns in sitting submerged in the tub.

Early night, when the moon was not yet up, and while for a brief space no lightning illumined the breathless sea, an apprentice reached into the carpenter's room and stole his can of fresh water without disturbing his slumbers. Late in the night he woke and strode to the deck blaspheming. He wakened the sailors and they damned him. He wakened the apprentices and they laughed at him. He went up to the poop to complain to the mate. Paying no attention to him, the mate leaned on the taffrail and whistled for a wind: It was three weeks a-coming!

344

CHAPTER XI

DUTCH FLAT

Here's a little description of my new home. I came here on a Monday evening, just before sunset. On Tuesday evening I bought an old house that was built by the owner of the saw-mill in Dutch Flat's palmy days. I couldn't resist it. I've seen no such daffodils since I saw them at Dymock, Gloucestershire; no such narcissus. I have two lovely maples by my front fence, a huge old oak by my kitchen door, a very lofty poplar by my work-room window. From my back, I look down from a bluff upon the mined-out area. In front, I look across a little dip with a clear creek flowing down it to a pine-clad hillside. The birds are marvellous. Robins, the American robin, a bird the size of your blackbird, or rather larger, brown back, black head, bright buff breast and underpart, sing before day and after dusk. The red-headed golden oriole nests close to me. Brilliant yellow warblers, bright blue-crested jays and many other birds sing all day long.

Twenty miles away, down the mountains, is a town of some thousands of people, where are many Cornishmen. It is a goldmining town still. The Cornishmen came in numbers to the goldmines. They still make saffron cakes! The old gold towns of Red Dog and You Bet are seven miles down mountain, both quite dead. Just a few old-timers live at each. How this place has escaped being commercialized I can't think. I hope that till I'm gone it will not be! It is a little bit of New England and a little bit of Old England. I have a gorgeous old house—the newest house in the place. Forty years old! In California, forty years is about the equivalent of four hundred in the Old Country!

Dutch Flat's a grand place. I've been here a month and not a soul has asked my business!

There's no 'Chamber of Commerce' at Dutch Flat, no 'Booster's Club'. There's none of the modern ballyhoo that makes an old sailor wish he were becalmed in a tough windjammer on the line, or picking up a frozen topsail down in sixty degrees south latitude in the dead of winter. They've a great idea nowadays of this thing called 'Progress'. You can't have progress in a society in which the chances of a man lying back and trying to do his own thinking are getting rarer all the time.

It was only by accident that I happened to hear of Dutch Flat, by one of life's lucky chances. "Where is the place?" said I to the old fellow who told me of it.

"Did ever you hear tell of the Donner party?" he asked me.

"I did that," said I. Anyone who knows anything of California's early history knows something of the Donner party.

"Well," said the old fellow, "Dutch Flat's about thirty mile down the mountains from where the Donner party perished. It's an old dead gold-mining town."

Next day I came to Dutch Flat. It's history, pure and simple, that after Donner and his party of emigrants became snowed in just across the divide of the high Sierras, on their way to California, the living ate the dead. They did worse that that, too. For after a few of them, seeking relief, had managed to get down to Sutter's fort on the Sacramento, where Sacramento city stands to-day, Sutter sent back a couple of Indian guides with them, to help the party find its way out. On the way down from the terrible mountains, one of the Donner party shot the two Indians from behind and their bodies were used for food. There still lives an old woman who, as a child, was a member of the Donner party. But she can't tell you anything much about it. Though grown people boiled and ate their shoes, though human flesh was devoured before her eyes, she was too little then for any memory of it to remain. To-day there are pleasure resorts by the shores of the lake beside which Donner and his people perished. There's a dance hall. In summer-time the place is thronged with people who dance and fish and swim and row and hold gay parties. The golden day

116.   *Caulking decks—aboard the INVERCLYDE.*

of California is gone and where the emigrant trail once wound, monstrous locomotives haul huge trains, with three locomotives to the train—one in front, one in the middle and one to push from behind. Where oxen that had hauled them from beyond the far-off plains across the wide Missouri River once drew groaning wagons laden with emigrants and their chattels down the mountain sides, a concrete highway winds to-day. In a dip of the hills below the gleaming railway and the highway, Dutch Flat lies sleeping.

It was a sunny day, with here and there a vagrant cloud, when I came up the mountains seeking Dutch Flat. Dipping down a steep hill between tall pines, I left the highway and presently saw below me a sun-bathed basin.

An aged Chinaman seated at the roadside looked up as I passed by. A lean man with a bushy beard nodded to me from his saddle. Soon I saw a little ramshackle dwelling half hidden amongst old apple trees, then another and another. When I asked a grey-haired man the way to the town of Dutch Flat; he pointed to a row of tall poplars on the other side of the basin. Making my way toward the poplars, I passed old warped houses over which trailed rose bushes with flowers of yellow, white and red. Locust trees drooped sweet-scented blossoms above the narrow road. On every hill-slope pines swayed in a little breeze.

The town of Dutch Flat consists of one store, which is also the post office. As age goes in the West, it is a hoary building. It was built in the days of the gold-rush, of stone quarried from the hill behind it. Across the street from it stands the hotel. In front of both, lofty poplars wave in the mountain breezes. Along the hilly street below, rows of deserted, crumbling buildings stare at one another through the poplar trunks.

On my first night in Dutch Flat I slept in a vast walnut bed that came over the plains in a wagon drawn by oxen, long ere the railway spanned America. In each room of the little hotel are similar beds. On the lobby table is a pile of dog-eared registers and ledgers from the gold-rush days. You may read in faded ink of how such-and-such a miner brought in so many ounces of gold and took out a new pick, a sack of flour, tobacco and so many bottles of schnapps.

At the height of the gold-rush there were nigh three thousand white people at Dutch Flat, as well as more than two thousand Chinese. When the white men had worked out their claims, had taken the free-est gold, the yellow men bought them and worked them over again for themselves. Behind Dutch Flat the mountains have been upturned, torn down, scoured away, mile upon mile, by hydraulic mining. When, because it was filling the streams with silt, raising the levels of the rivers, and thereby endangering the existence of the towns in the valleys far below, hydraulic mining was forbidden by the law, Dutch Flat died.

In its heyday there was a saw-mill at Dutch Flat. There were lumber yards, livery stables, blacksmiths, groceries, druggists, and a score or so of saloons. There was a newspaper and an opera house. There were three hotels, one of them of three storeys. There were churches and a school. To-day you'll find no board of the opera house, no sign of the three-storey hotel. The forest has taken back to itself the spot where the saw-mill stood, as it has taken back to itself the site of dwelling after dwelling. Here and there in little clearings, upon which the forest creeps closer every year, you may come upon a few old rotted boards, beneath which the great black wood ants nest. Neglected rose bushes trail above the boards, smothering them with blooms. In long-abandoned apple orchards robins build and sing. Young pines are springing up amongst the apple trees. Thimble-berry and manzanita come creeping in from the forest.

Beside the little stream that wanders through Dutch Flat the wild azalea flowers. The band-tailed pigeon, the robin and the crested jay, feast in unowned, uncared-for cherry trees. Oriole and grosbeak, willow goldfinch and warbler and red-headed linnet nest and sing about the street and pathways of Dutch Flat. Hawk and martin and violet swallow nest in the cliff holes. Through pines and dense grown brush the red fox and the badger make their way. Deer wander the hill-slopes. In fall, the brown bear comes to gorge himself upon ungathered fallen apples.

To-day there are perhaps a hundred people at Dutch Flat. Most of them are old. In the school are nine pupils only. One church still stands, its stone steps cracked and crumbling. Sometimes, on Sunday, a preacher comes from twenty miles down the mountain. The parsonage has long since fallen to ruin—you'll find no board of it.

Meet a Dutch Flat man upon the street and he'll say "Good-day" to you. Say to a Dutch Flat woman in her garden, "You have fine flowers there," and she will answer you, "You can have any you wish."

Upon my first day in Dutch Flat I found white English may in flower. I've found it often since, single and double, white and pink. An aged woman said to me, "Them that was homesick for it brought it here." Pheasant's-eye narcissus and daffodil, lily of the valley and tiger lily, peony and pansy thrive. By every house is lilac, white or purple. Bleeding heart, dog wood, lemon verbena and syringa, flower at the forest's edge. Laburnum droops its yellow blossoms o'er the street, where cows, with bells on their necks, wander at will. Maple and oak, poplar and elm, beech and cottonwood and willow shade Dutch Flat windows. By every little creek, in every little canyon, blackberries sprawl wild.

349

"How long have you lived in Dutch Flat?" I asked a white-haired man sawing wood by his shanty of unpainted boards.

"I'm seventy-two," he answered, "I came when I was three."

"You've lived here all your life?" I asked.

"Thirty year ago I went away. I was gone a year," said he, and added. "'Twas a wasted year. The mountains called me back."

Passing along the road, a man I hadn't seen before nodded to us. "He's an old-timer, too?" I asked the mountain man. "No," said the mountain man. "He's one of the newcomers."

Later, I met the man who'd passed, and talked with him. He's been here twenty years!

On a high hill above the little town I came upon a bracken-grown spot where tombstones stand amidst great oaks and towering pines. Bending to read the faded lettering of one, I saw, "A native of Cornwall, England." Perhaps he brought the may. It was Vermonters brought the tiny elms that stand so wide, so high, to-day. Beyond the picket fence where sleeps the Cornishman is the old cemetery of the Chinese. Most of the Chinamen have long since been exhumed and taken home to China. Only here and there a wooden marker leans, half hid amidst the bracken. The aged woman who used to wail at Chinese funerals is long since dead and gone beyond the sea.

Some day, perhaps, Dutch Flat will be discovered and commercialized. Tourists will come and hurriedly set up their radios. There'll be a dance hall here perhaps and 'hot dog' stands. Vandals will rob the wild azaleas of their blooms, dig up the ferns and carry them away. Perhaps, just as one meets them everywhere along the concrete highway now, there'll be great, flaring advertising hoardings and gaudy 'service stations'. One more lost corner of a lovely land will have been modernized. Then I'll go on again, seeking some spot where old world beauty dwells.

June, 1929.

350

CHAPTER XII

NEIGHBOURS AND RECOLLECTIONS

DUTCH FLAT. *August 30th, 1929.*

T here is something of an excitement this morning in Dutch Flat. Not far from me there lives a woman who was born and raised and has lived all her life here. She lives all alone in a log cabin house surrounded with ferns, flowers and trees. Yesterday, as I came from the post office, I handed her a copy of 'The Blue Peter' containing an article on Dutch Flat. This morning she brought it back. Her eyes were bright, and her smile was happy. The people of Dutch Flat have a deep love for the old forgotten place, and it seems to have given them some pleasure to have had the spot that of all places on earth is, to them, the loveliest written of in your magazine. A few minutes ago I came in from the post office. Just as I left it the proprietor of the hotel came from his door. He hurried across the street to me and, smiling all over his face, asked me if it would be possible for him to get a half-dozen copies of 'The Blue Peter' containing the article on Dutch Flat. By a curious coincidence there happens to be a lady staying in the Flat just at present who has a friend who takes 'The Blue Peter'. The issue containing the Dutch Flat article has been sent to her, and, what with her copy and mine, a good many of the local people have read it. I am very glad that they so much approve of it, for I have never lived amongst kindlier people.

There are in the world many people the souls of whom are dead to beauty. Such as they hold an amused contempt for this old dead city. Blind to its loveliness, they see but a spot that once was rich and is now

351

fallen from prosperity. To these, Dutch Flat is a laughing-stock; a place to be spoken of with superior smiles—a place that will never again enrich men with gold. My neighbours, who have known it in its heyday, whose childhood playmates sleep on the quiet hill beneath the pines and manzanita, who have known laughter and love, sorrow and death, here, in whose ears is yet heard the jingle of the harness of the stage-coach horses, and who, now, watching the rush and hurry of this modern world, remember a day when their little mountain community was the largest town in its county, live contented in the memory of the past, and in the peaceful beauty that to-day surround them. If, as sometimes happens, they leave the Flat to go down to the busy city in the valley sixty miles away, or to the canyon streets of San Francisco, they return as soon as may be. For the stars above Dutch Flat are stars indeed. The wind is a pure wind. The riches of the mountains are their own, and they are wealthy in them.

Now that I have been some months in the Flat I begin to get acquainted with its people. They are mostly old. This year there will be but five pupils in the school, instead of nine as there were last year. 'The boys,' a somewhat grizzled company, who spend much of their time seated in easy chairs upon the porch of the little pool hall that was once bank and express office, at first, I think, regarded me with some suspicion, supposing me to be, perhaps, a federal officer come to spy upon them. Since prohibition became the national law one can never tell just who a newcomer may be, and distrust is rife throughout the land. Now I sometimes sit on the pool hall porch myself and listen to 'the boys' as they discuss the best spots wherein to find good trout fishing; to tales of great deer hunts in past years; to arguments as to the respective merits of their various 'hound dogs'. Last night they told me of the time an Indian entered the pool hall and shot two men dead. At that day the pool hall was a saloon. They told me, too, of the last occasion upon which a prisoner was locked in the Dutch Flat jail. The jail is a diminutive building hidden away at the back of an abandoned apple orchard; a building with thick stone walls, a vast iron door and two-foot-square, iron-barred windows. Having come upon an Indian behaving oddly at the edge of the town, two of the citizens conducted him to the jail. As they pushed him in he fell to

352

117. *STAR OF GERMANY, in her prime.*

the floor. One said, "He's dying." The other said, "He's drunk."
They fetched the doctor, for at that time there was yet a doctor in the
Flat. The doctor said, "He's dead." The coroner was sent for from
down the mountains. Having seen the Indian conveyed to a temporary
morgue, he set out and arrested the man from whom he had obtained
his liquor. On going to the jail next morning to give the new prisoner
his breakfast, they found him dead also. The Chinaman had hung
himself from a rafter.

The Justice of the Peace delivers me my milk each evening. Sometimes, while wandering in the starlight, I catch a glimpse of him as he
plods up and down the steep streets. Sometimes I seem to hear him
muttering to himself. I think that perhaps he is trying to work out a
problem in mental arithmetic, a problem that has to do with the high

353

price of shoe leather and the small profits to be obtained from delivering a few bottles of milk.

My nearest neighbour is a woman of seventy-three. In as far as human company is concerned, she lives all alone. But she has a cat named Clara, and a dog named Mike. Also she has six canaries. Since the cat's one desire is to eat the canaries, and Mike's is to eat the cat's two kittens, her days pass busily. Amongst the kindly people of Dutch Flat she has a name for being very tender-hearted; the proof of her kindness being that whenever Clara has so many kittens that some must be disposed of, she invariably sets a pan of water on her stove to warm that they may feel their drowning less.

I have a letter from a reader of 'The Blue Peter', who asks how Dutch Flat came by its name.

Years ago, when Red Dog and You Bet were both busy mining camps, an old Dutchman had a small vegetable patch on a spot of level land seven miles away on the opposite side of Bear River. On Sundays, the miners of Red Dog and You Bet, laying off from their labours, would say to one another, "Let's go over to the Dutchman's," or "Let's go over to the Flat." Rumour has it that, in addition to growing vegetables, the Dutchman made excellent liquor. In later years, after gold was mined from the gravel beds about the Dutchman's flat, after a town was grown there, there arrived from San Francisco a high-toned city lawyer, who, thinking Dutch Flat to be a name too lacking in style, tried to have it changed to one that, containing his own initials and some of the letters of his name, should perpetuate his memory instead of that of the Dutchman. After much talk the matter was put to the popular vote. The Dutchman was dead. But his two grown daughters were living. When polling day came both were in bed with high fevers, their faces blotched and unsightly with a red rash. Anxious to know how the voting was going, they rose from their sick beds, and tottered off arm-in-arm to the polls; to be met with the cheers of the men of Dutch Flat. To-day the last of the Dutchman's family are gone. The place where once the Red Dog and the You Bet miners made merry amongst his beans and peas is no longer recognizable. Stages no longer clatter down the hill toward Bear River, and over the stream to Red Dog and You Bet. Dutch Flat sleeps on in peace.

354

118.   ROSS-SHIRE.

The picture of old *Ross-shire* on 'The Blue Peter' cover gives me a quick twinge of home-sickness. Seeing such a picture, one who has known the feel of them desires to have stiff spray-wet ropes within his hands again! What was there ever better than steering a tall swift ship, by day or by night? I was once in 'Frisco with *Ross-shire*. I remembered particularly one of her apprentices whose sailor luck went hard. While unbending sail in the bay he fell from aloft and was terribly smashed up. It took months in hospital, took the utmost skill of clever surgeons, to mend him. We all agreed that they ever did mend and make him sound again was marvellous. But they did, and later he sailed for England in another of the company's ships. I think it was *Kinross-shire*. On the fair day upon which she sighted the Lizard he fell from a topsail yard and was lost! To some the sea was a bitter hard mistress.

119. KINROSS-SHIRE.

Reef points pattering their low tune in the moon-light. A full moon overhead. Sails on the hatch, with his concertina. Silvered sea. Men and apprentices dancing. Skipper leaning on the taffrail, taking a moment's respite from continual care. Mate walking the poop, with an eye on the royal leech. Wind at full and bye. Shipmate, how'd you like to be back there again?

Bumper stays upon the main and crojack weather yard arms. Black sky. Black sea. A howl in the air. Dusk, the towering mast-heads dimly visible. Slippery wet deck. Lifelines rigid. Fifty-nine south latitude. Mid-June. Salt-water boils at wrist and neck. Palms split wide open. Sea-boots full of water. Bedding soaked. No dry rag left. Who wouldn't sell a farm and go to sea?

Remember how it felt when a shipmate was lost overboard by

night, and the next dawn came coldly over the fast following sea?

Remember how it felt when you were ashore, and chancing to pass by a church of a fine Sunday evening, heard, sonorous through the open door, the choir boys singing:

> *Eternal Father, strong to save,*
> *Whose arm hath bound the restless wave,*
> *Oh, hear us, when we cry to Thee,*
> *For those in peril on the sea.*

There are some things that into human speech cannot be put.

The wind that whispers through the pines and cedars of Dutch Flat is that same wind that whispered in the royal leeches long ago!

So-long Shipmate!

W·M·BIRCHALL.
1927.

120.   *STAR OF FRANCE, setting sail.*

CHAPTER XIII

GOLD'S WHERE YOU FIND IT

It's a grand morning in Dutch Flat, California—there's not a trace of cloud in the sky. Except for bird-song and the tinkle of a distant cow-bell, there isn't a sound, and the air's full of scent. While wandering in the canyon last evening I came upon a bush of sweet-brier. I'd not seen nor scented sweet-brier in thirty years—now my house is full of its sweetness.

Why, while sitting on my porch in the morning sunshine of Dutch Flat, should memory suddenly leap backward through the years to the old Liverpool Sailors' Home? I couldn't reason that out for a time. Now I know—it's because of the stillness of the pines, and the sweetness of the brier.

A man might wonder what the stillness of the pines at Dutch Flat upon a summer's morning could possibly have to do with the old Liverpool Sailor's Home. It was through pines that we once carried a good shipmate to his grave. His memory's sweet as the scent of the sweet-brier. It was in the Liverpool Sailors' Home that I first met him.

I'd not swap my memory of that evening in the Sailor's Home for all the gleaming gold that lies hidden deep in the hills about Dutch Flat. They say that there are millions of dollars' worth, and I've no doubt at all that it's there—the trouble is that they don't know where to look for it!

"Gold's where you find it," was an old saying of the forty-niners. Geologists might tell you different, but I'll take the word of the withered old prospector. My gold is in the memory of the golden age at sea,

359

121. AUSTRASIA as the German GUSTAV. Later Erikson's MELBOURNE.

when there were still fine square-rigged ships upon the waters; when there were little sea-apprentices in brass-buttoned suits who, ere they came to the sea, imagined that all a sea-apprentice would have to do would be to walk up and down in his blue serge suit with a big telescope tucked under his arm.

Some artist-fellows ought to paint a picture of the old Sailors' Home. It's too late now, though; and we who knew it don't need the painted picture, anyway—the memory is indelible.

*   *   *   *   *   *

"Gold's where you find it!"

CHAPTER XIV

'FRISCO

I am farther from the sea than I have ever been in my life, and though well content at my moorings, find 'The Blue Peter' more than ever welcome. Old memories flood back to me at sight of names of ships I used to know. Some time ago I saw the *Austrasia* mentioned. Instantly I was taken back to thirty years ago when my ship lay at the 'Frisco sea-wall with big *Austrasia* tied up just ahead. What a big brute she was! I remember her well—painted slate colour; double topgallant sails. I can see her plainly as I saw her that yesterday that is so long ago. I was fool enough to lend her third mate a dollar! I, too, was third mate, and in the happy fashion of the sea that young idiot was a brother of mine. What comradeship has ever been like to those dear old comradeships of the sea?

In those days there were all manner of crooks along the 'Frisco water-front. I suppose that there were always crooks where sailors were plentiful. It was owing to a crook that I lent *Austrasia*'s third mate a dollar. I should recognize the particular crook did I meet him to-day—he was short, plump, yellow-complexioned, bulge-eyed, and wore a pale grey, somewhat shabby suit, and in his hand he carried a little black bag. Plenty of readers of 'The Blue Peter' have no doubt seen similar little black bags.

It was on my second visit to 'Frisco that *Austrasia* lay ahead of my ship. I was used to the tricks of the water-front, so when I saw the shabby fellow with a black bag in his pudgy hand come over our gangway, I ordered him off. He didn't want to go; he tried to argue. He didn't go until I informed him that unless he did so, and did so

361

quickly, I should chuck him over the rail. I'd been four years at sea then and had a certain amount of beef—weighing close to two hundred pounds. The other apprentices (for, though third mate, I was still an apprentice, of course) were youngsters and I had something of a fatherly feeling toward them. I did not intend to let them be skinned by the yellow-faced water-front crook.

Feeling pretty well pleased, though at the same time regretting that I hadn't chucked that shabby dick over the rail, I watched him go mumbling ashore. He didn't love me. When I saw him make for *Austrasia*'s gangway I decided that he should love me yet less. I knew the boys of the big ship's half-deck. It was their first visit to 'Frisco.

As the swab with the black bag entered the door of *Austrasia*'s half-deck, I entered at his heels. "You chaps had better dump this swab over her side," I said; but of course I couldn't take matters into my own hands. The crook knew that, and he promptly opened his little black bag.

I'd like to know, how many sailors' dollars went into the pockets of that slimy water-front crook. Why were young sailors (and old ones, too, for that matter) so simple? I was simple enough myself, heaven knows. But a year or so ago that fellow had had one of my dollars, and I meant to be even with him now, or at least to check-mate him if I anyhow could.

Once you'd seen into it, it was a fine appealing bag that the swab carried. In it were envelopes some of which contained five-dollar bills. Some contained ten dollars. Some contained nothing. Pay the fellow a dollar and you could have your pick! And you did not have to take his word for it that there were five- and ten-dollar bills in some of the envelopes. He'd open some of them before your eager eyes! He'd wave a five- or a ten-dollar bill before you. Think of it! Pay one dollar, and get, maybe, ten in return! Fine new crisp bills they were that he took from his envelopes!

It was useless for me to try to argue with the *Austrasia* apprentices. In fact, I didn't try to argue for very long. The sight of those crisp bills began to influence my own simple mind. Perhaps, after all, I'd been a bit too hasty in ordering him ashore from my own ship. It was Saturday evening, and, according to custom, the skippers of

122.   *SUSIE M. PLUMMER—an American West Coast schooner.*

both ships had given to each of their apprentices the sum of one dollar. I had my dollar in my pocket; each of the *Austrasia* boys had a dollar in his pocket—each of them but the third mate, that's to say. During the week her third had borrowed a dollar from her second mate, and this evening he'd paid it back. The third was broke, but I was a pal of his, and I had a dollar.

"Bill," said the *Austrasia*'s third mate, "lend me a dollar, will you?"

I lent *Austrasia*'s third mate a dollar. He handed it to the water-front crook. The crook opened the little black bag. My pal dived his hand in and brought out an envelope. He opened the envelope—there were a couple of slips of blank paper in it.

The third mate of the *Austrasia* sighed. I sighed.

"That's too bad," said the swab with the bag, "you didn't have any luck." And before our eyes he dived his own hand into the bag and fished out an envelope. "See there!" said he, and held up a crisp ten-dollar bill. "You pay only one dollar and maybe you gets ten back!"

The third mate of the *Austrasia* took his cap from his bunk. Leaving the *Austrasia*'s youngsters to their fate we went ashore together.

Before another week was gone the *Austrasia* pulled out. Once again that slimy water-front swab had skinned me out of a dollar!

If an apprentice knew his way about in 'Frisco he could do a good deal with a dollar in those days. Down on Third Street was a little eating-house where for fifteen cents you could get soup, fish, meat and a slice of pie. A feed every night of the week and ten cents left over! It was not a very high-class eating-house, of course. Cockroaches crawled over the floor, walls and tables. But then cockroaches crawled about the half-decks, too! Then, too, there was that place that every apprentice who was ever in 'Frisco will remember—Clark's on Kearney Street. 'Clark's bakery'. You'd see dozens of apprentices there of a Saturday night, for ten cents would buy you a big cup of first-rate coffee and a whopping big doughnut, cream puff, slice of pie, or snail. Put down your dime, go to the long counter and help yourself. But Clark's burned up in the big fire after the earthquake, and Kearney Street is altogether different to-day.

Speaking of doughnuts—I don't like 'em. It was Clark's bakery that was responsible for my present-day dislike for them. One Saturday

364

123. *STAR OF ALASKA, ex BALCLUTHA, towing to sea.*

midnight another apprentice and I went to Clark's with sixty cents between us. We wanted doughnuts. The doughnuts were not out yet. The man behind the counter said they'd be out at two o'clock. So, night and day being all one to a deep-water sailor, we sat on the kerb outside and smoked our pipes and gammed till two o'clock. Then, with a whopping big paper bag chock-a-block full of hot, greasy doughnuts, we started down to the sea-wall where the ship lay; and as we walked we ate doughnuts. There were still quite a few in the bag when we reached the ship. One of the other boys happened to be awake in his bunk, and he finished them for us. How many we had eaten I don't know—but enough to cure me for all time of doughnuts.

Speaking of that eating-house where one could get soup, fish, meat and pie all for fifteen cents, reminds me of a night when my pal and I went ashore together. Paddy and I always went ashore together. It was our first visit to 'Frisco. Paddy never made another—*'Lost overboard'* on the road home.

Many a deep-water Jack must remember old St. Mary's Hospital. I've reason to remember it myself—I lay there one Christmas, in a ward full of disabled sailors; I'll never forget the picture of it. There was an old ship's carpenter named McFee: he must have been well over sixty. He lay in the next bed to me, with one of his hips smashed. Next to him, on the other side, was the second mate of the *Falkland*, with a pipe put into his lungs to drain them. A cheery, joking chap he was, always trying to hold the hand of Miss Moran, the nurse who nursed so many of us deep-water men. One morning he died. Across the ward from me was a little cockney A.B. who had been knocked down and swept against a hatch coaming by a big sea. From shoulder to hip he was wrapped rigid in a plaster cast. "*'What cheer,' all the neighbours cry! 'Who're ye going' to meet, Bill? Have ye bought the street, Bill?'*" he used to sing. And there was a little apprentice chap from a big four-poster. They operated on him for appendicitis one day and on the next his ship went to sea and he went with her; carried aboard on a stretcher! The last thing he said to me was, "If you're in South Shields before me, remember me to——," and mentioned the name of a girl. Long afterwards I met the girl and the first thing she said to me was, "Jimmie's dead. Did you hear about it?" I hadn't heard.

124. *STAR OF FRANCE as a Packers' ship.* (*Note the added wheel-house.*)

Excuse me for gamming so long. I'm living up in the Sierra Nevada Mountains now in the old gold-mining country; in the land of Bret Harte. There's not a soul about me who has ever seen a ship. 'The Blue Peter' comes in, and of a sudden, instead of hearing the wind in the pine trees, I hear a wind that blows along the sea. Old faces come back to me, and luring, lovely names, and all the world is young once more—my own world, a sailor's world, where glorious ships roll by.

"Falmouth for orders!"

Cheer-oh!

WM BIRCHALL
1931

CHAPTER XV

GHOSTS IN OAKLAND ESTUARY

Seated in a boat on the muddy waters of Oakland Estuary, I talked last night with ghosts. A clear night it was, and starry.

It was at a bit past sunset that I pulled from the Oakland shore, and headed across the estuary to where lie the last of the square-rigged ships. Always when I am by 'Frisco Bay I take a boat, and pull off to the other side of the estuary where, a few years ago, lay the large fleet of the Alaska Packers. Year by year I've watched the fleet diminish. Long ago the *Star of Russia* was sold, to go to the islands as a store-ship. One by one, I've seen them pass away. *Star of France*, and *Star of Italy*—star by star passing from the sky of a sailor's memory. To-day only the *Star of Alaska* and *Star of Finland* remain.

To an old square-rigger man 'Frisco Bay brings a heart-ache. Progress is having her way. They are spanning the bay with a great bridge: the Golden Gate with another. Where once twinkled the riding-lights of the ships of the grain fleet, anchored between Goat Island and the 'Frisco ferries, waiting their turns to go to the wharves, to-day there dazzle the flaring electric lights of the bay bridge. Never a ship comes in through the Golden Gate, where, in place of the winking green and red sidelights of ships from round the Horn, blaze from dusk to dawning the lights of the thing called Progress. Progress it may be: it doubtless is. And an old sailor bows to the inevitable and, bowing, pulls across the estuary to dream awhile in the starshine under the sides of the last of the white-winged ships of his youth.

A long time I sat, my boat made fast to the rudder of the *Star of Alaska*, that long ago was the old *Balclutha*. And looking up to her

369

125. Alaska Packers' fleet laid up at Alameda.

hull, dim in the starshine, I thought of a pal of mine who, in that bygone day, was second mate of her; and of the night when, a foremast hand having gone overboard, he leapt into the sea, risking his life for a man who couldn't swim.

Squally the night was, the ship driving under three topgallant sails; and men standing by the topgallant halliards, ready to lower away in a hurry when the order came. No night to stop a ship and put a boat out. And had not the second mate leapt to the wild sea, the skipper would not have stopped her; for with each squall came a beat of rain and a blackness blacker than the night's common blackness. The barometer falling steadily. But with his second mate gone, as well as a foremast hand, the skipper brought her to, and a boat was cleared away. And it was at just that moment when the mate said to the men at her oars: "No good, lads, they're gone," and was about to turn the boat back to the ship, that the second mate's cry was heard, faint on the yell of a

126.   STAR OF ITALY.

squall. Holding fast to the foremast hand, he was; and his strength nigh done. So they dragged them into the boat, and back to the ship they went, and the ship sailed on.

I have heard that cry; that once heard can never be forgotten, *"Man overboard!"* I remembered men lost from my ship, far out in mid-ocean, on dark midnights. I remembered how we used to stand, gathered under the mizen rigging, all staring out into the impenetrable blackness. "Is there anything more that you want me to do, men?" I heard the skipper ask. And heard, after a long minute of silence, from some old wrinkle-eyed foremast sailor, the gruff "Nothing more to do, sir."

And sitting there in my boat I said to myself, thinking of how ships are gone from our sea, "Nothing more to do." Morose I was, sad-hearted.

And then it was that of a sudden I was aware that I was not alone in the boat. Beside me in her stern-sheets sat a shadowy figure, and on each of her thwarts sat another. And the shadows talked in low voices, one to another.

I heard one shadow say to another: "I was fourteen when I went to sea. I was ordinary seaman in one o' them Fernie ships, and was killed by a fall from her fore-royal yard when I was painting it as she lay at anchor 'tween Goat Island and the ferries."

And the shadow spoken to replied: "Ordinary seaman, was ye? Me, I was boatswain o' one o' Brocklebank's tall gals, and got drunk one night on the Barbary Coast and fell offen her gangway going aboard an' was drownded. Twenty-five year I'd been at sea, me son. And sometimes the skipper'd send for me and ask of me, on the quiet, the two of us out of sight behind the mast, maybe, like as it was a secret atween us two: 'Bos', what d'ye think?—D'ye think as she can stand it if I keep the main topgallant sail on her, eh, Bos'?"

"And did I say, 'Sir, she can stand it all right,' or did I reply, 'Ye'd best be takin' yon sail off her, sir, or she'll be losin' the stick,' he'd act accordin'. W'y, lad, me, I was well-nigh as much skipper o' that tall gall as was the skipper hisself. But not a soul in her knew it, but just him an' me only."

And then a dim shadow seated in my boat's bow spoke up and

372

127. *STAR OF FINLAND* ex *(and later)* *KIAULANI*.

said: "Me, I was master gunner wi' good Francis Drake that day
w'en he dropped 'is anchor in Drake's Bay outside the Golden Gate.
Drumming round the seas we was after the ships o' Spain, an' booty
was fat. I died o' the scurvy and never saw Plymouth Hoe no more.
They put one of me shot at me feet, an' dropped me over her side.
How was it i' Devon when last ye was there? Or was none o' ye ever i'
Devon, lads?"

"The primroses was bloomin' all up along and all down along
Bickley vale when I was last there. 'Twas fifty year gone an' more,
though," came answer from a shadow seated amidships.

And there another shadow interrupted, saying, with a cackle o'
laugh in its throat, "Aye! I mind I heerd tell as ye died from eatin'
yer own plum-duff." And from shadow to shadow a ripple of throaty
laughter ran.

"Ye're wrong there, son, for never was no plum-duff served
aboard that little barky," replied the speaker. "I was killed by the

373

falling of the main tops'l halliard block on me bare head when, as we was pilin' the sail on her, homeward-bound just out the Golden Gate, an' me lendin' a hand at the halliards, the tie carried away. The skipper was for puttin' back into the bay an' havin' me buried ashore, but the old hands in her fo'c'sle said as 'twould fetch bad luck to the ship. So they kep' me till evenin' an' buried me from her quarter railing, an' the bark made a fine fast run home, so I've heard since."

"No decent sailor'd be wantin' any shore buryin'," muttered the wraith of Drake's old gunner, and a murmur of assent ran from one to all.

And then a shadow amidships asked: "Will we not sing a bit of a song, for the days wot used to be?"

And a song rose, started by the old gunner of Francis Drake's ship:

Haul on the bowline, our bully ship's a-rolling

And all the shadows came softly in on the chorus:

Haul on the bowline, haul!

And as that song ceased one of the shadows growled: "Gunner, 'tis always that same song ye sing when we foregathers together."

"I know naught o' the song ye later-day seamen sang," retorted the gunner. "But that one I know right well; for I've heard Drake himself sing it, lending a hand on the rope when most o' his lads was down wi' the scurvy an' the ship short-handed. Sing what ye will! 'Tis good songs they all be."

And then that old boatswain who had gotten drunk on the Barbary Coast and fallen from his ship's gangway and drowned sang:

Whiskey is the life of man

And a murmur of approval rose from stem to stern of my boat, the lot of them singing softly the chorus:

Whiskey for my Johnnie!

"A good song, but I never touched lip to that drink whereof ye sing, sons. 'Twas on rum we chased, caught, an' whipped the Spaniard," said the old gunner.

And so they sang, on and on, chanty after chanty, soft in the star-

374

128.   Packers' Fleet at Alameda, Oakland. (STAR OF HOLLAND on right.)

shine on the muddy waters of Oakland Estuary. And, being grown sleepy, I fell into a drowse by and by, one of them as I began to drowse off singing:

> *Boney was a warrior.*

And the old gunner interrupting to ask: "What sort of a warrior, now, was this Boney, eh? An' did ye singe the beard of him?"

"'Twas long after your day," came the answer, "an' we singed him well."

When presently, after I know not how long a time, I wakened, I was aware of a flight of gulls that came wheeling in the dim star-shine toward my boat. And above my boat they paused, and they hovered. And then, all in a moment, there were no longer any shadows in my boat. Alone I was. And the gulls, all save one gull, were gone.

That one lone gull stayed, hovering above me, and I saw its beady eyes down-turned on me. And that lone gull seemed as though

375

it fain would speak to me. But speak it, of course, could not; being but a gull. And looking upward, looking above its outspread wings, I saw the web of the rigging of the old *Balclutha*. And while yet that lone gull remained there, hovering in that forlorn sort of way, it came to me that the gull was my gull. And to it I said: "Wait. Lone you are, I know, and lone you must be awhile yet. I know not how long it will be, but the day will come."

And so I know that, when my day does at last come, my spirit has waiting for it a gull, and that I shall foregather at nights with those other shadows of old sailors. For well known to be a fact it is, amongst all good sailors, that when a sailor dies his spirit enters the body of a sea-bird. So I'll have company, and progress will not hinder the flight of my wings to and fro over the waters of 'Frisco Bay.

And when at last I pulled back to the Oakland side of the estuary and stepped ashore and turned my boat over to the man from whom I had hired it, the man, a bit growly because I had kept him so long a time up awaiting my return, that fellow said, looking into my face, which was illumined by the lantern he held: "Man, it's a chill, dank night and what in the name of all time do you find to smile about so? One might think you'd been having a grand time all alone. Who you may be I don't know, but mad you surely must be."

"Mad I may be," I answered him, "but I've had a good time, and there's a good time coming for me also."

CHAPTER XVI

SWANS WITH WHITE WINGS

I was rowing once again in Oakland estuary, and in the stern-sheets sat Apple Dumpling, who is eleven years old. Apple Dumpling had never before been in a boat, and was chattering nineteen to the dozen. Of what she was talking I had not the least idea, for my thoughts were elsewhere. Indeed it might be said that I did not hear her chatter, was aware of it only as a sort of distant monotone. My eyes were on the bottom of the boat, but likewise it was not the bottom of the boat that I saw. I was seeing those things of which I thought.

I was a lad, a sea apprentice, and the time was some forty years ago. I was pulling an oar in a ships' gig, one of four apprentices, and upon me were the eyes of my Old Man, who sat in the stern-sheets. It was my first time in a boat, and my Old Man's face was grim. Grim because we were rowing him ashore from the ship at anchor between Goat Island and the 'Frisco ferries, and our course lay past other ships at anchor. I was aware of many eyes upon the gig, eyes of skippers, mates, foremast sailors and apprentices aboard those other ships. On the preceding day the gig of another ship had rowed past my ship, and laughter had risen from my ship's deck at sight of the clumsy rowing of inexperienced rowers in her.

Now lest, those aboard other ships laugh as those aboard my ship had laughed yesterday, my Old Man eyed me sternly. And well do I remember with what effort I managed to keep stroke with my fellow oarsmen. My arms, my wrists, my shoulders and back ached, and perspiration was heavy on my face. By the time we brought the gig to the landing steps I was exhausted. But my exhaustion was at

377

129. *The Alaska Packers' cannery ships. L. to R.: STAR OF ALASKA, STAR OF INDIA, STAR OF FINLAND and STAR OF RUSSIA.*

once forgotten when, looking at me dourly and yet with a something that was not disapproval in his cold eyes, my Old Man said, harsh-voiced and yet not unkindly, "Ye never pulled an oar before, eh, boy?" I knew then that I had not brought disgrace to my ship, and my heart was glad.

And as now I sat, unheeding Dumpling's chatter, I thought of later days when our Old man grinned approval while we, his gig's crew, drove her past the gigs of other ships until we came to be known as the best gig's crew in port. A proud lot we were, and those days were very good days.

From thinking of my old ship's gig my mind wandered to other well-remembered scenes in 'Frisco bay. I saw again the swans with white wings coming in through the Golden Gate and clewing up their white wings. I heard the cheering and the throaty songs of sailors. And I saw also swans with white wings going forth seaward, laden for the ports of home; passing out from 'Frisco bay, their white wings not yet unfurled, the tow-lines taut before them and the tug-boats

130.   *Towing in – a swan folds her wings. (Norwegian barque SUPERB, ex AIRLIE.)*

straining ahead. And then my mind went to tug-boats I had known
in that other day so long ago.

There was the tug that took me seaward on my first voyage, on a
day of murk and grey weather. Again I saw the smoke pouring from
her funnels, the sombre waters churning under her stern. Small love
has any sailor for vessels driven by steam, yet for tug-boats there is in
his heart a something of affection. For the tug-boats were, in a manner
of speaking, as godmothers to our tall ships; sending us out on our
long voyages with, as they cast us off and set us free to the ocean winds,
a toot from their whistles that was as a blessing; greeting us when we
came homing, meeting us often when we yet were far offshore—the
first to bid us welcome to the ports of home. So always that first tug,
the *Sarah Joliffe*, remains in my memory as a pleasant memory. And
other tugs also I remembered. The *Conqueror* of London, the *Lorne*
of the Puget Sound ports, the little tugs of Hull, the great tugs of Durban,
the puffing tugs of the Bristol Channel darting to and fro by Lundy,
and in 'Frisco the *Relief* with her black hull and high black funnel.

131. Tug LORNE.

Oftener than any other tug, the *Relief* had my ship in tow; oftener than any other heard us chantey the topsails to their mastheads, casting us off upon our homeward way.

Presently I was aware of Apple Dumpling, insistently asking a question, and I looked up from the boat's bottom into her youthful face.

"What sort of a ship's that, daddy?" asked Dumpling, and, turning to look where her young hand pointed, I saw, resting on the mud at the edge of the estuary, a small craft, her side all rusty, her tall funnel red with rust. Little more than a wreck she was, her railings broken, plates dented, the name on her low stern indecipherable. I gave her but a brief glance and, rowing on, said contemptuously, "That thing isn't a ship."

But Dumpling begged that we stop and go aboard the old wreck, so to humour the child I pulled under her low stern, and we climbed over it and to her rotted deck. Her engines had long since been taken out, and she was but a shell.

"Why isn't it a ship? I think it's nice, daddy," said Dumpling,

380

peering into what once had been the vessel's tiny galley. I grunted, in scorn, and led the way back to the boat. And as I helped Dumpling into the boat she asked, "May I row, daddy?"

"The boat's too heavy for you," I replied, "and there's but one pair of rowlocks. You're too little to pull two oars, and the thwart's too narrow for us to sit side by side each with one oar."

"I'd like to try," insisted Dumpling, and so I went to the stern-sheets to humour the child. It would be but for a minute or two, I knew, even though the oars were short and light. Had Dumpling been a boy maybe I'd have felt differently.

But with no question as to the right way of doing it, Dumpling took the oars and pushed them out. All eagerness she was, her eyes shining, her hair glossy in the sunlight, her small hands firm and determined.

"Easy, now! Take it easy," said I, and as I spoke saw that I need not have spoken. For the child lay back as to the manner born, and pulled as though she'd been often in a boat before, making but slight effort.

Thought I then, "If she were a boy there'd be the makings of a sailor in her."

"Am I doing it right, daddy?" she asked, and when I replied that she was doing finely, looked at me with her lips parted in a proud smile. But when she turned to look again at that old wreck that we were now passing, I at once said sternly, "Eyes in the boat! You'll not learn to row if you don't learn that first."

So she looked then at the bottom boards at my feet, and I said, "That's better."

And then of a sudden she cried, "What is it, daddy?" For I had risen and was staring amazed at the old wreck on the mud at the estuary's edge.

"Look! Look at her name on her bow! Can you make out the letters?" I said, for my own eyes I could not believe.

And Dumpling, resting on the oars, spelled out the letters that, though rusted and dim, were yet faintly legible.

"R-e-l-i-e-f"—she read.

Then to Dumpling I said, "You were right. She's a ship." And I

381

132. Tug RELIEF alongside French barque NANTES.

told her how, nigh forty years ago, that old stranded vessel on the mud had taken my ship out through the Golden Gate, over the swells of the bar beyond, and how, having cast us off, she had sped back to fetch another tall ship seaward.

"What is it makes you look so sort of sad, daddy? Don't you like to be on the water in a boat?" asked Dumpling.

"I'm not sad, and I like to be on the water in a boat very well," I replied. The first was not fact. There was a long silence then, while I sat dreaming; forgetful that at the oars was a child who, till that day,

133.   *Tug RELIEF laid up alongside ANNIE M. REID,*
ex HOWARD D. TROOP.

had never had oars in her hands. Little by little the *Relief* grew smaller astern, and presently I looked away from her to Dumpling. And I saw that her face was tired, that her arms and shoulders ached, and that the perspiration was heavy on her forehead.

"You'd best let me take the oars," said I. "Your hands will be getting blistered."

"My hands are all right. Please let me row," remonstrated Dumpling.

So I let the child row, and she rowed till she was exhausted. Yet

383

not till she was so weary that she no longer could keep the boat moving would she give over the oars to me. "How are the palms of your hands? Let me see them," said I then.

"They're all right, daddy," she answered me, seated in the stern-sheets now, with her hands clasped in her lap.

"Let me see them," said I again.

"Daddy, you're being funny," she laughed, her eyes shining and eager, her hands still clasped in her lap.

"Well, you're tougher than I thought," said I.

"If I were a boy I'd be a sailor," replied the child.

"You're boy enough, and sailor enough," said I, and her eyes shone brighter yet.

So I rowed again, and again heard little of Dumpling's chatter as she chattered on and on. But by and by I looked up and saw that her head nodded. I turned the boat then, and pulled back past the old *Relief* to the landing stage where I'd hired the boat. "Wake up, sleepy head!" I said. And, waking, she murmured, "I wasn't asleep, daddy."

"Oh, you weren't, weren't you? "I laughed.

'Well, maybe I was, daddy," she replied, full awake now, and added, "I was dreaming I was in a ship and that the little ship called the *Relief* was pulling the ship."

Soon we were seated together in a street car, and Dumpling's young head was on my arm. And while she slept I sat dreaming idly of that other day when there were swans with white wings on the sea. And it came to me that maybe a day might come, in years far ahead, when all the petrol in the earth would be used up, and all the coal. And maybe also there might come a day when the Ruling Hand would cause to come a cataclysm that would block and close for all time the ditch at Panama, and that ditch at Suez, also, which first drove the knife into the hearts of the swans with white wings. Cataclysms greater than that have been in times past. And I thought how, with those ditches done away with and no petrol nor coal left, men would again build swans with white wings. The idle dream of an old sailor, yet an idle dream is a very pleasant thing.

So we came home, and soon were called to the table to eat. And

384

134. *French barque VINCENNES sailing towards Alcatraz Island and making her numbers to Fort Point, on right.*

after we had eaten and the table had been cleared, Apple Dumpling's mother called to her, "Dumpling, what in the world have you got on your serviette?"

"Gravy, I suppose, mother. I'm sorry," answered the child.

And then Dumpling's mother called to me to come and look at the serviette, and on it I saw what very plainly was vaseline. "I told her to wash her hands before coming to the table. I wish you'd give her a talking to," said Dumpling's mother to me.

So I went to Dumpling, and I said, "Show me your hands."

And the child replied, "My hands are all right, daddy."

"I didn't say they were not," said I. "Why didn't you wash them before going to the table?"

"I did wash them," replied the child.

"Let me see them," said I again, and took her hands and opened them, though she tried to keep her small fists clenched.

"You washed them, did you?" I asked, looking from her palms, which were all blistered, with many blisters broken and raw, into her eyes.

"Yes, daddy. I greased them after I'd washed them," replied the child.

Having explained how things were to Dumpling's mother, I sat smoking my pipe and thinking how in that day that some day yet may come when men will build swans with white wings again, the child of the child of the child of my child will walk a ship's deck, and when the ship comes to port will row her Old Man ashore.

"You're looking very pleased about something." said Dumpling's mother, when the child was in bed and asleep, "as though relief had come to you about some troublous thing."

"It has," said I.

So-long!

386

CHAPTER XVII

LIFE'S A QUEER JIG

It's as the sailmaker said to me one day soon after I set forth upon my first voyage. It was my watch below, and I was seated close to him where he sat at work on the main hatch repairing a sail. I had not spoken a word to him, nor he to me, till, looking up, gazing straight into my face, he said, "Life's a queer jig, son, an' ye got to take it as it comes."

I recall a night when the eight of us, apprentices, sat puffing our pipes in the half-deck during the second dog-watch. And, by the way, what a blessed period the second dog-watch was, wasn't it, when the weather was fine and there was no work to be done? Looking back along my life I think that, of all good times that ever I have lived, the second dog-watches of my apprentice days bring me the best memories.

Some of the finest scoffs that ever I had were in the second dog-watch. And, thinking of my apprentice days, it seems to me that of all happy times an apprentice was happiest when he was scoffing good scoff. We had a little oil stove in the half-deck. I am proud to say that I owned it. A small affair with a wide wick, and a little chimney upon which one could cook burgoo or make chocolate. Some of us had brought a store of sweet, sticky, canned milk to sea. Some of us had brought burgoo. Excellent! Most excellent of all, the esteemed maiden lady who raised me had provided me with some cans of Thomas Lipton's chocolate. What scoffs we had off the Horn that voyage! For, wisely, we kept our shore grub till we were off that infernal Cape. We scoffed burgoo and hot chocolate till our belts were let out to the last hole, and our young stomachs were tight as the bellies of the lower topsails. What a dire and tragic thing it was when a fellow had to be at the wheel in such a second dog-watch! One night when we were scoffing the mate came in. We offered him some of our scoff; not that we were trying to suck up to him. Just out of the goodness of our youthful hearts. Who ever heard of a mean, close-fisted apprentice? I never did. The mate shook his head, but the second mate sat down with us, and scoffed as much as any one of us, and was welcome, though heaven well knows that he was a hard driver of apprentices, with that nasty habit of breaking a royal buntline stop in the middle of a fine night—just for the fun of sending an apprentice aloft to overhaul it.

And, of course, singsongs were frequent in the second dog-watch. For some queer reason the favourite song seemed to be that one about poor old Jeff:

> *For poor old Jeff is gone to rest*
> *We know that he is free;*
> *Disturb him not, but let him rest*
> *Way down in Tennessee.*

Why on earth should Limey apprentices sing such a song as that over and over again? Not one of us knew where Tennessee was within a thousand miles.

Of course, too, one of the favourite themes of conversation in the second dog-watch was girls. As a rule, any healthy apprentice— and who ever heard of an unhealthy apprentice?— joined his ship with the picture of at least one girl in his pocket. After getting a bit offshore we swapped them round. Rare was the apprentice who reached a foreign port still the possessor of the picture that he joined with.

Yes, we had a deal of fun in the second dog-watches. Only, of course, it happened sometimes that it was a case of "All hands shorten sail! Clew up the fore and mizzen topgallant sails! Step along!" And then out to the howling dark we went, to be bowled over like as not by a green sea and soaked to the hide before we started up the rigging to feel our way to the lofty yards, and cling to them with toe-nails and eyelashes, as the saying was, with the jerking foot-ropes beneath our sea-boots, and the frozen canvas knocking the skin from our knuckles.

135. *STAR OF LAPLAND bowing to the swell. (Note triangular crossjack.)*

Life's a queer jig, an' ye got to take it as it comes, son! It is close
to eight o'clock as I sit writing. The second dog-watch is almost done.
The snow is blowing against my window panes, the wind is howling
up the canyons, the forest tops are swaying in the pitchy night.
Doubtless the cathedral bells still chime in that old city by the sweetly
flowing river. Annie has grey hair long since, doubtless; and so have I.

136. Making sail—the American WILLIAM H. SMITH.

And there are no more royal buntlines to overhaul, no scoffs of burgoo and chocolate, no singsongs.

To-morrow is another day, and we will take it as it comes; and whatever it brings, we'll make it All-Sir-Garney-Oh!

Meet me off the Western Islands, and we'll roll up the Channel together. Would God that we might!

CHAPTER XVIII

FESTIVE POPPETS

In the October, 1934, 'Blue Peter' I found the answer to a riddle that puzzled me when I was at San Francisco bay a short time ago. Down by Oakland's waterfront lay a five-masted barquentine. By her rickety gangway, and at the end of the dusty street that led to the wharf where she lay, were 'Keep Out' and 'Absolutely no Admittance' signs. Such signs mean naught to a sailor and, ignoring her gangway, I grasped a rope that hung down from her rail and hove myself aboard. One thing I knew ere I climbed to her deck—she was of British build. But, what was she now? Well, whatever she was, she awakened old dreams in me. She had a weird little boom, so short that her bows were made hideous by its stumpiness. Her fore-lowermast and fore-topmast appeared to be her original masts; but her topgallantmast was plainly not as it had once been. Like her boom, it had been cut short; stumped down; giving her a bald-headed look. Her main, mizzen and jigger, fore-and-aft rigged, were sorry things for an old Cape Horner to see. I tried to find where, in other days, her main and mizzen masts had been, but could only guess. Yet I knew full well that she had once been a full-rigged ship. Though her decks were rotten and filthy, she spoke of strength. Some-one had fitted her with a crazy jury-wheel; six pieces of two-by-four timber bolted together. I knew that, once, she had had a teakwood wheel, but what had become of it the shipkeeper could not tell me. Her present dining saloon, after saloon and captains cabin had been dismantled and were now all one big room, had in its centre a dirty old cook stove for the use of the shipkeeper. Seeking a hint of her

391

former nationality, though I knew it well enough, I found at last, hidden under flakes of rust, the faint lettering, 'To accommodate one seaman'. Within the door beneath those words was what once had been her mate's cabin. Bunk, desk, and settee were gone: as was the glass from the port. In one corner lay a rusty marline-spike. Her bells were gone. Her teak taffrail had been replaced by a stranded old rope. Utterly forlorn from stem to stern she looked; and her shipkeeper was just as dirty and forlorn. Her name, *Monterey*, in dirty old white letters on her bow, told me nothing. In a locker under the starboard side of the break of her poop were a number of lanterns, which I knew at once had been hers in a long-gone better day, a stern-light, and two riding-lights. There was also a brass binnacle top. For a long time I tried to bribe the dirty shipkeeper into selling me one of the lanterns for five dollars. He was poor and dishonest as myself, but also he was afraid of losing his job. Not even one of her old iron belaying pins would he let me slip into my breast pocket. "You could turn your back," said I. He replied, "Mister, I daren't do it."

Seeming to hear from down the long years the mate's order, *"Lee fore-brace!"* I laid my hands upon her fore-brace and managed to move the fore-yard a little.

In 'The Blue Peter' I read that this poor old ship was once the proud *Cypromene*. The shipkeeper told me that she had been in the trade to Honolulu carrying sugar. Though it saddened me, yet, in a way, it somewhat gladdened me to walk her rotten decks: for beneath them was the feel of a strong and valiant hull. The shipkeeper also said that she was shortly to be towed to San Pedro, to be broken up. He gave me the name of her owner in San Pedro, and I wrote that day to ask if I might buy one of her lanterns. Writing that letter, I lied, saying, "I was mate of her, more than thirty years ago. I'd like to have one of her lanterns for old time's sake." These shipbreaker people have no soul, for the reply informed me that the owner was unable to sell any of her fittings.* To them an old ship is merely so much scrap. Never beneath the stars have they seen a ship's lights winking across a trade-wind sea. Never have they heard the piping voice of a young first voyage apprentice, keeping look-out, cry to the mate upon the poop, "All's well, sir, and the lights are bright!" Never

---

* The *Monterey* was broken up at Los Angeles in 1934. [Ed.]

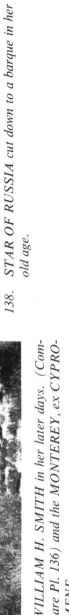

138. *STAR OF RUSSIA cut down to a barque in her old age.*

137. *WILLIAM H. SMITH in her later days. (Compare Pl. 136) and the MONTEREY, ex CYPROMENE.*

have they seen a royal shake; nor listened to the quiet patter of the reef points upon a swelling topsail. Never have their souls been delighted by the whip of clean salt spray upon their faces. Never have they sat astride upon a weather fore yard-arm, hauling out upon a reef earring; the hail-stones bouncing from their sou'-westers and their oilskinned shoulders.

Upon my study wall there hangs a photograph of Fernie's old *Cypromene* slipping along with her six topsails, foresail, main topgallant sail, and two jibs set. There is a hand aloft, loosing her mainsail. At her tall peak there flies the old Red Duster. Doubtless the picture was taken from the tug that had just let go her tow-line. Long ago I met *Cypromene* on a dark and almost windless night, south of the Horn, with a great swell running threateningly up from the west. We wore ship after we saw her green side-light. She wore soon afterwards. When morning came we were close together, with topgallant sails set; and the wind coming ever fresher from the gloomy west. Before mid-day we lost her in the driving snow: both ships stripped down to lower topsails. She came into 'Frisco a few days after we did and tied up a little ahead of us at the old sea wall. My fellow apprentices and I often went ashore with her apprentices; to drink beer together in the 'Last Chance' saloon at the foot of Market Street, and then to stroll on to the Missions to Seamen a little way down Steuart. In those days there was usually a Fernie ship in any port that one entered. *Chrysomene, Pythomene, Sardomene* and the great four-masted barque *Eulomene*, with ponderous double topgallant yards on each mast. *Melanope*, too. I have a photo of *Melanope* on my wall, also. Her fore and main top-masts are gone, and she is lying far over to starboard; with a tug-boat ahead. Her old skipper is a pal of mine and lives by the bay. To hear him talk, you'd think him still as young as he was when he was in the old training ship *Conway*; and there is still the bright sea-twinkle in his furrowed eyes.

Once when I came into 'Frisco, *Melanope* was there; dressed in all her flags. A competition had been held to determine which was the best-kept ship in port, and she had won it. Had my own ship been there in time, she would have lost. (Of course, any decent sailor would say the same of his own ship.) *Eulomene* lay alongside us in

139.   The picture on Adam's wall of the MELANOPE, listing and dismasted.

Portland one winter. Her skipper had his bride with him: a gentle lady, sorry for the hard lot of sea apprentices. One day she went forward along the long bridge, to the top of the deck-house, in which was the apprentices' half-deck. Thinking to do a kindly act, she lowered through their skylight a package containing tins of sardines and other delicacies. But, though hungry, the big four-poster's apprentices were an uppish lot. Offended, thinking that she should have taken the trouble of going to their door, they threw the gift back through the skylight, calling, "We don't want your charity!" The poor lady went back to the cabin, wiping tears from her eyes. When we apprentices in my old barque heard of it we told them they were a lot of fools, and used a strong adjective before the 'fools'. There was no false pride in our half-deck! We would beg, borrow or steal, at the least chance. Wherever we went, we were soon known as the hungriest apprentices in port. We were known for other things, too. It was

395

when we were bending sail in the African dock, Antwerp, that the skipper of the barque *Cumbrian* alongside us, called over to our old Blue Nose from his poop, "I wish I had your apprentices, Gibson!" We were on the crossjack-yard at the time, and plainly we heard our old Blue Nose answer in his harsh, metallic voice, "You ain't the only one!" It was nothing for the eight of us to bend all sail, ere the old barque went to sea. We saved our owners much money in rigger's wages, and got devil a red cent for our pains, of course. Little we cared!

Thirty years ago, on October 18th, I had dinner at a London hotel, with a chap who had made three voyages with me as an apprentice. Having served a year in the old *Patriarch* ere he came to our old four-poster, he finished his time before I did, and left to go up for his second mate's ticket. When we dined together that night, drinking a big bottle of Moet & Chandon, and laughing much, he was second mate of the *Umgeni*, of Bullard, King & Co. I was second mate of Rennie's little *Illovo*. After dinner we went to see 'The Importance of Being Earnest'. From the time we parted outside the theatre I have never heard of him again until yesterday. Often I have wondered what became of him. Yesterday, opening my mail box in the little store that is also the Post Office, I found a letter with a Chinese stamp on it. A six-page letter, in a neat close-written hand.

"It isn't often that I see 'The Blue Peter'," I read, "but a few days ago I happened to see one in Shanghai, with, in it, a letter from Bill Adams. I wondered if it could be the old Bill, and very soon I saw that it was."

I am vastly obliged to 'The Blue Peter'. While I came up the hilly street, reading my old chum's letter, the years rolled away. For twenty-two years he has been on the China coast. Master, long ago, of course. Said he, "Do you know anything of any of the rest of the old Festive Poppets?" Who it was gave that name to the apprentices of our old four-poster, I do not remember. I had, indeed, forgotten it, until his letter came; and walking up the hill, I laughed aloud: so that the old mountain man walking beside me asked, "What's the joke?" A score of memories came flooding back to me. I remembered the time when we gave a minstrel show in the old wooden 'Opera House' at the smelly little fishing village of Steveston, at the mouth of the

141. *CUMBRIAN (distant) and DUDHOPE towing in tandem into the Fraser River.*

140. *French barque TURGOT clearing the land.*

Fraser: where we loaded canned salmon for Liverpool. We sang chanteys and nigger minstrel songs, all our sailor faces blackened with burned cork. At the cannery astern of us lay the *City of Benares*, a very lovely ship. Ahead lay the bluff barque *Balmore*, a fat and graceless cargo carrier. Their skippers and ours sat in free seats on the hard wooden bench in the front row. We charged everyone else, except the apprentices and the few sailors of the *Benares* and *Balmore*, twenty-five cents admission. The place was jammed. And we came away with fifty iron men in our pockets! An iron man, in case you do not know, is a dollar. Fifty dollars, amongst eight apprentices! And then, alas, we did a very foolish thing. It was our eldest apprentice who suggested it, and I have never forgiven him. There was a heated argument before he had his way. He suggested that we keep fifty cents apiece, and give the rest of the money to old MacDonald!

Old MacDonald was the minister of the little Presbyterian church that stood out in the country a short way from Steveston. We used to go to his church on a Sunday night. Always, after the sermon, we sang the hymn beginning: "Eternal Father, strong to save".

The rest of old MacDonald's congregation never sang a word of that hymn. They left it to us sailors, and always turned their heads to watch us while we sang. We sat, always, in the rearmost seat, near to the door, that we might slip out quickly as soon as the service was over.

On our last night in Steveston, a Sunday night, this lad who wrote to me from the China coast, and I, parted company with the other apprentices as soon as church was over. Each of us had hidden a large gunny sack near the church door. In front of old MacDonald's house was a row of well-laden apple trees. Beneath each was a beehive. The night was dark, and while old MacDonald stayed to chat with his landsman flock, we ran for the apple trees. We had our sacks well filled when old MacDonald's dog barked. He was coming home, down his drive. We saw the glimmer of his lantern. We ran; and, running, my chum fell over and capsized a beehive. An angry buzz arose. We reached the ship with not an apple lost, but with our faces much swollen!

Festive Poppets! where are they now? Fair winds to them, in all their voyaging!

CHAPTER XIX

BARE WALLS—AN EXTRAVAGANZA

I never cared much for curios, for relics or heirlooms, or any junk of that sort. At one time and another I have possessed a good many of the things that a sailor is apt to pick up while wandering here and there. I set no store by them. I have given parrots, parakeets, or cockatoos, to a dozen different girls. I gave an old maid a monkey once, and once I gave a pair of Madagascar cats to a widow with whom I boarded between voyages. Here and there I've distributed canary birds from Teneriffe, roibecks from Durban, cardinals from South America, love-birds from Java. To an estaminet man in Antwerp I gave an armadillo in trade for two bottles of hock. I have had walking-sticks made from the backbones of sharks, whale teeth with scrimshaw work on them, sealed jars containing sargasso-weed, stuffed flying fish, coral, coconut shells with little pictures painted on them by natives of the Marquesas and the Solomons, native-made baskets with worsted patterns worked on them by dusky island women: assegais, knobkerries, rhinoceros-hide whips, silks from Japan, peacock fans from China. A drunken native at Inhambane once gave me an elephant's tusk in trade for a handful of old brass buttons that I had cut from the jacket of a drowned shipmate. I've had models of ships, in bottles, and out of bottles. To-day I have nothing to show for my wanderings, save an old bruise here and there, or scars gained in fighting the sea-winds. Looking at my walls, bare but for a few ship pictures, I do not regret. Sailors were ever generous with the simple harvests that they gathered from their sea! Yet there is one fragment of flotsam that I should like to own.

399

The first time I saw Pitcairn was on a dark night. The islanders saw our side-lights before we were aware of their island, so that the first indication we had of it was the blaze of their bonfire. Whenever they saw a ship's lights by night, if the weather was fine, without too much of a sea running, they lighted a bonfire on the island's summit to let her know that she was seen. If she burned an answering flare it meant that she was stopping, and they started off to her, their two whale-boats laden to the gunwales with sweet green oranges, green coconuts, mummie apples, pineapples, bananas and so forth.

We hove the ship to when we could just make out the dark mass of the island on our beam. We were to leeward, and the scent of it blew down to us—fresh and wonderful after our forty days at sea. There is not on earth fragrance sweet as is the scent of tropic island to the sailor long from shore; but because the wind was fair for the Horn, the skipper soon ordered trading to be stopped, and the ship set on her course again, for home—nine thousand miles away. So that time we had but little chance to become acquainted with the descendants of the mutineers of the *Bounty*.

The second time that I saw the island was by day. We came close to it, to windward, and so had no scent of it; there was a strong, squally wind, with a lumpy sea running. Under topgallant sails the ship was making fifteen sea-miles an hour; more when the squalls struck her. Even had it been fit weather for boats, the skipper would not have hove his ship to while she was making that good speed toward home. Regretting, that once, a good fair wind, we sailed on.

The third time that I saw Pitcairn was on a bright, cloudless dawn. What little breeze there was, was dying. I was on the poop that forenoon, painting the ship's name on her three poop life-buoys. Now watching the island, now with a sharp eye to my work, the skipper paced to and fro: "Do a neat job, boy! See that you do a neat job!"

By mid-forenoon, when we came abeam of the land, the life-buoys were painted; the breeze had died utterly. The natives soon came aboard; while some brought fruit to us for barter, the headman went up to the poop where the skipper and his wife waited him. Ordinarily the people of Pitcairn were not given to making friends with sea-faring men. Deeply religious, they feared contamination, and,

142. The clipper PATRIARCH.

excepting in case of shipwreck, allowed no sailors ashore; but with our Old Man and his wife they were friendly, for, during their more than thirty years of sailing together, their ship had called there many times.

Some of the natives were at the forecastle door, bartering with the foremast sailors, others in the apprentices' half-deck, where I and my comrades were eagerly trading, when the mate's whistle sounded. "Clear away the gig!" he ordered.

The headman had invited our Old Man and Old Woman ashore to a feast.

I was one of the gig's crew. Let me live to be a hundred, I will not forget that day! The ship under full sail, with her mainyards aback; her snow-white canvas drooping idly from her spars, and the blue, transparent sea silent, motionless about her. Our Old Man

401

in his shore suit, smoking a fine cigar; our Old Woman rigged in her best, carrying a green parasol. A whale-boat, pulled by the grand-children of the *Bounty* mutineers, making shoreward on either side of us; flying fish darting; birds circling ship and boats.

"Show 'em a sailor pulling, now, boys!" says our Old Man. With never a splash we feather our oars, making the teak gig fly till the natives are hard put to it to keep abreast of her.

On the beach, in Bounty Cove, a crowd of natives waits us. Seizing the boat as we toss our oars, they haul her high and dry.

"You boys stay with the boat," orders our Old Man.

"Oh, no sir! Oh, no, sir!" remonstrates the headman.

Up the steep path to the village we go, smiling natives all about us. For forty days we have eaten salt pork, hard-tack, pea-soup—the hard fare of sailors. Now a table laden with roast chicken, roast kid, yams—more food than a hungry young sailor can believe exists, well-nigh! The headman asks a blessing. Our Old Man and Old Woman, we and the natives, stand with bowed heads.

Opposite each other at the end of one table sit our Old Man and Old Woman, waited on by the headman himself, with men and women eager to help. At another table sit the four of us, waited on by laughing girls and young men. Hole by hole, we let out our belts.

Dinner is barely done when our Old Man rises. A whisper of wind is come.

We leave them calling long farewells from Bounty Cove: "Come again, captain! Lady, come again! Come again, young sirs!"

White caps break about us while we speed toward the ship, waiting with the wind in her sails. The bells break out as we come alongside. I hurry to the poop to take my trick at the wheel.

"South-east by south a quarter south," says the Old Man beside me, giving me the course for the distant Horn; for home—nine thousand miles away.

Seven and a half years went by—a year and a half later, with my apprentice days finished, I had left my old ship. Now, with a gale in her topsails and a thunderous sea running, a ship bound in to Valparaiso sights, as night falls, the glow of fire upon the darkening sea ahead. Gloom deepens while she hastens toward where smoke columns whirl over the stormy sea. By the light of leaping flame her people spell the letters, familiar to me, of the doomed ship's name;* see that her boats have gone. Leaving the abandoned ship, they have sped away for port. No man was ever found from that burned ship.

It was a full thousand miles from Pitcairn that my old ship perished. It was one year later, to the day, that a native found, in Bounty Cove, a fragment of flotsam from her. With all the broad Pacific to drift in, with wind and tide to swirl it hither and yon, one of the old ship's three poop life-buoys had washed ashore at the one small accessible spot along the precipitous coast of Pitcairn; on it, to identify it, the mossy, faded lettering that I had put there on the fine bright forenoon long ago.

Until, long afterwards, the master of another vessel told them that he had retired before the voyage that saw his ship's doom, the natives mourned our Old Man and our Old Woman.

*See Introduction, p. XXII. [Ed.]

W. M. Birchall.
1928

WM BIRCHALL . 1928

CHAPTER XX

THE PARK GATES

Much water has passed between the banks of Thames, and Severn, of Wye, and Dart, and Avon, since last I wrote to 'The Blue Peter'. Dear rivers of England, how fair they flow! Thinking of them brings to my mind willow-bordered banks whence flash the kingfishers; meadows where grow the daffodil and cowslip, rows of tall elms by deep lane sides, little copses where at eve the thrushes sing, furzy banks where rabbits disport themselves at dawning. It is over thirty years since I lost the white shape of St. Catherine's in the mists of the channel. How plainly I see that dim white shape still, and the line of the shore beneath it, and the tossing white caps in between! How plainly I feel the south-west wind upon my face! Ah, dear south-west wind that blows the sailor home! But I was outward bound that day, and my face was turned shoreward; and not yet have I been back. But never mind! Three years ago an Englishman sent me some primrose seed. For a long time there was no sign of any seedlings, and, at last, I gave up hope. But more than a year after I had scattered the seed I found myself looking down upon a primrose in flower! A wonderful morning that! Now I have a number of primrose plants, and each spring am a small boy wandering in little English lanes again.

Somehow speaking of my primroses has brought to my mind the park gates. There was, beside the park gates, no gatekeeper's lodge. There were no trees near by—no flowers. No rooks passed, cawing, overhead, at evening. No hedge-sparrow laid her blue eggs in any near-by hedgerow.

405

How we apprentices of the old four-post barque, in which I served my apprenticeship, used to abominate the park gates!

The bridge ran forward from the break of the poop, between the two quarter-boats, and ended in a 'T' abaft the mizzen-mast. It had brass rails which were kept dazzlingly bright. We apprentices who did the polishing were very glad when the Old Man decided to have them painted white. The bridge deck, of pine, was always kept spotlessly white. When the after hold was being discharged the fore and aft parts of the bridge were hoisted, the 'T' remaining stationary upon teak stanchions.

It was at Steveston, the dismal little fishing village at the mouth of the Fraser river, where we went to load salmon for Liverpool, that the park gates came into being. At the outskirts of the village was a little wooden Presbyterian church, close to which was the little wooden house in which the old minister lived. One afternoon the minister's wife called on our Old Man's wife. The Old Man's wife returned the call. And when the Old Man's wife saw the minister's wife's flower garden she decided that she must have a flower garden too.

Chips, the carpenter, was called upon to construct upon the 'T' of the bridge a strong, deep wooden box. It stood on four short wooden legs, some six inches from the bridge deck. When it was completed we apprentices were ordered ashore, directly after breakfast one hot morning, each carrying a gunny sack which was to be filled with soil wherewith to fill the box.

When the box was full of earth the Old Man's wife planted a number of little rows of seeds, with, at the end of each, a stake, and a label bearing the name of the seed in the row. Columbine, Canterbury bell, wallflowers, larkspur, sweet-william, primroses. It was a few weeks before we went to sea that the garden was completed, and thenceforth, each morning after breakfast, the mate would blow his whistle for an apprentice. Aft one of us would go to the bridge, where awaited him the Old Man's wife. Morning by morning an apprentice would take from her hand a watering-can, walk ashore, fill it with water, return, and hand it to her that she might water her seeds. Apparently she judged that the water in the ship's tanks was not good enough for her seeds. Morning by morning, noon by noon, evening by evening, the Old Man's wife would visit her garden and, peering at the soil, search for signs of growth. There was still no sign of any growth when we went to sea.

On the first day at sea Chips was very busy in his shop. When the dog-watch came, the mate blew his whistle for an apprentice. "Two of you boys go to the carpenter's shop," he ordered. And to the carpenter's shop we went, to carry thence to the bridge a heavy glass cover for the Old Woman's garden. Morning by morning, noon by noon, evening by evening, the Old Woman peered at her garden, hoping that, with glass above them, her seeds would sprout. Nothing sprouted, and at last she gave up her hope for flowers. But if flowers would not grow, perhaps something else would. On the top of the midship house was a hen house with some hens in it. And in the lazarette were some sacks of wheat for the hens. One morning an apprentice was called to the bridge. With the Old Woman for overseer, he dug up the soil in the garden. Then the Old Woman planted wheat in place of her flower seeds.

One morning after we had left astern the chill mists of the North Pacific, and were rolling down the trades, the mate blew his whistle for an apprentice. "Go to the bridge. The Old Woman wants you," said the mate, and to the bridge I went.

"Adams, open the park gates," ordered the Old Woman, and, not at first catching her meaning, I stared at her perplexedly. She repeated the order, and, understanding, I raised the glass cover of her garden that the sun might shine direct upon the little rows of pale green wheat that had sprouted during the night.

Morning by morning after that, just when a hungry apprentice was ready to hasten to the half-deck, the moment eight bells struck, the mate's whistle would blow for the opening of the park gates. Evening by evening, just when a tired apprentice had put away his deck broom after the regular evening sweeping of the long decks, and was ready to hasten to his supper, it would blow for their closing. Added to the countless little jobs that fell to the lot of an apprentice, the greasing of the royal-masts, the overhauling of buntlines, the coiling of ropes, the taking a pull here and a pull there on some rope not quite tight enough to please the Old Man's fancy, the park gates

407

became a byword, and were hated with the hate that none but a sea apprentice knows. And as her park gates were hated, so also did we come to hate the Old Woman. The Old Woman and her garden were the cause of more bad language in the half-deck than were all the bunt-lines put together, all the brasswork that must be polished, all the little annoying jobs that, falling to an apprentice just when he thinks he is entitled to be free to go below and have a peaceful pipe in the half-deck, or a cheery sing-song on the main hatch, rile his youthful soul. Yes, an apprentice had plenty to do besides being nursemaid to a few straggling stalks of pale green wheat! But all the way down the Pacific we opened and we closed the park gates, and the wheat grew taller and taller, and the Old Woman came and went with her watering-can. And one evening, passing by where she stood with the Old Man, I overheard her say, "Well, wheat's better than nothing at all. It's not much, but at least it's something green and growing." And I repeated her words when I came to the half-deck, and the eight of us all jeered; making great fun of her. Roundly we cursed her, and her garden too.

And then one evening, not long after we had passed Pitcairn Island, the mate's whistle blew, and we ran out to the deck to see a great dark cloud coming up in the west. We were losing the south-east trade winds and picking up the westerlies. And the westerlies came with a rush and a roar. We braced the yards, and, taking the wind upon our starboard quarter, ran away at a grand clip for the Horn. And now, because the air was full of little salt sprays flying, the park gates were very seldom opened. The wheat was grown high, so high that its tops touched the glass.

One morning, when, at the mate's whistle, I went to the bridge to lift the glass for the Old Woman, the Old Woman had a pair of scissors in her hand. She was going to cut some of the wheat and set it in a vase in the saloon! She smiled at me that morning. And, smiling at me, she said, "I've followed the sea for nearly thirty years, Adams. I've never had any flowers." And when I went forward to the half-deck I repeated that to my comrades, and we all laughed and jeered. Young lads we were, hot-headed; without much understanding or caring for the strange deep things of life. Full bellies, and as little work as possible, were the things we cared most about. And God knows

143. CITY OF BENARES.

well that our young bellies were seldom full enough in those hard days, and that the tall four-poster, with her great spread of sail, with her braces, halyards, buntlines, leechlines, downhauls, lifts, brails, vangs, with her decks to be holystoned and her kicking wheel to be fought, gave us more than plenty of work for our young muscles.

Day by day after that, the Old Woman had the park gates opened so that she might cut a few stalks of the green wheat to set in a vase in the saloon. And soon most of the wheat was gone and the earth in the box was bare. The Old Woman wore a sad look that day. "It would be nice to have some flowers, Adams," she said to me. And that day, somehow, a something in her face, in her tones, kept me from making fun of her when I came back to the half-deck where my young comrades were.

409

It was a night or two after the wheat was all gone, and the vase taken from the saloon table, that the west grew black as thunder and the moon went out; lost behind a mass of fast advancing cloud. And just as the moon went out, and a deep gloom fell upon the ship, hiding her arching sails, hiding the length of her long white decks, the mate's whistle shrilled. "All hands shorten sail!" came the order. So out ran the watch below, to join the watch on deck. Blacker grew the night, and blacker; till sail and spar were hidden, and we were hauling on the ropes in utter darkness, but before we had the topgallant sails off the flying ship the squall struck her. The Old Man's voice sounded from the poop, "Look alive there!" Sails crashed, flapping high in the darkness above us. Ropes skirled through their blocks. "Watch out!" came the voice of the mate, as the ship braced herself to take the blow of a great sea rushing upon her in the utter blackness. And in the utter blackness men and apprentices laid hold tight to stanchions, to hand rails, to shrouds; lest, when it break aboard, the grey-back sweep them to their deaths. It burst with a thundering roar, coming over the bulwark all the way from just before the mizzen rigging to the cross-jack brace belaying pins. The quarter-deck was filled with roaring, raging white water. And for a little space no man gave thought to aught save his own life, for to do aught else was impossible. But presently the decks cleared, and, without having lost a sail, we at last got the old ship shortened down to six topsails and a reefed foresail. Away she went, running for the Horn and home like a stag with the hounds at his heels. And not till the cold dawn broke did anyone know that the great sea had smashed up the Old Woman's garden utterly. Not a trace of soil was left. It was gone completely; not a thing, save the cleats in which its four legs had stood, remaining. So we apprentices laughed and were merry. "You'll never have any flowers now," we said mockingly.

Some fifteen years had passed by since we loaded the old four-poster with salmon at Steveston. I was living ashore, nigh four hundred miles from the sea. And by the sea, four hundred miles away, were living the Old Man and the Old Woman, retired long since. One day word came to me that the Old Woman was gone to her last long watch below. Then it was I remembered the days when I was a young sea apprentice, full of the devil, caring for little save a full belly and to avoid work whenever possible. I remembered the old ship— how she looked with her thirty sails all set, and drawing well in a fine fair wind. I remembered the park gates, and how at morning, noon and night the Old Woman used to stand by them. I remembered how, sometimes, I'd see the Old Man and the Old Woman standing side by side, and how, as I passed them by, they would sometimes look at me. No expression in their eyes, save one of infinite patience— that infinite patience which is to be seen in the eyes of all such as, having long served the sea, know that of all qualities needed by the sea's servitors patience is the one most essential. For me, a reckless young apprentice, filled with youth's devilment, there was neither judgement nor anger. It was as though those two minds were unaware of me. That Old Man and that Old Woman were grown grey in the hard service of the sea. Little ease had been theirs—ever. The joys of them who dwell in security upon the shore were unknown to them. No gay blackbird had ever whistled for them at the dawning from his ivy-clad perch, no thrush from a green larch top at evening. No skylark had ever winged upward in the sunny noontide for them, pouring his heart out in ecstasy of song. Only for them had been the grey gulls, the petrels, the sea pigeons, the mollymawks, the albatross, the marline-spike bird; birds of hoarse voices, homeless wanderers upon the great deep sea.

For that Old Man and that Old Woman had never had any flowers. Never had rose bloomed at their bedroom window, never pansy nor peony, primrose, forget-me-not, larkspur, nor any other bright blossom by their doorstep. For them had been only the white flowers that, when the rolling sea curls and breaks, fall ever from its broken ridges. Thinking of those old days it came to my mind how the Old Woman had said to me that day, "I've never had any flowers." So then I went out into my garden, where grew many flowers in great profusion. And for the Old Woman, for the dead wife of that Old Man of mine, I gathered an armful, and with light twine bound them together in the form of a great white anchor. All white flowers they were, and when the anchor was ready I started for the place, four hundred miles away, where the Old Man was now alone. It was long

411

past dark when I came to his door. He was sitting apart, all alone, with a puzzled look in his much-wrinkled eyes, in a room in which were several people; friends of his and of his Old Woman's: friends who held him and the Old Woman in high regard, and were come to try to comfort him now that the Old Woman was gone. As I entered he looked up and, in a moment, saw me.

Then, instantly, there passed from his face that look of loneliness, and there came to his aged eyes a look such as I had often seen upon it in the old days at sea. He rose, and he stretched out a hand and took in his hand my hand. And then, with my hand in his, he looked round upon those people in the room and spoke; and in his words there was a something of the old bold, proud murmur of the great salt sea. I saw sails arching to a brave wind as he spoke. I saw the bow wash breaking from a good ship's swift advance. I was a lad once more: a young apprentice boy—and he was again my Skipper. To those people who were come to try to cheer him, he said, "Here's one of my old boys, come four hundred miles to stand by me now." And in his voice there was gladness and surprise. Though I was a man, in the prime of my manhood, he called me "one of my old boys," and I was proud to have him so call me. And soon the room was empty, save for him and for me. We sat silent for a long time, for there was no need for any speech. Two seafaring men together. Let them who dwell upon the shore talk. We had no need of it.

Next day the Old Woman was borne away, from the spacious room in which she had lain; all surrounded with flowers. That spacious room and the wide hall without it were filled entirely with flowers. But of all the flowers there left the house but one garland, and upon it was a little card on which I had written. "From the boys of the old ship." And as, with the Old Man leaning on my arm, I followed the Old Woman to her last long watch below, I seemed to hear, faint, from far away, the shrill of the mate's whistle. Once again, from down the long years, there came to me the mate's voice, "The Old Woman wants you."

Please pardon my having wandered thus. It was your little note, suggesting that I write something for 'The Blue Peter', that started me wandering. I would that the Blue Peter were gaily flying at the fore-

412

truck of a tall ship, and that she was heaving up anchor, homeward-bound for the land where the primroses grow in the deep little lanes. But that is quite all right. Nothing can rob one of one's memories. If I have seemed too sentimental I ask your pardon.

Fair winds to you!

144. *DRUMCRAIG.*

CHAPTER XXI

ALL IN A LIFETIME

A few evenings ago I had a very delightful experience. I was sitting rather moodily at my desk, thinking of old times, when the door-bell rang. It is very, very rarely that my bell rings, even by day; and rarer yet that it rings by night. Dutch Flat folk are not given to visiting one another's houses. We foregather down at the old building that in the busy mining days, when this old town was a hustling little city, was the bank and express office; and seldom, unless in case of rare emergency, intrude on one another in our homes. So I went to my door expecting to hear that some fellow townsman was in trouble, or that a forest fire had broken out, and that every able-bodied man was needed to fight it. But at my door was a young girl from the hotel. There was a friend of mine just come to the hotel, she told me. He was crippled and, having driven many miles during the day, did not feel up to climbing the steep hill to my house. He wondered if I would come down and see him. His name was strange to me. I could not place him, for I could think of no friend crippled as she told me he was.

A fellow whose name gets into magazines receives letters from all sorts of people, and I supposed that this man was someone who had at some time written to me. For aught I knew he might be a first-rate chap, or then again, as at times happens, he might be a waster—some man who would ask me for financial assistance, or who might turn out to be a plain bore. I had put in a long day and did not feel at all like being bothered by anyone, let alone a stranger. And, moody though my meditations had been, they had, since I had been thinking of my days at sea, been somewhat pleasant. So I decided to stay at home. I hated the thought of talking with some landsman with whom, in my present mood, I should feel nothing in common.

But on second thoughts I decided that I was being rather bearish. The fellow might, after all, be interesting, too. One is apt to get into a rut, living up here in the mountains; and to get into a rut is not good for one. So I took my pipe and my hat, and went downhill with the lass.

I found the fellow sitting on the hotel porch. He sat with one leg outstretched, and I told him not to rise. We shook hands. "I can't place you," I said, "I'm sorry, but you seem to have slipped my memory."

"I served my time in the old *Clan Graham*," said he. "I wrote to you two years ago, and you answered my letter."

So there we were—two old sea apprentices, sitting on the porch of a little old hotel in a little old dead town in the mountains. A great gam we had! And after a while we came up the hill together, to sit here in my room, with pictures of ships all round its walls. We talked far into the night. We stole the skipper's stores from the lazarette again. We reefed the topsails, and sang the anchor up, and visited old Salthouse dock, and the African dock in Antwerp, and the Hamburg sailing ship dock, and got into a long calm on the Line, and made cracker hash, and "strike me blind," and caught a shark or two, and fished for bonito, and spoke the names many a long-lost old windjammer. We discovered that when he was almost lost in the great gale at Port Elizabeth*, I was in Durban harbour. We found that we had both lain in the same ward in the same hospital in a far foreign port, and that the same doctor had tinkered us both. We found that he knew many a man that I had known in years long gone. He told me how he once fell from the fore-topgallant yard, and, after having his fall broken by the belly of the foresail, dropped over the rail and had a leg very badly smashed. He was a long time in hospital, and when at last the doctor told him that he might walk about again the doctor added, "Keep away from those damned ships. D'ye hear? Don't go fooling round any damned ship now." So, being a sailor, he, of course, went straight down to the waterfront and went aboard a square-rigger, and, just as luck would have it, he had a bad fall and

* This was in 1902! [Ed.]

145. *CLAN GRAHAM.*

broke the mended leg again, so that it was almost as bad as it had ever been. The doctor damned him up and down, naturally. He lay long in hospital once more, and by and by he was once more mended up and able to get about in good shape.

Then, after a while, the war came, and he joined up with the the Canadians. And, over there in France, the Germans shot clear away from him the leg that he had twice had broken, so that he was left crippled for life. Well, he made no howl at all about that. There was never a more philosophical fellow. He talked of things in the same fashion as if a man might read aloud a tale from a book. It was all of it just thus and so, and that's that.

It's queer how every once in a while I meet up with some old sea apprentice. They pop up unexpectedly in all sorts of places; and they do all sorts of jobs. This chap is an automobile insurance man. Just what I am, only the good Lord knows. I'd not even try to say myself. A bit of flotsam is as near as I can come to it. One ex-apprentice that I know is a chiropractor in a little cow-town away in the cow-country.

417

I met him first when he was a first voyager, in Portland. That's round thirty-four years ago now. He writes me about the way the cow-punchers come in to have their lame backs and sprained limbs rubbed. "It's a great old graft," he says. "Rub a lame back, and you pull in a couple of dollars."

Another ex-apprentice is a house painter. I should say 'was' a house painter, for not long ago I had a letter from his little daughter, who told me of his death. He and I were in 'Frisco together years ago. He was in the old four-poster *Springburn*, and she lay alongside us at the wharf. She had gone ashore on a coral reef on the passage out, and forty grand pianos in her hold had been smashed to splinters. Some hundreds of tons of cement in her hold had been so damaged that all the cement was frozen, as it were, into a solid mass, and had to be dug out and dumped overboard.

Another old apprentice travels all up and down California selling sewing machines to the farmers' wives. He is an old-timer, much my senior, and writes me of the ship he first went to sea in for all the world as though she had been the first and only girl that he has ever loved. And another ex-apprentice is vice-president of an Air Line. I haven't heard from him in a year or more. Perhaps he has crashed and is gone below, like the *Springburn* lad. Speaking of that *Springburn* lad and his job of painting houses for a living, reminds me that painting houses was also my first shore job after I quit the sea. The boss, knowing that I was a sailor, used to send me up to paint all the high, steep roofs, and once he sent me up to paint a church steeple. I didn't like working high up ashore. It was one thing to work aloft on a ship's mast, with the salt sea to fall into if one fell; but quite another to work on a high roof or steeple, with hard concrete down below to drop and get smashed on. I did not work very long at that painting job though for, one fine morning, when I was on a high roof, I looked round and saw a sailing schooner coming into the wharf of the little coast town where I lived. I was never in a fore-and-after, and I never much admired the rig; but, at any rate, she was a ship, and she looked good to me then, with her canvas all white in the warm sun. I set my paint-pot and my brush down, and down the ladder to the ground I went in a hurry.

146. *SPRINGBURN*.

"Where are you going? What are you doing?" asked the boss.

"There's a ship coming into the wharf," said I, "I'm going down to have a look at her."

The boss flared up at once. "You get back on the job," said he, "I don't take any sailor monkey business."

And I said again, "I'm going down to take a look at that schooner."

The boss said, "You get right back on the job, or you're fired right now."

And, of course, being a decent-minded seafaring sort of party, I said to the boss, "You can have your old job. I don't want it." So I lost my job. In all the blessed world I had just less than thirty dollars, and I had the missus and the kid to take care of. But I went aboard the schooner, and I had a good yarn; and that was that, and here I am.

It's a rummy deal when a sailor who has not long left the sea goes to work for landsmen. They don't understand a fellow. They think he has bats in his belfry, as a rule. And maybe they think right. But I'd far rather have bats in my belfry, and a clean whiff of salt sea air blowing through it, than have nothing but bats and cobwebs the way they sometimes have, poor fellows!

What puts me in mind of bats in the belfry is an old farmer I worked for many years ago. It was a hard winter, and times were tough. I was broke. I was out of a job. There were no jobs to be had. So one night, when it was raining hard, and this old farmer met me on the street as I was going disconsolately home after a day of useless searching for a job of some kind, and asked me if I could milk, I said "Yes," of course; though I'd never milked a cow in my life. I climbed into his buggy with him, and away we went, out into the country. When a farmer asks a man if he can milk, he means, "Can you milk thirty cows twice a day, and separate the cream afterwards, and feed the calves, and the pigs, and the cows, and keep the cow barn clean?" That's a milker's job in the state of California! And, of course, he has to wash the separator, and the milk cans, too.

When we came to the farm the farmer's wife had milked the cows, helped by a neighbour; but I was called at three next morning to get them into the barn, and go to work.

420

"How many's the most cows you ever milked?" asked the old farmer.

"I never milked a cow before," said I.

You should have heard him swear! I couldn't see what all the fuss was about. All a man needs as a milker is an easy-going disposition and a strong wrist and fingers. A sailor has naturally an easy disposition, and as for a strong wrist and fingers, if a man does not get them from pulling a long oar, I don't know how else he could get them. I milked my thirty head twice a day for two years. The farmer had no kick, but when he heard me telling a cow to starboard her helm, he put me down as a crazy man, and told all his neighbours about it. Such is life!

Excuse my rambling, please. I beg your pardon. Blame it on that chap who served his time in the old *Clan Graham*. It was he who started me off on this long gam.

Well, it's all in a lifetime.

Report me 'All well'. Thank you, and good luck!

147.   *CLAN GALBRAITH, sister of the CLAN GRAHAM.*

CHAPTER XXII

BLOW THE MAN DOWN

We of the old-day square-riggers talk with a queer longing of the days that are done, and remember wide sea-ways which, once well known to the keels of our sailing ships, are in these days become as lone as they were in the days before Drake and the Dons trailed on them. It is strange to remember those black and frowning foreshore rocks by the eastward point of Staten Island, some ninety-eight miles north and east of the Horn, and to think that the summer and winter months go by while never a stretch of storm canvas, never a sea-lashed bow, staggers away to the southward, seeking a good offing, a chance to come up to and about the cold corner that we used to hate and to dread so.

Three years ago there came to my home one evening a quiet little man who, introduced to me by a friend, sat in silence, apparently indifferent, in an easy-chair while we others talked. It was then over twenty years since I had been at sea. When my wife chanced to move the table lamp, and its ray fell upon a photograph of a fine four-master with her topsails reefed to a Cape Horn blow, he leaped to his feet.

"Where did you get that?" he asked, in surprise, and added, with an intense tone in his voice, "I used to know that ship."

"That was taken off the Horn," said I, and added, "I was with her."

He stood, voiceless, gazing at her noble top-hamper, at the great seas that broke all about her.

"Did you ever know a clipper called *Province*?" he asked.

"Yes," said I, "she lay alongside us, in Oregon—somewhere

round twenty-two years or so ago."

"My heaven, man; I believe I remember you—we used to go ashore together!" he cried.

Brought together quite by accident in a tiny inland village, where no one knew anything whatever of the life we used to lead, we sat and talked till the daylight came again.

He had in his pocket an "extra master's certificate," and had served all through the war in steam. But the war, the dreary horror of man's foolish battlings, was all forgotten that night. We said never a word of steam; but talked unendingly of the world as it used to be in the days when we were boys, each ambitious to sail his own good ship, each imagining that there would always be the same world as the boyish world we sailed in.

We remembered those hard days, those ill-fed ships, those weary periods of torturing calm upon the line, which were to be so soon followed by the insensate savagery of snow-laden hurricanes, as men who are grown to manhood, who are coming toward old age, recall the faces of the kind women who were good to them as little children. Our world was then filled with glamours of romance. The very ships we sailed were part and parcel of the sea herself, their canvas sisterly amid low driving clouds, their mast-heads glittering, gilded, un-ashamed in the sunshine of wonderfully lovely days.

We recalled evenings when crews sang on the main hatch, when fiddles and creaky concertinas played for naked feet to dance. In those days newspapers meant naught to us. Politics were things as much out of our ken, as much devoid of interest, as to-day are the spring-time plans of the cave men to a modern dairy farmer. We lived in a world that had no bearing on us, no bearing that we recognized.

I went to sea three weeks after the declation of America's war with Spain, and arrived, under sail, on the other side of the world a week after that war's conclusion.*

The old sailing-ship man was something akin to the turtle, the seal, or the whale himself.

A glamour that we did not understand lay over our days. We cursed not seldom the hardships of our life, yet were unable to leave them.

*Adams' second voyage. The United States declared war on April 21st, 1898, and peace was signed on September 10th. [Ed.]

148.   *CRAIGERNE, later the Finnish MARGARETA.*

When to-day we seem to speak scornfully of the modern seaman and his craft, it is but the inexpressible yearning for our youth that we utter.

Now and again I meet by chance some old deep-water man. They all say the same. The hardest of them, the men in whose faces one can see no sign, in whose tones there seems to linger no regret, all say, after a little while of talking, "There was no life like it."

Not many months ago I took a journey by auto stage, beside me a severe old patriarch with a drooping white moustache. We said not a word for over three full hours. Then, while passing the creek at Oakland, where lie a few old-time ships, he grunted, and I spoke.

"Tough old hookers," I said.

He flared at me, as though I had insulted something, and said nothing.

"I was in company with *that* ship," said I, "on the night she lost her mate and all his watch overboard," pointing to *Star of Russia*.

"Vell! you iss deep-vater man—vy you ain't said so?" he said.

He had a little garden, one hundred miles from the sea; an old ship's carpenter who had known, and sailed with, ships I used to know.

We ambled off up Market street, talking nineteen to the dozen, discussing sailors' boarding masters, ships, seaports, and men we used to know.

"Eet voss hard life," he said, when at parting we shook hands at a street corner, "but, py Gott, eet voss *man's* life, eh?"

Shore folk, hearing his words, turned to stare at us.

They would not, could not, have understood why two old men should get so excited and should part with regretful faces, with perhaps a hint of moisture in their eyes, in the throbbing traffic of a busy street.

JM BIRCHALL
1935

CHAPTER XXIII

THE HELMSMAN OF THE *STAR*

Upon the end of an old wharf whither to-day no ship, dropping cork fenders over her side, comes to moorings, the old man told me his story; a man who stared at me from sunken eyes, his voice a wind murmur, his accents mingling strangely with the lap of water amongst the piles, his face continually turning toward the horizon of the south.

"I was helmsman of the *Star* that night," said he.

"*That* night?" I asked, for the *Star* is an old story on the sea.

"Aye! *that* night," he answered.

A grey gull dipped past us, flying southerly, the eyes of the old sailor following it.

"I'm no flying-fish man," said he.

"Nor I," I replied.

Flying-fish sailors are they who, when wild weather is upon the sea, go to their bunks under the pretext of sickness, sprain, or bruise.

"When I was a boy aboard the old *Balclutha* a foremast hand jumped from her lee railing to a cake of drifting ice alongside her, and, bracing his feet, shook bare fists at her as she passed by, cursing her for having taken him to sea."

"A shanghaied landsman?" I asked.

"Aye! Shanghaied; clerk in a shoe store near the water-front. He cursed the old *Balclutha*, his face whiter than the ice he stood upon, the wind drowning his voice, though you could tell that he was cursing her. The sea birds hovered near him. The ice blink enveloping him, we saw him no more."

427

"Tell me about the *Star*," I said.

The old man's eye were lit with water lights, filled with green reflections. "She was bound for Chiloe, making westerly south of the Diegos. I was at her wheel, a freshening breeze taking her along at her fifteen knots," said he, and paused.

"It was one of *those* sort of nights," he continued. "You've seen them?"

I nodded.

"She was a good ship to steer," said the old sailor, gazing southward.

"I played with her, listening to the roar of the seas that swept her fore-deck when I luffed; seeing, in my fancy, the high, white water at her weather bow, the green twists in her wake. I knew how lovely she would look were daylight on her, but it was night, and her beauty was a hidden thing. I sang to myself. I was young then. The mate came to stand beside me, staring at the compass card. With him to watch me I steered her carefully, not luffing her at all, keeping her head away from the great seas, and her fore-deck dry.

"'A fine ship to steer when she gets it this way,' said the mate, his voice pleasant upon the wind.

"'A fine ship sir,' I answered him, holding her very steady on her course.

"'Don't let her luff,' said the mate, his pipe glow lighting his eyes so that it was as though the eyes of a bodyless man looked up at me.

"I did not see him again. He went to the bridge, leaving her to me. I played her along that noisy sea south of the Diegos, the wind freshening, and the old *Star* lifting high to the swell, the weather continually more murmurous about her."

The eyes of the old sailor glowed with green lights, as though seeing those waters beneath the Southern Cross.

"She was beginning to take water. I could hear the thunder of the seas along her deck. Once I heard a crackling, abrupt sound, as though the edges of a continent dropped into the devouring sea. Ice. I didn't like that, wishing the mate would take sail off her, but soon, hearing it no more, laughed at my timidity. I gave her a touch

428

of lee helm, and let her luff, smiling to hear the sea rumble along her main deck as I did so.

"I seemed to hear the mate's voice say, *'Don't let her luff.'*

"Look at the gulls! They hover close to the water," cried the old man, rising to stare at the sea fowl screaming by.

He stood up, a bent old man, his beard white, his eyes upon the inshore waters, his hands twitching as though he held the wheel spokes of the *Star*.

Gulls flew close by, peering at him. The old man stared at them as though defiantly—a mad old man.

"You heard of *Guiding Star*?" he asked me suddenly. I nodded, recalling stories of the wreck of *Guiding Star*, in April, '55, the year *Red Jacket* lost three days amidst the ice, and *Champion of the Seas* lay fast in it a week.*

"*I saw them*," said the sailor, turning solemn eyes upon me.

"There were seven men from *Guiding Star*, high on an iceberg ridge; frozen stiff, their eyes pecked by the sea birds, their cheek bones bare."

I watched the sea outside.

"The berg lifted suddenly as we passed by," he continued, "and, toppling, spilled over. It broke the water to a hundred rainbows on that wintry morning. Those seven slid to the sea, all rainbow-wrapped, and very misty seeming."

"That was the end of them," I muttered, thinking of the funeral of those men of *Guiding Star*.

"No—" said the old sailor, stooping above me where I sat.

"Killer whales passed by directly after, seeking their ocean nourishment."

I shuddered, wishing the old man would leave me—a man to whom the sea was old when I was young.

"She flew along the night," he cried, then grew serene, pacing the wharf, eight paces up, eight paces down, as though upon the lookout of the old *Star*.

"It wasn't my fault. *It was the sea*," he said.

Green wavelets danced below us as he spoke.

"The mate's eyes looked up at me as eyes without a body," he

---

* *Red Jacket* was in bad ice that year. *Guiding Star* was condemned in Hong Kong in 1870! [Ed.]

continued—"I sometimes see them now, in the middle of the night.

"It was cold, as those south winds are cold down there. With oilskins on, and soul and body lashings, and mittens on my hands, I was most bitter cold. Snow flew across the binnacle. She grew hard to handle. I fought her to hold her to her course; knowing that, to ease her pitching, the mate must soon take sail off her forward. She was wasting good time by her high stepping manner. Hearing a comber rumble on her deck, I knew that she must be waist-deep in water; then, faint, yet distinct, I heard the mate's whistle, shrill upon the night.

"'He's going to take a head sail off her. That will ease her, and she will fly again,' said I.

"After that I was alone, singing to myself cheerily, playing with her again, chiding her to each thump of water on her decks and hatches. Once, as though a sail blew from its bolt ropes, I thought I heard a crack, and then, at once, a scream. Knowing that no voice could reach me from the forecastle head, where, well I knew, they were taking in a jib, I laughed at my imagination, giving her a spoke of weather helm.

"'The mate says not to let you luff, old girl,' said I. 'Keep your big nose up, well above the sea, so they can get that sail off you all dry.'

"The *Star* ran easily again, the wind still freshening.

"'They will take off more sail,' thought I, as, in an increasing wind, she staggered to the sea, the roar of water continuing upon her.

"No one came near me. I knew that my time at the wheel must soon be up, and that a man would come to my relief. I was cheerful, singing aloud, stamping my feet. I made grimaces at the binnacle, putting my tongue out at an imagined face within the compass card.

"'When's that fellow coming to relieve me?' thought I presently. 'I bet it's old Scot Dougal—the old whale! Why don't he step along?'

"Time passed, the *Star* ripping ahead as though grown savage, independently assertive of her personality.

"'Ah, my beauty, would you, then?' said I, shoving the helm up.

"She flung a spray over me at the wheel, a thing I'd never known her to do before, for she was a fine ship, always dry aft.

"'I'm your master, beauty,' said I. 'Keep still, now, while I sing.'

430

149.   *STAR OF RUSSIA.*

And, so saying, sang a chorus through, aloud.

"'Where's that old Dougal?' said I, at the end of my song. 'Why don't he come? They are long at coiling up those ropes.'

"Presently, wondering at the length of time that I was left, I called, half jestingly, 'Aye! Mister Mate, relief here, please!'

"Then, growing morose, cold, and swearing silently, I gripped her hard, steering her as an arrow on the water. She flew, the sea raging beside me.

"'Rage, you old sea. I'm master here,' said I.

"I was a young man then.

"The *Star* staggered, the wind mightier, the mighty sea increasing.

"'Scot,' said I aloud, 'where are you, Scot Dougal?'

"I steered into the blackness, the *Star* as cleaving through a wall; the sea, unwilling of her passage, swamping her decks. She shook, hesitating in that lash.

"'Steady now, old lady! You are grown old,' said I, laughing at her.

"As though wrathful at my insult, she flung a spray over me."

"'Aye, Mister Mate!' I shouted, aware that I was too long at the wheel, my arms aching, salt thick upon my face.

"'I'll tell old Scot some things when he does come,' said I.

"The wind was hard. I wondered what was doing on the deck.

"' Maybe they've split a sail in furling, and are getting out another from the locker. Well—let them hurry, then,' I said.

"Midnight crept in upon me. Throwing up my head, my arms aching, I breathed deep of that strong wind.

"'I'll sing a bit,' thought I. 'That'll pass the time till they are done. Then Scot will come, and I shall go below.'

"I sang, very loud, a sort of creeps upon me.

"I stamped my feet, shouting to frighten the darkness farther from me, snow fluttering across the compass card.

"'Scot!' I yelled, grown suddenly afraid of something.

"The ship needing my utmost strength, fear passed. A roller, raising her bow aloft, her stern deep in the water valley, my breath ceased. My hands were rigid upon the spokes, and the *Star* was as though she would never rise again. I wrenched at her wheel, heaving

432

it hard up, and, paying off, she rolled easily across that mountain ridge that had lifted her against the sky.

"'There! I win again,' said I.

"I was wet with sweat, my breath a mist, my body trembling.

"'Mister Mate, relief here, please!' I called.

"I swore aloud, cursing Scot Dougal, calling that old whale all names I knew.

"'You old man-swallowing killer! It's your trick at the wheel! Relief here!' I shouted. No one answered me; the night's great wall was about me, the gale madder. The *Star* drummed heavily along the sea.

"I heard a sea bird scream.

"The sweat upon me was cold, I was exhausted.

"'Scot! Relief here!' I cried again.

"As though we two were alone in mystery, the ship whispered; I, knowing by her tremble, that she was all awash.

"'If the mate don't take in sail she'll lose a stick, or all her sticks,' I thought, trying to hold her to her course, but humouring the sea.

"My strength of body gone, my mind rose uppermost. No longer swearing at Scot, no longer calling to the mate, I was becoming a spirit of the night, steering the ship, my fellow spirit.

"Together we waited.

"Stepping from the wheel grating, holding the wheel in one hand, my knee steadying the lower spokes, reaching forward to the lanyard of the bell amidships of the cabin skylight, I beat upon it.

"There was no response.

"Again I beat the bell.

"Its clamour, awakening me from stupor, maddening me, I was again the helmsman of the *flying Star*.

"Shouting to Scot Dougal to relieve me, I crashed upon the bell.

"Then, neither flesh nor spirit, I became an automaton of night.

"Suddenly a figure was beside me; two questioning eyes peered into my face. I had awakened the captain with the clamorous bell.

"His arm pointing forward in the dim arc of the binnacle light, his lips framing words unheard, he left me.

"The trembling ship raced beneath my confident feet.

433

"In a few moments I was relieved, my relief repeating the course I gave him. He did not look at me, nor I at him—two helmsmen relieving one another in the darkness of a windy night.

"Passing the chart house, I heard voices; the second mate was saying, 'The jib is blown away.' The captain's voice replied in words I did not hear.

"Clinging desperately to life lines, paying no heed to men who, shortening sail in a hurry, now shouted upon the gear, I battled my way to the forecastle. Without removing my oilskins or sea boots, with soul and body lashings yet upon me, crawling exhausted into a bunk, I fell immediately asleep.

"When I awoke, grey day was in the forecastle and I was alone. Conscious again of that gripping terror that had crushed me at the wheel and, rising, I stepped across the slopped forecastle deck to peer through a misty port, seeing naught save the ice covered shrouds, and, beyond them, the high, black ridges of the windward sea. Seeking one whom I could question, I went on deck. A new jib bellied to the gale as I came through the forecastle door; the wind was terrible, the sea in uproar, the ship forlorn.

"Aloft upon the main topsail yard I saw seven sailors, but no man of my own watch was to be seen. Hungry for companionship, I started aloft to help them reef that topsail, the gale holding me pressed against the rigging as she lurched to leeward. In quick dashes, as she made her windward rolls, I came at last to the spar, and stepped upon the foot-rope beside a sailor of the second mate's watch.

"That sailor, seeing me, edged away quickly, as though afraid lest I come near to him.

"I shrieked a question at the fellow, who, ghastly white, stared at me from eyes of extraordinary and most baneful expression. Seeing me about to approach him, he threw an arm up, as though to ward me off.

"The second mate, upon the foot-rope beyond him, now looked up, and, observing that the fellow was afraid of me, shouted unheard words into his ear. Then, with a look of hate, that sailor again went to tying the reef points.

"The sail reefed, they descended to the deck. Each man, in passing me, either avoided me or scowled savagely.

"The second mate hastening aft to the bridge, I, most cold and hungry, a horrid fear upon me, followed his men along the swamped deck to the forecastle.

"I entered the forecastle behind the last of them.

"They stared at me.

"'Where are Scot Dougal and the mate?' I cried. 'Where are my watch?'

"A sailor stepped toward me then.

"'They've drowned,' said he. *'You luffed!'*"

*This imaginative story is based on an actual incident in the *Star of Russia* a couple of years before Adams went to sea, when the helmsman did let the ship come to the wind as the mate and his watch were hauling down the flying jib. All were lost. [Ed.]

W. M. BIRCHA

150.   *The French barque BOILDEAU hove-to for her pilot.*

CHAPTER XXIV

DAYS THAT ARE OVER, DREAMS THAT ARE DONE

It is six o'clock of a windless winter morning. I have been up for half an hour. The fires are lighted and the doors flung wide open to freshen the house for another bright day. I have just let my dog out of the wood-shed, and, seated by the fire, he looks up at me with cocked ears and with a question in his eager eyes—"Will it be a good walk for us to-day?" he is asking. He has probably been dreaming of jack-rabbits and squirrels; but I have had dreams of my own.

We are far from the sea, my dog and I; but last night I dreamed of the sea, and this morning my thoughts are of the days of long ago when I followed the sea, ploughing her rolling prairies from one side of the world to the other and back again, year after year.

I wish that I were sitting up in the fore cross-trees, with the big topgallant sail bellied out close by and the slim symmetry of the main truck clear against the cloudy sky each time that I glance up from my work. What a lot of fine pictures an old sailor has to look back upon!

There was the pitch-black night when, after we had been at sea but a few days, I went aloft all by myself to furl the fore royal. Though there was but very little breeze, there was a something ominous about the night, so that the skipper had ordered the royals taken in. From the fore royal yard all I could see was the thin wedge of phosphorus that broke about the bow. There was nothing else in the universe but myself and that little glow of sea-flame a hundred and seventy feet below me. The ship was lifting gently to a light swell; motion was barely noticeable. In that utter darkness I could not see the white

437

canvas beneath my hands. I could hear nothing. The low breeze fanned my face lightly. I would that I might have those moments back, could know once more the first awed wonder of a boy. For it was upon that night, up there upon the swaying royal yard, that the mystery, the marvellous beauty of the sea first sank into my being.

Days have passed, and I see a ship under full sail in the trade-winds; beneath her, a bright blue sea; above her, a bright blue sky, across which pass unceasingly the legions of soft white trade-wind clouds. Day after day, week upon week, she sweeps steadily onward. We go barefoot and wear the lightest of clothing. By day, those who are off duty sit out at the end of the long boom and fish for bonito and skipjack or perhaps albacore. By night, those who are off duty sleep on the hatches and upon the bare deck. Beside them sleep those who are on duty, for as long as we are in the trades no rope need be touched, no sail need be handled, from one evening till the next. Evening by evening we tighten braces, and sheets, and halyards, singing as we haul. By day, those on duty work aloft in the web of her rigging—splicing and knotting, seizing, painting or tarring down. Some work on the wide spars; some sit in boatswains' chairs slung by the slowly-rolling masts and, wielding their paint brushes, call now and again to a lad on the deck far below, "Lower a little." Night and day the warm wind caresses us; we know no care. When day is done and the dog-watch comes, all hands gather by the hatch to pass away the evening. Barefooted, we dance to the music of a concertina; we sing old songs that have been heard on every ocean and in every seaport; we box, wrestle, and challenge one another for a race to the masthead and back. From the poop, skipper and mate look on. The tropic sun dips, leaving the sky aflame with gold and sapphire, with turquoise and with amethyst. Purple shadows linger awhile on the dimming sea; they fade to darkness and a myriad stars awaken. All voices hush while an old man commences a yarn of the sea he has served since boyhood. He finishes his tale, silence falls. A flying fish skims over the weather rail and falls flapping on the deck near by. All hands leap up and dash for the prize, each eager for a fine breakfast next morning. While we scrimmage and push, the music of the bells breaks clear. The look-out man calls, *"All's well, sir!"* The mate replies, "All right." Night

151. Perhaps not appreciated in a picture, this sea was taken in a hurricane!

begins. To-morrow, and to-morrow, and to-morrow will each bring an evening alike.

Years have passed. A ship is south of Cape Horn; she is under six topsails and foresail. It is mid forenoon. At six o'clock all hands were called on deck to take in the three topgallant sails, the mainsail, and crojick. I have been three years at sea and am third mate. Because, since I am a big fellow, the owners feared that it would cost too much to feed me at the cabin table, I still live and eat with the other apprentices in the half-deck; for I am only an apprentice yet, and shall not be 'out of my time' for a twelvemonth. Except for myself, the apprentices are all little chaps; most of them first voyagers. The foremast crew is a terribly poor one. There are half a dozen of them who cannot so much as tuck an eye splice. There are wastrels who jumped from the pier-head at the last moment, when we towed from the dock out to the stream, to take the places of some who had failed to put in an appear-

439

ance. There are several jail-birds. Amongst the fourteen men in the forecastle many nationalities are represented—Greek and Italian, Brazilian and German; there are two Finns; there is a negro, and there is one Englishman. Amongst them all there is but one man fit to call sailor—a Norwegian named Pedersen. And on the preceding night, when the rest had run to save their skins as a greyback came roaring aboard, he, by staying at his post and holding fast to the main brace, has had his hand caught and badly crushed in the block, between sheave and shell.

Throughout the forenoon I stay with the mate on the poop, only going forward for a few minutes now and again to see that the crew, who are making robands beneath the forecastle head, are not loafing too much. It is July; the wind is biting cold. Having lost two hours of my watch below, when all hands were called on deck, I am tired, and anxiously waiting my time to go below again, when one bell is struck at 12.30. But at one bell the order comes to take in the fore upper topsail. As third mate, it is for me to lead the way. Looking down as I go up the ratlines, I see the mate and second mate beating the crew aloft; pounding the hangers-back; fisting and cursing them. The mate is a fine man—we get along famously, he and I. At the end of his last voyage he was hauled into court and heavily fined for beating his crew up. No honest judge could fine him, seeing him beat our crew to-day.

The first hand into the rigging after me is an apprentice, a happy-go-lucky youngster of seventeen. It is his second voyage. There is a grin on his lips, as though the madness of this exuberant morning brings him delight; strikes him as humorous. The little first-voyage lads come after him, youngsters of fifteen and sixteen. The foremast scum follow, with the second mate cursing at their heels. The mate goes back to the poop.

A snow-squall drives upon us ere we are yet to the topsail yard. I come to the yard with my hands numb with the cold. As I begin to gather up the frozen canvas, the blood starts to circulate; the agony is well-night unendurable, but I hang on, and somehow we get the heavy sail stowed. Thinking that I shall now be able to go to my dinner and my bunk, I come down from aloft light-heartedly, but when I drop

440

from the rigging to the deck the mate is there, waiting me. "Mizzen topsail!" says the mate. So up we go again, to repeat the performance on the mizen and, having come down again, we go aloft once more, to take the main upper topsail off her. Now at last I can go to my food and my long-overdue sleep. But before I am well out of the rigging the order comes to haul the foresail up. By the time that that huge sail is made fast I am listless with weariness. To be listless is no use. The skipper is on the poop, bawling, *"All hands wear ship!"* So we wear her round, and while doing so become thoroughly soaked, and well bruised, and nigh half drowned; for, shipping enormous seas, she floods the length of her decks when, having put her helm up, we bring her stern to the gale and then fetch her into the wind upon the other tack.

Now at last comes the order, "Go below the watch!" The order is of small comfort. In fifteen minutes, at four o'clock, the mate's watch must be back on duty. I hurry to the half-deck, eager for the pea-soup and the boiled salt pork I should have eaten almost four hours ago. There is no pea-soup. A sea has swamped the galley and filled the soup-kid with salt water. All that is left for dinner is a hunk of salt pork that one of the younger apprentices has found washing about in the scuppers. We gulp it down, and to fill out our meal munch weevily hard-tack. Then, having changed into dry clothing, I return to the poop as eight bells strikes. The early darkness of the Cape Horn winter is setting in. The wind screams, in full gale force. Snow whirls by in the fast gathering gloom. Greyback after greyback lifts its lumpy head and roars aboard, to crash over the hatches and burst in clouds of spray about the midships and the forward deck-houses.

At five o'clock the mate leaves me, to go down to the cabin for his supper with the skipper. I smell, for an instant, coffee and fried liver and bacon, as the steward hurries by me with their meal in his hands. Longingly I wait the coming of four bells, at six o'clock, that I may go below to such supper as is for famished apprentices. Wearily I look up at the dim shapes of the masts, reeling incessantly against their background of deepening night and driving storm cloud. For a time, at any rate, there will be no occasion to go aloft! For that I am thankful.

The mate rejoins me. A moment later the skipper looks from the chart-room door. "Better be getting the bumper stays rove off, mister," he calls to the mate. "There you are. There's a nice little job for you," says the mate to me. So down to the swamped deck I go, to call out the watch. Since I am third mate, and the watch is worthless, I must myself go aloft and supervise the hoisting from the deck and the hooking to the main and crojick yard-arms of the heavy tack tackles. In semi-darkness and whirling snow I cling to the reeling main yard-arm and at length, without too great trouble, succeed in reeving off the bumper stay that, steadying the eighty-four-foot spar, shall ease the strain on the mast. I am half-way up the mizzen rigging to reeve off the stay on the crojack when four bells strikes. It is my turn to go below. But on a night such as this one does not go below with a job half done. I continue my way aloft, hoping that I can manage on the crojack with no more trouble than I had upon the main. But it is pitch-dark now, and blowing harder every minute. Wind of well-nigh hurricane violence. The snow has changed to hail. Hail lashes my bare hands, beats on my sou'wester, on my back and shoulders.

It is after seven o'clock when I at last drop to the deck once more. In an hour my time below will be up and I must return to the deck to stay there till midnight. Clinging to a life-line, I start towards the half-deck. As I hurry by the main hatch, well away from the shelter of any deck-house or from the comparative safety of a fife-rail, the ship takes a monstrous sea aboard; my feet are swept from under me. Soaked and gasping, I am washed to and fro, hanging for dear life to the line till the deck clears.

Famished and frozen, I come to the half-deck. For supper there is skilly and hard-tack. Skilly is supposed to be tea. Perhaps it was made from old tea-leaves that after being served to the folk who dwell ashore were dried out and repacked for us seafaring people. One benefit it has—it is hot. One can warm one's icy hands upon the dirty tin pot. To warm one's miserable belly, hot water would do as well.

So ends a sailor's common day. Nothing out of the ordinary has happened. The ship is safe, has suffered no damage. Not a sail has been split. Though I have no change of clothing left, there is at any rate time to smoke a pipe when supper is done. There is time to rub vaseline on my skinned knuckles and into the deep cracks in the thick skin of my palms and finger-joints.

Eight bells clangs out upon the big iron bell at the break of the forecastle head. I return to the poop, to rejoin the mate and to stay there till midnight, when, provided nothing happens to prevent it, I shall get below to sleep for almost four full hours ere going on duty once more at four in the morning.

From down the seas of memory there comes to me the sound of sailors singing. We are come to port again, at voyage's ending. Sunshine and starry night, trade-wind and storm, are forgotten. I hear the tramp of feet as a crew warps in a mooring-line upon the quarter-deck capstan.

> *I thought I heard the Old Man say,*
> *Leave her Johnnie, leave her!*
> *You can go ashore and draw your pay,*
> *And it's time for us to leave her!*

FLOWER CHILD

"Oh, where are you a-goin' to?" says Liza.
"I'm a-takin' of a trip to sea," says Pete.
"Oh, what is it that's makin' of you do so?"
"There is somethin' that's a-both'rin' in my feet.

"Where will I next meet up with you?" says Liza.
"You can meet me off the Horn, maybe," says Pete,
"Or maybe on the line in the Atlantic
Where the outward and the homing clippers meet."

"Oh, it's hard to be a poor sad-hearted female
With a man that's got to follow the cold sea."
"Does you think as it's soft to be a sailor,
When the ice cakes rides a-cracklin' down to lee?"

"Oh, Peter, won't you stay and pick the flowers
That are climbing up beside the kitchen door?"
"I hears the big iron bell break out the hours,
An' there's buds that breaks to blossom off the shore."

*   *   *   *   *

"There are flowers fairer far than lady's slippers,
There are blossoms that are sweeter than the rose;
They break to brightest bloom beneath the clippers—
S's's's'h—they're whisp'rin' now. I hears 'em—an' I goes."

BILL ADAMS

444

APPENDIX

MOVEMENTS OF THE *SILBERHORN* COVERED BY THIS BOOK

First Voyage:

February 25th, 1897	Adams signed indentures and joined ship.
February 28th, 1897	Sailed Liverpool.
March 4th, 1897	Put into Barry Roads with loss of sails and weather damage.
March 13th, 1897	Sailed Barry Roads, with new crew.
March 15th, 1897	Spoken 50°N. 8°W. (2 days out.)
August 4th, 1897	Arrived Victoria, B.C. (144 days from Barry Roads, 157 days from the Mersey. Adams gives 166 days. Possibly, as a first voyager, he took the time to her berth.)
October 25th, 1897	Sailed Vancouver.
October 27th, 1897	Passed Tatoosh.
January 28th, 1898	Spoken 14°S. 33°W. (93 days out.)
March 18th, 1898	Arrived Liverpool. (142 days out from Tatoosh.)

Second Voyage:

May 14th, 1898	Sailed Liverpool.
June 11th, 1898	Spoken 9°S. 33°W. (28 days out.)
September 17th, 1898	Arrived Astoria. (126 days out.) It is not clear when she passed Cape Flattery.
November 12th, 1898	Sailed Astoria.
April 5th, 1899	Off Isle of Wight. (144 days out of Astoria.)
April 7th, 1899	Arrived Antwerp. (146 days from Astoria.)

445

Third Voyage:

June 3rd, 1899	Sailed Antwerp.
June 4th, 1899	Passed Dover.
October 2nd, 1899	Arrived San Francisco. (120 days from Dover.)
December 5th, 1899	Sailed San Francisco.
April 3rd, 1900	Arrived Falmouth for orders. (119 days out.)
April 9th, 1900	Sailed Falmouth.
April 10th, 1900	Passed Prawle Point.
April 16th, 1900	Arrived Hull. (7 days from Falmouth.)

After discharging, the ship was shifted up to the Tyne.

Fourth Voyage:

June 6th, 1900	Sailed Tyne.
June 13th, 1900	Passed Portland. (7 days out.)
October 29th, 1900	Arrived San Francisco. (146 days out of the Tyne, 139 from Portland.)
February 26th, 1901	Adams left the *Silberhorn*.

The ship left San Francisco on February 27th, 1901, and arrived in Scattery Roads, Limerick, to discharge, on July 1st, 1901 (124 days out).

152.   *Latterly French square-riggers, aided by State bounties, took the lion's share of the 'Frisco grain trade. Here are LA FONTAINE and MARGUERITE MOLINOS in the foreground.*

153. *"There's a lilting tune I seem to hear . . ."*
The CHRISTOBAL SOLER spreads her wings.

ALL'S WELL

There's an ache in my heart, and I can't tell why,
Something to do with the sea and sky
And maybe a star or so;
Maybe a whirl of wind and snow
And the easy lift of a sailing ship
Gliding away from her landing slip,
Heading at dawn for the misty west
In her little white royals and skysails dressed.
There's a lilting tune I seem to hear,
A roving chorus, a quavered cheer;
The air is chill as there rumbles past
A berg as tall as her tall mainmast.
There's the creak of her gear in the stilly night,
With her braces and sheets and halliards tight.
Dear God! But I'd give my soul to go
To the open sea and the wind and snow,
To that old clear cry of the ocean night:
"All's well, sir, and all of her lights are bright!"

BILL ADAMS